THE DIVINE
SPARK

THE DIVINE
SPARK

A GRAHAM HANCOCK READER

Psychedelics, Consciousness, and the Birth of Civilization

GRAHAM HANCOCK, EDITOR

Published by Disinformation Books,
an imprint of Red Wheel/Weiser, LLC
with offices at
665 Third Street, Suite 400
San Francisco, CA 94107
www.redwheelweiser.com

ISBN: 978-1-938875-11-3

Library of Congress Cataloging-in-Publication data available upon request.

Cover and text design by Jim Warner.
Cover photograph © xrender / istock.
Printed in the United States of America
EBM

10 9 8 7 6 5 4 3 2

Disinformation® is a registered trademark of The Disinformation Company Ltd.

CONTENTS

EXPANDING THE MIND

SERIOUS RESEARCH

EXPERIENCING PSYCHEDELICS

SUPERNATURAL

INTRODUCTION
BY GRAHAM HANCOCK

I've been very lucky; I feel I've been blessed; I've lived a blessed life. I'm grateful to the universe for giving me the chance to live this life.

But why am I here? Why are you here? Why are we *all* here on planet earth? Why are we conscious? What are our lives *for?*

In answer to such questions, I can't offer any facts. I can only give you my view, which is that this world is a theatre of experience and that consciousness is fundamentally *nonphysical* and one of the driving forces of the universe like gravity or electricity. My guess is that consciousness has chosen to manifest in physical form and perhaps has invested in a very long process of manifestation on the earth—a four-and-a-half-billion-year process using evolution.

So . . . I'm not against evolution. Evolution is obvious. It's a fact. It's there. But the fact that it's there gets over-interpreted. It gets loaded down with a lot of baggage that it shouldn't really be carrying. For example, materialist scientist Richard Dawkins, author of *The Selfish Gene*, goes so far as to claim that the existence of evolution *proves* that there's no transcendental meaning to life, that there's no such thing as spirit, that consciousness cannot survive physical death—and so on and so forth.

What Dawkins doesn't consider is the possibility that "the spirit world" (for lack of a better phrase) has *used* evolution to manifest physical entities in which consciousness can emerge and express itself and learn lessons. What he doesn't consider, in other words, is the possibility that consciousness comes first while physical realms and beings are manifestations or projections of that primordial consciousness—as above, so below, as many ancient wisdom traditions state.

According to these traditions, the world is indeed a theatre of experience and we find ourselves on its stage in order to learn lessons that can only be taught in a physical realm. Moreover, we are enjoined to be aware that we have been given a precious opportunity to be born into this world of matter and consequences as human beings (rather than as fruit flies, or slime molds, or cockroaches, or stones). After all, the whole biosphere is here to support us. Four billion years of evolution on earth have led us to a point where we can make very fine distinctions between good and evil, darkness and light, love and fear—where we can make conscious choices that will impact us and others in profound ways.

This is why, in my view, modern technological society can only be described as demonic. It appears to have been expressly engineered to switch people off to the wider implications, and the wider mystery, of being alive. It bombards our consciousness with sterile, soulless messages of production and consumption, of envy and greed, that never get to the fundamentals of anything. It seeks to convince us that we're just meat—just accidents of physics and chemistry—that our only purpose is to produce and consume as much as possible, and that when we're dead, we're dead and that's the end.

I don't believe those messages! I think we're part of a very long journey—and that we may manifest in human form many times upon this earth. Reincarnation makes perfect sense to me precisely because I don't see consciousness as a mere "epiphenomenon of brain activity," as a man like Richard Dawkins must, but as the true source of all created things.

I am not alone in this intuition of the primacy of consciousness; indeed, it is shared by all the contributors to this volume and, I suspect, in various guises, by a great many others, all around the world, who have successfully resisted the mental virus mind-programming of modern technological society. But how to take that resistance further? How, if we are beings of consciousness, are we to attempt to penetrate the mystery of consciousness itself and perhaps even discover who or what we really are and why we're here?

At the level of scientific research, I'm not sure how much further scope there is for physical probing of the brain, whether directly through surgical procedures or dissection, or indirectly by means of CT scans, MRI scans, PET scans, intracranial electrophysiology, and so on and so forth. Yes, we can compare healthy and diseased brains, and we can map brains and arrive at fairly definite conclusions about the functions of different brain areas, and we can even digitally reconstruct neurons, but I suspect the real breakthroughs in our understanding of consciousness are going to come from an entirely different direction.

That direction, controversially, has to do with psychedelics—which, as many of the contributors to *The Divine Spark* argue, offer spectacular potential for the investigation of the "hard problem" of consciousness. After a hiatus of nearly half a century, this potential is again beginning to be explored by science—although as yet only in tentative and limited ways that focus on therapeutic outcomes and that shun the use of psychedelics to explore the deeper mysteries of consciousness. Indeed, even in the therapeutic arena, continuing delays, sidetracking, and shortage of funds are still the norm and arise entirely from the ideology of the mind-programming exercise called the "war on drugs" that we have been subjected to by our governments since the 1970s and that continues to undermine the most basic values of Western democracy.

SOVEREIGNTY OVER CONSCIOUSNESS

What, after all, is Western civilization all about? What are its greatest achievements and highest aspirations?

It's my guess that most people's replies to these questions would touch—before all the other splendid achievements of science, literature, technology, and the economy—on the nurture and growth of freedom.

Individual freedom.

Including, but not limited to, freedom from the unruly power of monarchs, freedom from the unwarranted intrusions of the state and its agents into our personal lives, freedom from the tyranny of the Church and its Inquisition, freedom from hunger and want, freedom from slavery and servitude, freedom of conscience, freedom of religion, freedom of thought and speech, freedom of assembly, freedom to elect our own leaders, and freedom of sexual orientation.

The list of freedoms we enjoy today that were not enjoyed by our ancestors is indeed a long and impressive one. It is therefore exceedingly strange that Western civilization in the 21st century enjoys no real *freedom of consciousness*.

There can be no more intimate and elemental part of the individual than his or her own consciousness. At the deepest level, our consciousness *is* what we are—to the extent that if we are not sovereign over our own consciousness, then we cannot in any meaningful sense be sovereign over anything else either. So it has to be highly significant that, far from encouraging freedom of consciousness, our societies in fact violently deny our right to sovereignty in this intensely personal area and have effectively outlawed all states of consciousness other than those on a very narrowly defined and officially approved list. The war on drugs has thus unexpectedly succeeded in engineering a stark reversal of the true direction of Western history by empowering faceless bureaucratic authorities to send armed agents to break into our homes, arrest us, throw us into prison, and deprive us of our income and reputation simply because we wish to explore the sometimes radical, though always temporary, alterations in *our own consciousness* that drugs facilitate.

Other than being against arbitrary rules that the state has imposed on us, personal drug use by adults is not a crime in any true moral or ethical sense and usually takes place in the privacy of our own homes where it cannot possibly do any harm to others. For some, it is a simple lifestyle choice. For others, particularly where the psychedelics such as LSD, psilocybin, and DMT are concerned, it is a means to make contact with alternate realms and parallel dimensions, and perhaps even with the divine. For some, drugs are an aid to creativity and focused mental effort. For others, they are a means to tune out for a while from everyday cares and worries. But in all cases, it seems probable that the drive to alter consciousness, from which all drug use stems, has deep genetic roots.

Other adult lifestyle choices with deep genetic roots also used to be violently persecuted by our societies.

A notable example is homosexuality, once punishable by death or long periods of imprisonment, which is now entirely legal between consenting adults—and fully recognized as being none of the state's business—in all Western cultures. (Although fourteen US states, at time of writing, retain "anti-sodomy" laws banning homosexuality, these statutes have rarely been enforced in recent years, and in 2003 the US Supreme Court invalidated those laws.) The legalization of homosexuality lifted a huge burden of human misery, secretiveness, paranoia, and genuine fear from our societies, and at the same time, not a single one of the homophobic lobby's fire-and-brimstone predictions about the end of Western civilization came true.

Likewise, it was not so long ago that natural seers, mediums, and healers who felt the calling to become "witches" were burned at the stake for "crimes" that we now look back on as harmless eccentricities at worst.

Perhaps it will be the same with drugs. Perhaps in a century or two, if we have not destroyed human civilization by then, our descendants will look back with disgust on the barbaric laws of our time that punished a minority so harshly (with loss of reputation, financial ruin, imprisonment, and worse) for responsibly, quietly, and in the privacy of their own homes seeking alterations in their own consciousness through the use of drugs. Perhaps we will even end up looking back on the persecution of drug users with the same sense of shame and horror that we now view the persecution of homosexuals, the burning of witches, and the imposition of slavery on others.

Meanwhile, it's no accident that the war on drugs has been accompanied by an unprecedented expansion of governmental power into the previously inviolable inner sanctum of individual consciousness. On the contrary, it seems to me that the state's urge to power has all along been the real reason for this "war"—not an honest desire on the part of the authorities to rescue society and the individual from the harms caused by drugs, but the thin end of a wedge intended to legitimize increasing bureaucratic control and intervention in almost every other area of our lives as well.

This is the way freedom is hijacked—not all at once, out in the open, but stealthily, little by little, behind closed doors, *and with our own agreement.* How will we be able to resist when so many of us have already willingly handed over the keys of our own consciousness to the state and accepted without protest that it is okay to be told what we may and may not do, what we may and may not explore, even what we may and may not *experience,* with this most precious, sapient, unique, and individual part of ourselves?

It may even be, by allowing the demonization and criminalization of altered states of consciousness to continue, that we are denying ourselves the next vital step in our own evolution as a species.

THE GREAT LEAP FORWARD

During most of the first seven million years of human evolution, there is no evidence at all for the existence of symbolic abilities amongst our ancestors. No matter how intensively we examine what is known about the fossil record, or speculate about what is not yet known about it, all that we see evidence for throughout this period is a dull and stultifying copying and recopying of essentially the same patterns of behaviour and essentially the same "kits" of crude stone tools, without change or innovation, for periods of hundreds of thousands, even millions of years. When a change is introduced (in tool shape, for example), it then sets a new standard to be copied and recopied without innovation for a further immense period until the next change is finally adopted. In the process, glacially slow, we also see the gradual development of human anatomy in the direction of the modern form: the brainpan enlarges, brow ridges reduce in size, and overall anatomy becomes more gracile.

By 196,000 years ago, and on some accounts considerably earlier, humans had achieved "full anatomical modernity." This means that they were in every way physically indistinguishable from the people of today and, crucially, that they possessed the same large, complex brains as we do. The most striking mystery, however, is that their behavior continued to lag behind their acquisition of modern neurology and appearance. They showed no sign of possessing a culture, or spiritual beliefs, or self-consciousness, or any interest in symbols. Indeed, there was nothing about them that we could instantly identify with "us." Dr. Frank Brown, whose discovery of 196,000-year-old anatomically modern human skeletons in Ethiopia was published in *Nature* on February 17, 2005, points out that they are 35,000 years older than the previous "oldest" modern human remains known to archaeologists: "This is significant because the cultural aspects of humanity in most cases appear much later in the record ... which would mean 150,000 years of *Homo sapiens* without cultural stuff."

Brown's colleague, John Fleagle of Stony Brook University in New York State, also comments on the same problem: "There is a huge debate ... regarding the first appearance of modern aspects of behaviour.... As modern human anatomy is documented at earlier and earlier sites, it becomes evident that there was a great time gap between the appearance of the modern skeleton and 'modern behavior.'"

For Ian Tattersall of the American Museum of Natural History, the problem posed by this gap—and what happened to our ancestors during it—is "the question of questions in palaeoanthropology." His colleague Professor David Lewis-Williams of the Rock Art Research Institute at South Africa's Witwatersrand University describes the same problem as "the greatest riddle of archaeology—how we became human and in the process began to make art and to practice what we call religion."

Contrasted with the endless, unimaginative cultural desert extending from 7 million years ago down to just 40,000 years ago, the appearance of the first great, fully representative symbolic art in caves and rock shelters between 40,000 and 30,000 years ago represents a spectacular enigma. That art, moreover, was already perfect and fully formed from the moment that it began to be created. What ushered it in? Why did it happen? And why was it accompanied by other significant changes in human behavior—including but not limited to better and more sophisticated stone and bone tools, better hunting strategies, and the first evidence for spiritual beliefs? Correlation is all we can prove, but looking at the overall suite of new behavior that appears at this time, it is difficult to avoid the conclusion that whatever divine spark led our ancestors to start creating art *caused* all the other changes as well.

In other words, if we can explain the art, we can explain the origins of modern humanity. It is therefore of the greatest interest that such a theory has been proposed and does indeed completely explain the special characteristics of Stone Age art from as far afield as Europe, the Americas, Africa, and Australia, and moreover, why identical characteristics are found in art produced by the shamans of surviving tribal cultures today. The theory was originally elaborated by Lewis-Williams and is now supported by a majority of archaeologists and anthropologists. In brief, it proposes that the reason for the eerie similarities and universal themes linking all these different systems of art is that in every case—both ancient and modern and wherever in the world they are found—the shaman-artists responsible for them had previously experienced altered states of consciousness in which they had seen vivid hallucinations, and in every case their endeavour in making the art was to memorialise on the walls of rock shelters and caves the ephemeral images that they had seen in their visions. According to this neuropsychological theory, the different bodies of art have so many similarities because we all share the same neurology, and thus share many of the same experiences and visions in altered states of consciousness.

There are lots of ways of inducing the necessary altered state. The Bushmen of South Africa get there through night-long rhythmic dancing and drumming; the Tukano Indians of the Amazon do it through consuming the psychedelic beverage Ayahuasca, the "vine of souls." In prehistoric Europe, it's most likely that the requisite altered states were reached through the consumption of *Psilocybe semilanceata*—the popular little brown magic mushroom that is still used throughout the world to induce hallucinations today. In Central America, the Maya and their predecessors used other *Psilocybe* species (*P. mexicana* and *P. cubensis*) to induce the same effects.

TERRA INCOGNITA

I took LSD once in my twenties, at the Windsor Free Festival in England in 1974, and had a fantastic, exciting, energizing twelve-hour trip in a parallel reality. When my normal, everyday consciousness returned—and it did so quite abruptly, like a door slamming—I felt grateful for such a wonderful experience but so much in awe of its power that I doubted if I would ever want to embrace it again. Suppose things had gone the other way? Suppose instead of an exciting medieval Otherworld through which I had been allowed to travel like a knight-errant, I had been ushered into some hell realm for twelve hours? How would I have handled that? Would I have handled it at all?

It was not until I reached my fifties and began work on my book *Supernatural: Meetings with the Ancient Teachers of Mankind* that I decided to confront the psychic challenges of major hallucinogens again. In order to research my subject properly, and to know what I was talking about when I spoke of altered states of consciousness, I drank Ayahuasca with shamans in the Amazon and self-experimented with DMT, psilocybin, and the African visionary drug known as Iboga—"the plant that enables men to see the dead."

The extraordinary experiences I went through convinced me that David Lewis-Williams is right and that visionary states of this sort, brought on by the accidental discovery of plant psychedelics, did indeed provide the inspiration for ancient cave and rock art traditions all around the world.

Lewis-Williams is also right to insist that it is to the proper examination of such altered states of consciousness that we should turn if we wish to discover the source of the first spiritual ideas ever entertained by our ancestors.

It was precisely at this point, however, that I began to part company with Lewis-Williams and his theory. Whatever the cave artists saw in their trances, and no matter how devoutly they may have believed that what they were seeing was real, the South African professor is adamant that the entire inspiration for 25,000 years of Upper Paleolithic cave paintings reduces to nothing more than the fevered illusions of disturbed brain chemistry—i.e., to hallucinations. In his scientific universe, there is simply no room, or need, for the supernatural, no space for any kind of otherworld, and no possibility that intelligent nonphysical entities could exist.

I found I couldn't leave the matter there, with the inspiration for cave art and the birth of religion neatly accounted for by disturbed brain chemistry, with the earliest spiritual insights of mankind rendered down to mere epiphenomena of strictly biological processes, with the sublime thus efficiently reduced to the ridiculous. To have established the role of hallucinations as the inspiration for cave art is one thing—and David Lewis-Williams, in my opinion, has successfully done that. But to understand what hallucinations really are, and what part they play in the overall spectrum of human experience and behaviour, is another thing altogether, and neither Lewis-Williams nor any other scientist can yet claim to possess such knowledge, or to be anywhere near acquiring it. Gifted and experienced shamans the world over really do know more—much more—than they do. So if we were smart, we would listen to what the shamans have to say about the true character and complexity of reality instead of basking mindlessly in the overweening one-dimensional arrogance of the Western technological mind-set.

Because I had been shaken to the core by my experiences with Ayahuasca and Iboga, I decided to take my investigation further and to explore the extraordinary possibility that science is unwilling even to consider and that David Lewis-Williams dismisses out of hand. This is the possibility that the Amazonian and African psychedelics had obliged me to confront face-to-face—and that shamans contend with on a daily basis—the possibility that the "spirit world" and its inhabitants are real, that supernatural powers and nonphysical beings do exist, and that human consciousness may, under certain special circumstances, be liberated from the body and enabled to interact with and perhaps even learn from these "spirits." In short, did our ancestors experience their great evolutionary leap forward of the last 40,000 years not just because of the beneficial social and organisational by-products of shamanism but because they were literally helped, taught, prompted, and inspired by supernatural agents? Could the "supernaturals" first depicted in the painted caves and rock shelters—and still accessible to us today in altered states of consciousness—be the ancient teachers of mankind? Could it be they who first ushered us into the full birthright of our humanity? And could it be that human evolution is not just the "blind," "meaningless," "natural" process that Darwin identified, but something else, more purposive and intelligent, that we have barely even begun to understand?

If so, then we demonise altered states of consciousness at our peril, and rather than sending our fellow humans to prison for seeking them out, we should encourage, reward, and support them as the true explorers and adventurers of our time. I have brought together this series of essays in *The Divine Spark*, written by researchers and activists in the field of consciousness whose work I respect, as a contribution to this exploration of terra incognita.

ON CONSCIOUSNESS

TO INFINITY AND BEYOND:
THE HOLOGRAPHIC NATURE OF MASS

BY NASSIM HARAMEIN

EXPLORING REALITY

Have you ever wondered about the structure of reality? Where did it come from? How did it get here? And how did it self-organize to result in my observing it? These are fundamental inquiries that most people have asked themselves at some point in life. They might have thought of these questions in many different ways, perhaps not exactly as stated above, but most people have wondered about the source of existence, about a beginning and an end, or about an eternal continuous dynamic.

From an early age, I have felt these questions are most worthy of investigation, and in a certain way, my earlier adventures in the various sports industries became tools that I could use to investigate the reality I am in, my interaction with it, and my capacity to modify it or at least push it to the extreme. And to the extremes I pushed it: whether it was skiing, climbing, or deep-sea diving, my tendency was to see how far I could push the edge of the structure of reality by my intent and capacity to overcome physical limitations. It was a test of mind over matter, and in every case I felt that a resonance field could be established with the structure of reality—what athletes typically call "the zone"—where, as best I can describe it, I felt a flow, a type of harmony with all the various dynamics I was encountering in these extreme situations.

Whether it was the forces involved, such as gravitational in skiing, or the sensations of the material world feeding back information to my body and my body responding to it—such as the fine edge of my ski slicing through an icy surface, or the sensations in the tips of my fingers conforming to sharp crystals while I climbed a thousand-foot rock face—these moments of high communion with nature taught me that there must be a fundamental feedback relationship. Some kind of a feedback/feedforward in the structure of space-time that produced a sense of complete integration within the wheelworks of nature that I was experiencing (in the zone). In these moments of high awareness, it felt like I had reached a harmonious relationship with the self-organizing properties of the material world, which I could clearly observe everywhere in the natural environment where highly organized and complex systems can be found.

Yet there was more. My early interest in exploring the more mystical side of our experience led me to investigate the internal world of meditation, a world that is in complete reference to the event of consciousness, of a deep and fundamental self-discovery and exploration of the observer experiencing this reality. Therefore, it was both an external exploration, in which I could push the boundary of my influence on the external world (what one could call the material world), as well as an exploration of how far I could push the boundary of the internal world to identify the source of the observation. And to my great surprise, the two seemed to feedback on themselves. For instance, in those states of "the zone" during peak experiences in sporting events, nature seemed to be speaking to me beyond the receptor sites of my five senses to a deeper, more profound sense, as in a unity between my physicality and the physicality of the world around me. Similarly, in deep meditative states and moments of rapture, a profound sense of unity with the material world around and inside of me seemed to take place. The question then was: what are the mechanics of the apparent feedback between me, the observer, and the material world, and is there an information medium that makes the connection between the observed and the observer? Such discovery would generate a unified view of natural processes and the physics of our world.

In order to answer these questions appropriately, I had to conduct, on the one hand, an in-depth study of the physics of our world and, on the other hand, a study of the mores (the customs and ritual practices) of various societies that could reveal a deeper understanding of the relationship between the observer and the material world. In my opinion, both were equally important, although the task of studying both in parallel, which encompassed fields ranging from applied physics to cosmology and quantum mechanics as well as archaeology, psychology, and spirituality, seemed insurmountable. Therefore, it was with great procrastination and reluctance that I finally abandoned my professional career in the sports industry to dedicate all of my time and energy to the studies necessary in order to begin answering some of these questions.

This led to a prolonged, isolated period of my life, when I lived in a van with the bare minimum necessary to survive, living the simplest life possible in order to dedicate every second of my day (and most nights) to the study of these various fields. Still, to this day, I consider those times as some of the most wonderful, productive, and mystical times of my life. I was completely free—free of telephones, appointments, and interactions with the outside world. I was completely free to think whatever I wanted to think, to study whatever I wanted to study, and to move wherever I wanted to move, as all I had to do was put the key into the ignition, press on the gas pedal, and I was instantaneously relocating. My home was wherever I parked, and I was fortunate enough to be in some of the most beautiful and remarkable natural environments on our planet. From the alpine meadows of British Columbia and Alberta, Canada, to the high deserts of the American Southwest and everything in between, I spent many months in communion with the natural world while in deep contemplation of its physics and of the relationship between these physical structures and my observations of them.

I continued a routine of physical activities to balance the typical fifteen to eighteen hours a day I spent studying. At the time, most of my physical activity consisted of rock climbing, as I would typically start my morning with a sunrise climb after some time meditating, or I would get out of the van at sunset for a little fresh air and a quick multipitch climb to get my blood flowing. Since I was usually alone, these climbs mostly consisted of free solos (no protective gear).

At the fine edge of these experiences, where any mistake would surely result in the obvious outcome of a body falling through space being rudely arrested by the ground, I could get into that zone where, however extreme the experience of reality was, there was a complete sense of comfort, a sense of absolute trust, of harmony with all of nature at the same time as complete relaxation—and that stuff was addictive. I was in love with nature, and it felt like nature was in love with me.

I distinctly remember moments when my cheek was glued to the face of sheer rock walls, with the exposure of a few thousand feet unravelling below me, and I was gazing at teeny crystals glistening in the rising Sun and thinking about the molecules and atoms and subatomic particles that make up those crystals. Where did they begin, and where did they end? After all, these crystals I was climbing were part of a larger crystal, a large geode called the Earth, and the Earth was part of a solar system, and the solar system was part of a galaxy, and the galaxy was part of a cluster of galaxies, which was most likely part of a supercluster, and so on. Furthermore, every crystal was made out of millions and millions of molecules, and each molecule was made out of atoms, and these atoms were made out of subatomic particles, and so on. Was it appropriate to think that the Universe ended somewhere, whether on the infinitely large scale or on the infinitely small scale?

These moments often brought on trance-like states in which I would completely lose track of my whereabouts and either dive down the rabbit hole into the molecular structure of these crystals or expand into galactic and universal structures, imagining and contemplating!

A MATTER OF SCALE

From the study of the physics I was conducting and from various discoveries I had made in exploring my internal experience, I realized that if we were truly to look for a complete picture of the dynamics and mechanics that produce both the material world and the observer that experiences it, the model would have to be based on an infinite relationship of scales.

I discovered within myself what seemed to be an infinite division of the scales. This seemed to be beyond the concept of a bubble Universe from which everything started with a bang without any clear understanding of either what produced the bang or how the material/energy got there to bang in the first place.

I remember being very young, probably about seven, when it was explained to me that the Universe was like a big balloon expanding. My first question to myself was: expanding in what? Surely, if the Universe were expanding, it must be expanding inside another Universe, larger than the one we are in. And then again, if that one were expanding as well, surely it must be expanding in a larger one, and so on. There was no easy solution to the riddle. The only thing that made sense was that the Universe was infinitely large and infinitely small, that we lived in a continuum of divisions, and that our world was defined by the mere fact that we observed the Universe from a very specific scale. Therefore, from this scale (that is, the scale of our Universe) there would be a fundamental lower size that defined the pixel of our scale. Not that this pixel would be the smallest thing the Universe does but that this pixel size is the fundamental building block for a universe of our specific magnitude.

For instance, if you were experiencing the Universe from the scale of an atom or even a subatomic particle, your experience would be widely different from the experience you have of your Universe as a human being. And if I were to grow you from an atom to the size of a human, you would most likely think that you had changed universes or even changed dimensions (although that would be partially true, as you have literally changed in dimension).

These thoughts had come to me in various ways throughout the years, but how could they be appropriately expressed in physics? Were there any physics already written in our world that indicated such a principle? Furthermore, did these concepts agree with thousands and thousands of years of advanced thinking in philosophy, mysticism, and religious belief?

The first clue had come in my teenage years, when I initially realized that for almost a hundred years, a chasm had existed in physics between the mathematics and models we use for large objects, which predicts a continuum that tends toward singularity and infinities (Einstein's field equations), and the quantum world of atomic and subatomic particles, which predicts linear functions of bounded states, well-defined and with finite behaviors. Yet big things are made out of small things, so how could the Universe use two completely different sets of physics?

How could the Universe be both finite and infinite at the same time? Truly, day-to-day experience seems to point to the existence of well-defined finite boundaries. After all, your body's dimensions are defined by what appears to be a very specific scale. The same applies to the chair you're sitting on, or the pole you're holding on to while you're reading this article on the bus on your way to work. But wouldn't an infinite universe have no definition, no distinct way of identifying a boundary to define all other ones? All of this became the subject of many years of contemplation, and the answer, interestingly, came from an unexpected source.

THE ORGANIZING PRINCIPLE OF NATURE

From my study of ancient civilizations, there seemed to be a persistent, recurring theme, and that theme, to cut to the chase, seemed to have something to do with geometry and some fundamental medium permeating everything, being omnipresent, omniscient, and the organizing principle of nature. I looked to find if similar concepts were present in our history of physics and the advanced physics of today, and indeed I found similarities.

On the geometric side, for instance, was Einstein's geometrization of the structure of space-time. As well, in mathematics, fractal theory resembled many ancient concepts and symbols and provided a perfect relationship between infinities and the boundary condition, as an infinite amount of boundaries could be embedded within a finite initial boundary (the scale at which you are observing). As far as an omnipresent permeating energy was concerned, it occurred to me then that maybe, just maybe, the all-prevailing intensely energetic vacuum of the quantum world might fit the bill.

Maybe the space between all of the molecules and atoms that I was observing on my cliff face inside the crystal that my hands were so firmly gripping, the space between our planet and the Sun, the space inside our galaxy and the space between galaxies was full instead of empty. Maybe space was permeated with all the information of all things in the space and was the great connector between all these things. After all, from infinitely large to infinitely small, space is always present, since even the extremely small radius of an atom still contains some 99.99999 percent space. Perhaps space defined matter, rather than the material world defining the space.

What if matter were only the result of a discrete boundary condition of the space itself, like the feedback iterations that produced the divisions of a fractal? Was the world-space experiencing itself? Were we an extreme extension of the space, looking back at ourselves and experiencing matter? Einstein seemed to think so, as in his famous statement: "Physical objects are not *in space,* but these objects are *spatially extended.* In this way the concept 'empty space' loses its meaning."

But if space were the great medium that connected all things, gathering information from all places so as to self-organize and create the complexity we observed in our natural world, then space would have to be nearly infinitely dense—infinitely dense with information or energy. Was this possible, and if so, was there any evidence as such? I was probing deeper and deeper into the physics that had been written and into the experiments that had been performed throughout nearly three hundred years of modern physical theory, and I came across something significant.

THE ENERGY DENSITY OF THE VACUUM

It seemed that in the quantum world, a difficulty had been encountered when physicists tried to calculate the energy density of an oscillator such as an atom. It turned out that some of the vibrations still existed even when the system was brought to absolute zero, where you would think that all the energy would be gone. In fact, the equations showed that there was an infinite amount of possible energy fluctuation even within the vacuum.

To understand this better, physicists applied a principle of "renormalization," using a fundamental constant to cut off the number and get a finite idea of how dense the vacuum energy must be with all its vibrations. The cut-off value used was the Planck's distance or length, named after the great physicist Max Planck, who is considered to be the founder of quantum theory. This value is thought to be the smallest vibration of the electromagnetic field possible, being in the order of 10^{-33} centimeters and having a mass energy in the order of 10^{-5} grams.

To better understand the scales involved, here is an analogy. There are approximately 100 trillion cells in the average human body, and each typical cell is made of approximately 100 trillion atoms. If you were to take one of those minute atoms and make it the size of the dome at the Vatican (138 feet or 42 meters diameter) the proton in the middle nucleus would be approximately the size of a tiny head of a pin. Now, if we were to put a Planck unit on the end of your finger and then grow it to the average size of a grain of sand, then the minuscule proton would all of a sudden have a diameter equal to the distance from here to the nearest star, Alpha Centauri or approximately 25.5 trillion miles or 40 trillion kilometers in diameter. Therefore, although the proton is already an extremely small entity, the Planck size is mind-bogglingly tiny.

Thus, the calculations that were done to derive the Planck vacuum energy density entailed working out how many teeny Planck's volume vibrations could coexist in a cubic centimeter of space. The answer is then the number of Plancks that fit in a centimeter cubed of space multiplied by each of their mass (10^{-5} grams) to obtain the mass/energy density that existed in a centimeter cubed of space. Of course, the result was enormous since the Planck is so tiny! The vacuum energy density, or what is typically called the Planck density, was, when it was first calculated, in the order of 10^{93} grams per cubic centimeter of space and was quickly dubbed at the time "the worst theoretical prediction in the history of physics"[1] or "the vacuum catastrophe."

To give you an idea of how dense this value is, if you were to take all of the matter we observed in our Universe today with billions of galaxies containing billions of stars, most of which are much larger than our Sun, and we were to stuff them all into a centimeter cube of space, the density of that cube would only be 10^{55} grams/cm^3. This is still some thirty-eight orders of magnitude less dense than the density of the vacuum. Many scientists thought that this figure was ridiculous, and in general, it fell into obscurity. Even today, some trained physicists are not necessarily aware of this value. Throughout the years, I've received prompt criticism from certain physicists who either were unaware of its existence or simply discarded it, as if the largest energy quantity ever predicted could be completely ignored.

However, the vacuum fluctuations of energy are crucial to our understanding of particle physics at this point, as they are the source of virtual particle creation at the atomic level, which is essential to our current understanding of physics. This is what led John Archibald Wheeler, a colleague of Einstein, to eventually state, "The vision of quantum gravity is a vision of turbulence—turbulent space, turbulent time, turbulent spacetime . . . spacetime in small-enough regions should be not merely 'bumpy,' not merely erratic in its curvature; it should fractionate into ever-changing, multiply connected geometries. For the very small and the very quick, wormholes should be as much a part of the landscape as those dancing virtual particles that give to the electron its slightly altered energy and magnetism [Observed as the Lamb shift]."[2]

More importantly, in 1948 the Dutch physicist Hendrik Casimir calculated and elaborated a configuration that would ultimately allow an experimental validation of this vacuum energy. Casimir reasoned that if two plates were placed close enough to each other so that the longer wavelengths of the vacuum oscillations would be eliminated from between the plates and yet would still be present on the outside of the plates, then a minute density gradient could be generated where there would be more pressure on the outside and less on the inside, resulting in the plates being pushed together. However, when the distance by which the plates had to be separated to do the job was calculated, it was found that the plates had to be mere microns apart. This was an impossible task in 1948, and it wasn't until the early 1990s that this experimental test could be done successfully. The result agreed very well with the calculations done by Casimir, showing that this energy of the structure of space itself is truly present.

More recently, the Casimir effect has been able to be reproduced in a dynamic way called the dynamical Casimir effect, in which the plates are essentially replaced by a nano-scale mirror oscillating at a significant percentage of the speed of light. The result is that some of the pairs of virtual particles in the vacuum fluctuations cannot recombine quickly enough, as they usually do as they are being separated by the movement of the mirror disturbing their path, and thus become "real" photons being emitted directly from the vacuum.[3]

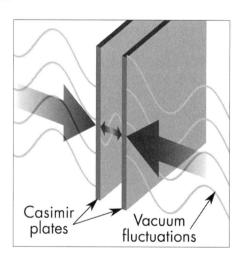

Casimir plates   Vacuum fluctuations

A CONNECTED UNIVERSE

So the energy was there in the vacuum at the quantum resolution. Could it be the energy that connects all things, the energy from which everything emerges and to which everything returns? Well, if so, it would have to be present at all scales. That is, there had to be evidence of this energy between stars and galaxies as well. I had studied quite a bit of cosmology by then, and at the time, there was zero evidence of this energy being present at the cosmological level. Nevertheless, I was in a highly creative mode, elaborating on many of the foundations that eventually brought me to form the various scientific papers I have written.

From the sense I was getting from my studies of both ancient civilizations and advanced physics, this vacuum energy could not be completely random. It had to have structure, some kind of geometry, and most likely it was polarized—that is, spin was involved. And it was these thoughts that eventually brought me to add a fundamental force to Einstein's field equations in order to show that space-time, in addition to curving to produce gravitation, twisted as well—like water going down the drain—to produce the spin of all organized matter from galaxies to stars and even to subatomic particles. That twisting of space would imply that space itself was imbued with gyroscopic and Coriolis effects that needed to be included in Einstein's geometrization of space and time. Yet if this torque really was present, then we should be able to detect it at the cosmological level.

I will always remember the day when this confirmation fell into my lap. It must have been around the late 1990s, when I was in Joshua Tree National Park, where I liked to spend part of the winter climbing and studying. Typically, I would go in and stay for weeks at a time before my supplies ran out and I would have to come out again to get a little bit of shopping done. My budgets were quite restricted (on average, three thousand dollars a year), so I would buy a very minimal amount of food (I mostly lived on prana—vacuum energy), but almost every time, I would buy popular science magazines to keep in touch with the latest scientific discoveries.

So on a beautiful morning after one such expedition the night before and then after my ritual climb, I sat on the edge of the stairs of my van and opened what I recall was an issue of *Astronomy Magazine*. And there it was: astronomers had found evidence that the Universe was not only expanding but was also accelerating as it did so.

This discovery produced a large amount of controversy at the time, and most theorists agreed that the best approach to deal with this anomaly was to reinstate a constant that was first used by Einstein. He had added this fudge factor, called the cosmological constant, in his early mathematical expressions to make the Universe static (which was believed to be the case at the time). It was later removed when astronomer Edwin Hubble discovered that the Universe was expanding, as Einstein's equations would predict without the fudge factor. Now astronomers reinstated the cosmological constant with a negative energy in such a way as to show the Universe accelerating as it expanded. The fudge factor was back. This eventually was dubbed "dark energy," and it wasn't until recently that it started to be associated with vacuum energy. For me, however, that was an easy and obvious leap, as I had already expected from my theoretical tenets that the polarized Coriolis dynamics of the vacuum structure would produce such an effect on the universal expansion and rotation.

So the vacuum energy was there at all scales, although in various densities—a density gradient in the structure of space itself. Was the vacuum dividing at specific densities from extremely large to extremely small? And if the vacuum energy was essentially infinitely dense, and all scales contained vacuum—since even the atom itself (as we saw earlier) contains a large percentage of vacuum—then all atoms inevitably contained enough vacuum mass–energy to be considered a black hole. The Universe had to be black holes, from all the way up—the Universe that we're in—to all the way down to every single atom. With this concept, I eventually coined the term *black whole*.

A BLACK WHOLE UNIVERSE

While pursuing various readings at the time and looking at the currently accepted mass of our Universe, I realized that the Universe as a whole obeyed the condition that described a black hole. Later on, with the help of Dr. Elizabeth Rauscher and afterwards Dr. Michael Hyson, we developed various scaling graphs that supported the concept of a fractal black hole universe.

Eventually, after some twenty years of being almost alone in thinking that we may live in a black hole universe, popular science reports appeared that elaborated on the research of a physicist at Indiana University. The first sentence of the university's communiqué asks: "Could our universe be located within the interior of a wormhole which itself is part of a black hole that lies within a much larger universe?"[4-5]

But could an atom, or the nucleus of an atom, the proton, be considered a black hole? I suspected so but I didn't know, and it was not until the year 2003 that I finally got to working out the calculations to make such a prediction.

At the time, I was living on the Big Island of Hawai'i and my daily routine started at sunrise with an encounter with the creatures of the ocean, usually wild dolphins, spinner dolphins in particular. The sensation of gliding in the ocean and the vorticular spinning hydrodynamics of the water around my body often reminded me of our daily "swim" through the vacuum structure and the Coriolis dynamic that was part of my views of the physics of creation.

It occurred to me that a certain percentage of the mass–energy of the vacuum must be contributing to the energetic event that we call the nucleus of an atom. Scribbling on a notepad in my office chair overlooking Kealakekua Bay, I calculated the tiny volume of a proton and then proceeded to pack it with Planck vacuum fluctuations and outputted their combined mass. Remarkably, the combined mass of all the Plancks inside the volume of a proton was equivalent to the mass of the Universe, approximately 10^{55} grams! Was this evidence of the holographic nature of this vacuum information network connecting the information of all other protons in the Universe in one proton? Of course, this value was large enough to make a single proton a black hole since this value even in the volume of our Universe makes our Universe a black hole. I called Dr. Rauscher right away and discussed the simple calculations that would tell us how much of the vacuum energy was necessary for a proton to be in the Schwarzschild condition, the condition of a black hole. It took a remarkably small amount of the energy of the vacuum available in the proton to do the job, but what was notable was that the energy it took was equivalent to the energy necessary to produce the force typically described as the strong nuclear force, or the strong force, the confining force that holds the protons together in the nucleus of an atom. That is, if the proton was considered a teeny black hole due to the vacuum energy present in it, then the attraction between two of these protons would be exactly the force we attribute to the so-called strong force. Coincidence? I didn't think so.

The strong force had always bothered me because, as in many other instances in modern physics (such as with dark energy and dark matter), this force had been simply invented, plucked out of thin air. When it was found that the protons were highly charged but confined to a very small radius in the nucleus of an atom, physicists went on to invent a force that would overcome the repulsion of the electrostatic fields of these particles, and they made it exactly what it was needed to be to do the job. Eventually it was believed that the proton seemed to have smaller constituents within it called quarks, which were confined in an even smaller space, and so the color force had to be invented, which is the base for quantum chromodynamics, or QCD. Furthermore, QCD predicts that it would take an infinite amount of force to separate two quarks in order to account for the fact that no free quarks have ever been observed. Now the original strong force near the radius of a proton was seen as only a remnant of this color force at the quark level.

Yet from decades of calculations with supercomputers, no analytical solution has ever been found to support the QCD model, and the idea that quarks cannot be found because it would require an infinite amount of force to separate them is circular at best. From my point of view, the infinitely strong nuclear color force was, instead, the result of the gravitational attraction of mini–black holes, and it was extremely confirming to find that, when one considered the proton as a black hole, the gravitational attraction of such an entity was exactly the energy typically associated with the strong force.

Furthermore, although these calculations were very rough at the time, as we were scribbling on pieces of paper and napkins, it seemed that certain values of the Schwarzschild proton, as I came to call it, nicely predicted certain measured values of the proton entity. This was, and still is, a radical idea—although more and more physicists are coming to these conclusions now. Imagine all of the atoms that make up your physical body, and the entire material world around you, are made out of mini–black holes the size of a proton.

Although these initial calculations were somewhat conclusive, it took until 2008 before a first version of the calculation was published in one of our papers titled "Scale Unification: A Universal Scaling Law for Organized Matter." A more complete version titled "The Schwarzschild Proton" was eventually presented at a scientific conference in Belgium in 2009, where it won a Best Paper Award.

Of course, the publication of that paper created many controversies in the scientific community and the public at large. Many argued that the mass of a black hole proton, being some forty orders of magnitude larger than the measured value in a laboratory, was not acceptable. Yet there were no qualms with throwing a force into the standard model that has infinite strength in order for the model to work, giving no explanation of the source of energy required to produce such a force nor any mathematics or analytical solution to back it up. At least my solution was well-grounded in the analytical mechanics of gravitation. Yet I certainly had to expand the understanding in order to complete the model and account for these forty orders of magnitude that were contributed by the vacuum energy present within the volume of a proton. What were the mechanisms that made this energy express itself as a gravitational force between two protons? And would this mechanism demonstrate that the range of such a gravitational field matches the short range typically associated with the strong force?

From 2009 to December of 2012, I worked continuously almost day and night in an attempt to uncover this mechanism. The Schwarzschild Proton approach had given me some very important hints. The mass of all the vacuum fluctuations inside the volume of a proton was equivalent to the mass of the Universe, or all other protons in the Universe. Maybe the holographic nature of the vacuum fluctuations' information network was the source of the mechanism that made the proton act as a mini–black hole. I started to think that maybe the vacuum energy inside the proton and the vacuum energy outside the proton relating information through the surface event horizon of the proton may be the source of this pressure we call gravity.

I set out to study holographic concepts and found that in the same period of time, some of the most advanced physicists on the planet were attempting to solve the black holes information paradox problem utilizing what eventually was dubbed the Holographic Principle. The so-called information loss paradox resulted from the consideration that all the information that falls into a black hole would be lost as the black hole evaporates to nothing, due to an earlier postulate by Hawking—known as Hawking radiation—which describes the emission of quantum Planck vacuum fluctuations' "virtual particles" producing a slight loss of the black hole's energy over time, eventually leading to its complete evaporation.[6] But if the whole thing evaporates, where does the information go? The conservation of information or energy would be violated. The Holographic Principle states that all of the information that falls into the volume of the black hole is imprinted in terms of little Planck bits on the surface of the black hole, and by using this approach, physicists arrived at the correct answer for the temperature, or entropy, of the black hole.[7]

But what if the information that fell into the black hole was shared across all other black holes through the wormhole network of the vacuum fluctuations, like a huge information superhighway at the Planck and proton level? Maybe that's what allowed extremely complex systems to self-organize in such a rapid evolution since the early Earth, such as the biological structures all around us (including us) which cannot be accounted for under random functions in such a short amount of time. Maybe the feedback between the network structures is the source of the neuronal structure of our brain and the basis of what we think of as self-awareness or consciousness. Furthermore, what if the information back and forth across the event horizon surface of the black hole, whether cosmological or a proton, is the source of its gravitational mass? Yet how would I define the mechanics of this information structure and extract from it meaningful results? After all, the numbers involved with the vacuum fluctuations were extremely large (the mass of the Universe) and it was tentative at best that such large numbers would yield precise values for objects like a proton for instance, with a mass in the order of 1.6726 x 10^{-24} grams (0.0000000000000000000000016726gm), an extremely small number.

After years of manipulations of algebraic relationships and geometric explorations, finally a solution emerged. In fact, the solution was so simple, it had completely eluded me all these years. It turned out that a simple volume-to-surface ratio of the Planck vacuum fluctuations (but only if they are Planck spherical units, which I call PSU) generated the correct answer for the gravitational mass of any black hole in the cosmological Universe and that a simple inverse relationship yields the exact value of the mass of the proton. This was a remarkable result; all of a sudden I could give a solution to Einstein's gravitational equations by simply deriving the discrete Planck quantities of electromagnetic fluctuation of the vacuum interacting with the surface of the black hole. Of course, this was a quantum gravity solution since it was quantized in discrete Planck units, and when I applied it to the quantum world of the proton, although the numbers were extremely large, the resulting mass was within 0.001 x 10^{-24} grams of the measured value.

Knowing that we are able to measure the mass of the proton extremely precisely but that the measurement of the radius has been a source of great difficulties, I then reversed my equation to predict from the mass what the exact radius of the proton should be. In December of 2012, I sent a paper titled "Quantum Gravity and the Holographic Mass" to the Library of Congress containing these results and my prediction. A few months later, on January 25, 2013, a new most-precise-to-date measurement of the radius of the proton was made by the proton accelerator in Switzerland and published.[8] Incredibly, my predicted value was within 0.00036 x 10^{-13}cm of the new measurement and inside one standard deviation, or loosely speaking, the margin of error of their experiment. Therefore, my predicted value from theoretical tenets may be the most precise value and the experiments are slowly approaching it. This would make sense since I am making the calculations utilizing the smallest unit of measurement possible, the Planck units, and the smaller the units of measurement, the more precise the result.

However, the paper did not predict just the radius of the proton and that gravity can be described by discrete chunks of Planck quantities but as well that such a geometric approach of the pixilation of space-time with Planck spherical units yields as well, the correct value for the strong force and its correct range—demonstrating that the force that confines protons in the nucleus of atoms is actually gravity in terms of discrete Planck quantities of vacuum electromagnetic fluctuations.

REFLECTIONS ON A REVOLUTION IN PHYSICS

We live at a remarkable time. It is a time of great changes, including fundamental changes in our understanding of the physics of our world and its relationship to consciousness. There is a quiet revolution occurring in physics that will modify our understanding of the atomic structure as many other researchers are now starting to realize that atoms may be considered as mini–black holes[9–12] and that the vacuum structure may be a crucial player in the existence of our world.

Why is this exciting? Because if we understand the source of energy that generates our Universe, its forces, and the mechanics under which the creation process occurs, then we can reproduce these dynamics with advanced technological means and completely transform our relationship to nature. Such discoveries will change our world from a society that believes that there are only limited amounts of resources and available land—and the wars fought over them—to a society that realizes that there is an infinite amount of energy all around and within us, and a whole Universe to explore with the means literally to reach for the stars.

However, we don't need to wait for these advances to start to transform ourselves and our environment. We need only take a few moments every day to connect with the infinite potential present at the center of our entire material world, which makes up our existence, and experience its infinite nature and beyond.

NOTES

1. MP Hobson, GP Efstathiou & AN Lasenby (2006). General Relativity: An introduction for physicists (Reprint ed.). Cambridge University Press. p. 187. ISBN 978-0-521-82951-9.
2. J. A. Wheeler, "Geons, Black Holes and Quantum Foam: A— life in Physics," W. W. Norton, New York, pg. 248, (1998).
3. C. M. Wilson, G. Johansson, A. Pourkabirian, et al. "Observation of the dynamical Casimir effect in a superconducting circuit" Nature 479, 376–379 (17 November 2011) doi:10.1038/nature10561

4. "Our universe at home within a larger universe? So suggests IU theoretical physicist's wormhole research," Indiana University press release, 6 April 2010, http://newsinfo. iu.edu/news/page/normal/13995.html

5. Poplawski, Nikodem J., "Radial motion into an Einstein–Rosen bridge," Physics Letters B 2010 Apr 12; 687(2- 3):110–113

6. Hawking, S. W. (1974). "Black hole explosions?" Nature, Volume 248, Issue 5443, pp. 30–31 (1974 doi:10.1038/248030a0

7. t'Hooft, Gerard. "The Holographic Principle" 1 Mar 2000, revised 16 May 2000 arXiv:hep-th/0003004

8. A. Antognini, et al., "Proton Structure from the Measurement of 2S-2P Transition Frequencies of Muonic Hydrogen," Science, vol. 339, (25 January 2013).

9. "Could the Universe Be Made Up of Mini Black Holes? Two Leading Experts Say 'Yes'," The Daily Galaxy, 7 April 2010, available at http://tinyurl.com/y2p7lpe

10. Coyne, D.G. and D.C. Cheng, "A Scenario for Strong Gravity in Particle Physics: An alternative mechanism for black holes to appear at accelerator experiments," at http://arxiv.org/ftp/arxiv/papers/0905/ 0905.1667.pdf

11. Holzhey, C.F.E. and F. Wilczek, "Black Holes as Elementary Particles," Nuclear Physics B 1992 Aug 10; 380(3):447–77, at http://arxiv.org/abs/hep-th/9202014v1

12. Oldershaw, R.L., "Hadrons As Kerr–Newman Black Holes," Journal of Cosmology 2010; 6:1361–74, at http://arxiv.org/abs/astro-ph/0701006

THE CONSCIOUSNESS REVOLUTION
BY GRAHAM HANCOCK

Consciousness is one of the great mysteries of science—perhaps the greatest mystery. We all know we have it, when we think, when we dream, when we savor tastes and aromas, when we hear a great symphony, when we fall in love, and it is surely the most intimate, the most sapient, the most personal part of ourselves. Yet no one can really claim to have understood and explained it completely. There's no doubt it's associated with the brain in some way, but the nature of that association is far from clear. In particular, how do these three pounds of material stuff inside our skulls allow us to have experiences?

Professor David Chalmers of the Australian National University has dubbed this the "hard problem" of consciousness, but many scientists, particularly those (still in the majority) who are philosophically inclined to believe that all phenomena can be reduced to material interactions, deny that any problem exists. To them, it seems self-evident that physical processes within the stuff of the brain produce consciousness rather in the way that a generator produces electricity—i.e., consciousness is an "epiphenomenon" of brain activity. And they see it as equally obvious that there cannot be such things as conscious survival of death or out-of-body experiences since both consciousness and experience are confined to the brain and must die when the brain dies.

Yet other scientists with equally impressive credentials are not so sure and are increasingly willing to consider a very different analogy—namely that the relationship of consciousness to the brain may be less like the relationship of the generator to the electricity it produces and more like the relationship of the TV signal to the TV set. In that case, when the TV set is destroyed—dead—the signal still continues. Nothing in the present state of knowledge of neuroscience rules this revolutionary possibility out. True, if you damage certain areas of the brain, certain areas of consciousness are compromised, but this does not prove that those areas of the brain generate the relevant areas of consciousness. If you were to damage certain areas of your TV set, the picture would deteriorate or vanish but the TV signal would remain intact.

We are, in other words, confronted by at least as much mystery as fact around the subject of consciousness, and this being the case, we should remember that what seems obvious and self-evident to one generation may not seem at all obvious or self-evident to the next. For hundreds of years, it was obvious and self-evident to the greatest human minds that the Sun moved around the Earth—one need only look to the sky, they said, to see the truth of this proposition. Indeed, those who maintained the revolutionary view that the Earth moved around the Sun faced the Inquisition and death by burning at the stake. Yet as it turned out, the revolutionaries were right and orthodoxy was terribly, ridiculously wrong.

The same may well prove to be true with the mystery of consciousness. Yes, it does seem obvious and self-evident that the brain produces it (the generator analogy), but this is a deduction from incomplete data and categorically *not* yet an established and irrefutable fact. New discoveries may force materialist science to rescind this theory in favor of something more like the TV analogy in which the brain comes to be understood as a transceiver rather than as a generator of consciousness and in which consciousness is recognized as fundamentally "nonlocal" in nature—perhaps even as one of the basic driving forces of the universe. At the very least, we should withhold judgment on this "hard problem" until more evidence is in and view with suspicion those who hold dogmatic and ideological views about the nature of consciousness.

It's at this point that the whole seemingly academic issue becomes intensely political and current because modern technological society idealizes and is monopolistically focused on only one state of consciousness—the alert, problem-solving state of consciousness that makes us efficient producers and consumers of material goods and services. At the same time, our society seeks to police and control a wide range of other "altered" states of consciousness on the basis of the unproven proposition that consciousness is generated by the brain.

I refer here to the so-called "war on drugs" which is really better understood as a war on consciousness and which maintains, supposedly in the interests of society, that we as adults do not have the right or maturity to make sovereign decisions about our own consciousness and about the states of consciousness we wish to explore and embrace. This extraordinary imposition on adult cognitive liberty is justified by the idea that our brain activity, disturbed by drugs, will adversely impact our behavior toward others. Yet anyone who pauses to think seriously for even a moment must realize that we already have adequate laws that govern adverse behavior toward others and that the real purpose of the "war on drugs" must therefore be to bear down on consciousness itself.

Confirmation that this is so came from the last British Labour government. It declared that its drug policy would be based on scientific evidence, yet in 2009 it sacked Professor David Nutt, chair of the Advisory Council on the Misuse of Drugs, for stating the simple statistical fact that cannabis is less dangerous (in terms of measured "harms") than tobacco and alcohol and that ecstasy is less dangerous than horse riding. Clearly what was at play here were ideological issues of great importance to the powers that be. And this is an ideology that sticks stubbornly in place regardless of changes in the complexion of the government of the day. The present Conservative-Liberal coalition remains just as adamant in its enforcement of the so-called war on drugs as its Labour predecessor and continues, in the name of this "war," to pour public money—our money—into large, armed, drug-enforcement bureaucracies which are entitled to break down our doors at dead of night, invade our homes, ruin our reputations, and put us behind bars.

All of this, we have been persuaded, is in our own interests. Yet if we as adults are not free to make sovereign decisions—right or wrong—about our own consciousness, that most intimate, that most sapient, that most personal part of ourselves, then in what useful sense can we be said to be free at all? And how are we to begin to take real and meaningful responsibility for all the other aspects of our lives when our governments seek to disenfranchise us from this most fundamental of all human rights and responsibilities?

In this connection, it is interesting to note that our society has no objection to altering consciousness per se. On the contrary, many consciousness-altering drugs, such as Prozac, Seroxat, Ritalin, and alcohol are either massively overprescribed or freely available today, and they make huge fortunes for their manufacturers but remain entirely legal despite causing obvious harms. Could this be because such legal drugs do not alter consciousness in ways that threaten the monopolistic dominance of the alert problem-solving state of consciousness, while a good number of illegal drugs, such as cannabis, LSD, DMT, and psilocybin, do?

There is a revolution in the making here, and what is at stake transcends the case for cognitive liberty as an essential and inalienable adult human right. If it turns out that the brain is not a generator but a transceiver of consciousness, then we must consider some little-known scientific research that points to a seemingly outlandish possibility, namely that a particular category of illegal drugs, the hallucinogens such as LSD, DMT, and psilocybin, may alter the receiver wavelength of the brain and allow us to gain contact with intelligent nonmaterial entities, "light beings," "spirits," "machine elves" (as Terence McKenna called them)—perhaps even the inhabitants of other dimensions. This possibility is regarded as plain fact by shamans in hunter-gatherer societies who for thousands of years made use of visionary plants and fungi to enter and interact with what they construed as the "spirit world." Intriguingly, it was also specifically envisaged by Dr. Rick Strassman, professor of psychiatry at the University of New Mexico, following his groundbreaking research with human volunteers and DMT carried out in the 1990s—a project that produced findings with shattering implications for our understanding of the nature of reality. For further information on Strassman's revolutionary work, see his book *DMT: The Spirit Molecule*.

WHY RICHARD DAWKINS IS THE BEST ARGUMENT FOR THE EXISTENCE OF GOD

BY RUSSELL BRAND

I'm glad I get the opportunity to prove the existence of God. You may think me unqualified for a task that has baffled the finest theologians, philosophers, and physicists since the dawn of time, but don't worry, I've been unqualified for every job I've ever embarked on, from learning to drive to working as a postman for the Royal Mail, and both these quests were successfully completed, aside from a few broken wing mirrors and stolen letters. So, unlike the Christmas money of the residents of Ockendon, Essex, you're in good hands. Atheists are all around us, sermonizing from the godless pulpit on the benefits of their anti-faith with some pretty good arguments like, oh I dunno, "evolution" and oddly, I think, given the stated nature of their motives, being incredibly reductive in their line and manipulative in their targets.

ZERO FUN AND TOO MUCH MENTAL

I once had the pleasure of talking to the brilliant Richard Dawkins, who has been called the "Abu Hamza of atheism." (It was me who called him it, just then.) In his remarkable documentary *The Genius of Charles Darwin*, the professor excellently relayed the information within his hero's *On the Origin of Species*, gave us some key information from his own masterpiece *The Selfish Gene* (which I only read because I took it to be an unsanctioned biography of the Kiss bassist Gene Simmons) and set about unraveling religion and spirituality with the adorable fervor of the Andrex puppy making off with some scriptural lavvy paper. Choice among Dawkins's targets were the kind of daft apeths we're accustomed to tolerating on our telly; low-browed creationists gurgling up Genesis like (forbidden) apple chutney and knee-jerk fundamentalists, who are always zero fun and far too much mental.

Who could fail to concur with Dawkins's erudite dismissal of these hapless saps? No one. I have Dawkins to thank for my own understanding of the fantastic discovery that is evolution; his passion and expertise in this documentary hugely enhanced my knowledge and illuminated what for many spiritual people can be a difficult subject.

It is only in his absolute renunciation of God that the professor and I part company and, heaven knows, I'd understand if you wanted to join his party. In almost any expedition in which the rival guides were myself and Richard Dawkins, I wouldn't be surprised to find myself pulverized by the converted horde stampeding toward the professor.

However, it's not just swivel-eyed haters and mad mullahs who live a religious life, and to condemn all religion and spirituality on the basis of their slack-jawed, knee-jerk, saliva-flecked vitriol (spit-triol?) is as unfair as the simplified dogma that the choir of pious atheists harmonizes against. Gandhi, as I recall, was quite a religious man.

Saint Francis of Assisi was a straight-up believer. And while the tenets of Buddhism are varied on the notion of God, the creator, I think it would be fair to describe the Dalai Lama as a spiritual chap. I don't see atheists queuing up to call the Dalai Lama a dickhead. These are the examples to which we should turn when questioning the existence of a power beyond man. Not Glenn Beck or some other capillary blob on Fox News.

Dawkins, the patron saint of atheists, would say that all religions are simply wrong—a baffled blanket of cozy lies to warm dopes into snug compliance, unproven ideologies based on faith. I think God exists beyond the current reach of science, that one day our fast-evolving minds will know God empirically as they do now only intuitively. That the mystical will become physical.

Galileo Galilei, the man credited with being the first to point a telescope skyward (all previous users had presumably been Renaissance Peeping Toms), speculated that heliocentrism was viable: that the Earth likely circled the Sun. He was imprisoned for this observation, which, viewed retrospectively (through my invention, the retro-speculars), seems unfair. He was, after all, correct. Evidently the persecution of scientists by religion has irked the members of that community, but I think that the theoretical annihilation of God is a reprisal too far.

We must, on both sides of the debate, show compassion. I, for example, have overlooked the bald fact that Galileo's parents gave him a bloody stupid first name considering their surname was Galilei. Galileo Galilei. He would have gone through hell at my school, not for being a heliocentric heretic but for being a ridiculously titled child. We already had another lad in my year called David Dave (honestly), so his problem wouldn't have even been original.

THE DIVINE SPARK

Religion has rightly been cited as the cause of much suffering and conflict, way beyond what ol' star-gazing "two names" went through with his prison stretch and forced retraction. Plus the Pope (I think it was Pope Benedict Benedicto) recently pardoned GG, so let it go.

A CROISSANT CONFLICT

It has been said that "man is never more vehement in killing his brother than when it is in God's name"; perhaps that's true, but we humans can seek out conflict in any situation. My last serious argument was about a croissant. It had been placed in the fridge beneath a meat product and could have been contaminated by dripping. If I'd had a sword on me, I would have happily carried out a jihad in the kitchen, and I'm a vegetarian. It is our nature to quarrel and fight just as it is to inquire and to empathize.

Frankly, I think atheism is a commodity we cannot currently afford. "No atheists on a sinking ship," they say, and a quick glance out the porthole reveals icebergs aplenty, but I'm not suggesting God as some demented alternative to desperation—no, this is a phenomenon that touches my life every day.

Through Transcendental Meditation, twice daily I feel the bliss of the divine. Through the mental repetition of a mantra, eventually my chattering monkey mind recedes, gently banishing concerns of the past and drawing the inner eye away from speculation and want. I connect to a boundless consciousness that has no palpable relationship with my thoughts, fears, or desires.

In this impersonal state of awareness, I recognize that consciousness exists beyond time, beyond the individual. There was a time when the universe did not exist, this we know. We also know that energy cannot be created or destroyed, only transformed. This means that something, not nothing, existed before the universe. We do not know what, but there is wonder and intelligence enough to suggest that design may have been a component.

Could a witless miasma of molecules and dust ever have created anything as ingenious and incredible as Richard Dawkins? I don't think so, but I'm prepared to listen and tolerate any theories and arguments, a concerto of contemplation, a requiem of speculation, to divert us till we know the truth.

STELLAR CONSCIOUSNESS
BY GREGORY SAMS

Have you ever wondered why your spirits are lifted on a sunny day and not in a hot bright room—or paused to consider that the energy of your life is itself the recycled light of the Sun? Have you spent more of your life thinking about suntans, sunglasses, and sunblock than about the nature of the star in your movie—the movie of Life? As you read these words, the energy that moves your eyes and the energy with which you comprehend their meaning is the light of our Sun being expressed through a new medium: you. It's no wonder that we enjoy bathing in Sun's light.

Is there any reason why we cannot consider whether that which brings us the light of life might be conscious of life itself? It was once a common understanding. History's most enduring monuments were built with the Sun and other heavenly bodies in mind. As we explore the history of these cultures, we can easily overlook the one underlying principle common to the Egyptians, Maya, Celts, and Greeks, not to mention the Sumerians, the Chaldeans, the Assyrians, the Gnostics, the Khmer, the Norse, the Inca, the Aztec, the natives of South and North America, and countless other cultures through the world, including today's Hindu, Zoroastrian, and Shinto religions. This is the recognition that our local star is a conscious entity—a celestial being worthy of divine status. Yet despite being the world's most worshipped deity, the concept of a living Sun became one of the most powerful and unspoken taboos of the Western world and one which modern researchers of the above cultures are often reluctant to breach.

Many scientists question the existence of consciousness itself. Since they have no tools with which to weigh or measure it, and no formula to express it, they find no alternative but to deny its existence. They believe consciousness to be an illusion created by our brain to serve some evolutionary purpose, as yet undetermined. Some of this "Grand Illusion" camp have a corollary to their belief, which is that human beings have no free will—that every single thing we do or think (every word, each wink or inadvertent stink) was somehow predetermined by the arrangement of particles immediately after the Big Bang.

For scientists who do acknowledge the existence of consciousness, it was assumed until recently that human beings were the only vessel that it could possibly inhabit. Nothing else was deemed to be aware of its own existence, or functioning on anything other than the level of a biological machine solely driven by the need to propagate its species. Some in this camp now argue that orangutans and dolphins and a handful of other species, mainly primates, might just share this "rare" facility. But worms and trees rarely figure in their consideration, even though bacteria colonies are seen to act like a unified intelligence.

Scientists who may disagree over whether or not consciousness is an illusion will agree that it is the greatest mystery of our existence; this, even though it is consciousness that is seeking to understand itself. So how can we be sure that nothing else experiences this mysterious experience that we cannot understand? We cannot be sure; we simply perpetuate a well-entrenched Church tradition. It was not science that made us look on Sun worship as primitive and ignorant, but the Roman Church that took an extremely dim view of anybody who disagreed. Scientific thought does not even entertain the idea of stellar consciousness, dismissing it out of habit, not by the application of science.

Were you to have told a Zoroastrian or Mayan Sun worshipper of the fusion reaction in the core of the Sun, describing the very different functions of the next six layers, explaining the corona and the solar wind that spins from it, their jaw would have dropped in delighted awe. Our scientific understanding would give them greater cause to revere the character bringing light and the power of life to our world. The knowledge of anatomy does not diminish our status as conscious living beings.

However, unlike the ancients, we now view the Sun as little more than a dumb ball of hot gas that happens to accidentally provide us with the light of life. But science has found out an awful lot about this hot ball of highly charged plasma (it's not actually gas) and its stellar siblings. Unlike the ancients, we know Sun and others stars turn simple hydrogen and helium into all the elements that make up us and the world around us—from carbon and oxygen, to iron and gold. They are the transmutation engines of the cosmos. By weight, 93 percent of the matter in your body was born in the body of a star.

We know that stars turn matter itself into the energy of light, agent of the electromagnetic force. Light informs us of the world around us and brings it energy. Light is the catalyst in photosynthesis, on land and in the world's oceans, where water molecules and carbon dioxide from the air are rearranged into the basic building blocks of the entire vegetable world. During this process, the energy of Sun's light is stored in plants and their seeds, transferring to us when we eat those basic foods or another animal that ate them. This is the energy that powers life and consciousness.

We are made of stardust and powered by starlight. This much we know.

Unlike the ancients, we know that stars are complex and interconnected balls of plasma. Our Sun has seven distinct layers, all performing different functions with some of them rotating around each other at different speeds. Its powerful corona, an invisible energy field, occupies more space than Sun itself and is thought to manage various solar features including sunspots, solar flares, coronal filaments, and coronal mass ejections. We identify and measure electromagnetic field lines connecting the corona to Earth. In 2008 NASA discovered a magnetic portal the diameter of Earth that connects Sun's corona to our planet's geomagnetic field, through which tons of high-energy particles are believed to pass at eight-minute intervals in what is called a "flux transfer event." We know that the solar wind spinning off Sun's corona twists into a giant electromagnetic bubble, the heliosphere, which embraces and protects the solar system as it travels through the galaxy at an estimated 45,000 miles per hour. Scientists rank Sun's corona as its most mysterious feature. Perhaps it is as great a mystery as human consciousness. Perhaps it embodies the mind of Sun.

Unlike the ancients, we know that all those stars in the night sky are related to our Sun. We see that most stars live as couples, called "binary systems" by astronomers, and that they are not scattered randomly but live in communities called "stellar clusters." Every star sends its own unique signature into space and may have undiscovered connections to other stars, like those recently discovered connecting Earth to Sun. Electromagnetic fields have been discovered spanning deep space, connecting galaxy to galaxy.

Unlike us, the ancients felt connected to the heavens and believed that the consciousness of the Sun and planets influenced our consciousness, and thus the course of our lives. They carefully constructed monuments designed to connect our human energies to those of the Sun and other celestial beings. Today we know little of their knowledge and skills, of why and how they created the structures that survive to this day.

The harnessing of light in its multiple wavelengths underpins nearly all our technology of information transfer, from radio to TV, smartphones to wi-fi, optic cables to MRI scans. Within its narrow "visible" spectrum, light informs us and other animals of the world around us. Our cells and those of other species use photons to communicate with each other, and we discover plants communicating with photons. It does not seem far-fetched to consider that when stars are dispatching photons of many frequencies into the cosmos, they are serving the same purpose—the exchange of information.

Perhaps if scientists abandoned that old religious taboo against considering consciousness in anything other than us or things like us, they would not need fixes like "dark matter" to explain why galaxies do not behave like accidental mechanical systems. Essentially, "dark matter" is little more than the name given to the solution for a problem that has not yet been solved—it might as well be called "Factor X." Perhaps the reason galaxies don't fall apart is because they are not dumb balls of gas reacting to nothing more than the laws of physics, but are instead joined-up communities of intelligent dynamic beings. Just a thought.

I do not claim that Sun's behavior proves it and other stars to be conscious beings—simply that from an unbiased viewpoint and considering all the science, this looks like the most likely option. It is the default option humanity had always held until it was burned from our culture, literally, by a jealous Church. Now, with the supporting data to hand, and burning at the stake out of vogue, let us reconsider this idea with an open mind, free of irrational taboos.

Acknowledgment of stellar consciousness changes everything, and I explore the inevitable implications of this within my book *Sun of gOd*. Perhaps the most profound of these recognizes the status of light itself, for which our Sun is the local agent. And from a personal perspective, can there be anything more important to our spiritual well-being than reestablishing a connection with the life-giving star in the movie of Life?

REFLECTIONS IN A REAR-VIEW MIRROR: SPECULATIONS ON NOVELTY THEORY AND THE END TIMES

BY DENNIS J. MCKENNA

JUNE 6, 2014

When Graham recently invited me to contribute to his new anthology on consciousness, *The Divine Spark*, I was pleased at the invitation but didn't really know what to submit. Then I ran across two rather peculiar essays that I had written in the fall of 2011 while writing my memoir, *The Brotherhood of the Screaming Abyss*, which was published at the end of November in 2012. For various reasons, I eliminated them from the final draft of the book and relegated them to the limbo of some backup hard drive.

One, titled "This Just In . . . ," is a speculation on Terence's Novelty Theory that was prompted by an unusual announcement by a group of physicists at the Large Hadron Collider at CERN in Geneva. In September 2011, these researchers announced that they had observed an extremely anomalous phenomenon, the detection of neutrinos that travel faster than light, in clear violation of Einstein's Special Theory of Relativity. This event, if proven to be true, would have certainly been novel, or at least the measurement of it would have been novel, so it seemed like an excellent opportunity to muse on the Time Wave (TW0) and Novelty Theory and the nature of Novelty itself. The Time Wave, or more accurately the basic tenets of its construction, was downloaded into Terence's bemushroomed brain while we were in the grip of our shared psychedelic/shamanic odyssey at La Chorrera, Colombia, in April 1971.

The second essay, titled "The Day the World Ended," was written a few weeks after the first, on October 28, 2011, which happened to be the date that some Mayanist scholars had postulated was the real correct date for the end of the Mayan calendar, not December 21, 2012. This essay provided a good opportunity to reflect on humanity's seeming mass obsession with the End Times and the associated eschatological hysteria that infected the collective zeitgeist in the years and months preceding the postulated end date of the Mayan Calendar, December 21, 2012. Now, nearly two years downstream from that much anticipated and much dreaded event, we can look back on that date and wonder just what got into our collective heads. It was arguably the greatest non-event in human history; viewed as a cultural phenomenon, it can tell us little about the nature of time, eschatology, or history, but it can tell us volumes about our problematic human nature, and our endless capacity for distraction and denial.

THIS JUST IN . . .

September 24, 2011 1:43 PM

Over the last few days as I have been working on this section, a research group[1] at the CERN Large Hadron Collider facility in Geneva has reported that they have detected a population of neutrinos that apparently travel faster than light. The group reported an "anomaly" in experiments in which a beam of neutrinos sent 454 kilometers from Geneva to Italy arrived at the detector 60 nanoseconds faster than the speed of light. This is an infinitesimally small amount of time (a nanosecond is a *billionth* of a second), but nevertheless, it can be measured accurately, so the researchers claim. This announcement has rocked the world of physics, as well it should, and now other groups of researchers are piling on to either find the errors in the measurements (as well they should) or verify the results. This is the way that science is supposed to work. Extraordinary claims require extraordinary evidence, and this is one of the most extraordinary claims to come out of physics in a good long while. So therefore, independent confirmation by other research groups is the first step. Most likely, there is an error somewhere in the measurements, the math, or some other factor (these experiments are extremely delicate) but the researchers claim to have repeated the experiment multiple times and are standing by their results. If, however, the experiment *is* confirmed, it's extremely big news, because it means nothing less than the complete collapse of Einstein's Theory of Special Relativity, and with it, much of the foundation of modern physics.

I decided to comment on this development in midstream, because time does not stop in the real world and interesting things are constantly happening. And much of what has preoccupied Terence and me has been the nature of Novelty, and that preoccupation led to the Time Wave theory. The Time Wave that Terence conceptualized (or channeled) at La Chorrera purports to be a mathematical construct that describes the structure of time, a map of novelty and its "ingression" (to use Whitehead's term) into the continuum, that is, into reality. I am actually one of the harsher critics when it comes to TW0, or Novelty Theory as it has come to be known. I do not believe it's a real theory, and there are gaps and loopholes in the conceptual foundations of Novelty Theory that on close scrutiny are extremely hard to defend. However, much of the TW0 "theory" is based on Alfred North Whitehead's metaphysics, which is much more carefully reasoned. And based on Whitehead, I'm willing to grant that there is such a thing as "Novelty" (which, loosely characterized, means that occasionally there really *is* something new under the sun), and that, somehow or other, Novelty does "ingress" into reality. But some of the more animated discussions that Terence and I had about Novelty Theory were precisely about the questions: what is a truly novel event, and how does it "ingress" into the continuum, and how do we recognize it when it does (or more specifically how does the Time Wave map it or identify it)?

Now we have been handed, in the lovely waning days of September 2011, a report of an event that may be truly novel! We have been given the gift of a case study. We can watch novelty unfold in real time, so we can learn something (maybe) about just how novelty does express itself in reality and how that really plays out in our experience of reality. Much of the controversy over the Time Wave (and the subject of many an argument between Terence and me), had to do with the question of how one "fits" the wave to time, how to set the "end date" which you have to do because the theory postulates that there is a definite instant, a moment in time in which the wave collapses presumably at the instant of the Ultimate Novel Event, whatever that might be. Some have referred to this moment as the Singularity, but this is a deliberately vague term and possibly is misleading as well. The concept of the Singularity implies that at some point we cross a threshold where all of our assumptions, about causality, time, space, and virtually everything else, no longer apply. The Singularity could be just about anything, so the term is not particularly helpful in predicting what it's likely to be.

As anyone familiar with TW0 and Novelty Theory knows, Terence settled on the exact moment of the winter solstice on December 21, 2012, as the end point for the Time Wave based on a number of criteria and assumptions that may or may not be valid. This date corresponds to the generally accepted date for the end of the Mayan Calendar as well (though ever-industrious revisionists have recently come up with a much more alarming, because more imminent, date for the end of the Mayan Calendar of October 28, 2011.[2] About this, we shall see, it's just around the corner. But that's the subject of another conversation and probably another rant.).

In his conception of Novelty Theory, Terence favored what might be called the "punctate" theory of Novelty. Novelty ingresses into the continuum as dramatic events that have a global impact. Events like the detonation of the atomic bomb over Hiroshima, or the assassination of JFK, or the crucifixion of Christ, or Hurricane Katrina, or the terrorist attack of 9/11/2001 (though of course he did not live to see the latter two). But his idea was that these kinds of events had an enormous impact on history and the subsequent unfolding of human affairs, so they were truly "novel" and thus could be used as markers when trying to fit the Time Wave to the major novel events of history (and on larger scales even geological and evolutionary events, such as the impact of the Chicxulub asteroid in the so-called K-T extinction event that is thought to have spelled the end of the dinosaurs some 65 million years ago) and thereby arrive at an End Date for the Time Wave.

In contrast, I argued in favor of the "gradualist" theory of Novelty. Major historical or geological events like these may appear to erupt into time, but it's an illusion; it ignores the necessary chain of cause and effect that leads up to the dramatic event. Which is truly the novel event? When the bomb detonates over Hiroshima, or when it is first detonated in the desert at Alamagordo? Or when the first sustained fission reaction is triggered in the Field House at the University of Chicago by Oppenheimer's group? Or when Einstein first conceives his Theory of Relativity and comes up with the famous equation $E=MC^2$, which provided the mathematical framework that enabled the invention of the bomb? Or some even more ancient event, perhaps Democritus's early intuition that the world is made of atoms in the 4th century BCE? Is the assassination of Kennedy more novel than his election, or his birth, given that it would not have happened without these preceding events? Is the crucifixion of Christ more novel than his supposedly miraculous birth, and his remarkable career, prior to his crucifixion?

You can see my point: Novelty does not erupt into history as much as it oozes into history, and this makes the identification of truly novel events much more problematic. The wave becomes much harder to fit against the historical, geological, or evolutionary record because there are very few punctuate points against which to lay the map. And there is no way to quantify these events, no criteria that Terence ever defined whereby we can say a given event is more "novel" than another on some kind of measurable scale. This is, to my mind, the major and probably fatal flaw in Novelty Theory. Science works on measurement and quantification; to qualify as a scientific theory, it must be validated using measurable, quantifiable, and ideally mathematical criteria. A true theory must also state what will *invalidate* it; it must postulate what new data or new discovery will disprove it. (And here it is worth noting that no theory can ever be regarded as proven. All theories are provisional, some more than others, but there is always the possibility that new data will come along that overturns the theory. You can disprove theories but never definitely prove them.) The Time Wave does none of this. Thus it is not really a theory. It is a speculation, an interesting idea, a hallucination or fantasy; but it is not a theory. Terence never provided a quantifiable definition of Novelty, I don't really think he knew how, and I'm not sure anyone does. But the result is that unfortunately, Novelty in the Novelty Theory was defined as whatever Terence postulated it to be. So, interesting as it is, TW0 is utterly useless as a map of time, a predictor of events, or in any way as a mathematical theory that describes something fundamental and profound about the world.

So now, thanks to those industrious scientists at CERN, we have a rare opportunity to study the ingression of Novelty into our continuum. And the same questions apply. First of all, it's important to note that they are probably wrong. There is some error, somewhere, in the measurements or the design of the experiment. This is the conservative and parsimonious position to take for the moment, the provisional position. More data, please, from independent and unbiased researchers! What if such data is provided? That would be fantastic! We all hope that this discovery can be verified, especially us science fiction nuts, because *if* verified, it opens the way to the wildest of science fiction canards, faster than light travel and even time travel. Oh, we *so* want this discovery to be true!

If it is found to be true, if the consensus emerges that (until disproven, see above) this discovery holds up—that is, it can be independently verified under carefully controlled conditions—then it is novel indeed. It means the complete collapse of everything we thought we knew about physics since Einstein postulated the Theory of Relativity. Begging for the moment *when* the actual novel event took place. Presumably, if true, neutrinos have been traveling faster than light ever since there were neutrinos to do so, so these events have been occurring everywhere for about 13 billion years, give or take a few billion, ever since the Universe took form. So, neutrinos traveling faster than light? Nothing novel there. What was novel was the *measurement* of the phenomenon; so was the first measurement event the truly novel event, or the umpteenth measurement? After the initial measurement, the researchers scratched their heads and figured that they had made some mistake. They went back and checked their data, repeatedly. Ran the measurement numerous times, finally felt confident enough to report it to their colleagues. *The New York Times* (and the global media machine) first published the report on September 22. Was that the novel event? Colleagues immediately shouted,

"Pshaw! This can't be true!" and got to work to try to verify it (or actually, to knock it down; Nobel prizes and careers depend on this, in a big way). But suppose another group verifies the data. They are "me too" runners up, but their work is essential; the theory can't become the scientific consensus until at least one other group, and ideally several groups, verify this data. Just what event, exactly, out of this series of events, does one fit the Time Wave to, that defines the emergence of the novelty? I submit that it can't be done.

And further: one of the unspoken assumptions always looming in the background in discussions of the Time Wave and the Ultimate End Date, the ultimate novel event, is that the event is going to be either a catastrophic global event (though if the Time Wave purports to describe the structure of time for the entire Universe, it's hard to see why anybody should get too excited about some global catastrophe here on Earth, such as an asteroid impact or even a supernova; after all, we're pretty small potatoes on that scale). But the assumption has been that, on Earth, the End will be marked by some global event, either a catastrophe, which we'd rather didn't happen (most sane people, anyway, do not look forward to global disaster and the death of millions), or some kind of more hopeful scenario—the benevolent alien Space Brothers show up in their mile-wide ships and provide gentle advice and advanced technology to help us get our act together (the Child-hood's End scenario), or a wrathful Jesus comes riding in on his golden char-iot to smite the wicked and take the righteous up to heaven for an eternity of harp playing and bingo, or whatever they are going to do up there to pass the time (no sex or drugs allowed, remember!). Or the embryonic AI lurking in the Internet will suddenly cross the threshold into self-awareness and realize, in about three nanoseconds, that the reason things are so screwed up is because of the damn monkeys running all over the place, fouling the nest, so it will pull the plug on the whole show by causing all the world's nuclear reactors to go into critical meltdown while simultaneously launching the entire nuclear arsenal of the world's superpowers. All of these events would certainly be dramatic; all of them would be novel enough to qualify as a validation of the Time Wave if they occurred at or close to the postulated End Date (if the date is off by a few weeks, months or even years, we can still grant that the theory is verified; Novelty Theory, after all, is nothing if not an inexact science). All of them would have really dramatic consequences for life on Earth, if there was any life left, post–End Date. None of them is very likely to happen.

But now we have a discovery come along that might, just might, demol-ish the foundations of physics as we know it. If verified, that is an enor-mously significant discovery. It might even qualify as the Ultimate Novel

Event, or at least the most novel event to come along in historical memory. What difference will it make to our daily, humdrum, dreary lives? Practically none. A thousand years from now, it might mean that we will have FTL starships and time machines. That's certainly wonderful, and to be hoped for.

But in the first year of the second decade of the third millennium CE, it's not going to make a damn bit of difference, except that it will give physicists plenty to ponder and the rest of us geeks plenty to yak about. We will still have global warming, vast unemployment, widespread disease, poverty, wars, famine, and even unhappiness. It will not make a damn bit of difference to the way we live our daily lives. And yet . . . and yet, in some respects, you would have to say that if verified, this discovery, in some lab in Switzerland, amounts to a novel event that changes everything. Most importantly it changes (or will change) the way we think about and understand the world. But perhaps that is Singularity enough; a fundamental re-understanding of reality and the way it is constructed will not immediately change the way we conduct our daily lives, but over time, as that understanding permeates the collective world view, it may indeed have profound impacts. The pity is that no one alive today is likely to live to see any of those impacts. So perhaps this is indeed how the world ends, as T. S. Elliot said, not with a bang but a whimper.

And as I review this piece and reflect on it, I can't resist mentioning another novel event, one that also took place in a Swiss laboratory a few decades ago, that has had a much more profound impact on human history than this discovery is likely to do, at least in any foreseeable future. That discovery, of course, was Albert Hofmann's accidental (?) discovery of the remarkable properties of his new molecule, LSD. Now *there* was a novel event! We had better keep a watchful eye on those Swiss; you never know what they might get up to!

THE DAY THE WORLD ENDED

October 28, 2011 12:51 PM

The time has come to step away from my reminiscences, time to return to 2011 for a moment to note an event that is most germane to the theme of our story, and thus, too important to ignore.

I'm referring, of course, to the end of the world. It's supposed to happen today, but I expect most of us will be too busy to notice. Hopefully we'll be able to catch it on the ten o'clock news, except we won't because it's well off the radar of even the most eclectic journalists.

According to some Mayanists, who pay close attention to matters related to the Mayan calendar[3] and thus its imminent end, the calculations that postulate an end date of 12/21/2012 are in error, due to the discrepancies between the Mayan and the Julian calendars. After the necessary corrections needed to bring the two calendars into sync are made, it turns out that the real date is today, October 28, 2011.

The calculations needed to reconcile these discrepancies are not trivial. It seems that there is not one Mayan calendar, but at least three. There is the Mayan Long Count calendar, which is a nonrepeating, vigesimal (base 20 or base 18) calendar defining the number of days that have passed since a mythical creation date that correlates to August 11, 3114 BCE in the Gregorian calendar or September 6, 3114 BCE in the Julian calendar. There is also the 365-day solar calendar, the Haab, also used by the Maya as well as other Mesoamerican civilizations. Then there is the Tzolk'in, a 260-day calendar based on thirteen twenty-day cycles. These two calendars measure days but not years. The combination of a Haab date and a Tzolk'in date represents a specific date that does not occur again for fifty-two years. The two calendars based on 365 days and 260 days repeat every fifty-two years. For periods longer than fifty-two years, most Mesoamericans relied on the Long Count calendar. There is controversy over the correlations between the Long Count calendar and the Julian and Gregorian calendars. In the Long Count calendar, the B'ak'tun, the largest subdivision of the calendar, is 144,000 days, or 393.4 solar years. Creation was initiated in 3114 BCE with the beginning of the Long Count, thirteen B'ak'tun, and the count will end with the end of the second cycle of thirteen B'ak'tun, on December 21, 2012, or perhaps on October 28, 2011, or perhaps on December 24, 2011, or perhaps it already happened sometime in February 2011.

The fact is, nobody knows what the correct calculated date of the Mayan Long Count calendar is, as there is no consensus on the correlations to the Julian and Gregorian calendars. The most accepted correlation is the so-called Goodman, Martinez, Thompson (GMT) model, in which 584,283 Julian days is equivalent to the thirteen B'ak'tun. According to this correlation, creation started on September 6, 3114 BCE (Julian) or August 11, 3114 BCE (Proleptic Gregorian). The completion of another Long Count of thirteen B'ak'tun corresponds to December 21, 2012.

Most credible Mayanists do not interpret the end of this cycle as corresponding to the end of time. It was an occasion to celebrate the end of a long cycle, but was not viewed as a doomsday event. From the Wikipedia article, Sandra Noble, executive director of the Foundation for the Advancement of Mesoamerican Studies in Crystal River, Florida, believes: "To render

December 21, 2012, as a doomsday event or moment of cosmic shifting . . . is 'a complete fabrication and a chance for a lot of people to cash in.'"

"There will be another cycle," says E. Wyllys Andrews V, director of the Tulane University Middle American Research Institute (MARI). "We know the Maya thought there was one before this, and that implies they were comfortable with the idea of another one after this.'

I certainly make no claims to be an expert on the Mayan calendar, nor am I a mathematician. The endless debates over the correlations with the Julian or Gregorian calendars and the reasoning behind the arguments seem opaque to me. The reason for this is partly because I have not bothered to study them in great detail to draw a conclusion as to which one is "right." In fact, they are all wrong. They have about as much relevance to our current historical, and existential, crisis as the disputes of medieval theologians who tried to calculate the number of angels that could fit on the head of a pin. It just strikes me as the wasted effort of a number of excellent minds that could have been better occupied spending their time on other matters. To that we can add in the insights of other theorists who claim to have privileged information from extraterrestrials, extra-dimensionals, or other unverifiable sources. And there is the 2012 "franchise" to serve and a chance to cash in on that—have you purchased the iPhone app yet? There is still time to sign up for the latest workshop, pilgrimage, seminar, or combination package in some exotic location such as Palenque or Tikal. You had better get your reservations in soon because slots are filling fast, and frankly, you're not going to be able to find a parking place.

As the brother of Terence McKenna, arguably the person who has done more than all the Mayanists to seed the meme of 12/21/12 as the end date of history into the collective consciousness, I suppose I could be accused of being at best unsporting and at worst an annoying curmudgeon on this issue. I have to plead guilty on both counts. Certainly Terence's selection of 12/21/2012 as the end point of the Time Wave was a matter of convenience as much as it was the result of a serious mathematical analysis. The Time Wave and the Mayan calendar have nothing to do with each other, but they have been conflated in the delusions of the current cultural zeitgeist.

The Time Wave is so wrong in so many ways, and I have previously discussed some of them. The Mayan calendar may end today, or it may end on 12/21/12 or some other date, but trust me on this: the only people who are going to take this seriously are those who either have a financial stake in the 2012 mythos or those who are so completely deluded that they are ready to grasp at any straw to avoid honest consideration of our current environmental and historical crisis. For the rest of us, the event will be noted as a human-interest story presented as a wrap-up item by chirpy bubble-headed anchorpeople at the end of your evening newscast. We will awake up on 12/22/12 faced with the same set of intractable and horrifying problems that we were faced with the previous day. Jesus is not coming in his chariot of fire to save the righteous and smite the wicked; neither are our space alien brothers going to materialize in mile-wide ships over the major cities of the world to hand over the keys to galactarian citizenship. God knows I wish they would; if I'm wrong and it happens, I'll be the first to queue up to eat a mountain of crow. Nor is there going to be a massive asteroid impact, a supervolcano eruption, a gamma ray burst from a distant supernova that wipes out 99 percent of terrestrial life. These things may, and probably will, happen someday. I just don't believe they can be predicted. As a rule, this is not the way that Novelty ingresses into reality. With rare exceptions, such as global natural catastrophes that occur every few million years, Novelty ingresses more locally, and more slowly, than these disaster scenarios would have us believe.

As a species, we are extremely adept at denial. We can expend enormous effort on developing models to predict events that a moment's reflection will tell us are extremely unlikely. This is far preferable, certainly a welcome distraction, from the depressing contemplation of our current existential crisis. Every great civilization, every historical era, probably believes that it lives at the end of time, and that the end of its particular exceptional situation will define the end of history. The fact that this has never happened—that somehow history just rolls on whether or not civilizations rise and fall, continents and cultures are devastated by plagues and famines, environments or economies collapse—is dismissed in our longing for some resolution to our dilemma, some final outcome no matter how catastrophic.

What we should be doing is doubling down on the problems we face, now, and trying to figure out what we do about them, if anything is to be done, now. It's what we need to be doing, yet it is so damned hard. We are like the dysfunctional Congress of 2011; it needs to focus on jobs, jobs, jobs but instead wastes time on culture war issues, passing yet more restrictions on abortion, naming a post office, all the other trivia that fills its agenda while meanwhile Rome burns. We are a stupid species. Darwinian mechanics is not kind to stupidity, the dumb do not survive, and if we destroy ourselves due to our own stupidity (as it appears we are bent on doing), then perhaps that's for the best. The problem is that we have now developed toys and technologies (but not the wisdom to use them) that can bring down a good deal of the planet with us when we finally do implode, or more likely, explode.

We yearn for an escape from the prison of history. We long for what Eliade called the Eternal Return, a mythical, timeless era outside of time, before history, or after it (there is really no difference). Linear, historical cultures are trapped in history in much the same way that each individual is trapped in the time frame of his or her life. Every life has a beginning and an end; we are pushed along, inexorably, by time from the moment we are born to the moment the plug is pulled and the sheet drawn up. Nobody has ever escaped from time, though all of the world's religions are scams predicated on the notion that if we toe the line in certain ways, pay homage to the authoritarian structures, accept the dogma, behave ourselves, and of course have "faith," somehow we are going to beat the system. This may serve the agenda of whatever authoritarian hierarchies run these institutions, but it's a lie. Every person confronts their own personal Singularity at the end of time, the end of their own personal history. This is the only eschaton we can realistically look forward to. No one can say, definitively, what happens to consciousness when that Singularity is breached, whether it is extinguished forever or translates into some sort of virtual reality, whatever that means when talking about post-death survival. Someday, we may understand this. Someday, technology may advance to a point where it's possible to consider uploading one's consciousness or "soul" (whatever that is) into some kind of virtual environment maintained by supercomputer networks that are vastly more powerful than anything we have today. If that day ever comes (and I don't expect to see it in my lifetime) it will mark the collapse of all of the world's religions, and this is an unintended consequence to be relished.

Until that day comes, here we are, trapped in our own personal history that is in turn nested inside our cultural and national history, and that in turn is embedded in biological, evolutionary, geological, and cosmological history. It's not going to end today, or tomorrow, or on December 21, 2012. Like an insect stuck in amber, we are imprisoned in time, and rather than waste energy trying to escape, or predict its end, we should rather devote our efforts to making the time we are afforded the best it can possibly be.

History ended today. I am looking forward to tomorrow's sunrise.

NOTES

1. http://www.nytimes.com/aponline/2011/09/22/world/europe/AP-EU-Breaking-Light-Speed.html?_r=1&scp=1&sq=faster%20than%20light%20particle&st=cse
2. http://www.calleman.com/content/articles/end_of_creationcycles.htm
3. http://en.wikipedia.org/wiki/Mayan_calendar_ending#2012_and_the_Long_Count

FROM COSMIC CONSCIOUSNESS TO CONVERGENCE: PSYCHEDELICS, ENTHEOGENS, AND SPECIES ACTIVATION

BY RAK RAZAM

Rushing tunnel of light like hyperspace in Star Wars, and each bead is a frozen liquid angel, a condensed vibrational being, another drop in the cosmic ocean all around. And the angels are alive, they pulse with welcoming light-love, they caress and become me as I enter the DMT space and everything becomes infused with holiness, with a sacredness beyond words, felt in every fiber of my being. This is what the saints say, what the enlightened ones experience, the lower bardos and the shores of the heavenly realms. . . . All I have to communicate it to you, dear reader, is these poor words, these little niños. . . . The vehicle of the Word is like a freshly minted wave packet to contain energies that are burst open here as I swim through—in—become one with the core, the Source of all things, the Logos that creates and is pure Creation itself.

—Rak Razam, *Aya Awakenings: A Shamanic Odyssey*, 2013

I have, in my career as an "experiential journalist" covering issues around technology, spirituality, counterculture, and the global shamanic resurgence, been exposed to many illuminating states of mind and mystic traditions of indigenous tribal people and esoteric Western mystery cults, old and new. An invisible landscape has opened up for me that is every bit as real and potent as the baseline reality we experience around us in the material world. Indeed, this inner dimension seems inextricably bound and intertwined with the world we know, underscoring and perhaps animating it with a spirit or consciousness—as one paradigm would have it; others might use equally exotic terms like *coherent quantum processes* and *entanglement*. However we define it, consciousness is still at the heart of our reality, and it is a mystery that is yet to be fully explained.

Philosopher Alfred North Whitehead once defined consciousness as the "awareness of awareness, or the apperception of pattern as such." The mind-brain relationship has been debated all the way back to the ancient Greeks, and around the turn of the 19th century, philosophers like Henri Bergson and psychologist William James were still debating the brain's relationship to consciousness. James himself also famously experimented with another consciousness alterant of the time, nitrous oxide, and the use of other psychoactives like mescaline, opium, and peyote was prevalent in the medical underground and the bohemian intelligentsia. These substances also paralleled a rise in spiritualism, alternative religions, and interest in psi phenomena that seems to eerily parallel the later psychedelic revolution of the 1960s.

In 1898, James delivered a lecture at Harvard University that opposed the idea that consciousness is solely produced by the brain. Like Bergson before him, he believed that the "fangs of cerebralism" alone could not explain the full function of the brain and consciousness, which was, "as far as our understanding goes, as great a miracle as if we said, thought is 'spontaneously generated,' or 'created out of nothing.'" He went on to say, "Our normal waking consciousness, rational consciousness as we call it, is but one special type of consciousness, whilst all about it, parted from it by the filmiest of screens, there lie potential forms of consciousness entirely different." (*The Varieties of Religious Experience*, 1902)

Richard Maurice Bucke was a contemporary of James's, a Canadian who worked with the American Medical Association. In 1901, he wrote the book *Cosmic Consciousness: A Study in the Evolution of the Human Mind*, in which he explained that "cosmic consciousness is a mystical state above and beyond self-consciousness . . . which is man's natural state, which is in itself above pure sentient animal consciousness," and so on. This stepping-stone gradation of consciousness itself is something that modern science usually says ends with the current human condition, perhaps recognizing flashes of difference with geniuses like Einstein or Hawking.

But instead of just an increase in *intellect,* Bucke envisaged a type of consciousness that was itself conscious of "the life and order of the universe," an interconnected perspective "which is more of an intuitive knowing than it is a factual understanding." While it was evidently only possessed by a select few in his day, the increase in this awareness in the species over time promised a stage of human evolution where it would be eventually shared by all humanity.

The idea that consciousness continues to aggregate above our current plateau, and parallel to it, is deeply intuitive. We can recognize consciousness in ourselves, in animals, and in the shamanic paradigm, in plants as well. There are all different levels of consciousness in the indigenous understanding of the world as a living organism, and in that macro organism, there seems to be a cascading effect where one state of mind can build upon another for an interdependent whole that is greater than the sum of its parts.

Indeed, we can see the stratum of collective consciousness at work in different species in nature, as with many insects that work synergistically together, even though individually they might only have a rudimentary self-consciousness, or in partnership with plant species. Together they act in a synergistic way to actually perform more as a collective than they can individually, and that lesson is reflected in examples of collective consciousness developing in 21st-century human culture as the drive toward retribalization increases and a collective gestalt emerges in the social media–nonlinear-mesh-networks of the Internet.

This collective consciousness in nature may be a stepping stone for Bucke's idea of cosmic consciousness itself, which Wikipedia defines as: "The concept that the universe exists as an interconnected network of consciousness, with each conscious being linked to every other. Sometimes this is conceived as forming a collective consciousness which spans the cosmos, other times it is conceived as an absolute or godhead from which all conscious beings emanate." (*http://en.wikipedia.org/wiki/Cosmic_consciousness*) This theory has echoes and resonances with the Buddhist concept of Indra's net, Pierre Teilhard de Chardin's noosphere, and James Lovelock's Gaia hypothesis, amongst others.

While many mystics and seers both exhibited and talked about the concept of cosmic or expanded consciousness, Bucke was one of the first Victorian-era gentlemen to tease new ground with the concept by mapping it across the history books with individuals who achieved altered states. Bucke graphed and compared the experiences of saints and mystics like Jesus, Mohammed, William Blake, etc.—the list was pretty well-developed for a pre-20th-century demographic, but it raised a lot of questions, like whether or not some of these people were actual historical figures, and did they, in fact, have an elevated consciousness?

Still, perhaps because of his Victorian-era prejudices, one thing that Bucke didn't comment upon was shamanic cultures. Bucke's mapping of manifestations of cosmic consciousness in individuals across history ignored the sacramental use of indigenous peoples and the plant sacraments that connected them to the divine, however temporarily. Indigenous peoples the world over have used *entheogens* (Greek for "substances which evoke the divine within," usually natural plants and fungi, as opposed to *psychedelics* which are made-in-the-lab chemicals). Preeminent amongst modern entheogenic use is Ayahuasca and San Pedro in South America, peyote in

North America, and psilocybin-magic mushrooms through Mesoamerica and Siberia—and all of the above in the Western-led Shamanic Resurgence that is currently blossoming across the world.

The altered state of consciousness of shamanic culture also provides a deep connection to the great green-mind of nature, developing a sense of cultural equilibrium and sustainability for man's place in the web of life. In many instances, it also provides brief flashes of contact with an exploration of higher-dimensional realms for the tribal shamans and their patients. In higher doses, especially with the right entheogenic keys, locks are said to open to deep states of core consciousness and a perception of unity with all living things—that is, an awareness of the individual as an emanation of the Godhead, or as Bucke would call it, *cosmic consciousness.*

But this is still largely an individual affair, a global subculture protected from the mainstream in the West, although rapidly gaining in popularity and mainstream media attention. Traditionally, plant-based gnosis has often been sanctioned as part of village life in the old world, mediated by the village shaman in indigenous societies. Sometimes it was something the entire tribe would do—other times, depending on the dogma of the tribe, it was used by the hunters or other specialists. With the Shipibo-Conibos tribe in Peru, the shaman himself would take the Ayahuasca on behalf of the patient and go into the realms as a medicinal tool. So these states of higher consciousness have often been compartmentalized within the larger village life, until the mid to late 20th century, when modern Western culture "discovered" altered states en masse via LSD.

In the 1950s, psychedelics like LSD were still legal and were widely used in experiments by psychiatrists, corporations, the military, and the intelligentsia to boost creativity, remove mental blockages, and experiment with a reliable "truth serum." Writer Aldous Huxley helped coin the term *psychedelic* (Greek for "mind-manifesting") in letters with Dr. Humphry Osmond, who suggested the term in counterpoint to Huxley's phanerothyme. Huxley was also one of the first modern intellectuals to continue the idea that the function of the brain and the nervous system was as a filtering agent of consciousness. He argued the brain was not just an epigenetic nodal point where thought originates from; rather, he thought the brain was actually something that filters down the tsunami of overwhelming sensory information on all the different frequencies to make it more palatable for down here on the baseline level:

> According to such a theory, each one of us is potentially Mind At Large . . . [but] to make biological survival possible Mind At Large

THE DIVINE SPARK

has to be funneled through the reducing valve of the brain and nervous system. What comes out at the other end is a measly trickle of the kind of consciousness which will help us stay alive on the surface of this particular planet . . . temporary bypasses may be acquired either spontaneously, or as the result of deliberate "spiritual exercises" . . . or by the means of drugs. (Huxley, *The Doors of Perception*, 1954).

One of the key attributes of psychedelics and entheogens, and perhaps the reason they are often approached with trepidation, is that they dissolve the ego. In a 2013 presentation, by Brazilian neuroscientist Dráulio Barros de Araújo, he argued that fMRI brain scans proved that the hallucinogenic brew Ayahuasca reduces neural activity in what is called the Default Mode Network (DMN) regions of the brain. (*http://maps.org/conference/ayahuascafriday/*) Science is still grappling with the DMN's role but believe it may trigger our sense of being itself, our identity and ego. Similar tests by the Beckley Foundation in the United Kingdom in 2012 found that psilocybin mushrooms also inhibit the DMN, which suggests this is how psychoactive substances tune us in to that mystic sense of oneness with all things.

As our paradigms deepen and seem to parallel, the scientific, spiritual, and psychedelic experience all present valid models to understand the world around us and find the meaning we so desperately crave. And yet, as philosopher and raconteur Terence McKenna once said: "The psychedelic experience is as central to understanding your humanness as having sex, or having a child, or having responsibilities, or having hopes and dreams, and yet it is illegal." As increasing attention is focused on the use of both manmade psychedelics and plant-based entheogens as potent psychological tools in legal medical studies across the world, a wider context must also be established to integrate the proper understanding of these substances in the role of consciousness itself.

Investigations into the suppression of the DMN by psychoactive substances could be crucial to finding the truth about consciousness in general. Current models of how consciousness works includes the "electromagnetic field theory," which states that the brain produces an electromagnetic field that orders neuronal activity into coherence. Other theories posit a "quantum brain dynamic" interpretation where water molecules in the brain create a "cortical field" that interacts with quantum coherent waves in the neuronal network. Both of these dominant models still propose an unresolved assumption—that the brain itself *creates* consciousness within the brain-mind dynamic.

If consciousness isn't simply created from the "hardware" of the brain itself, the inverse possibility is that it is received and filtered through the quantum-neuronal interface. The original analogy for this was of that of a radio and the signals it receives—if the radio is destroyed, the data it transmits is not lost; the music and audio signals are, of course, broadcast from an external source. The radio is simply the receiving and filtering mechanism to convert radio signals to audible sound. In the same way, William James and others argued that when the brain is damaged and consciousness is impaired, this does not mean that the full spectrum of consciousness is destroyed, merely that the receiving device is debilitated.

This, of course, then raises the larger question of where does the stream of consciousness that is being broadcast originate from? If it's not local to the hardware of the brain, it must be "nonlocal." Dr. Larry Dossey, in his book *The Power of Premonitions*, also reminds us that the radio (or even the updated analogy of a TV set) picks up electromagnetic (EM) signals that weaken according to distance and can be blocked, whereas consciousness does not appear to be limited in the same ways the EM bandwidth is.

Dossey goes on to say that:

> My conclusion is that consciousness is not a thing or substance, but is a *nonlocal* phenomenon. *Nonlocal* is merely a fancy word for *infinite*. If something is nonlocal, it is not localized to specific points in space, such as brains or bodies, or to specific points in time, such as the present. Nonlocal events are *immediate;* they require no travel time. They are unmediated; they require no energetic signal to "carry" them. They are *unmitigated;* they do not become weaker with increasing distance. Nonlocal phenomena are *omnipresent,* everywhere at once. This means there is no necessity for them to go anywhere; they are already there. They are infinite in time as well, present at all moments, past present and future, meaning they are *eternal.* (*The Power of Premonitions: How Knowing the Future Can Shape Our Lives*, 2009)

Here we start to delve into the territory of quantum physics and the ideas of leading physicists like Einstein and David Bohm. Einstein famously posited in his Theory of General Relativity that space and time are not separate but are actually parts of a larger time continuum. Bohm went further than Einstein, saying that everything in the universe is part of this continuum and that on the "Explicate" level (the manifested world that springs from a primal "Implicate," or Source) everything is seamlessly connected. "The universe may be nothing more than a giant hologram created by the mind," said Bohm. He further argued that consciousness itself is a subtle form of matter that is intrinsically embedded in all things on the Implicate level.

This model of a "conscious universe" changes the typical Western view of reality and what consciousness is. There is no longer a need for any distinction between living and nonliving things, as everything is alive and has consciousness, including energy itself and everything made from it. This announcement has immediate parallels to the worldview of shamans, mystics, and the indigenous wisdom of tribal people. Still, if consciousness is a field of being not just broadcast but "on," underlying and perhaps animating the material world, through what interface does it work? How does the brain then receive this omnidirectional signal given off by this Implicate Source? How do other living creatures without a centralized brain structure—for instance, plants—receive this signal?

The modern science of quantum biology examines how the theories of quantum physics interact with biological life forms, and in recent years, plants have played a central role in deepening our understanding of these processes. A 2007 paper in *Nature* magazine saw "evidence for wavelike energy transfer through quantum coherence in photosynthetic systems." (*http://www.nature.com/nature/journal/v446/n7137/full/nature05678. html*) Plants have long been posited as conscious entities, and as far back as 1966, Cleve Backster, an ex-interrogation specialist for the CIA during the infamous MK Ultra days, conducted his now-infamous plant intelligence experiment. Backster attached polygraph electrodes to a Dracaena cane plant and was amazed to see that it was alive and was reading out in much the same way a human polygraph readout would display. He went on to experiment with biocommunication in plant and animal cells, which led to his theory of what he called "primary perception," or extra-sensory perception by plants to external stimuli.

This interspecies communication becomes more possible as our understanding of energetic frequencies increases. We currently know that the human brain has five different frequencies it operates at: Beta, Alpha, Theta, Delta, and Gamma, measured in cycles per second (Hz), each of which have their own set of characteristics and produce a specific brain function and type of consciousness. Beta (14–40 Hz) gives us waking consciousness and reason and logic; Alpha (7.5–14 Hz) is a state of deep relaxation, light meditation, and intuition; Theta (4–7.5 Hz) is present in the REM dream state, deep meditation, and spiritual and psychoactive states of unity and oneness. Delta (0.5–4 Hz) is the slowest brain frequency, manifesting in deep, dreamless sleep or egoless meditation; and Gamma (above 40 Hz) is the fastest frequency, thought to produce insight, flow, and rapid information processing.

Gamma was only discovered with the advent of EEG machines that read the brain, and that in itself proves that states of consciousness can and do exist that we are sometimes unable to measure. Modern scientific tests have also proven that plants respond and improve their growth when exposed to signals of consciousness in the 0–15 Hz frequency range (Delta through Alpha), the same bandwidth as ecstatic states, meditation, and out-of-body experiences.

Modern science has discounted Backster's experiments as misinterpretations of galvanic skin responses (and indeed, later testing hasn't been able to replicate his extreme findings), but the idea of plant sentience, and a larger reservoir of consciousness embodied in nature herself, is at the heart of the indigenous perspective of the Amazon. The shamans, *brujos, vegetalistas, tobaqueros, ayahuasqueros,* et al., all work with unseen entities and forces of embodied consciousness that do not have discreet corporeal form. These medicine people say they are in direct communication with the plant and earth spirits that animate their jungle canvas. The vegetalistas in particular work with thousands of medicinal plants and understand the delicate ecosystem as a living entity. The ayahuasqueros work with the power plant Ayahuasca and a number of other plant additives in the Ayahuasca brew to produce an astounding visionary entheogen that is also a remarkable physical purgative and emotional cleanser.

While Western science has proven that Ayahuasca is a rich source of serotonergic agonists and reuptake inhibitors, the effect of the Ayahuasca brew is not just a neurochemical one. The shamans believe it is the relationship with the spirits both in the plant ("madre ayahuasca") and in the astral or consciousness ecology that engage with their patients to aid in their healing, often mediated through the shaman's use of *icaros,* sacred songs transmitted by the plants themselves that are, in essence, vibrational codes. By singing the vibration, or essence, of a plant into the patient, the shaman connects the energetic bodies of plant and patient in a symbiotic gestalt. All of this is part of the deeply researched, tested, and proven efficacy over hundreds of years of knowledge (within their culture) of their science of *curanderismo.*

Stephan Beyer, author of *Singing to the Plants*, wrote an article in the *Journal of Shamanic Practice* titled "What Do the Spirits Want from Us?" In it he said:

> Shamans in the Upper Amazon have established a relationship of trust and love with the healing and protective spirits of the plants. To win their love, to learn to sing to them in their own language, shamans must first show that they are strong and faithful, worthy of trust. To do

this, they must go into the wilderness, away from other people, and follow *la dieta*, the restricted diet—no salt, no sugar, no sex—and ingest the sacred plant that is the body of the spirit.... The spirits are all here, with us, right now. This world is as magical—as filled with ogres and allies, signs and mysteries—as the miraculous world of the vision fast.

The modern world is too caught up at a denser energetic state to hear the singing of the plants, the shamans say. It is fixated to computer screens, TVs, iPhones, and the like, trapping consciousness at Alpha levels. But when you take entheogens like Ayahuasca, the DMN is subdued, and the transmission of higher consciousness is revealed and remembered.

Dennis McKenna, an ethnopharmacologist known for his work with Ayahuasca and its effect on the brain with pioneering studies like the Hoasca Project (1990), and brother of psychedelic philosopher Terence McKenna, has also had his fair share of mind-expanding shamanic experiences. Integrating them into the Western scientific paradigm forced him to examine many basic concepts anew, such as: "If the brain is a receiver of consciousness, then perhaps consciousness itself is a singularity point much like black holes, where energy is compacted so densely in on itself that it collapses. That collapse in the brain may be what causes consciousness." (Dennis McKenna, quoted in *Aya Awakenings: A Shamanic Odyssey,* 2013) Is this what psychoactives do when they subdue the Default Mode Network? I once posited that "adding an injection of DMT to the endogenous levels of DMT already in the brain ... may act like the collapse of a star into a black hole, as the brain receiver tunes into an ultra-dense state, reading deeper than ever before." (Rak Razam, *Aya Awakenings: A Shamanic Odyssey,* 2013).

The science of black holes is still an evolving field, and despite recent headlines by Steven Hawking claiming black holes don't exist (he was actually proposing a hypothesis that the event horizon around a black hole doesn't behave the way models suggest), the relationship to black holes as singularities in space time, and consciousness as a singularity, is an intriguing one. Astrophysicists have recently used computer simulations to model how the universe evolved, with visual representations of that growth showing clusters of young galaxies surrounded by stars, older galaxies and dark matter in a complex web eerily identical to the synaptical pathways of the brain, with individual neurons in the same place as galaxies. Ancient alchemical wisdom had an axiom "as above, so below," and in this, and so many other examples, nature may use the same principles in unfolding her creation on different scales.

Interestingly enough, there is another culture that believed the source of consciousness was in the center of our galaxy—the ancient Maya. The Maya had an amazing ability to map the stars and create calendrical systems that proved astoundingly accurate over vast periods of time, but for them, it wasn't a dry, scientific affair. The spiritual intimacy of their science is reflected in the language they used to describe the stars—for them, galactic center, which they knew about and revered as the source of their knowledge and of all consciousness in our galaxy—they called Hunab Ku, which translates as "the womb of the great mother." The Maya, and many of their contemporary Mesoamerican cultures, were also entheogenic based and used San Pedro cactus, Ayahuasca, and DMT-containing plants and snuffs both in their consciousness exploration and to facilitate the underpinnings of their science and culture.

Interestingly enough, since the launch of the latest generation of space telescopes like the Swift Gamma-Ray Burst mission in 2004 and the Fermi Gamma-Ray Telescope in 2008, our understanding of black holes has deepened. NASA has confirmed that the center of our galaxy *is* actually a supermassive black hole, which according to current theories doesn't just suck matter into its event horizon but also spits out jets of ionized gas into space. The jets are bits of matter accelerated by the event horizon they entered, rebounded so fast, they give off gamma rays, converting energy to light. This then heats space and changes the cosmic environment, which may help spark new stars into being. So black holes are not just a source of death, but—like the Maya said about Hunab Ku, the womb of the great mother—they are a source of life.

So what if the Maya were also right about the center of the galaxy being the seat of consciousness, a "pan-galactic cloud computer," if you will, that creates, stores, and transmits consciousness itself? Other exotic theories also posit the potential for black holes to be wormholes to other points in space-time or to parallel universes or higher dimensions. Like our current mapping of the structural similarities of the galactic star structure and neuronal pathways in the brain, could the galactic superstructure itself be the macro-receiver for higher dimensional consciousness from an Implicate Source? And like the way different regions of the brain filter and modulate consciousness for specific tasks, does the distribution of consciousness in the form of energy blanket the galactic-neuronal pathways to activate subprograms, i.e., life forms?

We do know that these galactic emissions affect the magnetic fields of both our sun, and through it the earth, and from there our brains directly.

In 2008 *New Scientist* magazine interviewed Kelly Posner, a psychiatrist at Columbia University in the United States, who said: "The most plausible explanation for the association between geomagnetic activity and depression and suicide is that geomagnetic storms can desynchronize circadian rhythms and melatonin production." The pineal gland, which regulates circadian rhythm and melatonin production, is sensitive to magnetic fields. "The circadian regulatory system depends upon repeated environmental cues to [synchronize] internal clocks . . . Magnetic fields may be one of these environmental cues." (*http://www.newscientist.com/article/dn13769-does-the-earths-magnetic-field-cause-suicides.html*) The pineal gland in rats has recently been confirmed to secrete endogenous dimethyltryptamine, or DMT, a powerful psychoactive chemical that also exists in our brains as well as in most mammal and many plant species. The pineal gland is directly affected by sunlight and the magnetic fields tripped by the light, and through the pineal, the metabolism of the body is regulated.

So if this celestial daisy chain we are all embedded in has a verifiable effect on the earth, and the health of us as individuals, what then can we say about the alignment of our solar system with galactic center and the supermassive black hole in the cosmic circuit? To the Maya, it was 0.0.0.0.0 on their calendar, or the moment when the 26,000-year orbit concluded and a new cycle began. The grand 26,000-year galactic orbit took in a series of successive world ages, or quadrants, each of which they believed affected consciousness. Heading toward the super-information highway of galactic center, their cosmology suggests, should see a peak in the cosmic-consciousness-connection. You could make an analogy of a mobile phone: Halfway through the galactic orbit of 13,500 years, you go down to a one- or two-bar signal. And as you align closer to galactic center, you receive more consciousness signal, like getting four-bar reception on your mobile phone. And if you use up all your galactic bandwidth allowance, consciousness itself may be "shaped" until you roll over to the next installment, or world age. . . .

Which is just where we seem to find ourselves in the post-2012 Gregorian era, a critical turning point within history. The exponential march of consciousness has created a technological transformation that has simultaneously drained the planet of resources while creating an ever-complexifying web of interconnected information (the Internet), startlingly similar to Vladimir Verandsky and Pierre Teilhard de Chardin's conception of the "sphere of human thought" they called the "noosphere." A cross between atmosphere and biosphere, the noosphere was defined by Verandsky as the third phase after the geosphere and the biosphere, and was marked by the emergence of human consciousness transforming the environment.

But human consciousness is not the only one on the planet transforming the environment—in fact, humans, animals, plants—all the sentient species have different levels of consciousness that make up and transform the biosphere. Collectively, we may act as an *organic mesh network,* a terrestrial-DNA-receiver for the galactic signal, a "species satellite dish," for receiving consciousness itself. To update the old analogy of the radio or TV set receiving signal, what if the planet creates the hardware (each species) to host the software (consciousness), downloaded like a *bit-torrent from galactic center?* What if the quantum entanglement of consciousness file-shares the source code from higher dimensional space on the other side of the black hole? And what if those clever plants, themselves deep in the egoless 0.5 Hz frequency of consciousness and connected to the broadcast signal, have been grooming us to come back to the garden, to balance with nature and *four-bar Godhead consciousness* through their entheogenic brethren?

Isn't that just where the resurgence of global shamanism and the popularity of entheogens like Ayahuasca and psilocybin is heading? A return full circle? These entheogens give us a brief flash of the interconnected web of life embodied in the DMT frequency, and in doing so, they may be training us for that experience of full-spectrum consciousness embedded in nature and connecting us back to the Source.

If there is some truth in these theories of consciousness that unites the macro-galactic with the micro-neuronal levels, mediated by the plants and the entheogenic frequencies they enable, it would reposition our understanding of consciousness in the same way that Galileo's discovery that the earth actually revolves around the sun changed our worldview centuries ago. It would take us from the egoic role of consciousness creators to consciousness receivers, and in a way, relieve us of at least some of the guilt the ego brings. For when we go into the egoless state and merge with a sense of unity consciousness, we're actually present in real time, outside linear time and inside eternity.

And in that moment you might, as William Blake said:

> . . . see a World in a Grain of Sand
> And a Heaven in a Wild Flower,
> Hold Infinity in the palm of your hand
> And Eternity in an hour.

EXPANDING THE MIND

THE CREATIVE PROCESS AND ENTHEOGENS
BY ALEX GREY

with thanks to Allyson Grey

On the evening of May 30, 1975, I took my first dose of LSD in Allyson's apartment. The experience was so rich and profound, coupled as it was with the meeting of my future wife, Allyson, that there seemed nothing more important than this revelation of infinite love and unity. As an artist, this became the only subject worth my time and attention. Spiritual and visionary consciousness assumed primary importance as the focal point of my life and art. My creative process was transformed by my experience with psychedelics, also called entheogens, because of their uncanny ability to reveal the God within.

Due to its visionary power and richness, the psychedelic experience has played a tremendous role in fueling an artistic and cultural renaissance. Offering artists access to deeper and higher aspects of their soul, the psychonaut is given a subject worth making art about. The transformative vision is a critically important discovery, a magnetic passion that burns in their souls and artworks. A worthy subject is an artist's most important discovery and can impact whether their work will evoke the deepest and highest resonance with their viewers.

Oscar Janiger's studies of LSD and creativity showed that many artists felt the work done while tripping or post-tripping was more inventive and inspired work than their previous work. Keith Haring, one of the most celebrated artists of the 1980s, credited LSD with stylistic breakthroughs that brought him to his own unique work. Sacramental substances in every culture have been treasured by certain members and not recommended for all. It seems a crime against cognitive liberty, however, to punish self-discovery through sacraments that can empower our spiritual and creative lives.

"How can we bring the insights of the entheogenic state into our lives?" For the visionary artist, their work is a translation of a mystical state and represents, to the best of their ability, the depth of feeling and perception in subtle inner worlds they experienced in that state. Utterly unique to each

65

individual, the entheogenic state is yet characterized by archetypal states of being reported by scores of psychonauts, some through art. Stages of the psychedelic experience can be translated into works of art.

1. Body signals or symptoms: Jitteriness or rushes of energy may shoot through our body. The chest or the top of our head may have an opening or lifting sensation. We feel a heightened sensitivity to colors and notice wavy or slowly billowing distortions of our outer world perceptions. Turning our attention inward, we may perceive dynamic geometric forms and cartoon-like figures morphing into strange and inventive shapes. The unconscious is surfacing toward consciousness. As we release the depth of mystery and meaning our conceptual mind has been keeping at bay, our ordinary perception floods with portent.
2. Psychodynamic visions: Unresolved repressed emotions emerge. Dramatic personally meaningful imagery confronts us face-to-face. Frightening encounters with suppressed memories can emerge and resolve to ultimate completion in a healing environment.

Next come transpersonal stages:

3. Birth, death, and rebirth experiences: The ego/small self is frightened, crushed, overcome, and reborn through intense cythonic and cathartic visions.
4. Archetypal and mythic visions: Meditating on each other's faces, Allyson and I simultaneously saw the "everyface" of humanity wash across the face of our adored one. In my view, Allyson became every woman, every man, and every animal, and for her, I transformed into all beings.
5. Energy release: Kundalini movements in body, chakras opening, awareness of subtle energy systems.
6. Universal mind: Cosmic unity, voidness or emptiness as the ground of being beyond polarities. Vistas of subtle, pulsating fountains and drains of energy. Looking down infinite turning, activated suck-holes and blow-holes of energy.

Each of these stages or structures of higher consciousness and the subtle inner worlds can be evoked in our art. As with sacred art traditions in a multitude of cultures gone by, the Integrative Entheogenic Vision in art brings together the opposites of dark and light, reason and intuition, the known and the believed, male and female, life and death, matter and spirit.

Heinrich Kluver studied the effects of mescaline on normal subjects and found visual and perceptual "form constants" that recur in psychedelic voyages. Particularly relevant to developing our entheogenic artistic vision, these form constants include the spiral, the lattice or fretwork, tunnels, funnels, and passageways. There is a perception of "greater dimensionality," both visual multidimensionality and ontological dimensions of meaning. Iridescent and finely filigreed organic and complex geometric shapes evolve and dissolve, referencing both nature and sacred architecture. Colors appear more radiant and overwhelming. Light itself takes on a palpable character. The white light is everywhere present, the "glue" of creation.

An experience of such overwhelming power can influence an artist's approach. In order to bring forth the deepest work, an artist needs to be sensitive and courageous toward their own process. There are many stages in realizing a work of art and the mysterious phases of creativity:

1. Formulation: Discovery of the artist's subject/problem
2. Saturation: A period of intense research on the subject/problem
3. Incubation: Letting the unconscious sift the information and develop a response/solution
4. Inspiration: A flash of the artist's unique response/solution to the subject/problem
5. Translation: Bringing the internal response/solution to outer form
6. Integration: Sharing the creative answer with the world
7. Interpretation: Collecting and integrating feedback

The most important question for any artist is, what is my subject? The formulation of a problem arises from the artist's worldview and, if the problem is sufficiently broad, the stage may be set for an entire life's journey. The problem is the "well" dug to reveal the Source, the Vision, the creative matrix of questions and obsessions that drive you. Solving your aesthetic problem becomes your mission.

The journey of creating the painting *Transfiguration* clearly illuminates the evolution of an artwork and the stages in my creative process. The subject of the body/mind has long been my passion and making visible multiple dimensions of reality among my greatest challenges. Initial experiences on LSD compelled me to make mystical consciousness itself the subject of my art. The subject of consciousness and the artistic problem of how to portray it became my life's work.

In the stage of saturation, I immersed myself in the subject, researching and scouring many libraries for tracts on transpersonal psychology and the art of diverse cultures. Transfiguration became the subject of an illustrated lecture with artistic representations of transcendental light or energy in relation to the body, created by artists all over the world today and in cultures throughout human history. The painting *Transfiguration* had not yet been envisioned.

In the incubation stage, the vast womb of the unconscious takes over, gestating the problem. The embryonic artwork grows effortlessly at its own pace. For the painting *Transfiguration*, this phase took about half a year.

Then, in a dream, I had been painting a piece called *Transfiguration*. The painting had a simple composition, two opposing spherical curves connected by a figure. Floating above the earth sphere, a human, fleshly at the feet, became gradually translucent as the figure rose between the globes. At about groin level, the figure "popped" into a bright hallucinogenic crystal sphere. The dream revealed a unique solution to my simmering aesthetic problem.

This illumination, or inspiration phase, my aha! moment provided by the dream, was underscored later that week when I smoked DMT for the first time. As I inhaled the immediately active and extremely potent psychedelic, I experienced the transfigured subject of my painting firsthand. In my vision, my feet were the foundation of the material world. As I inhaled, the material density of my body seemed to dissolve, and I "popped" into the bright world of living geometry and infinite spirit. Strange jewel-like chakra centers glowed within my wire-frame spirit body. Spectral colors appeared that had been absent from my dream painting. Fully inside my future painting, this image was clarified in order to better create a work of art.

After two visionary encounters of the same painting, I began drawing my inspired impression in a sketchbook. This started the translation phase. Bringing the inner solution of my artistic problem to an outward form, I drew the body and computer-plotted an accurate texture map of the electric grid around the hypermindsphere. Assembling the various elements, I stretched a 60 x 90 inch canvas to create a life-sized figure centered between two large spheres. After a long period of drawing and refining, I started painting. After months of painting the figure and the spheres, Allyson, my partner in all things, continued to ask about the unconsidered area of the painting, the blue negative spaces around the lower body below the hypermindsphere and above the earth. This was a dark area that went unnoticed in my previous visions.

When we are aesthetically "stumped" and need to see our work with fresh and creative eyes, Allyson and I, studio mates for most of our lives, smoke cannabis together and gaze at the work of art (or blank canvas) in question. Suggestions of what should appear in the empty space of *Transfiguration* did coalesce. Stars obviously, but this was not just outer space—this was inner space, the place of numinous angels or demons, of Terence's "self-dribbling basketballs," beings with skin like a Fabergé egg, the oddly glowing mindspheres anticipating the transformative megasphere above. The painting took almost a year to complete.

Integrating the inspired moment by creating an artifact and bringing that artifact into the world outside the studio is a prime function of the creative process. I sculpted an elaborate 104 x 156 inch frame to honor this life-altering vision. A poster was published, the work has been widely exhibited, and it was reproduced in my book titled *Transfigurations*. Allyson and I have decided to retain the original framed painting to share at CoSM, Chapel of Sacred Mirrors, a sanctuary of visionary art.

Although entheogens have played a crucial role in the creative process of many artists, including Allyson and me, we cannot responsibly advocate the use of these sacraments for everyone and certainly do not promote a constant haze of chemically altered consciousness for anyone. Some—and they often know who they are—should completely steer clear of psychoactive substances without guidance from a qualified physician. Vision drugs catalyze our inherently visionary and potentially mystical dimensions of consciousness. May they be recognized and honored for the powerful and sacred substances they are, proof of the importance and infinite vastness of the subtle inner worlds of imagination and illumination, and may they open an endless source of inspiration for new universal sacred art.

POSTSCRIPT

Since writing this essay nearly fifteen years ago, a tribe of visionary artists has emerged, developing and refining the subject of altered and higher states of awareness. The visionary art movement is largely underground, appearing at transformational festivals worldwide, and the resulting visionary artworks form a body of evidence that testifies to the recurring motifs of the inner worlds and beings that dwell there. Allyson and I believe this is a new sacred art pointing to the emergence of a planetary civilization.

HOW EXPANDING CONSCIOUSNESS AND OUR CONNECTION TO SPIRIT MIGHT HELP THE SURVIVAL OF LIFE ON PLANET EARTH

BY MARTINA HOFFMAN

With the latest International Climate Report in place, we now know that climate change is a definitive reality and that there are ways to keep things at bay. Also, we are told that there are certain changes that are irreversible, like losing species that have graced Gaia for a long time.

On a brighter note, it appears that growing numbers of humans worldwide have started to take inventory of their state of consciousness and spiritual lives. The idea of looking within reveals a new frontier, and now millions of people worldwide are meditating.

As we are navigating through these greatly accelerated times of global change, this might come in handy with the way we'll be able to stay focused and strong. As we experience changes in the weather, we are simultaneously changing the way we see and have to make adjustments in how we exist on planet Earth.

This is good news, and we are beginning to see new streams of consciousness expressed on select television shows, social media in the increasing amount of spiritual awareness sites, as well as the multitude of YouTube videos. The Internet is a world wide web with a technical pathway where one can inquire on a variety of consciousness-, spirituality-, and environment-related subjects. And finally when mainstream media begins to stir, it will become a new star and will champion the support of an awakening that is as necessary for the successful and healthy continuation of life on Earth as it is timely. Granted, many of these shows are a watered-down level of how deep we truly need to go, but they are a start.

This gives us at least some hope that whatever challenges we may encounter, as a collective we can discover a sustainable solution and act upon it. Should our balance of problems and solutions be serendipitous with natural flow, we will be in harmony with Gaia.

Tree of Knowledge

I've been asking myself how we can accelerate the process of positive and healthy change for our humanity as well as Gaia, and the term *raising Consciousness* seems to offer an excellent place to start.

Consciousness is an ancient term and has always been a part of our human existence. And while it appears that we are in the process of rediscovering it as an integral part of our reality, in actuality, we are just reinventing the wheel.

Regardless of how much or how little the concern for Consciousness has grown in the hearts and awareness of the masses, it has always existed as part of our evolution. And most of us will agree that our graceful survival as a species will largely depend on it.

Unfortunately, the Western mind and world at large seem to have denied the essential role of "Consciousness," this age-old connection to the Universe, the key ingredient throughout human evolution. They have placed it into the category of a rare and isolated human experience, reserved for secret societies, mystical groups, and the chosen few: the saints who seek strange experiences and visions while meditating for extended periods of time on isolated mountaintops, and the spiritual weirdos and lunatics. But nothing could be further from the truth.

The ancients and tribal cultures in particular have for millennia lived an awareness that is our innate birthright. They have spoken about this most essential connection to the cosmos and to spirit and kept it at the heart of their spiritual practices and lives. They have continuously, since the beginning of humankind, lived in close relationship with the earth and used rituals, methods, and tools to build, increase, and maintain their awareness in Consciousness. In the Western context however, these practices have largely been

Caught in the Web

kept a secret, reserved for those who choose to live an ascetic life away from the world. Often, such individuals are marginalized by society. But if we pay attention, we find that these tools are still available at all times to us in the form of dream work, fasting, drumming, and other shamanic/spiritual practices, and that they allow us to connect deeper with the fundamental energies that drive and support us. Sometimes these rituals might even involve the ingestion of today's criminalized, Consciousness-enhancing plant teachers that have the potential to help us to expand our awareness, our spiritual connection, and our enlightenment as well as physical healing. While these ancient practices are here for us to tap in to for support in our evolution as a species, the majority of the world follows well-guided, rehearsed, repeated, and dogmatic religious practices, which foster the dependence on religious institutions, formulae, and the powers that be, as well as creating great separation within humanity. Meanwhile, the ancient indigenous rituals provide us with a profound experience of knowing to be an integral part of the Universe and of being deeply interconnected, interrelated, and interdependent with all of Life. This offers us a vast and tremendous view of the seemingly unlimited landscape of Consciousness.

Ultimately it appears to me that the "renegade" versions of paths to greater Consciousness traditionally seem more universal and all accepting. They afford us a greater-encompassing worldview and connection to the larger reality, one that considers all sentient beings, all peoples bound into a living "Web of Life" and Consciousness which is eternal and infinite. With every thought, feeling, and action being an integral part of the Web, we directly influence how it vibrates, contracts, expands, and ever changes. In this ancient cosmology, all beings and all that is are intimately connected. To know and see all that is as an important part of the whole, and us not just at the mercy of the Gods but rather as an individualized reflection of the "One"

Cusp

Curandura

provides us a precious gift and opportunity: to become instrumental in the creation of our reality, hopefully conscious cocreators for our planetary existence as well as aware guardians for our planet.

It is quite remarkable to see that it is often our indigenous brothers and sisters who have kept the connection between this world and the Spirit World alive through their way of living closer to the earth and through their rituals. But the old Shamans are slowly vanishing, and they are now facing, just as the Western world, a reality that does not harmonize with the same ancient Gaian rhythm. We now all have to become "shamans" in our own right and find new ways of working and approaching reality together. And if we add play and joy to the mix, evolution is inevitable.

Of course, greater Consciousness can be developed and reached by following many paths or spiritual traditions as long as the path is tread upon with honesty, humility, and our interconnectedness in heart and mind.

This new path that wants to emerge worldwide includes all peoples and traditions—indigenous as well as Western—and all religions. It is nondenominational, nongenerational, nongender, and nonracial, and its development lies in our own hands.

Many feel a continuous and all-pervasive revolution happening, which we wish will transcend all differences and move our evolution forward.

There is no earthly authority that has a patent on it.

With this, we are free to develop and attain a higher understanding of it by ourselves. If need be, we can utilize the help of age-old practices—prayers, meditations, sacred shamanic journeys, sacred medicines, simple personal interactions with nature, being in silence, fasting, singing, chanting, making art, simply loving, and being of service to others.

This revolution begins at home in the intimacy of our own bodies, minds, and hearts, and luckily there is no middleman or institution needed to achieve it. As long as we are willing to listen inside with abandon to the individualized voice of "Source Energy" that is as eternal and infinite as our spirits, we will grow.

As an artist, my personal path to Consciousness has led me on a magical journey of discovering the ways through expressing in form and color. But

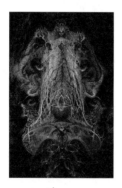

La Chacruna

Lysergic Summer Dream

Alien Ascension

Snake Egg

Snake Helix

whether we are actual artists or not, we still remain cocreators of the divine, all instrumental in changing and creating our world and reality one step, one person, and one day at a time. So it is paramount that we are becoming conscious of our great power and importance in this game of life and of how we are influencing and shaping reality every second of our existence. This is no longer a dress rehearsal. We all have to show up.

With this awareness comes responsibility and the need to be present and conscious of our actions at every moment. The world and all life within it, us included, lie in our own hands and depend on it.

Having Consciousness means holding this responsibility with absolute respect for all life and existence. We hold the powerful and precious tool for transformation in our own hands and hearts, one loving thought and action at a time.

Each individual's gift and contribution to the whole will vary but has equal importance. Mine, as a visionary painter, lies in making visible the more subtle and intuitive states of our existence by encoding them in my work and thereby producing symbols and maps that reflect Consciousness. These symbols and otherworldly blueprints, now manifested on canvas, have become part of the human field and thereby directly shape our world, reality, and culture. Further, I like to use art as a portal for spirit-communication and as a conscientious tool for manifesting spiritual, physical healing and transformation.

My work is an attempt to show spirit as the one universal force beyond the confines of cultural and religious differences.

Gayatri

I feel that we all need to become artists with our gifts and talents, as we are all called to raise our Consciousness and awareness. As the light dawns upon our Consciousness, we learn to embrace our Oneness as a global human family—our interconnectedness, interrelatedness, and interdependence with Nature and all that is.

Through this, we have a real chance to heal and transform the planet's existing state of woundedness and the opportunity to create a reality as beautiful, healthy, and strong as our imagination can fly.

Let's do it! The "divine intervention" that many of the "awakened ones" have been waiting for might come in the form of each and every one of us individually and all of *us* together finally taking charge. The world is a better place because you are in it.

Hawk Medicine

THE DIVINE SPARK

WHISPERING LEAVES: INTERSPECIES COMMUNICATION?[1]

BY PAUL DEVEREUX

Societies of the past have used the psychedelic experience to strengthen, renew, and heal the spiritual underpinning of their social structures. The ever-deepening social unease that Western civilisation seems to be caught in is the real source of our "drug problem": natural hallucinogens are not the problems in themselves; it is the context in which they are used that matters. If there were orderly and healthy structures and mechanisms for their use and the cultural absorption of the powerful experiences—and knowledge— we could separate these from the culture of crime that surrounds them now. In short, the problems are not in the psychoactive substances themselves, but in a society, which on the one hand wants to prohibit mind expansion altogether and on the other chooses to use mind-expanding substances in a literally mindless, hedonistic fashion.

Perhaps only a shock of some kind could break our society free from the patterns of thought and prejudices that lock it into this crisis. The desire for such a shock may be hidden within the widespread modern myth of extra-terrestrial intervention. In fact, we do not have to look to science fiction for a real otherworld contact: it already exists in the form of plant hallucinogens. If we see them in the context of a "problem," it is only because they hold up a mirror in which we see our spiritual, social, and mental condition reflected. And they hold that mirror up to us as one species to another just as surely as if they were from another planet. Indeed, that champion of the psychedelic state, the late Terence McKenna, argued that the ancestral spores of today's hallucinogenic mushrooms may have originated on some other planet.[2] (This is not as fringe an idea as it sounds, for even some "hard scientists"—the late Francis Crick, codiscoverer of DNA, among them—have suggested that the germs of life may have had extraterrestrial origins, brought to Earth by means of meteorites or comet dust.) The psilocybin family of hallucinogens, says McKenna, produces a "logos-like phenomenon of an interior voice that seems to be almost a superhuman agency . . . an entity so far beyond the normal structure of the ego that if it is not an extraterrestrial it might as well be." Precisely.

Other "psychonauts" have emerged from the altered mind states enabled by plant substances with similar impressions. For instance, New York journalist Daniel Pinchbeck wrote about his various initiations with plant hallucinogens in his book *Breaking Open the Head* (2002). In one Ayahuasca session with Amazonian Secoya Indians, he found himself wandering in a visionary space where he encountered beings that "never stopped changing" their forms. "The shaman and the elders seemed to be inhabiting this space with me. . . . They sang, their words unintelligible, to these creatures, interacting with them. . . . I had no more doubts that the Secoya engaged in extra-dimensional exploration." Or, again, two of the three molecular biologists taken to the Amazon to experience Ayahuasca trances by anthropologist and writer Jeremy Narby felt that they had communicated with an "independent intelligence." Narby himself feels that in their Ayahuasca altered states, shamans plumb the molecular level of nature and that, to put Narby's idea crudely, Ayahuasca—with its trademark visionary snakes—has the ability to communicate information concerning the double-helix coil of DNA (*The Cosmic Serpent*, 1998). Indeed, to allow contact with what we might call the mind of nature.

The idea that ontologically independent beings ("spirits") or intelligences are contactable through plant-induced trances is standard in most if not all shamanic tribal societies, but to posit such a thing in modern Western societies is viewed as tantamount to insanity, a nonsense notion to be dismissed out of hand. In other words, we can't discuss it without forfeiting all credibility. This problem concerning the inability to explore certain ideas has been addressed by Oxford-based researcher Andy Letcher.[3] He uses Foucauldian discourse analysis to critique the models, the "discourses" employed by the West in dealing with the content of altered mind states. These include pathological, prohibition, psychological, recreational, psychedelic, and entheogenic discourses. Each has its own imposed boundaries; they are cognitive constructs. Letcher notes that some of these discourses or approaches to hallucinogenic substances ignore the subjective experience of the altered mind states involved, or else place it within an inner psychological framework rather than it being a case of simply seeing more, of being in a wider frame of consciousness. He critiques even the entheogenic discourse as relying on a "God within" model, divine revelation that does not by any means occur in all altered states. However diverse they might be, all these discourses can be used within the norms of Western culture. Only one discourse crosses that "fundamental societal boundary," what Letcher refers to

THE DIVINE SPARK

as the animistic discourse—the belief that the taking of, say, hallucinogenic mushrooms occasions actual "encounters with discarnate spirit entities." Because of the deep-rooted modern Western assumption that consciousness cannot occur in any other guise than human (the ultimate hubris of our species, perhaps), discussion of a conscious plant kingdom, or of that providing a portal through which contact with other, ontologically independent beings or intelligences can occur, is simply not possible within the mainstream culture. "It nevertheless remains a phenomenon in need of further scholarly research," Letcher rightly insists.

It is a remarkable fact that plant hallucinogens are hallucinogenic precisely because they contain the same, or effectively the same, chemicals as are found in the human brain and so act on us as if we were indeed engaged in an interspecies communication. "The chemical structure of the hallucinogenic principles of the mushrooms was determined . . . and it was found that these compounds were closely related chemically to substances occurring naturally in the brain which play a major role in the regulation of psychic functions," Schultes and Hofmann have observed, for instance.[4] This challenges the view held by many people that taking a plant hallucinogen is somehow "unnatural." Certainly, mind-altering plants take the brain-mind to states that are not normal by the standards of our culture, but the "normal" state of Western consciousness cannot claim to be the one-and-only "true" state of consciousness. (Indeed, judging by the mess we manage to make of our societies and of the natural world around us, it may even be an aberrant or pathological state of mind that we are culturally locked into.)

Peter Furst writes:

> If one were to reduce to its essentials the complex chemical process that occurs when an external psychoactive drug such as psilocybin reaches the brain, it would then be said that the drug, being structurally closely related to the naturally occurring indoles in the brain, appears to interact with the latter in such a way as to lock a nonordinary or inward-directed state of consciousness temporarily into place. . . . There are obviously wide implications, biological-evolutionary as well as philosophical, in the discovery that precisely in the chemistry of consciousness we are kin to the plant kingdom.[5]

These are probably the same kind of chemical changes that occur during the course of long and intensive spiritual exercises, but it takes a rare person to achieve sufficient expertise in such techniques to arrive at experiences that match those accessible through hallucinogen usage, which are certainly very "real" in a subjective sense. It is a culturally engineered cliché to dismiss such states as being somehow delusional. They are subjectively no more delusional than the experience of daily life. The human body is an open system, taking in material from the environment and expelling matter into it all the time, and we really shouldn't think of taking in natural chemicals for visionary and mind-expanding functioning as any different, any less natural, than taking in gases from the air for their chemical benefits to the body; or chemicals and compounds in animal and vegetable matter to provide food; or fermented fruits and vegetable matter to provide delicious, refreshing, or inebriating beverages; or vitamins to augment healthy functioning; or medicines when we are ill; or caffeinated teas and coffees when we want to be energised. "Ethnobotanists now realize that psychotropic plant species extend further than had been suspected, as though nature truly wanted the human species to get in touch with its floral neighbors," Richard Gehr muses. "As plant species die off at a furious rate, the issue is no longer what they are trying to tell us, but whether we will get the message in time."[6]

That message may be to do with the need for us to change our minds, or at least, to broaden our cognitive horizons. The plant kingdom could be urging us to allow the ability to "switch channels" in consciousness terms to let them become a recognised and acceptable part of our emerging global culture. Hallucinogen-using ancient and traditional societies had and have exceptional sophistication when it comes to understanding and navigating alternative states of consciousness, whereas we are still quite primitive and inexperienced in this regard. The manual for using expanded consciousness is a textbook we have not read—or, more accurately, recalled. Not that simply widening our collective experience of consciousness will act like a magic wand and remove all problems and obstacles, but it would help us to make wiser, more wholesome decisions in coping with them. If Western civilization is truly to advance, we surely must learn to operate within the multidimensional capacities of our minds rather than using the police to conduct an indiscriminate war on the means of doing so. A workable balance has to be struck between protecting the well-being and the orderly functioning of society as a whole, and allowing the human brain-mind to explore its full potential. We are smart enough and complex enough and able enough to make it possible to do both. There are no excuses.

References

1. This essay is an adapted extract from Paul Devereux's *The Long Trip* (Penguin Arkana 1997; Daily Grail Publishing 2008).
2. McKenna, Terence, *The Archaic Revival*, HarperSanFrancisco, 1991,San Francisco. (pp. 39–40)
3. Letcher, Andy, "Mad Thoughts on Mushrooms: Discourse and Power in the Study of Psychedelic Consciousness," 2007, in *Anthropology of Consciousness*, Vol.18, No.2. (pp. 74–97)
4. Schultes, Richard Evans, & Hofmann, Albert, *Plants of the Gods*,(1979), Healing Arts Press edn., 1992, Rochester, VT. (p. 27)
5. Furst, Peter T., *Hallucinogens and Culture*, Chandler & Sharp, 1976, Novato, CA. (p. 15)
6. Gehr, Richard "Notes from a Psychedelic Revival Meeting," in *Village Voice*, 5 July, 1995.

THREE HUMONGOUS IDEAS AND A DOZEN MERELY BIG ONES
OR
THE PSYCHEDELIC FUTURE OF THE MIND LITE

BY THOMAS B. ROBERTS

These three excerpts from The Psychedelic Future of the Mind *present a trimmed-down form of what I see as the book's three biggest ideas. Their importance rests on what I judge as their answers' broad scope to the question, "What does it mean to be a human?" A list of the "merely big ideas" follows at the end of this article. But first, a few words about this book's unique perspective on psychedelics.*

A SHORT TRAIL GUIDE TO THE BOOK

The book *The Psychedelic Future of the Mind* looks forward, not backward. Experiences beget ideas, and the book is an exploration of some ideas psychedelics engender. Based on a collection of pieces of scientific research, case studies, anecdotes, and other information about psychedelics, the book asks, when all these pieces are assembled, what do they tell us about what it means to be a human, about our minds, and about the future?

- It is not a book about the discovery and history of LSD and all the strange and wonderful characters who are part of that story.
- It is not a book about psychotherapy and the seemingly miraculous cures psychedelics sometimes produce.
- It is not a book about how psychedelics plug in to receptor sites on neurons and set the brain adancing.
- It is not a book of the I-drank-Ayahuasca-puked-and-saw-the-anaconda-goddess kind.

Where might psychedelic ideas take us?

IDEA 1: THE NEW RELIGIOUS ERA—FROM RITUAL TO WORD TO EXPERIENCE

In Western culture, we are transitioning from an era of word-based religion to an era of experience-based religion, a change that may turn out to be as broad and as deep as the religious transformation five hundred years ago when text-based religion replaced the then-dominant rite-based religion's place at the center of religion. Two other ideas support this one: 1) mystical experiences form a foundation of religion that gives rise to beliefs, rituals, ethics, and organizations, and 2) under the right conditions, psychedelic plants and chemicals can—but do not always—produce mystical experiences.

DEMOCRATIZING TEXT—AROUND THE YEAR 1500

Around 1500, moveable type and the printing press democratized access to religious texts. The Reformation and the Counter-Reformation followed. General literacy and public education became important so that people could read religious texts. The growing importance of words nourished reason and science. While older religious observances of the prior period continued, new word-centered activities such as reading texts and interpreting them overlaid and overcame the older religion-as-rite era. New interpretations resulted; new churches flourished. Most important, text became an increasingly powerful source of religious ideas and a standard for judging them. Over time, the locus of Western religious activity shifted from rites to reading, from observances to Bible, from participation to verbalization.

We need only look at our current religions to see. In contrast to pre-1500, we approach religion verbally—through words. Texts, speaking, beliefs, sermons, catechisms, creeds, dogmas, doctrines, theology, and so on—all these are words. This overemphasis on words shows up today in the way we describe religions—as sets of wordy beliefs. To us, thoughts (cognitive processes) form religion. If we ask someone about his or her religion, we expect to hear about beliefs, not what rituals that person performs. The older rites certainly remain but lie obscured beneath a five-hundred-year blizzard of words.

DEMOCRATIZING PRIMARY RELIGIOUS EXPERIENCE—AROUND THE YEAR 2000

Four questions and their respective answers point to a new stage of religious development that is unfolding: a transition from word-based religion to a new era of experience-based religion, one whose foundation is an intense, personal experience of the sacred.

How would a direct primary spiritual experience affect someone?

A volunteer in the psilocybin study at the Johns Hopkins Medical Institute's Behavioral Pharmacology Research Unit answers this way: "The complete and utter loss of self . . . the sense of unity was awesome. . . . I now truly do believe in God as an ultimate reality."

If this happened regularly, how might wider society change?

Stanislav Grof, summarizing one of the effects of LSD psychotherapy, says: "Even hard-core materialists, positively oriented scientists, skeptics and cynics, and uncompromising atheists and antireligious crusaders such as Marxist philosophers suddenly became interested in a spiritual search after they confronted these levels in themselves."

What if religious studies programs, divinity schools, seminaries, religious orders, and similar religious educational institutions could teach their students to know this?

Psychotherapist Frances Vaughan, describing her own LSD-based experience, conducted when LSD was legal: "I understood why spiritual seekers were instructed to look within. . . . My understanding of mystical teaching, both Eastern and Western, Hindu, Buddhist, Christian, and Sufi alike, took a quantum leap."

What if this happened fairly regularly?

Data from the fourteen-month follow-up of the Johns Hopkins psilocybin study states that "33 percent of the volunteers rated the psilocybin experience as being the single most spiritually significant experience of his or her life, with an additional 38 percent rating it to be among the top five most spiritually significant experiences." Today entheogens—psychoactive plants and chemicals used in a spiritual context—democratize access to primary religious experience.

Just as the 1500s word-based reformation evolved into today's religious, social, and political world, will today's experience-based reformation give birth to its distinctive future?

IDEA 2: MULTISTATE THEORY—APPS ARE TO DEVICES AS MINDBODY STATES ARE TO MINDS

After recognizing the Singlestate Fallacy—the erroneous idea that all useful abilities reside in our ordinary, default mindbody state—Multistate Theory proposes substituting the word *mindbody* for *consciousness* in its theory. Then it challenges many of the social sciences and humanities into expanding into wider mindbody territories of human experience.

WHAT'S THE MATTER WITH CONSCIOUSNESS?

Mindbody states are overall patterns of cognitive and bodily functioning at any one time. They are composed of body plus mind considered as one unified whole, such as in the commonest states of wakefulness, sleeping, and dreaming. The word *mindbody* also avoids the ambiguity of the word *consciousness,* which is used in different ways in different disciplines and in common language. Confusion arises when people think that they are talking about the same thing when they use the same word. The uses of the word *consciousness* listed here, however, make it clear that the meanings are quite different, though at times overlapping.

- Common language 1: *Consciousness* means awake and interacting normally with the environment, for example, "She is *conscious* now, but last night she was asleep," and "After being in a coma for three days, he is *conscious.*"
- Common language 2: *Consciousness* refers to what one habitually thinks about, to what is typically "on one's mind" such as, "She has good ecological consciousness," or "His money occupies the center of his consciousness."
- Politics and the social sciences: *Consciousness* means the thoughts and feelings one has constructed due to one's place in society, for example, *proletarian consciousness* or *women's consciousness.*
- Philosophy: *Consciousness* refers to a self-reflective sense of "I": one thinks and can reflect on oneself and on one's thinking. In this case, the word *self-reflexiveness* would be more precise and avoid ambiguity.
- Religion and spiritual discussions: *Consciousness* means level of spiritual development, as in, "His mystical experience raised John's level of consciousness."
- Psychology 1: *Consciousness* is the sequence of what one attends to second by second; what passes through one's mind becomes the *stream of consciousness.*
- Psychology 2: Here *consciousness* refers to different overall patterns of mind and body functioning at any one time, as in Tart's "altered states of consciousness." This meaning is the one I suggest replacing with *mindbody.* This will allow cognitive studies to avoid ambiguity and will provide a way of specifying a particular pattern of mind plus body functioning at any one time.

BLOWING THE SINGLESTATE ROOF OFF THE HUMANITIES AND SOCIAL SCIENCES

Residence. One of the major concepts in the multistate theory is *residence*. Our mental and physical capacities reside within mindbody states; that is, mindbody states are the programs that express, or produce, outputs—our behavior, sensations, and thoughts. To access the outputs, we first achieve the states that contain them. As we move from one state to another, we observe that some of our cognitive processes, perceptions, feelings, and abilities become stronger in some states and weaker in others; processes in one state have their analogs in others. This leads to an enormous question that blows the roof off nearly all the topics that psychologists, cognitive scientists, and humanists study: how does [insert a topic here] vary from mindbody state to mindbody state?

Applying the Central Multistate Question

How does/do _____ vary from mindbody state to mindbody state?

To sample the opportunities that the Central Multistate Question and its paradigm offer, try inserting the topics below into the question above:

cognition	aesthetics	observation
consciousness	theology	values
movement	development	identity
meaning	emotions	reason
learning	perception	intelligence
memory	performance	creativity
language	sensations	relationships

To invent additional hypotheses, questions, and intellectual agendas, insert your favorite topics.

As we move from one state to another, we may also discover new, unsuspected abilities—ones that do not exist in our ordinary state. Systematic exploration of all mindbody states and inventorying their resident abilities are two huge mind-mapping tasks that remain in the quest to fully describe the human mind and to develop it fully.

Possible/impossible. Generally when we say a specific human behavior or experience is possible or impossible, we are tacitly implying but seldom acknowledging that we mean "in our ordinary awake state." Rare and unusual abilities and even some so-called impossible abilities and events may seem impossible to us because we have looked for them only in our default awake state. As we systematically examine other mindbody states, however, we are likely to find skills and experiences that don't reside in our ordinary state. In addition to alerting us to examine how an ability that we recognize—say, problem solving—varies from state to state, the concept of residence also alerts us to extend our vision of possible human functioning to abilities and events that do not reside in our default state.

Experimental Humanities. The section above, "The New Religious Era," hints at how it is now possible to develop a new specialty of experimental religious studies. Philosophers can do similar experiments. How does mind vary from mindbody state to mindbody state? Do default-state philosophical ideas hold in other mindbody states? What are we to make of these changes? Thanks to psychedelics and other psychotechnologies, philosophers can move beyond armchair speculation to study their topics experimentally too. Just as religion is moving beyond its word-anchored past, so can the humanities.

IDEA 3: DESIGNING AND INVENTING NEW COGNITIVE PROCESSES

Just as programmers can write a large number of new programs and apps for electronic devices, cognitive designers using psychotechnologies (ways of producing mindbody states) can compose a large number of programs for our minds. These programs and their applications are not limited to states we now know of; it may be possible for future cognitive scientists to invent new, hitherto unknown, synthetic mindbody states containing new cognitive processes, possibly with their respective applications for human needs. This might be done by inventing new psychotechnologies, by sequencing current or new psychotechnologies in innovative series, or by combining them into new recipes. The singlestate fallacy frowns on this possibility: multistate theory sees designing and creating new cognitive processes as inventing the future of the human mind.

Without our recognizing it, the Neurosingularity Project (the application of the neurosciences to building bigger and better brains) has already started. Much of the information above marks milestones along this road. Current neuropsychology is (among other things) mapping the human mind and many of its complexities. There is still a long and exciting way to go. A full map must include all mindbody states and all their respective abilities and biological correlates.

The multistate section mentioned the possibility of combining existing mindbody psychotechnologies, both chemical and behavioral, to produce new mindbody states. There we considered only new mindbody states as they might affect our current brains, but biological sciences raise the possibility not only of enhancing our current brains' activities but also designing and growing advanced brains, even bigger heads for bigger brains.

Existing psychotechnologies provide enough leads to keep generations of psychologists, biologists, and their many friends and relations busy. And the scope of the Neurosingularity Project will grow even more as new psychotechnologies are invented and imported from other cultures: the number of mindbody combinations and sequences multiplies. When brain enhancement is added, the number of possible psychotechnology recipes and sequences multiplies again.

For future mindbody inventors—perhaps we should we call them *neuroarchitects, cerebralengineers, mindartists,* or *cognidesigners*—the possibilities of the Neurosingularity Project and the human future are endless.

A DOZEN MERELY BIG IDEAS

In this brief article, we have tasted three psychedelic ideas that enrich the humanities and liberal arts, and although we haven't mentioned how the arts have benefited from psychedelics, this is already widely recognized. Besides the Humongous Three—1) the transition to an era of experiential relation, 2) Multistate Theory, and 3) mind design—psychedelics offer an additional swarm of "merely big" ideas. Here are where you can find some of my favorites in *The Psychedelic Future of the Mind*:

- Experimental humanities and abstract concepts, pages 129, 138, 142
- Experimental religion, page 139 and on
- Mind explorer as hero, page 176
- Residence and Central Multistate Question, pages 127–29
- Values developed from mystical experiences, chapter 3, especially altruism, page 48, and open-mindedness, page 51
- Transcendence as peak of Maslow's needs hierarchy, pages 33–36
- A company to offer psychedelic sessions, chapter 13
- Teaching psychedelic courses and units in higher education, chapter 15
- Another path to moral development, page 38
- Changing what well-educated means, chapter 14
- Singlestate Fallacy, page 123
- A method to discover rare and unusual abilities, page 128

Chapter and page numbers refer to *The Psychedelic Future of the Mind*. Book reviews and elaborations on these ideas reside at: niu.academia.edu/ThomasRoberts

SERIOUS RESEARCH

TRANSCENDING THE MEDICAL FRONTIERS: EXPLORING THE FUTURE OF PSYCHEDELIC DRUG RESEARCH[1]

BY DAVID JAY BROWN

When I was in graduate school studying behavioral neuroscience, I wanted nothing more than to be able to conduct psychedelic drug research. However, in the mid-1980s, this was impossible to do at any academic institution on earth.

There wasn't a single government on the entire planet that legally allowed clinical research with psychedelic drugs. However, this worldwide research ban started to recede in the early 1990s, and we're currently witnessing a renaissance of medical research into psychedelic drugs.

Working with the Multidisciplinary Association for Psychedelic Studies (MAPS) for the past four years as their guest editor has been an extremely exciting and tremendously fruitful endeavor for me.

It's a great joy to see how MDMA can help people suffering from post-traumatic stress disorder (PTSD), how LSD can help advanced-stage cancer patients come to peace with the dying process, and how ibogaine can help opiate addicts overcome their addiction.

There appears to be enormous potential for the development of psychedelic drugs into effective treatments for a whole range of difficult-to-treat psychiatric disorders.

However, as thrilled as I am by all the new clinical studies exploring the medical potential of psychedelic drugs, I still long for the day when our best minds and resources can be applied to the study of these extraordinary substances with an eye that looks beyond their medical applications, toward their ability to enhance human potential and explore new realities.

This appendix explores these possibilities. But first, let's take a look at how we got to be where we are.

A BRIEF HISTORY OF TIME-DILATION STUDIES

Psychedelic drug research began in 1897, when the German chemist Arthur Heffter first isolated mescaline, the primary psychoactive compound in the peyote cactus.

In 1943 Swiss chemist Albert Hofmann discovered the hallucinogenic effects of LSD (lysergic acid diethylamide) at Sandoz Pharmaceuticals in Basel while studying ergot, a fungus that grows on rye. Then, fifteen years later, in 1958, he was the first to isolate psilocybin and psilocin—the psychoactive components of the Mexican "magic mushroom," *Psilocybe mexicana.*

Before 1972, nearly seven hundred studies with LSD and other psychedelic drugs were conducted. This research suggested that LSD has remarkable medical potential. LSD-assisted psychotherapy was shown to safely reduce the anxiety of terminal cancer patients, the drinking of alcoholics, and the symptoms of many difficult-to-treat psychiatric illnesses.

Between 1972 and 1990, there were no human studies with psychedelic drugs. Their disappearance was the result of a political backlash that followed the promotion of these drugs by the 1960s counterculture. This reaction not only made these substances illegal for personal use but also made it extremely difficult for researchers to get government approval to study them.

THE NEW WAVE OF PSYCHEDELIC DRUG RESEARCH

The political climate began to change in 1990, with the approval of Rick Strassman's DMT study at the University of New Mexico.

According to public policy expert and MAPS President Rick Doblin, this change occurred because "open-minded regulators at the FDA decided to put science before politics when it came to psychedelic and medical marijuana research. FDA openness to research is really the key factor. Also, senior researchers who were influenced by psychedelics in the Sixties now are speaking up before they retire and have earned credibility."

The past eighteen years have seen a bold resurgence of psychedelic drug research, as scientists all over the world have come to recognize the long-underappreciated potential of these drugs. In the past few years, a growing number of studies using human volunteers have begun to explore the possible therapeutic benefits of drugs such as LSD, psilocybin, DMT, MDMA, ibogaine, and ketamine.

Current studies are focusing on psychedelic treatments for cluster headaches, PTSD, depression, obsessive-compulsive disorder (OCD), severe anxiety in terminal cancer patients, alcoholism, and opiate addiction.

The results so far look quite promising, and more studies are being planned by MAPS and other private psychedelic research organizations, with the eventual goal of turning MDMA, LSD, psilocybin, and other psychedelics into legally available prescription drugs.

As excited as I am that psychedelic drugs are finally being studied for their medical and healing potential, I'm eagerly anticipating the day when psychedelic drug research can really take off and move beyond its therapeutic applications in medicine.

I look forward to the day when researchers can explore the potential of psychedelics as advanced learning tools, relationship builders, creativity enhancers, pleasure magnifiers, vehicles for self-improvement, reliable catalysts for spiritual or mystical experiences, a stimulus for telepathy and other psychic abilities, windows into other dimensions, and for their ability to possibly shed light on the reality of parallel universes and nonhuman entity contact.

Let's take a look at some of these exciting possibilities.

THE SCIENCE OF PLEASURE

Almost all medical research to date has been focused on curing diseases and treating illnesses, while little attention has been paid to increasing human potential, let alone to the enhancement of pleasure.

However, one can envision a time in the not-too-distant future when we will have cured all of our most challenging physical ailments and have more time and resources on our hands to explore post-survival activities. It's likely that we'll then focus our research efforts on discovering new ways to improve our physical and mental performance.

A science devoted purely to enhancing pleasure might come next, and psychedelics could play a major role in this new field. Maverick physicist Nick Herbert's "Pleasure Dome" project seeks to explore this possibility, and although this is little more than an idea at this point, it may be the first step toward turning the enhancement of pleasure into a true science.

According to surveys done by the US National Institute of Drug Abuse, the number-one reason why people do LSD is because "it's fun." Tim Leary helped to popularize the use of LSD with the help of the word *ecstasy,* and sex expert Annie Sprinkle has been outspoken about the ecstatic possibilities available from combining sex and psychedelics.

Countless psychedelic trip reports have described long periods of appreciating extraordinary beauty and savoring ecstatic bliss, experiences that were many orders of magnitude more intense than the subjects previously thought possible.

With all the current research emphasis on the medical applications and therapeutic potential of psychedelics, the unspoken and obvious truth about these extraordinary substances is that, when done properly, they're generally safe and healthy ways to have an enormous amount of fun. There's good reason why they're so popular recreationally, despite being illegal.

When psychedelic research begins to integrate with applied neuroscience and advanced nanotechnology in the future, we can begin to establish a serious science of pleasure and fun. Most likely this would begin with a study of sensory enhancement and time dilation, which are two of the primary effects that psychedelics reliably produce.

Perhaps one day our brightest researchers and best resources will be devoted to finding new ways to enhance sexual, auditory, visual, olfactory, gustatory, and tactile sensations, and create undreamed-of new pleasures and truly unearthly delights.

Scientific studies could explore ways to improve sexual performance and enhance sensory sensitivity, elongate and intensify our orgasms, enlarge the spectrum of our perceptions, and deepen every dimension of our experience.

Massage therapy, Tantra, music, culinary crafting, and other pleasure-producing techniques could be systematically explored with psychedelics, and universities could have applied research centers devoted to the study of ecstasy, tickling, and laughter.

The neurochemistry of aesthetic appreciation, happiness, humor, euphoria, and bliss could be carefully explored with an eye toward improvement. Serious research and development could be used to create new drugs and integrate neurochemically heightened states with enhanced environments, such as technologically advanced amusement parks and extraordinary virtual realities. In this area of research, it seems that psychedelics may prove to be extremely useful, and countless new psychedelic drugs are just waiting to be discovered.

In addition to enhancing pleasure, psychedelics also stimulate the imagination in extraordinary ways.

CREATIVITY AND PROBLEM SOLVING

A number of early studies suggest that psychedelic drugs may stimulate creativity and improve problem-solving abilities. In 1955 Louis Berlin investigated the effects of mescaline and LSD on the painting abilities of four nationally recognized graphic artists.

Although the study showed that there was some impairment of technical ability among the artists, a panel of independent art critics judged the experimental paintings as having "greater aesthetic value" than the artists' usual work.

In 1959 Los Angeles psychiatrist Oscar Janiger asked sixty prominent artists to paint a Native American doll before taking LSD and then again while under its influence. These 120 paintings were then evaluated by a panel of independent art critics and historians.

As with Berlin's study, there was a general agreement by the judges that the craftsmanship of the LSD paintings suffered; however many received higher marks for imagination than the pre-LSD paintings.

In 1965 James Fadiman and Willis Harman at San Francisco State College administered mescaline to professional workers in various fields to explore its creative problem-solving abilities. The subjects were instructed to bring a professional problem requiring a creative solution to their sessions.

After some psychological preparation, subjects worked individually on their problem throughout their mescaline session. The creative output of each subject was evaluated by psychological tests, subjective reports, and the eventual industrial or commercial validation and acceptance of the finished product or final solution. Virtually all subjects produced solutions judged highly creative and satisfactory by these standards.

In addition to the scientific studies that have been conducted, there are also a number of compelling anecdotal examples that suggest a link between creativity and psychedelic drugs.

For example, architect Kyosho Izumi's LSD-inspired design of the ideal psychiatric hospital won him a commendation for outstanding achievement from the American Psychiatric Association, and Apple cofounder Steve Jobs attributed some of the insights which led to the development of the personal computer to his use of LSD.

Additionally, a number of renowned scientists have personally attributed their breakthrough scientific insights to their use of psychedelic drugs—including Nobel Prize winners Francis Crick and Kary Mullis.

There hasn't been a formal creativity study with psychedelics since 1965, although there are countless anecdotal reports of artists, writers, musicians, filmmakers, and other people who attribute a portion of their creativity and inspiration to their use of psychedelics. This is an area that is more than ripe for study.

Anecdotal reports suggest that very low doses of LSD—threshold level doses, around 20 micrograms—are especially effective as creativity enhancers.

For example, Francis Crick was reported to be using low doses of LSD when he discovered the double-helix structure of the DNA molecule.

I'd love to see a whole series of new studies exploring how cannabis, LSD, psilocybin, and mescaline can enhance the imagination, improve problem-solving abilities, and stimulate creativity. At the time of this writing, the Beckley Foundation in England is supporting a study into the effects of cannabis on creativity, which is getting positive results.

As more and more of our world becomes automated with advanced robotics, I suspect that creativity will eventually become the most valuable commodity of all. Much of the creativity in Hollywood and Silicon Valley is already fueled by psychedelics, and research into how these extraordinary tools could enhance creativity even more effectively may become a booming enterprise in the not-too-distant future.

However, creativity isn't the only valuable psychological ability that psychedelics appear to enhance.

ESP AND PSYCHIC PHENOMENA

Few people are aware that there have been numerous carefully controlled scientific experiments with telepathy, psychokinesis, remote viewing, and other types of psychic phenomena, which have consistently produced compelling, statistically significant results that conventional science is at a loss to explain. Even most scientists are currently unaware of the vast abundance of compelling scientific evidence for psychic phenomena, which has resulted from over a century of parapsychological research.

Hundreds of carefully controlled studies—in which psi researchers continuously redesigned experiments to address the comments from their critics—have produced results that demonstrate small but statistically significant effects for psi phenomena such as telepathy, precognition, and psychokinesis.

According to Dean Radin, a meta-analysis of this research demonstrates that the positive results from these studies are significant with odds in the order of many billions to one.

Princeton University, the Stanford Research Institute, Duke University, the Institute of Noetic Science, the US and Russian governments, and many other respectable institutions have spent years researching these mysterious phenomena, and conventional science is at a loss to explain the results. This research is summarized in Radin's remarkable book *The Conscious Universe*.

Just as fascinating as the research into psychic phenomena is the controversy that surrounds it. In my own experience researching the possibility of telepathy in animals and other unexplained phenomena with British biologist Rupert Sheldrake, I discovered that many people are eager to share personal anecdotes about psychic events in their lives—such as remarkable coincidences, uncanny premonitions, precognitive dreams, and seemingly telepathic communications.

In these cases, the scientific studies simply confirm life experiences. Yet many scientists that I've spoken with haven't reviewed the evidence and remain doubtful that there is any reality to psychic phenomena. However, surveys conducted by Sheldrake and me reveal that around 78 percent of the population has had unexplainable "psychic" experiences, and the scientific evidence supports the validity of these experiences.

It's also interesting to note that many people have reported experiencing meaningful psychic experiences with psychedelics—not to mention a wide range of paranormal events and synchronicities, which seem extremely difficult to explain by means of conventional reasoning.

Psychologist Charles Tart, PhD, conducted a questionnaire study of 150 experienced marijuana users and found that 76 percent believed in extrasensory perception (ESP)—with frequent reports of experiences while they were high, which were interpreted as psychic.

Psychiatrist Stanislav Grof, MD, and psychologist Stanley Krippner, PhD, have collected numerous anecdotes about psychic phenomena that were reported by people under the influence of psychedelics, and several small scientific studies have looked at how LSD, psilocybin, and mescaline might affect telepathy and remote viewing.

For example, according to psychologist Jean Millay, PhD, in 1997, students at the University of Amsterdam in the Netherlands did research to establish whether or not the use of psilocybin could influence remote viewing. This was a small experiment, with only twelve test subjects, but the results of the study indicated that those subjects who were under the influence of psilocybin achieved a success rate of 58.3 percent, which was statistically significant.

A great review article by Krippner and psychologist David Luke, PhD, that summarizes all of the psychedelic research into psychic phenomena can be found in the spring 2011 *MAPS Bulletin* that I edited about psychedelics and the mind/body connection. This article can be found here: *www.maps. org/news–letters/v21n1/v21n1-59to60.pdf.*

When I conducted the California-based research for two of Sheldrake's books about unexplained phenomena in science, *Dogs That Know When Their Owners Are Coming Home* and *The Sense of Being Stared At*, one of the experiments that I ran involved testing blindfolded subjects to see if they could sense being stared at from behind. One of the subjects that I worked with reported an unusually high number of correct trials while under the influence of MDMA. I'd love to run a whole study to see if MDMA-sensitized subjects are more aware of when they're being stared at.

It is especially common for people to report experiences with telepathy, clairvoyance, precognition, remote viewing, and psychokinesis while using Ayahuasca, the potent hallucinogenic jungle juice from the Amazon. There have only been several studies with Ayahuasca that demonstrate health benefits, but this is an area that is just crying out to be explored carefully and in depth.

Future studies could examine Ayahuasca's potential and accuracy as a catalyst for psychic phenomena, and all of the traditional studies that have been done with psychic phenomena, which generated positive results, could be redone with subjects dosed with different psychedelics to see if test scores can be improved.

Increasing our psychic abilities may open up the human mind to new, unimagined possibilities—and if you think that harnessing telepathic and clairvoyant abilities is pretty wild, then hold on to your hats for what's likely to come next.

HIGHER DIMENSIONS AND NONHUMAN ENTITY CONTACT

A primary ingredient in Ayahuasca is DMT, and it appears that this remarkable substance has the extraordinary power to open up an interdimensional portal into another universe. Some of the most fascinating psychedelic research has been done with this incredible compound.

DMT is a mystery. One of the strangest puzzles in all of nature—in the same league as questions like, what existed before the Big Bang? And, how did life begin?—revolves around the fact that the unusually powerful psychedelic DMT is naturally found in the human body as well as in many species of animals and plants, and nobody knows what it does, or what function it might serve, in any of these places.

Because natural DMT levels tend to rise while we're asleep at night, a role in dreaming has been suggested. But this is pure speculation, and even if true, it may do much more. Because of its endogenous status and unusually potent effects, many people have considered DMT to be the quintessential psychedelic.

DMT has effects of such strength and magnitude that it easily dwarfs the titanic quality of even the most powerful LSD trips, and it appears to transport one into an entirely new world—a world that seems more bizarre than our wildest imaginings, yet somehow, is also strangely familiar.

Psychiatric researcher Rick Strassman, PhD, who conducted a five-year study with DMT at the University of New Mexico, has suggested that naturally elevated DMT levels in the brain may be responsible for such unexplained mental phenomena as spontaneous mystical experiences, near-death experiences, nonhuman entity contact, and schizophrenia.

Strassman and others have even gone so far as to speculate about the possibility that elevated DMT levels in the brain might be responsible for ushering the soul into the body before birth and out of the body after death.

But perhaps what's most interesting about DMT is that, with great consistency, it appears to allow human beings to communicate with other intelligent life forms.

When I interviewed Strassman, I asked him if he thought that there was an objective reality to the worlds visited by people when they're under the influence of DMT and if he thought that the entities that so many people have encountered on DMT actually have an independent existence or not. Rick replied, "I myself think so. My colleagues think I've gone woolly-brained over this, but I think it's as good a working hypothesis as any other."

A 2006 scientific paper by computer scientist Marko A. Rodriguez called "A Methodology for Studying Various Interpretations of the N,N-dimethyltryptamine-Induced Alternate Reality" explores how to possibly determine if the entities experienced by people on DMT are indeed independently existing, intelligent beings or just projections of our hallucinating brains.

Rodriguez suggests a test that involves asking the entities to perform a complex mathematical task involving prime numbers to verify their independent existence. While it seems like a long shot that this method could lead to fruitful results, I think that any serious speculation about establishing communication channels with these mysterious beings is constructive.

Strassman's work could represent the very beginning of a scientific field that systematically explores the possibility of communicating with higher-dimensional entities, and this might prove to be a more fruitful endeavor for establishing extraterrestrial contact than the SETI project. What they can teach us, we can only imagine.

My own experiences with DMT lead me to suspect that Strassman's studies would have yielded far more fruitful results had the subjects been dosed with harmaline prior to receiving their DMT injections. Harmaline is an MAO-inhibiting enzyme that is found in a number of plants. It's found in the famous South American vine known as *Banisteriopsis caapi*, which composes half of the mixture in the sacred hallucinogenic jungle juice Ayahuasca, which has been used for healing purposes by indigenous peoples in the Amazon basin for thousands of years.

Harmaline is widely known as the chemical that allows the DMT in other plants, like *Psychotria viridis*, to become orally active. Orally consumed DMT is destroyed in the stomach by an enzyme called monoamine oxidase (MAO), which harmaline inhibits. However, it does much more than just make the DMT orally active. I've discovered that drinking a tea made from Syrian rue seeds—which also contain harmaline—two hours prior to smoking DMT dramatically alters the experience. Harmaline has interesting psychoactive properties of its own that are somewhat psychedelic, and it slows down the speed of the DMT experience considerably, rendering it more comprehensible, less frightening, and easier to understand. For thousands of years, indigenous peoples in the Amazon jungles combined harmaline and DMT, and this long history has cultivated a powerful synergism between how the two molecules react in our bodies.

In future studies, harmaline could be used in conjunction with DMT to more accurately simulate the Ayahuasca experience that strikes such a powerful primordial cord in our species. This would allow for the experience to become much more comprehensible and to last for a greater duration of time, which would allow for more ability to examine the phenomenon of nonhuman-entity communication.

Some readers may have noticed that this article has loosely followed a Christian theological progression, from the ego death and bodily resurrection of the medical studies with psychedelics, to the paradisical pleasures of heaven, where we discovered our godlike powers and met with the angels. Ultimately, it appears, this research will lead us to the source of divinity itself.

THE STUDY OF DIVINE INTELLIGENCE

Perhaps the most vital function of psychedelics is their ability to reliably produce spiritual or mystical experiences. These transpersonal experiences of inseparability often result in an increased sense of ecological awareness, a greater sense of interconnection, a transcendence of the fear of death, a sense of the sacred or divine, and an identification with something much larger than one's body or personal life.

Many people suspect that this experience lies at the heart of the healing potential of psychedelics—and that making this experience available to people is essential for the survival of our species. I agree that we need a compassionate vision of our interconnection with the biosphere to guide our technological evolution, or we appear doomed to destroy ourselves.

In his book *The Physics of Immortality*, physicist Frank Tipler introduces the idea that if a conscious designing intelligence is genuinely a part of this universe, then ultimately religion—or the study of this designer intelligence—will become a branch of physics. Psychedelic drug research may offer one pathway toward establishing this science of the future.

Recent studies by Roland Griffiths and colleagues at Johns Hopkins have confirmed that psilocybin can indeed cause religious experiences—which are indistinguishable from religious experiences reported by mystics throughout the ages—and that substantial health benefits can result from these experiences.

These new studies echo the findings of an earlier study done in 1962 by Walter Pahnke of the Harvard Divinity School, and it's certainly not news to anyone who has had a full-blown psychedelic experience. An online commenter by the username R.U. Sirius responded to this seemingly redundant research by saying "Wow! Scientists Discover Ass Not Elbow!" Nonetheless, this may represent the beginning of a whole new field of academic inquiry that explores those realms that have been previously declared off limits to science.

It appears that the integration of science and spirituality lies on the horizon of our adventure as a species, and that our future evolution depends on this. Without a transpersonal perspective of interconnection to guide our evolutionary direction, we seem to be firmly set on a path toward inevitable self-destruction. I think that psychedelics can help us get back on track and help us heal the damage that we've done to ourselves and to the earth. This is why I believe so strongly in psychedelic drug research.

There isn't much time left before our biosphere starts to unravel, and we may only have a small window of opportunity to save our fragile world.

I think that MAPS—and sister organizations like the Beckley Foundation and the Heffter Research Institute—are industrialized society's best hope for transforming the planet's ancient shamanic plants into the respectable scientific medicines of tomorrow and, in so doing, for bringing psychedelic therapy to all who need it.

This may not only help to heal a number of difficult-to-treat medical disorders and increase ecological harmony on the planet, but it may also open up a doorway to untold and unimagined new worlds of possibility.

NOTE

1. This essay also appears on the Acceler8or.com website (http://www.acceler8or. com/2011/07/transcending-the-medical-frontiers-exploring-the-future-of-psychedelic-drug-research/), and in the book *The New Science of Psychedelics*, by David Jay Brown, Inner Traditions, 2013.

PAHNKE'S "GOOD FRIDAY EXPERIMENT": A LONG-TERM FOLLOW-UP AND METHODOLOGICAL CRITIQUE

BY RICK DOBLIN

On Good Friday, 1962, before services commenced in Boston University's Marsh Chapel, Walter Pahnke administered small capsules to twenty Protestant divinity students. Thus began the most scientific experience in the literature designed to investigate the potential of psychedelic drugs to facilitate mystical experience (Pahnke, 1963, 1966, 1967, 1970; Pahnke & Richards, 1969a, 1969b, 1969c). Half the capsules contained psilocybin (30 mg), an extract of psychoactive mushrooms, and the other half contained a placebo. According to Pahnke, the experiment determined that "the persons who received psilocybin experienced to a greater extent than did the controls the phenomena described by our typology of mysticism" (Pahnke, 1963, p. 220).

This paper is a brief methodological critique and long-term follow-up study to the "Good Friday Experiment." Pahnke, who was both a physician and a minister, conducted the experiment in 1962 for his PhD in Religion and Society at Harvard University, with Timothy Leary as his principal academic advisor (Leary, 1962, 1967, 1968). Describing the experiment, Walter Houston Clark, 1961 recipient of the American Psychological Association's William James Memorial Award for contributions to the psychology of religion, writes, "There are no experiments known to me in the history of the scientific study of religion better designed or clearer in their conclusions than this one" (Clark, 1969, p. 77)

Since a classic means of evaluating mystical experiences is by their fruits, follow-up data is a fundamental importance in evaluating the original experiment. A six-month follow-up was part of the original experiment, and a longer-term follow-up would probably have been conducted by Pahnke himself had it not been for his death in 1971. For over twenty-five years, it has not been legally possible to replicate or revise this experiment. Hence, this long-term follow-up study, conducted by the author, is offered as a way to advance scientific knowledge in the area of psychedelics and experimental mysticism.

Lukoff, Zanger, and Lu's review (1990) of psychoactive substances and transpersonal states offers a recent overview of this topic.

Though all raw data from the original experiment is lost, including the uncoded list of participants, extensive research over a period of four years and enthusiastic cooperation of most of the original subjects have resulted in the identification and location of nineteen out of the original twenty subjects. From November 1986 to October 1989, this author tape recorded personal interviews with sixteen of the original subjects, meeting fifteen in their home cities throughout the United States and interviewing one subject (from the control group) over the telephone. In addition to the interviews, all sixteen subjects participating in the long-term follow-up, nine from the control and seven from the experimental group, were re-administered the six-month one-hundred-item follow-up questionnaire used in the original experiment.

Of the remaining three subjects from the experimental group, one is deceased. The identity of another is unknown. One declined to participate citing concerns about privacy. One subject, from the control group, declined to be interviewed or to fill out the questionnaire because he interpreted Pahnke's pledge of confidentiality to mean that the subjects should not talk about the experiment to anyone. This author's discussion of the meaning of confidentiality and mention of the explicit support for the long-term follow-up by Pahnke's wife failed to enlist his participation.

Informal discussions were also conducted with seven out of the ten of Pahnke's original research assistants for purposes of gathering background information about the experiment. At the time of the experiment, these people were professors or students of religion, psychology and philosophy at universities, colleges, and seminaries in the Boston area.

METHODOLOGY OF THE ORIGINAL EXPERIMENT

Pahnke hypothesized that psychedelic drugs, in this case psilocybin, could facilitate a "mystical" experience in religiously inclined volunteers who took the drug in a religious setting. He further hypothesized that such experiences would result in persisting positive changes in attitudes and behavior.

Pahnke believed the most conducive environment for his experiment would be a community of believers participating in a familiar religious ceremony designed to elicit religious feelings, in effect creating an atmosphere similar to that of the tribes which used psilocybin-containing mushrooms for religious purposes (Harner, 1973; Hofmann, Ruck & Wasson, 1978; Hofmann & Schultes, 1979; Wasson 1968). Accordingly, the experiment was designed to administer psilocybin to a previously acquainted group of Christian divinity students in church during a Good Friday service.

Methodologically, the study was designed as a randomized controlled, matched group, double-blind experiment using an active placebo. Prior to Good Friday, twenty white male Protestant volunteers, all of whom were students at the same theological school in the Boston area, were given a series of psychological and physical tests. Ten sets of closely matched pairs were created using variables such as past religious experience, religious background and training, and general psychological makeup. On the morning of the experiment, a helper who did not participate further in the experiment, and who did not know any of the subjects, flipped a coin to determine to which group, psilocybin or placebo, each member of the pair would be assigned.

Three different methods were used to create numerical scales quantifying the experiences of the subjects in terms of an eight-category typology of mystical experiences designed by Pahnke especially for the experiment. Blind independent raters trained in content-analysis procedures scored descriptions of the experiences written by the subjects shortly after Good Friday as well as transcripts of three separate tape-recorded interviews conducted immediately, several days, and six months after the experiment. A 147-item questionnaire was administered to the subjects one or two days after Good Friday, and a one-hundred-item questionnaire was administered six months after the experiment. The subjects' responses to the interview and the two questionnaires were transformed into three distinct scores averaging the percentage of the maximum possible score in each category. Each of the three complementary scores was then compared to each other.

Pahnke secured support and permission to use Marsh Chapel from Rev. Howard Thurman, Boston University's dynamic black chaplain. Several small meeting rooms and a self-contained basement chapel were set aside on Good Friday for the participants in the experiment while the main service led by Rev. Thurman was taking place upstairs in the larger chapel. The two-and-a-half hour service was broadcast into the basement chapel, where altar, pews, stained glass windows, and various religious symbols were permanently located.

Pahnke gave an active placebo of nicotinic acid to the controls who were expecting to receive either the psilocybin or an inactive placebo. This was done in order to "potentiate suggestion in the control subjects, all of whom knew that psilocybin produced various somatic effects, but none of whom had ever had psilocybin or any related substance before the experiment" (Pahnke, 1963, p. 89).

The ten research assistants worked as part of the experimental team in order to provide emotional support to the subjects prior to and during the service. Subjects were divided into five groups of four with two research assistants, known as group leaders, assigned to each group. These small groups met for two hours prior to the service to build trust and facilitate group support. Subjects were encouraged to "go into the unexplored realms of experience during the actual experiment and not try to fight the effects of the drug even if the experience became very unusual or frightening" (Pahnke, 1963, p. 96).

As a precaution against biasing the subjects toward the typology of mystical experience, leaders were told not to discuss specific aspects of the psychedelic or mystical experience. The lack of overt bias was confirmed by all of the subjects in their long-term follow-up interviews. In a typical long-term follow-up report, psilocybin subject S.J. (all initials used to identify subjects are coded to preserve anonymity) made the following remarks both about the preparation phase of the experiment and the conduct of the group leaders:

> None of the fine points of the mystical experience were given to us. We were not told to read any books such as Stace's book on mysticism or Jacob Boheme's books, nothing like that. They did not bias us in any way towards that, not at all.

At the insistence of one of the group leaders as well as Pahnke's faculty sponsor, Timothy Leary, but over the objections of Pahnke, all of the group leaders were also given a pill prior to the service (Leary, 1984, p. 107). This was done in a double-blind manner with one of each group's leaders receiving a half dose of psilocybin (15 mg) and the other the placebo. Pahnke was concerned this would lead to charges of experimenter bias being leveled against the study, but Leary and the group leader felt that the full involvement of the group leaders would create more of a community feeling and lend necessary confidence to the subjects. Though administered a capsule at the Good Friday service, the group leaders' reactions were not tape recorded, nor did they fill out questionnaires. Pahnke himself refrained from having any personal experiences with any psychedelic drug until after the experiment and follow-up had been completed.

DIFFICULTIES WITH THE DOUBLE-BLIND

The double-blind was successfully sustained through all of the preparation phases of the experiment up to and including ingestion of the capsule. The double-blind was even sustained for a portion of the Good Friday service itself because of the use of nicotinic acid as an active placebo. Nicotinic acid acts more quickly than does psilocybin and produces a warm flush through vasodilation of blood vessels in the skin and general relaxation. Subjects in the placebo group mistakenly concluded, in the early stages of the experiment, that they were the ones who had received the psilocybin (Pahnke, 1963, p. 212). The group leaders, unaware that an active placebo was going to be used, were also initially unable to distinguish whether subjects had received the psilocybin or the placebo.

Psilocybin's powerful subjective effects were eventually obvious to all subjects who received it, even though they had not previously ingested the drug or anything similar to it (Pahnke, 1963, p. 212). Inevitably, the double-blind was broken during the service as the psychoactive effects of the psilocybin deepened and the physiological effects of the nicotinic acid faded. At the end of the day of the experiment, all subjects correctly determined whether they had received the psilocybin or the placebo even though they were never told which group they were in (Pahnke, 1963, p. 210). Pahnke himself remained technically blind until after the six-month follow-up. The comments of subject O.W., gathered in the course of the author's long-term follow-up, are typical of members of the control group:

> After about a half hour I got this burning sensation. It was more like indigestion than a burning sensation. And I said to T.B., "Do you feel anything?" And he said, "No, not yet." We kept asking, "Do you feel anything?" I said, "You know, I've got this burning sensation, and it's kind of uncomfortable." And T.B. said, "My God, I don't have it, you got the psilocybin, I don't have it." I thought, "Jeez, at least I was lucky in this trial. I'm sorry T.B. didn't get it, but I'm gonna find out." I figured, with my luck, I'd probably get the sugar pill, or whatever it is. And I said to Y.M., "Do you feel anything?" No, he didn't feel anything. So I sat there, and I remember sitting there, and I thought, "Well, Leary told me to chart my course so I'm gonna concentrate on that." And I kept concentrating and sitting there and all I did was get more indigestion and uncomfortable.
>
> Nothing much more happened and within another 40 minutes, 45 minutes, everybody was really quiet and sitting there. Y.M. was sitting there and looking ahead, and all of the sudden T.B. says to me, "Those lights are unbelievable." And I said, "What lights?" He says, "Look at the candles." He says, "Can you believe that?" And I looked at the candles, and I thought, "They look like candles." He says, "Can't you see something strange about them?" So I remember squinting and looking.

I couldn't see anything strange. And he says, "You know it's just spectacular." And I looked at Y.M. and he was sitting there saying, "Yeah." And I thought, "They got it, I didn't."

The follow-up interviews yielded no evidence that the experimental team consciously used their knowledge of which pill the subjects had received to bias the results. However, unconscious bias resulting in an "expectancy effect" cannot be ruled out (Barber, 1976). Still, valuable information can be generated without the successful use of the double-blind methodology. Louis Lasagna, director of the Center for the Study of Drug Development at Tufts University, writes:

> We have witnessed the ascendancy of the randomized, double-blind, controlled clinical trial (RCCT), to the point where many in positions of authority now believe that data obtained via this technique should constitute the only basis for registering a drug or indeed for coming to any conclusions about its efficacy at any time in the drug's career. My thesis is that this viewpoint is untenable, needlessly rigid, unrealistic, and at times unethical. . . . Modern trial techniques [were not] necessary to recognize the therapeutic potential of chloral hydrate, the barbiturates, ether, nitrous oxide, chloroform, curare, aspirin, quinine, insulin, thyroid, epinephrine, local anesthetics, belladonna, antacids, sulfonamides, and penicillin, to give a partial list . . . (Lasagna, 1985, p. 48).

Commenting about the attempt to remove the experimenter from the experiment completely, Tooley and Pratt remark:

> In certain participant-observer situations (e.g. psychotherapy, education, change induction, action research) the purpose might be to influence the system under investigation as much as possible, but still accounting for (though now exploiting) the variance within the system attributable to the several significant and relevant aspects of the investigator's participant observation. . . . From this perspective, the quixotic attempt to eliminate the effects of participant-observation in the name of a misplaced pseudo-objectivity is fruitless, not so much because it is impossible but because it is unproductive. . . . From our point of view . . . the question becomes not how to eliminate bias (unaccounted-for influence) of participant observation, but how optimally to account for and exploit the effects of the participant observation transaction in terms of the purposes of the research (Tooley & Pratt, 1964, pp. 254–56).

The loss of the double-blind makes it impossible to determine the relative contributions of psilocybin and suggestion in producing the subjects' reported experiences. If the experiment were designed specifically to measure the pure drug effects of psilocybin, the failure of the double-blind would be quite damaging. In this instance the loss of the double-blind is of lesser significance because the entire experiment was explicitly designed to maximize the combined effort of psilocybin and suggestion. The setting was religious, the participants were religiously inclined, and the mood was positive and expectant. Pahnke did not set out to investigate whether psilocybin was able to produce mystical experiences irrespective of preparation and context. He designed the experiment to determine whether volunteers who received psilocybin within a highly supportive, suggestive environment similar to that found in the ritual use of psychoactive substances by various native cultures would report more elements of a classical mystical experience (as defined by the questionnaires) than volunteers who did not receive psilocybin. The loss of the double-blind may have enhanced the power of suggestion to some extent and suggests that restraint should be used in attributing the experiences of the experimental group exclusively to the psilocybin (Zinberg, 1984).

CRITIQUE OF THE QUESTIONNAIRE

Pahnke designed the questionnaire he used to measure the occurrence of a mystical experience specifically for the experiment. No similar questionnaires existed at the time (Larson, 1986; Rue, 1985; Silverman, 1983). Pahnke decided to measure the mystical experience in reference to eight distinct experiential categories. The categories include 1) sense of unity, 2) transcendence of time and space, 3) sense of sacredness, 4) sense of objective reality, 5) deeply felt positive mood, 6) ineffability, 7) paradoxicality, and 8) transiency. These categories are very similar to those elaborated by such well-respected scholars of mystical experience as William James (1902), Evelyn Underhill (1910), and W. T. Stace (1960) and are accepted as valid even by academic critics of the Good Friday experiment such as R. C. Zaehner (1972). At present, the scientific questionnaire most widely used by researchers to assess mystical experiences is a thirty-two-item questionnaire created by Ralph Hood, also based on categories developed by W. T. Stace (Spilka, Hood & Gorsuch, 1985).

Zaehner's critique of Pahnke's questionnaire is that it does not contain a category for experiences which are specifically Christian, such as identification with the death and rebirth of Jesus Christ. From Zaehner's perspective, this omission made it impossible to determine if the experiences were religious, since he thought a religious experience for Christians necessarily involves a theistic encounter with Christ. Zaehner objected to the claim that an experience of a generalized, nonspecific, apprehension of a transcendent reality beyond any specific cultural forms and figures could properly be called religious. Anticipating this critique, Pahnke asserted in the thesis that he was not attempting to resolve the question of what can properly be called religious but was simply investigating mystical experiences, regardless of whether or not they were considered religious. This author will also leave this delicate discussion to others.

The questionnaire used in the Good Friday experiment has been modified and expanded over the years by Pahnke, William Richards, Stanislav Grof, Franco Di Leo, and Richard Yensen for use in subsequent psychedelic research (Richards, 1975, 1978). From the initial creation of the questionnaire by Pahnke in 1962 to Di Leo and Yensen's computerized version, called the Peak Experience Profile, the basic items relating to the mystical experience have remained essentially unchanged (Di Leo, 1982). While the original follow-up questionnaire was composed of eight different categories, the Peak Experience Profile uses only six. The category of transiency was eliminated since it measures any altered state of consciousness whether mystical or not. The paradoxicality and alleged ineffability categories were combined into the ineffability category. Over the years, new categories measuring transpersonal but not necessarily mystical experiences were added. For example, new questions relate to the re-experiencing of the stages of birth and the perinatal matrixes as defined by Grof (Grof, 1975, 1980) and also to past-life experiences (Ring, 1982, 1984, 1988). A series of questions relating to difficult and painful nadir experiences, in some sense the opposites of peak experiences, has also been added.

In Pahnke's original questionnaire and in the subsequent revisions, the completeness with which each subject experienced each category is measured through numerical responses to category-specific questions. Pahnke's subjects rated each question on the post-drug questionnaire from zero to four, with zero indicating that the item was not experienced at all and four indicating that it was experienced as strong or stronger than ever before. The six-month follow-up questionnaire used a zero-to-five scale, with four indicating that it was experienced as strong as before and five indicating that it was experienced stronger than ever before.

The questions themselves are of two types. The predominant type asks the subject about experiences of a new perspective. For example, some of the questions used to determine the sense of unity ask subjects to rate the degree to which they experienced a pure awareness beyond any empirical content, a fusion of the self into a larger undifferentiated whole, or a freedom from the limitations of the self in connection with a unity or bond with what was felt to be all-encompassing and greater-than-self. These types of questions are sufficiently detailed and specific to be an effective test for the specific category.

The second type of question, used much less frequently, asks about the loss of a normal state. For example, two questions used to determine the presence of a sense of unity simply required subjects to rate the degree to which they lost their sense of self or experienced a loss of their own identity. This type of question is a minor weak point of the questionnaire because it can be rated highly without having anything to do with mystical experiences. For example, one subject reported in the follow-up interview that under the influence of psilocybin, he temporarily had difficulty recalling his career choice, home, names of his wife and children, and even his own name. This experience of a powerful loss of the usual sense of self and identity would be highly correlated with mystical experience in the questionnaire but may not actually be related because it can occur for a variety of reasons. Though the questionnaire has relatively few of this type of question, some overestimation of the completeness of the mystical experience could have been introduced into the data as a result.

In addition to asking questions about the experience itself, the follow-up questionnaire also sought to assess the effects of that experience on the attitudes and behaviors of the subjects. For example, the subjects' attitude changes were assessed by asking them to use a zero-to-five scale to rate whether they had experienced an increase or a decrease in their feelings of happiness, joy, peace, reverence, creativity, vocational commitment, need for service, anxiety, and hatred. Changes in subjects' behavior were assessed by means of questions asking whether or not they experienced changes in their relationships with others, in time spent in quiet mediation or devotional life, or whether they thought their behavior had changed in positive or negative ways.

Pahnke's questionnaire gathered information only from the self-reports of the subjects, resulting in a general sense of the subjects' own assessment of the direction of the effects of their Good Friday experience. The data do not yield specific information about the internal psychodynamic mechanisms at work within each subject, nor do they include the views of significant others regarding the effects of the experiment on the subjects.

In contemporary psychotherapy research, more sophisticated methods than Pahnke's are used to assess personality change (Beutler & Crago, 1983).

Reports from significant others such as family members and close friends of the subject are almost always used to add an important "objective" element in assessing personality change. Data from the follow-up questionnaires, administered by Pahnke at six months and by the author after twenty-four to twenty-seven years, should be considered valuable as far as they go, but this is not very far. Since no detailed personality tests were given prior to the experiment, results of such tests at the time of the long-term follow-up would have been of little value and were not conducted. The long-term follow-up interviews, because of their open-ended format and extensive questioning, yielded more detailed information than the questionnaire about the content of the experiences and the persisting effects.

FINDINGS OF THE ORIGINAL STUDY AND LONG-TERM FOLLOW-UP

Pahnke arbitrarily determined that for a mystical experience to be considered complete for the purposes of the experiment, out of the maximum total possible score, "the total score and the score in each separate category must be at least 60 to 70 percent" (Pahnke, 1967, p. 66). According to this cut-off point, "Four of the ten psilocybin subjects reached the 60 to 70 percent level of completeness, whereas none of the controls did" (Pahnke, 1967, p. 64). Looked at by subjects and categories, Pahnke reported that "eight out of ten of the experimental subjects experienced at least seven out of the eight categories. None of the control group, when each individual was compared to his matched partner, had a score which was higher" (Pahnke, 1966, p. 647). In every general category and in every specific question, the average score of the experimental subjects exceeded that of the control subjects. The differences between the groups in the scores on the questionnaires were significant at p<.05 level for all categories.

When asked at a conference if any of the controls had a mystical experience, Pahnke replied:

> To take an individual case, there was one control subject who scored fairly high on sacredness and sense of peace and that he himself, in his written account, said, "It was a very meaningful experience, but in the past I've certainly had one that was much more so" (Pahnke, 1966, p. 648).

Pahnke's six-month follow-up data and the author's long-term follow-up questionnaire data, both of which used the same instrument, are displayed in Table 1. The six-month scores are listed first, and the long-term follow-up scores follow in parentheses. For each category, the percentages in the chart represent the total scores of the subjects divided by the highest possible scores that could have been reported. The numbers measure the completeness with which each category was experienced.

Comparisons can reliably be made between the control group's six-month and long-term scores because nine out of the original ten control group subjects participated in the long-term follow-up and the variance in scores between control subjects was small. The absence of completed long-term questionnaires from three of the ten original subjects from the psilocybin group makes comparing their six-month and long-term scores more difficult. The long-term follow-up interviews produced specific information suggesting that one of the three missing psilocybin subjects had scores sig-

Table 1: "Good Friday Experiment" Experimental and Control Groups
at Six-Month and Long-Term Follow-Up
Shown as Percentages of Maximum Possible Scores

Category	Experimentals		Controls	
Unity	Six-Month	Long-Term	Six-Month	Long-Term
A. Internal	60	(77)	5	(5)
B. External	39	(51)	1	(6)
Transcendence of Time and Space	78	(73)	7	(9)
Deeply Felt Positive Mood	54	(56)	23	(21)
Sacredness	58	(68)	25	(29)
Objectivity and Reality	71	(82)	18	(24)
Paradoxicality	34	(48)	3	(4)
Alleged Ineffability	77	(71)	15	(3)
Transiency	76	(75)	9	(9)
Average for the Categories	60.8	(66.8)	11.8	(12.2)
Persisting Positive Changes in Attitude and Behavior	48	(50)	15	(15)
Persisting Negative Changes in Attitude and Behavior	6	(6)	2	(4)

At Six-Month Follow-Up, Exper. N = 10, Control N = 10
Long-Term Follow-Up (In Parentheses) Exper. N = 7, Control N = 9
P<.05 for all category comparisons at both six-month and long-term follow-ups

nificantly lower than average. No information was generated suggesting that the other two missing subjects had scores significantly different than average. The average scores for the long-term follow-up may thus overstate somewhat the scores from the entire psilocybin group.

The average scores for the eight categories of the mystical experience and the scores for persisting positive and negative changes in attitude and behavior have changed remarkably little for either the controls or the experimentals despite the passage of between twenty-four and twenty-seven years between the two tests. The questionnaire seems to be reliable and indicates that time has not substantially altered the opinions of the subjects about their experiences. In the long-term follow-up even more than in the six-month follow-up, the experimental group has higher scores than the control group in every category. For the long-term follow-up, these differences are significant at p<.05 in every category.

For the experimental group, the average score for the mystical categories at the six-month follow-up was 60.8 percent. They scored 66.8 percent at the long-term follow-up. In the six-month follow-up, the experimental group scored about 34 percent in all categories while in the long-term follow-up, they scored above 48 percent in all categories. The experimental group scored the highest in those categories that typify a different state of consciousness such as transcendence of time and space, alleged ineffability and transiency.

For the control group, the average score for the eight categories of mystical experience at the six-month follow-up was 11.8 percent. They scored 12.2 percent at the long-term follow-up. The highest score of the control group at either time was 29 percent, in the sacredness category. The control group scored the highest in the categories of experience that religious services are most likely to induce, namely sense of sacredness, deeply felt positive mood, and sense of objectivity and reality.

For the psilocybin group, the long-term follow-up yielded moderately increased scores in the categories of internal and external unity, sacredness, objectivity and reality, and paradoxicality, while all other categories remained virtually the same as the six-month data. Several decades seem to have strengthened the experimental groups' characterization of their original Good Friday experience as having had genuinely mystical elements. For the controls, the only score that changed substantially was that of alleged ineffability, which decreased.

A relatively high degree of persisting positive changes were reported by the experimental group while virtually no persisting positive changes were reported by the control group. In the open-ended portion of the long-term follow-up questionnaire, experimental subjects wrote that the experience helped them to resolve career decisions, recognize the arbitrariness of ego boundaries, increase their depth of faith, increase their appreciation of eternal life, deepen their sense of the meaning of Christ, and heighten their sense of joy and beauty. No positive persisting changes were reported by the control group in the open-ended section of the follow-up questionnaire.

There was a very low incidence of persisting negative changes in attitudes or behavior in either group at either the six-month follow-up or the long-term follow-up. However, the one psilocybin subject reported to have had the most difficult time during the experiment was the one who declined this author's request to be interviewed in person or fill out a questionnaire, placing in question the generalization of this finding for the long term.

Both the six-month and long-term follow-up questionnaire results support Pahnke's hypothesis that psilocybin, when taken in a religious setting by people who are religiously inclined, can facilitate experiences of varying degrees of depth that either are identical with, or indistinguishable from, those reported in the cross-cultural mystical literature. In addition, both the six-month and the long-term follow-up questionnaire results support Pahnke's hypothesis that the subjects who received psilocybin, more so than the controls, experienced substantial positive persisting effects in attitude and behavior.

THE LONG-TERM FOLLOW-UP INTERVIEWS: GENERAL OVERVIEW

This long-term follow-up was conducted roughly a quarter century after the subjects participated in the original experiment. All subjects contacted live in the United States, with five out of the eight psilocybin subjects and five out of the ten placebo subjects currently working as ministers. Other professions represented are stockbroker, lawyer, community developer, social worker, administrative assistant, and educator. Except for one of the psilocybin subjects, all are currently married. All are working and self-supporting. All but two welcomed the opportunity to discuss their participation in the Good Friday experiment.

Each of the psilocybin subjects had vivid memories of portions of their Good Friday experience. For most, this was their life's only psychedelic experience, in part because there have been no legal opportunities for such experiences for the last twenty-five years in the United States (or in any of the roughly 90 countries who are party to the international drug control treaties coordinated by the United Nation's World Health Organization). The experimental subjects unanimously described their Good Friday psilocybin experience as having had elements of a genuinely mystical nature and characterized it as one of the high points of their spiritual life. Some subjects reported that the content of their experience was specifically involved with the life of Christ and related directly to the Christian message, while others had experiences of a more universal, nonspecific nature. Most of the control subjects could barely remember even a few details of the service.

Most of the psilocybin subjects had subsequent experiences of a mystical nature with which they were able to compare and contrast to their psilocybin experience. These subsequent experiences occurred either in dreams, in prayer life, in nature, or with other psychedelics and seemed to the psilocybin subjects to be of the same essential nature as their Good Friday experience. Significant differences between their nondrug and drug mystical experiences were noted, with the drug experiences reportedly both more intense and composed of a wider emotional range than the nondrug experiences. The nondrug experiences were composed primarily of peaceful, beautiful moments experienced with ease, while the drug experiences tended to include moments of great fear, agony, and self-doubt.

The discussion of Subject T.B. about the relationship between his psilocybin and his other mystical experiences illustrates how the subjects saw the validity of their psilocybin experiences:

> I can think of no experiences [like the Good Friday experience] quite of that magnitude. That was the last of the great four in my life. The dream state . . . I had no control over when it was coming. It was when I [was about nine and] had scarlet fever and rheumatic fever, apparently at either similar or at the same times. And they thought that I was going to die. And I saw a light coming out of the sky, this is the dream, and it came toward me and it was like the figure of Christ and I said, "No, let me live and I'll serve you." And I'm alive and I've served. The prayer state when I was in seventh grade was very similar in the way it happened to me. I intentionally went for an experience with God. In seventh grade. And I also went for an experience with God at the Good Friday experience. And those were similar. The West Point experience was different. In that yes, it was prayers, it was on my knees, it was there, but the face of Christ was . . . it happened more to me than me participating in it. It was more like a saving experience kind of thing. So I've had that and can talk about "a salvation experience," a born again experience, it was that kind of dedication.

Each of the psilocybin subjects felt that the experience had significantly affected his life in a positive way and expressed appreciation for having participated in the experiment. Most of the effects discussed in the long-term follow-up interviews centered around enhanced appreciation of life and of nature, deepened sense of joy, deepened commitment to the Christian ministry or to whatever other vocations the subjects chose, enhanced appreciation of unusual experiences and emotions, increased tolerance of other religious systems, deepened equanimity in the face of difficult life crises, and greater solidarity and identification with foreign peoples, minorities, women, and nature. Subject K.B.'s description of the long-term effects is representative. He remarks:

> It left me with a completely unquestioned certainty that there is an environment bigger than the one I'm conscious of. I have my own interpretation of what that is, but it went from a theoretical proposition to an experimental one. In one sense it didn't change anything. I didn't discover something I hadn't dreamed of, but what I had thought on the basis of reading and teaching was there. I knew it. Somehow it was much more real to me.... I expect things from meditation and prayer and so forth that I might have been a bit more skeptical about before. ... I have gotten help with problems, and at times I think direction and guidance in problem solving. Somehow my life has been different knowing that there is something out there.... What I saw wasn't anything entirely surprising and yet there was a powerful impact from having seen it.

In addition to self-reports, several subjects who had stayed in contact with each other over the years spoke about the effects they noticed in each other. In the instances where such information was obtained, the observations of fellow subjects were similar to the self-reports and confirmed claims of beneficial effects.

Several of the psilocybin subjects discussed their deepened involvement in the politics of the day as one result of their Good Friday experience. Feelings of unity led many of the subjects to identify with and feel compassion for minorities, women, and the environment. The feelings of timelessness and eternity reduced their fear of death and empowered the subjects to take more risks in their lives and to participate more fully in political struggles.

Subject T.B. discussed how his perception of death during the Good Friday experience affected his work in the political field. He remarked:

> When you get a clear vision of what [death] is and have sort of been there, and have left the self, left the body, you know, self leaving the body, or soul leaving the body, or whatever you want to call it, you would also know that marching in the Civil Rights Movement or

against the Vietnam War in Washington [is less fearful]. . . . In a sense [it takes away the fear of dying] . . . because you've already been there. You know what it's about. When people approaching death have an out-of-body experience . . . [you] say, "I know what you're talking about. I've been there. Been there and come back. And it's not terrifying, it doesn't hurt. . . ."

Subject S.J. found that his Good Friday experience of unity supported his efforts in the political field:

I got very involved with civil rights after that [his psychedelic experience] and spent some time in the South. I remember this unity business. I thought there was some link there. . . . There could have been. People certainly don't write about it. They write about it the opposite way, that drugs are an escape from social obligations. That is the popular view. . . .

Only one of the control subjects felt that his experience of the Good Friday service resulted in beneficial personal growth. That particular control subject thought he was probably the one in the original experiment reported to have had a partial mystical experience. Ironically, he felt that the most important benefit he received from the service was the decision to try psychedelics at the earliest opportunity. The Good Friday service had that same effect on one another placebo subject, who also had a subsequent psychedelic experience.

The actual experiences of the original psilocybin subjects are best communicated by quoting from the transcripts of the long-term follow-up interviews. Rev. S.J. had an experience almost uniformly positive. He described his experience as follows:

Something extraordinary had taken place which had never taken place before. All of the sudden I felt sort of drawn out into infinity, and all of the sudden I had lost touch with my mind. I felt that I was caught up in the vastness of Creation . . . huge, as the mystics say. . . . I did experience that kind of classic kind of blending. . . . Sometimes you would look up and see the light on the alter and it would just be a blinding sort of light and radiation. . . . The main thing about it was a sense of timelessness.

The meditation was going on all during this time, and he [Rev. Howard Thurman] would say things about Jesus and you would have this overwhelming feeling of Jesus. . . . It was like you totally penetrated what was being said and it penetrated you. . . . Death looked different. It became in focus. . . . I got the impression, the sensation . . . that what people are essentially in their essence that somehow they would continue to live. They may die in one sense, the physical sense, but their being in heaven would survive. . . .

We took such an infinitesimal amount of psilocybin, and yet it connected me to infinity.

Subject L.J. confronted the issue of personal mortality, which he described as follows:

I was on the floor underneath the chapel pew and he [a group leader] was looking after me and sort of aware of, you know, "L.J. is down there, is everything all right?" I was hearing my uncle who had died [several months before], the one who was a minister, saying, "I want you to die, I want you to die, I want you to die" I could hear his voice saying. The more that I let go and sort of died, the more I felt this eternal life, saying to myself under my breath perhaps, "it has always been this way, it has always been this way. . . . O, isn't it wonderful, there's nothing to fear, this is what it means to die, or to taste of eternal life. . . ." And the more I died the more I appropriated this sense of eternal life. . . . While the service went on I was caught up in this experience of eternal life and appreciating what the peyote Indians or the sacred mushroom Indians experienced with their imbibing of the drug. Just in that one session I think I gained experience I didn't have before and probably could never have gotten from a hundred hours of reading or a thousand hours of reading.

I would have to say as far as I'm concerned it was a positive, mystical experience . . . confirmed by experiences both before and after.

Rev. L.R. had one of the most difficult experiences of all the psilocybin subjects. He described the early portion of his experience as follows:

Shortly after receiving the capsule, all of a sudden I just wanted to laugh. I began to go into a very strong paranoid experience. And I found it to be scary. The chapel was dark and I hated it in there, just absolutely hated it in there. And I got up and left. I walked down the corridor and there was a guard, a person stationed at the door so individuals wouldn't go out, and he says, "Don't go outside," and I said, "Oh no, I won't. I'll just look outdoors." And I went to the door and out I went. They sent [a group leader] out after me. We [L.R. and the group leader] went back into the building and again, I hated to be in that building and being confined because there were bars on the window and I felt literally like I was in prison. One of the things that was probably happening to me was a reluctance to just flow. I tried to resist that and as soon as resistance sets in there's likely to be conflict and there's likely, I think, for there to be anxiety.

In addition to his emotion struggles, Rev. L.R. discusses the mystical aspect of his experience as follows:

The inner awareness and feelings I had during the drug experience were the dropping away of the external world and those relationships and then the sudden sense of singleness, oneness. And the rest of normal waking consciousness is really . . . illusion. It's not real and somehow that inner core experience of oneness is more real and more authentic than normal consciousness. . . . I was also experiencing some of those same kind of states that produced anxiety, and I wanted to try to get at the bottom of it.

I personally feel that the experience itself was, and I know [Pahnke's] research came to the conclusion, that the effect of the chemicals like that is very similar, parallel to, perhaps the same as a classical mystical experience. . . .

Rev. Y.M. described his experience, which also had some difficult moments, as follows:

I closed my eyes and the visuals were back, the color patterns were back, and it was as if I was in an ocean of bands, streams of color, streaming past me. The colors were brilliant and I could swim down any one of those colors. Then that swirl dissolved itself into a radial pattern, a center margin radial pattern with the colors going out from the center. I was at the center and I could swim out any one of those colors and it would be a whole different life's experience. I could swim out any one of them that I wanted. I mean I could swim metaphorically. There wasn't the sense that I could actually paddle. I could choose any one I wanted, but I had to choose one.

I couldn't decide which one to go out, and eventually it connects to the decision I was in the midst of making about career choices . . . when I couldn't decide, I died. Very existential . . . for a brief moment there, I was physically dying. My insides were literally being scooped out, and it was very painful. . . . I said to myself . . . that nobody should have to go through this . . . it was excruciating to die like that. Very painful. And I died. . . .

After the psilocybin experience, I never consciously made the choice as to what I was going to do career-wise, but the choice was made. It was made while I was on the psilocybin. But it never had to be consciously, intentionally, "Ah, let's see, what I am going to do is. . . ." It was made, and I was confident of it, it was going to be. And I did it afterwards. . . .

Rev. K.B. described his mystical experience in the following manner:

I feel almost whatever I say about it . . . is a little bit artificial in terms of describing. What it is is something deeper and probably also more obvious and I think I endeavor to put it into some kind of category which may obscure the point in some way. I remember feeling at the time that I was very unusually incapable of describing it. Words are a familiar environment for me and I usually can think of them, but I didn't find any for this. And I haven't yet.

I closed my eyes, either thinking of meditating or maybe I was drowsy or something. I closed my eyes and it seemed to be darker than usual. And then there was a sudden bolt of light which I think was entirely internal and a feeling almost like a shock or something and that was only for an instant. It was violent but it was a definite tingling like taking hold of a wire or something.

I closed my eyes and . . . thought that this would be a fine time for [meditating on the Passion]. . . . So I did think about the procession to the cross. And with my eyes closed I had an unusually vivid scene of the procession going by. A scene quite apart from any imagining or anything on my part. A self-actualizing thing—kind of like watching a movie or something, it was apart from me but very vivid.

I had a definite sense of being an infant or being born, or something like that. I had a sense of death, too, but I think actually the sense of death came after the sense of birth. . . . I had my hands on my legs and there wasn't any flesh, there were bare bones, resting on my bones. That part wasn't frightening, I was just kind of amazed. . . . I think I must have gone along through the life of Christ identifying in a very total sort of way—reliving the life in some way until finally dying and going into the tomb.

I really am glad I took it. And glad that I was a subject. I don't think it would be a particularly memorable experience if I just had listened to the service. I've heard some good services and I imagine this was as moving as most. But I think it would be in that category instead of a once-in-a-lifetime sort of thing. . . .

I've remained convinced that my ability to perceive things was artificially changed, but the perceptions I had were real as anything else.

Subject T.B. was very comfortable with the effects of the psilocybin, perhaps because he had had mystical experiences prior to the experiment. He described his experience in the following way:

I was kneeling there praying and beginning to feel like I was in the seventh grade, eleven or twelve years old. It was the kind of experiences that you knew that something great was happening. I started to go to the root of all being. And discovered that . . . you never quite get there. That was my discovery during that time . . . it's a philosophy and a theology that I hold yet today. You can approach the fullness of all being in either prayer, or in the psilocybin experience. You can reach out, but you can't dive down . . . and hit that root.

The discovery within that experience is that you could approach God by two different ways. You either get to the root, the ground of all being, or the fullness of all being. And in getting to the root, you'll strive, you'll come closer and closer, but it's always half, and you'll think another half step, another half step, and you'll never quite get there. The fullness, to approach the fullness of God is the only way to approach God.

Subject H.R. told of his largely positive experience in the following way:

It was a feeling of being . . . lifted out of your present state. I just stopped worrying about time and all that kind of stuff . . . there was one universal man, personhood, whatever you want to call it . . . a lot of connectedness with everybody and everything. I don't think Christ or other religious images that I can remember came into it. That's the only reason I didn't think it was religious. I don't remember any religious images. . . .

I was convinced after the experiment that I had had quite an experience but that it was really into my psychological depths, and it was not a religious experience. . . . It was really the sense that I was discovering the depths of my own self. It did not have a sacredness kind of element to it. . . . I didn't think I had experienced a God that was particularly outside of me. What I experienced was a God that was inside of me. And I think that . . . made me say, I don't think this is religious, I think this is psychological. But that was because of the way I was defining being . . . the way I thought God was being defined by other people at that point.

After the Good Friday experiment, two out of the ten placebo subjects experienced psychedelics. Placebo Subject P.J. described his first psychedelic experience, which took place in a chapel with psilocybin Subject L.R. as his guide, as follows:

> I laid on the front pew and watched myself—it seemed like eternity—pour through my navel and totally become nothing. And I felt that this would never stop. It seemed like an eternity of being in heaven and everything. One of the most beautiful experiences in my entire life.
>
> It sure kicks the hell out of one being rigid with what could go on and what kind of experiences you could have. To take one of these drugs says a lot more can happen than what's been happening in your total experience. And I think that's good, and that's why I would want my kids to take it.

Placebo Subject L.G. received psilocybin in a hospital as a part of a subsequent experiment conducted by Pahnke (1966) in a fruitless search for a placebo substance which would permit a successful double-blind experiment. L.G. described his experience as follows:

> It was rather removed from the religious context. Certainly the environment we were in had no particular religious symbols. I recall they really stressed [the need to] be absolutely open and just relax and flow with the experience whatever comes. So, there was no context really to suggest a particular experience like there might have been with the Good Friday experiment. We didn't talk about the mysticism, as I recall, or religious symbols. . . .
>
> At one point I kind of felt like, "Well, maybe this is what it is like to be crazy." I never really panicked but I was acutely aware of anxiety. . . . As time evolved I just had this incredible sense of joy and humor, too. I was laughing, real ecstasy. . . . The thing that struck me was how anybody could worry or not trust, that just struck me as an absurdity. It was very exciting.
>
> There was an energy, it was almost a sexual thing, an intensity and a joy. The visual things that I experienced and the music, I think were aligned with the sense of unity, everything was unified. We were all part of the same thing. You didn't sense a difference between the music or the physical objects. . . .
>
> I think that you can certainly have a religious experience without the religious symbols. Certainly the religious symbols can lead you to a mystical experience. Unfortunately, they can also be divisive. The

sectarianism can flow from the different symbols and justify the differences rather than the commonality. I think the mystic experience as I understand it comes down more on the commons.

Contrasting with the desire of two of the control subjects to have their own psychedelic experience, several of the remaining control subjects decided during the course of the experiment that they had no desire to try psychedelics. The behavior of some of their fellow subjects who received psilocybin had frightened them. Placebo Subject B.A. remarked:

> I tend to look back on it as an historical curiosity, with intellectual interest to me, but you know, frankly not much else at this point. . . . The only change that I can think of that it brought about in my life was a conviction that I never wanted to go on a drug trip of any type ever. And I never have, except for booze. The sights I saw [during the experiment] were very disturbing to me, and I didn't see myself wanting to be in that kind of position. It appeared to be hopelessly out of control and life threatening in several instances.

The remaining control subjects viewed psilocybin with some equanimity but were not motivated enough to seek out their own experience. If the circumstances were right and the substances were legal, several indicated that they might be willing to participate in another experiment.

A SIGNIFICANT OMISSION

Out of the seven psilocybin subjects formally interviewed, only two had had Good Friday experiences that they reported to be completely positive without significant psychic struggles. The others all felt moments in which they feared they were either going crazy, dying, or were too weak for the ordeal they were experiencing. These struggles were resolved during the course of the Good Friday service and according to the subjects contributed to their learning and growth.

It appears that these difficult moments were significantly underemphasized in Pahnke's thesis and in the subsequent reporting on the experiment. Psilocybin Subject H.R. stated:

> The other thing I found unique that wasn't talked at all about in what I read, at least in the thesis, was that it was all on the positive up side. I don't know whether other people have said this but I had a down side. . . . It was a roller coaster. . . . I mean I had a very strong positive sense of the whole . . . one with humanity kind of positive glowing,

unity kind of feeling and then I went down to the bottom where I was really just . . . guilt . . . that's all I can say. It was a very, very profound sense of guilt.

Pahnke does mention that two of the subjects who received the psilocybin "had a little difficulty in readjusting to the 'ordinary world' and needed special reassurance by their group leaders until the drug effects subsided" (Pahnke, 1963, p. 219). Almost certainly, one of those subjects was L.R., who found the chapel to be like a prison and went outside for much of the service. The other subject is, almost certainly, the one who refused to participate in the follow-up study.

In one technical section of the thesis, and in none of his subsequent papers, Pahnke mentions that one of those two subjects later referred to his experience as "a psychotic episode" (Pahnke, 1963, p. 232). In another part of the thesis, Pahnke mentions that injectable thorazine was on hand for emergencies. What he does not report anywhere is that one subject was actually given a shot of thorazine as a tranquilizer during the course of the experiment. Several of the subjects and group leaders remembered this incident and reported in the long-term follow-up interviews that it involved the one psilocybin subject who refused to be interviewed by the author. Needless to say, this occurrence should surely have been mentioned in Pahnke's thesis and, by those few who knew that such an event had actually transpired, in any subsequent reporting on the experiment.

Pahnke probably did not report his use of the tranquilizer because he was fearful of adding to the ammunition of the opponents of the research. Fears that negative aspects of the experiment would be taken out of context and exaggerated may have been justified. In an example of just such a critique, Zaehner asserts in his book, *Zen, Drugs, and Mysticism*, that Pahnke, in an article Pahnke published several years after the Good Friday experiment, repudiated the results of his own study (Zaehner, 1972, p. 105). In that article, Pahnke does indeed say that mystical experiences were absent (Pahnke, 1967, p. 71). Pahnke was, however, referring to the control of subjects. This misreading of Pahnke by Zaehner is an indication of how, even in an educated scholar, bias can overwhelm facts. This observation, of course, is also true of Pahnke. His silence about his administration of a tranquilizer may perhaps have been good politics; certainly it was bad science.

Although an interview with the subject who was tranquilized would be necessary to understand the subtleties of his experience and its consequences, several long-term follow-up interviews generated secondhand information which may be summarized as follows: This subject was reported to be deeply moved by a sermon delivered by the very dynamic preacher who emphasized that it was the obligation of all Christians to tell people that there was a man on the cross. This subject was reported to have gone outside of the chapel possibly intending to follow the exhortation.

A struggle ensued when the group leaders, worried for his safety, tried to bring him back inside. After a time during which he seemed fearful and was not settling down, Pahnke tranquilized him with a shot of thorazine. He was then brought back into the chapel and remained calm for the duration of the experiment. He participated in all further aspects of the experiment and in the six-month follow-up reported that he considered his fear experience "slightly harmful" because "in a mob panic-situation I feel I would be less likely to maintain a calm objective position than I might have formerly" (Pahnke, 1963, p. 232).

Subsequent to the Good Friday experiment, the use of tranquilizers in controlled psychedelic psychotherapy research was largely abandoned in favor of simply providing a supportive environment and letting the drug run its course (Richard Yensen, personal communication, 1991).

DISCUSSION

The original Good Friday experiment is one of the preeminent psychedelic experiments in the scientific literature. Despite the methodological shortcomings of the unavoidable failure of the double-blind and the use of several imprecise questions in the questionnaire used to quantify mystical experiences, the experiment's fascinating and provocative conclusions strongly support the hypothesis that psychedelic drugs can help facilitate mystical experiences when used by religiously inclined people in a religious setting. The original experiment also supports the hypothesis that those psilocybin subjects who experienced a full or a partial mystical experience would, after six months, report a substantial amount of positive, and virtually no negative, persisting changes in attitude and behavior.

This long-term follow-up, conducted twenty-four to twenty-seven years after the original experiment, provides further support to the findings of the original experiment. All psilocybin subjects participating in the long-term follow-up, but none of the controls, still considered their original experience to have had genuinely mystical elements and to have made a uniquely valuable contribution to their spiritual lives. The positive changes described by the psilocybin subjects at six months, which in some cases involved basic vocational and value choices and spiritual understandings, had persisted over time and in some cases had deepened. The overwhelmingly positive nature of the reports of the psilocybin subjects are even more remarkable because this long-term follow-up took place during a period of time in the United States when drug abuse was becoming the public's number-one social concern, with all the attendant social pressure to deny the value of drug-induced experiences. The long-term follow-up interviews cast considerable doubt on the assertion that mystical experiences catalyzed by drugs are in any way inferior to nondrug mystical experiences in both their immediate content and long-term positive effects, a critique of the Good Friday experiment advanced primarily by Zaehner (Bakalar, 1985).

Unexpectedly, the long-term follow-up also uncovered data that should have been reported in the original thesis. Pahnke failed to report the administration of the tranquilizer thorazine to one of the subjects who received psilocybin. There is no justification for this omission no matter how unfairly the critics of this research may have used the information and no matter how minimal were the negative persisting effects reported by the subject. In addition, Pahnke underemphasized the difficult psychological struggles experienced by most of the psilocybin subjects. These very serious omissions point to an important incompleteness in Pahnke's interpretation of the effects of psilocybin.

Some of the backlash that swept the psychedelics out of the research labs and out of the hands of physicians and therapists can be traced in part to the thousands of cases of people who took psychedelics in non-research settings, were unprepared for the frightening aspects of their psychedelic experiences, and ended up in hospital emergency rooms. These unfortunate instances of panic reaction have many causes, yet some of them stem from the way in which the cautionary elements of the Good Friday experiment were inadequately discussed in Pahnke's thesis, in subsequent scholarly reports, and in the popular media. For example, *Time* magazine reported on the experiment in glowing, exaggerated terms stating, "All students who had taken the drug [psilocybin] experienced a mystical consciousness that resembled those described by saints and ascetics" (9/23, 1966, p. 62).

The widespread use of psychedelics, both in medical and nonmedical settings, which began in the 1960s, is still currently taking place, apparently largely underground. Such use was partially founded upon an optimism regarding the inherent safety of the psychedelic experience which did not fully acknowledge the complexity and profundity of the psychological issues associated with psychedelic experiences. With some proponents of psychedelics exaggerating the benefits and minimizing the risks, a backlash against these substances was predictable. With the intriguing connection reported by several psilocybin subjects between mystical experiences and political action, the backlash in retrospect may have been inevitable (Baumeister & Placidi, 1985).

Despite the difficult moments several of the psilocybin subjects passed through, the subjects who participated in the long-term follow-up reported a substantial amount of persisting positive effects and no significant long-term negative effects. Even the subject who was tranquilized in the original experiment reported only "slightly harmful" negative persisting effects at the six-month follow-up. Secondhand information gathered during the course of the long-term follow-up suggests that his experience caused no persisting dysfunction and may even have had some beneficial as well as detrimental effects.

The lack of long-term negative effects or dysfunction is not surprising. Strassman's literature review of all controlled scientific experiments using psychedelics in human volunteers found that panic reactions and adverse reactions were extremely rare. He concluded that the potential risks of future research were outweighed by the potential benefits (Strassman, 1984).

This long-term follow-up study, even in light of the new data about the difficulties of the psychedelic experiences of many of the subjects, adds further support to the conclusion that additional studies are justified. Future experiments should be approached cautiously and carefully, with a multidisciplinary team of scientists involved in planning and implementation. Such a team should include psychiatrists, psychologists, religious professionals from a variety of traditions, as well as drug abuse prevention, education, and treatment officials. Questions as fundamental as those raised by the Good Friday experiment deserve to be addressed by the scientific community and post special challenges to the regulatory agencies. Renewed research can be expected to require patience, courage, and wisdom from all concerned.

REFERENCES

BAKALAR, J. (1985). Social and intellectual attitudes toward drug-induced religious experience. *J. Humanistic Psychology,* 15(4), 45–66.

BARBER, T.X. (1976). *Pitfalls in human research.* New York: Pergamon Press.

BAUMEISTER, R. & PLACIDI, K. (1985). A social history and analysis of the LSD controversy. *J. Humanistic Psychology,* 23(4), 25–60.

BEUTLER, L.E. & CRAGO, M. (1983). Self-report measures in psychotherapy outcome. In M. Lambert, E. Christensen, & S. DeJulio (Eds.), *The assessment of psychotherapy outcome.* New York: Wiley.

CLARK, W.H. (1969). *Chemical ecstasy: Psychedelic drugs and religion.* New York: Sheed & Ward.

DI LEO, F. (1982). Protocol: LSD-assisted psychotherapy correlation of peak experience profiles with behavior change. Appendix C: Peak experience profile. Unpublished.

GROF. S. (1875). *Realms of the human unconscious: Observations from LSD research*. New York: Viking Press.

GROF, S. (1980). *LSD psychotherapy*. Pomona, CA: Hunter House.

HARNER, M. (Ed.) (1973). *Hallucinogens and shamanism*. New York: Oxford University Press.

HOFMANN, A. & SHULTES, R. E. (1979). *Plants of the gods: Origins of hallucinogenic use*. New York: McGraw-Hill.

JAMES, W. (1961, orig. 1902). *Varieties of religious experience*. New York: Collier Books.

LARSON, D. et al. (1986). Systematic analysis of research on religious variables in four major psychiatric journals, 1978–1982. *American J. Psychiatry*, 143(3), 329–34.

LASAGNA, L. (1985). *Clinical trials in the natural environment*. Boston, Tufts University: Center for the Study of Drug Development, Reprint Series RS 8695. 45–49.

LEARY, T. et al. (1962). Investigations into the religious implications of consciousness expanding experience. Newsletter #1: Research program on consciousness-altering substances. Cambridge, MA: Harvard University.

LEARY, T. (1967). The religious experience: Its production and interpretation. *J. Psychedelic Drugs*, 1(2), 3–23.

LEARY, T. (1968). *High priest*. New York: College Notes and Texts, Inc.

LEARY, T. (1984). *Flashbacks*. Los Angeles: J.P. Tarcher.

LUKOFF, D., ZANGER, R. & LU, F. (1990). Transpersonal psychology research review: Psychoactive substances and transpersonal states. *J. Transpersonal Psychology*, 22(2), 107–48.

PAHNKE, W. (1963). Drugs and mysticism: An analysis of the relationship between psychedelic drugs and the mystical consciousness. Ph.D. dissertation, Harvard University.

PAHNKE, W. (1966). The contribution of the psychology of religious to the therapeutic use of psychedelic substances. In Abramson, J. (Ed.), *The use of LSD in psychotherapy and alcoholism*. New York: Bobbs-Merrill, 629–49.

PAHNKE, W. (1967). LSD and religious experience. In DeBold, R. & Leaf, R. (Eds.), *LSD, man and society*. Middletown, CT: Wesleyan University Press, 60–85.

PAHNKE, W. (1970). Drugs and mysticism. In B. Aaronson. & H. Osmond. (Eds.), *Psychedelics: The uses and implications of hallucinogenic drugs*. Garden City, NY: Anchor Books. 145–64.

PAHNKE, W. & RICHARDS, W. (1969a). Implications of LSD and experimental mysticism. *J. Religion and Health*, 5(3), 175–208.

PAHNKE, W. & RICHARDS, W. (1969b). The psychedelic mystical experience and the human encounter with death. *Harvard Theological Review*, 62(1), 1–32.

PAHNKE, W. & RICHARDS, W. (1969c). Implications of LSD and experimental mysticism. *J. Transpersonal Psychology* 1(2), 69–102.

RICHARDS, W. (1975). Counseling, peak experiences, and the human encounter with death. Ph.D. dissertation, Washington, D.C.: Catholic University.

RICHARDS, W. (1978). Mystical archetypal experiences of terminal patients in DPT-assisted psychotherapy. *J. Religion and Health, 17(2)*, 117–26.

RING, K. (1982). *Life at death: A scientific investigation of the near-death experience*. New York: Quill.

RING, K. (1984). *Heading toward omega: In search of the meaning of the near-death experience*. New York: Quill.

RING, K. (1988). Paradise is paradise: Reflections on psychedelic drugs, mystical experiences and the near-death experience. *J. of Near-Death Experiences. 6(3)*. 138–48.

RUE, L.D. (1985). Our most outrageous blind spot: The academic study of religion. *Chronical of Higher Education, (29)*, 40.

SILVERMAN, W. (1983). Bibliography of measurement techniques used in the social scientific study of religion. *Psychological Documents 13(7)*. Washington, D.C.: American Psychological Association.

SPILKA, B., HOOD, JR., R. W. & GORSUCH, R. (1985). *The psychology of religion: An empirical approach*. Englewood Cliffs, NJ: Prentice Hall.

STACE, W.T. (1960). *Mysticism and philosophy*. London: MacMillan.

STRASSMAN, R. (1984). Adverse reactions to psychedelic drugs: A review of the literature. *J. Nervous and Mental Disease,* 172, 577–95.

TIME. (1966) Mysticism in the Lab. September 23, 62.

TOOLEY & PRATT (1964). Letter to the editor, *Behavioral Science,* 9(3), 254–56.

UNDERHILL, E. (1974, ori. 1910). *Mysticism*. New York: Meridian.

WASSON, R. G. (1968). *Soma: Divine mushroom of immortality*. Rome: Harcourt, Brace & Jovanovich, Inc.

ZAEHNER, R.C. (1972). *Zen, drugs and mysticism*. New York: Vintage Books.

ZINBERG, N. (1984). *Drug, set and setting*. New Haven: Yale University Press.

Bibliography of Related Literature

AARONSON, B. & OSMOND, J. (Eds.) (1970). *Psychedelics: The uses and implications of hallucinogenic drugs*. Garden City. NY: Anchor Books.

ABRAMSON, J. (Ed.) (1967). *The use of LSD in psychotherapy and alcoholism*. New York: Bobbs-Merrill.

BAKALAR, J. (1979–80). Psychedelic drug therapy: Cultural conditions and obstacles. *J. Altered States of Consciousness, 5(4),* 297–307.

BAKALAR, J. & GRINSPOON, L. (1986). Can drugs be used to enhance the psychotherapeutic process? *American J. of Psychotherapy, XL(3),* July.

CLARK, W. H. (1973). *Religious experience: Its nature and function in the human psyche*. Springfield, IL: Charles C. Thomas.

D'AQUILI, E. (1982). Senses of reality in science and religion: A neuroepistemological perspective. *Zygon, 17*(4), 361–84.

DEAN, S. (Ed.). (1972). *The observing self: Mysticism and psychotherapy*. Boston: Beacon Press.

DOBKIN DE RIOS, M. (1972). *Visionary vine: Hallucinogenic healing in the Peruvian Amazon*. Prospect Heights, IL: Waveland Press.

EFRON, D. (Ed.) (1967). *Ethnopharmacologic search for psychoactive drugs*. Washington, D.C.: Public Health Service Publication No. 1645.

GRINSPOON, L. & BAKALAR, J. (1979). *Psychedelic drugs reconsidered*. New York: Basic Books.

GRINSPOON, L. & BAKALAR, J. (Eds.) (1983). *Psychedelic reflections*. New York: Human Sciences Press.

HUXLEY, A. (1954). *Doors of perception*. New York: Harper.

LEE, M. & SCHLAIN, B. (1986). *Acid Dreams: Lsd, the CIA and the sixties rebellion*. New York: Grove Press.

MASTERS, R.E.L. & HOUSTON, J. (1966). *The varieties of psychedelic experience*. New York: Dell.

MASLOW, A. (1964). *Religions, values, and peak experiences*. New York: Viking Press.

MULLER, R. (1982). *New Genesis: Shaping a global spirituality*. Garden City, NY: Doubleday.

MYERHOFF. B. (1974). *Peyote hunt: The sacred journey of the Huichol Indians*. Ithaca, NY: Cornell University Press.

O'CONNELL, S. (1983). The placebo effect and psychotherapy. *Psychotherapy: Theory, research and practice, 20(3)*, 335–57.

PAHNKE, W. (1966). Report on a pilot project investigating the pharmacological effects of psilocybin in normal volunteers. Massachusetts Mental Health Center. Unpublished manuscript.

PERSINGER, M. (1987). *The neurophysiological basis for "God" experiences*. New York: Praeger Press.

PRINCE, R. H. & SALMAN, D. H. (Eds.). (1967). *Do psychedelics have religious implications?* Proceedings of the third annual conference, R. M. Bucke Memorial Society for the Study of Religious Experience, Quebec.

RAM DASS. (1974). *The only dance there is*. New York: Doubleday.

SCHMITZ-MOORMAN, K. (1986). Philosophical and theological reflections on recent neurobiological discoveries. *Zygon, 21*(2), 249–57.

SHULGIN, A., SHULGIN, L. A. & JACOB IIIM P. (1986). A protocol for the evaluation of new psychoactive drugs in man. *Methods and Findings in Experimental Clinical Pharmacology, 8*(5), 313–20.

SMITH, H. (1965). Do drugs have religious import? *J. Philosophy, LXI*(18), 517–30.

STAFFORD, P. (1983). *Psychedelics encyclopedia*. Los Angeles: J.P. Tarcher.

WEIL, A. (1972). *The natural mind*. Boston: Houghton Mifflin.

WILBER, K. (Ed.) (1984). *Quantum questions: Mystical writings of the world's great physicists*. Boulder, CO: Shambhala.

WOLMAN, B & ULLMAN, M. (Eds.) (1986). *Handbook of states of consciousness*. New York: Van Nostrand Reinhold.

THE DIVINE SPARK

THE SECOND COMING OF PSYCHEDELICS
BY DON LATTIN

Ric Godfrey had the shakes. At night, his body temperature would drop and he'd start to tremble. During the day, he was jumpy. He was always looking around, always on edge. His vibe scared the people around him. He couldn't hang on to a job. He started drinking and drugging, anything to numb out.

Years passed before a counselor with the Veterans Administration told him he had severe posttraumatic stress disorder, or PTSD. The former Marine had spent the early 1990s interrogating prisoners in Kuwait. Years later, he was still playing out the first Persian Gulf War.

Counseling helped a little, but the symptoms continued. He went to rehab for his substance abuse, then tried Alcoholics Anonymous. "That went on for ten years," he said. "I don't know how many times I hit rock bottom."

Then one of his Seattle neighbors—a woman who also suffered from PTSD—told him about a group of veterans who were going down to Peru to try a psychedelic drug called Ayahuasca, a jungle vine that is brewed into a tea. Indigenous Peruvians called it "sacred medicine." A wealthy veteran had started a healing center in South America and would pay all Ric's expenses.

The next thing Ric knew, he was crawling into a tent on a platform out in the middle of the Amazon jungle. The sun went down. The shaman gave him the tea, a blessing, and a pail in which to vomit.

"Your body will not keep it in you," Ric recalled. "At first, it's the worst thing you've ever done in your life. Then all of a sudden, you blink your eyes and you are not there anymore. You get out of your body and look back and see what is wrong with you. I saw the shell of the person I didn't want to be and stepped out of it. It was the most amazing thing. I've taken lots of drugs before, but I never remembered. I think this is the key. You actually gain knowledge from this. I don't even consider it a drug. It's an eye-opener. It makes you think about stuff. Your deepest darkest secrets, stuff you have been holding on to since you were eight years old. It washes out of you, and you feel like a totally different person. People look at you differently. Your whole world changes before your eyes."

Three years later, Ric Godfrey says he hasn't had a single symptom of the shakes or night terrors since he came back from the jungle. He's relaxed and holding down a great job.

"I've always been afraid that someone was out to get me, but I don't have that fear anymore," he says. "I still like to sit with my back to the wall. I still have certain military idiosyncrasies, but I'm not afraid anymore."

Psychedelic drugs are back. Not that they ever really went away. You could always find them on the street, in the psychedelic underground, and along the more enlightened edges of the drug culture. What's new is that these powerful, mind-altering substances are finally coming out of the drug counterculture and into the mainstream laboratories of some of the world's leading universities and medical centers. Research projects and pilot studies at Johns Hopkins, Harvard, Purdue University, and the University of California at Los Angeles are probing their mind-altering mysteries and healing powers. Psychedelic drugs like psilocybin and ecstasy are still illegal for street use and cannot be legally prescribed by doctors, but university administrators, government regulatory agencies, and private donors are suddenly giving the stamp of approval and the money needed for new research into beneficial uses for this "sacred medicine."

"This field of research is finally coming of age," said David Nichols, a veteran researcher who recently retired professor from the Purdue University College of Pharmacy and the Indiana University School of Medicine. "As Crosby, Stills and Nash said, it's been a long time coming."

Mainstream America's panic over psychedelics began after experiments at Harvard in the 1960s by notorious psychologists Timothy Leary and Richard Alpert spun out of control. What began as the Harvard Psilocybin Project morphed into a crusade to turn America on to the wonders of LSD. The researchers were eventually removed from the school's faculty, and Leary served jail time for marijuana. "Timothy Leary played a very significant role in the backlash," said Roland Griffiths, a professor in the departments of psychiatry and neurosciences at Johns Hopkins, who has emerged as one of the leaders in the new wave of research into the beneficial use of psychedelic drugs. "Leary was an iconic figure at the time, but he modeled the wrong outcome by departing from scientific method. He had a lot of interesting things to say about it but didn't pursue a systematic and cautious experimental approach."

The excesses weren't limited to Harvard. "Out on the West Coast we had the Acid Tests (of Ken Kesey and his Merry Pranksters) and all that—parties where psychedelic beverages were distributed," said Charles Grob, a professor of psychiatry and pediatrics at UCLA who has studied Ayahuasca rites in Peru and led research with psilocybin and cancer patients. "The culture was not prepared to handle these compounds."

The 1970 Controlled Substances Act reclassified common hallucinogens as schedule 1 drugs, meaning they were considered easy to abuse and had no legitimate medical use. New limitations were placed on human research, and federal funding disappeared.

But the times they are a-changin'. There's a new openness to the medicinal use of marijuana. In the November 2012 elections, the states of Washington and Colorado legalized the recreational use of pot. Baby boomers who came of age in the psychedelic sixties and seventies are now running government agencies and university administrations.

Leading the campaign in the new wave of government-sanctioned research is the Multidisciplinary Association for Psychedelic Studies (MAPS), an independent nonprofit which has raised millions of dollars to fund an ongoing study into the use of MDMA, also known as "ecstasy," to treat returning war veterans and rape survivors suffering from PTSD.

In the first phase of that study, MAPS researcher Michael Mithoefer, a psychiatrist from South Carolina, treated twenty-one patients. Some of the participants were given MDMA with psychotherapy, while some got a placebo along with their therapy. Researchers hoped to show that MDMA's ability to enhance trust, empathy, and openness would make it easier for patients to recount a traumatic event. It did. Over 80 percent of those who received MDMA had no PTSD symptoms two months later, compared to only around 25 percent of those who got the placebo. Patients with MDMA-assisted therapy did better than those treated with traditional prescription drugs, such as Zoloft or Paxil.

In September 2012, Mithoefer and his colleagues released more results in a paper published in the *Journal of Psychopharmacology*. It showed that the benefits of MDMA-assisted psychotherapy were sustained over an average of three and a half years since the last time the drug had been ingested, an exceptionally lengthy period for a follow-up study. Furthermore, there were no reports of lasting harmful effects from exposure to the drug.

Rick Doblin, the executive director of MAPS, envisions his organization as a sustainable nonprofit that will train therapists, run its own clinics, and distribute ecstasy to doctors and psychologists.

MAPS controls 960 grams of ecstasy that was legally manufactured in 1985 by Nichols, the Purdue University chemist. That's enough for between four and five thousand doses, and it has not lost its potency. "It's still the world's purest MDMA," Doblin said.

The use of psychedelic drugs for therapeutic purposes is not without controversy.

In the 1950s, writer Aldous Huxley warned that psychedelics can take users to "heaven or hell"—for some, a path to enlightenment; for others, the spark for psychosis.

Huston Smith, the scholar of world religions who was another early explorer, noted the drugs can mimic "authentic religious experience" but questioned whether altered states of consciousness actually change the way people live their lives.

Smith also issued early warnings that today's "Ayahuasca tourists" might consider. While "sacred medicine" may be helpful for a child or young adult raised in Native American religious culture, it may prove disastrous for an outsider unprepared for a mind-blowing trip. "History shows that minority faiths are viable, but only when they are cradled in communities that are solid and structured enough to constitute what are in effect churches," Huston writes in an essay titled "Psychedelic Theophanies and the Religious Life." More recently, the dangers of using psychedelics without medical supervision were illustrated when a man died after ingesting Ayahuasca at the same Peruvian retreat center where Ric Godfrey had his life-changing experience with the drug.

Doblin and other advocates of psychedelic-assisted therapy acknowledge that these powerful substances—while not as addictive as drugs like alcohol, heroin, or cocaine—can be abused by recreational users. They propose a system whereby the substances can be prescribed by doctors and administered by trained therapists.

Nevertheless, researchers and advocates argue that psychedelic drugs, used with close supervision, hold great promise for a deeper understanding of the connection between the brain and human consciousness.

"Where does our capacity for consciousness come from?" asked David Presti, who teaches graduate and undergraduate courses in neuroscience at the University of California at Berkeley. "It's still a huge mystery. It's the biggest mystery of all in science, and psychedelics are the most powerful probe to study that connection."

In an interview in his office in the Life Sciences Building on the Berkeley campus, Presti held up a large piece of dried Ayahuasca vine. He said brain scientists are confirming what shamanic cultures around the world have known for millennia. "These substances have a profound capacity, when used under appropriate conditions, to be catalysts for real transformation in people, for real healing."

A Johns Hopkins study of psilocybin and mystical experience is a good example. Follow-up surveys of thirty-six "hallucinogen-naive adults" who took psilocybin under Griffiths's supervision found that two-thirds of them rated the sessions as being "among the five most spiritually significant experiences of their lives."

Griffiths's work on the behavioral and subjective effects of mood-altering drugs has been largely supported by grants from the National Institutes of Health. Along with Grob, he has studied the effects of psilocybin to treat anxiety in cancer patients—their research found that low doses of psilocybin improved patients' mood and reduced their need for narcotic pain relievers—and has begun a new pilot study to see if the active ingredient in "magic mushrooms" can help people overcome their addiction to tobacco.

Griffiths's personal interest in meditation inspired his study of psilocybin-occasioned mystical experience in healthy volunteers. One research subject, Brian, who asked that his last name not be used, recalled, "I was unified with everything. I still had enough awareness to get up and walk to the bathroom, but everything was so incredibly beautiful that I laughed and cried at the same time. I was one with it. It was just incredible—one of the top five experiences I have ever had in my life."

The experience was so spiritually profound that Brian recommitted himself to his study of meditation and Buddhism, and in late 2012 was scheduled to be ordained as a monk in the Soto Zen tradition.

For Presti, outcomes like Brian's are not surprising. "One of the ways psychedelics work is by reducing our psychological defenses. They allow the person to become aware of uncomfortable feelings and thoughts so they can come to the surface and be therapeutically processed," he said. "Nobody knows exactly how these things work, but there may be some kind of hard rewiring that goes on in the brain. They may increase neuroplasticity—make the neurons more susceptible to forming new connections."

He believes the substances should also be studied as a possible treatment for depression. "But there is a lot of resistance to this from the pharmaceutical industry. The last thing it wants to see is a substance people only use once or twice. They want us to use something every day for the rest of our life. That's how they make money."

Other researchers are troubled that the new wave of psychedelic research is blurring the lines between spiritual experience and the hard science of medicine. "We are not purveyors of spirituality. Having an epiphany is not a part of medicine," said John Mendelson, a senior scientist at the California Pacific Medical Research Center in San Francisco. "Most of medicine is not predicated on making you better than you are. It's getting you back to where you were. There are lots of people and things out there [that] can make us feel better, but our job is to diagnose and treat and fix diseases." But that view is no longer going unchallenged.

At the same time, a new generation of dedicated psychedelic drug researchers has emerged on university campuses across the nation. Many of them gathered last September at a "Psychedemia" conference at the University of Pennsylvania in Philadelphia. They see their mission as "integrating psychedelics in academia."

"Psychedelic studies are entering the mainstream," said Neşe Devenot, young graduate student at Penn and a lead organizer of the multidisciplinary conference. "You can talk about this now at the dinner table without coming across as some kind of fanatic."

During a lunch break at the weekend conference, one of the wise elders in the field of psychedelic drug research, psychologist William A. Richards, sat in the cafeteria in the basement of Houston Hall, surveying the buzz of intergenerational excitement. Richards, who is nearing the end of a long career at Johns Hopkins, has been exploring these realms since the early 1960s with such luminaries as Stanislav Grof, Abraham Maslow, Walter Pahnke, and yes, Timothy Leary.

Richards knows there could be another backlash against psychedelic drug research, not just by those who are still fighting the "war on drugs" but also by academics who resist the idea that scholars should seriously study something as slippery as "spirituality."

"But if mysticism is to emerge from silent monastic cells into the bright light of scientific discourse, I see no alternative," Richards said. "We have arrived at that frontier where the growing edge of true science meets the mystery of the unknown. Here, faith takes over—either belief in something or belief in nothing. These experiences are not in any drug. They are in us."

Like Ric Godfrey, Judith Goedeke needed a way to heal.

Judith helped others through her work as an acupuncturist. She'd always taken care of her own body. Then she was diagnosed with kidney cancer in 2003.

"How has this happened to me?" she asked herself. "I was just obsessing over that question. I did not do the things that assault the kidney in my adult life." Then she thought of another possibility. "In my younger years I went a very long time in fear. My house was not a safe place, and I know from my work with Chinese medicine that fear does assault the kidney."

Judith had her left kidney removed. "By its removal, I am removing decades of trauma," she told herself. "I would see it then as a really deep healing, and I could live with that."

Over the next five years, she had three CAT scans a year. There was no indication of further disease, and she was released from the care of her oncologist.

A couple years later, Judith heard about a study at Johns Hopkins University School of Medicine in Baltimore, under researcher Roland Griffiths. Patients with life-threatening illnesses were being treated with psilocybin, a synthesized version of the drug found in "magic mushrooms," to help them deal with the psychological trauma of a cancer diagnosis.

"At first, I couldn't see myself doing this," she recalled. "I am a cancer survivor. I have tremendous respect for my body and am very careful."

Judith decided to enter the study after she got to know two staff members with the project who would guide her through the process. "They are very solid and generous, deeply spiritual, good people. I had a tremendous amount of trust in everyone I encountered who was part of the program."

She was led through two psychedelic sessions, one with a low dose and one with a high dose. She saw what seemed like the ornate work of a great medieval cathedral, patterns that would rapidly change color and texture. There were other hallucinations of strange, garish creatures—like something out of a carnival. They annoyed her, and scared her a bit.

"I said silently, 'Okay. Here's the deal. If I give myself over to you, will I get myself back in at least the same shape?' And what I heard was a voice that said, 'Do you think I would disrespect my own handiwork?'"

Three years later, Judith Goedeke felt that the session helped her to finally heal her decades-old trauma. "It was out of my brokenness that the disease got hold of me," she said. "So it helped me heal my life in a way that years of therapy and years of acupuncture and decades of journaling had not done. I felt like I could forgive all the folks who had unintentionally harmed me, and forgive myself of unintentionally harming myself. That has had tremendous ramifications in my family and stays with me on a daily basis. I've learned that we are not here to judge one another. Forgiveness is not earned. It is simply the way forward."

PREPARATION FOR THE JOURNEY
BY RICK STRASSMAN, MD

Important disclaimer: None of the authors of [**the book that this essay was first published in, INNER PATHS TO OUTER SPACE**], *condones any illegal activities, even when it comes to the potentially beneficial effects of altering consciousness with a psychedelic drug. In nearly the entire world, it is illegal to possess major psychedelics such as mescaline, DMT, LSD, and psilocybin. In some instances, the plants that contain these chemicals, such as mescaline-containing peyote cactus and psilocybin-containing magic mushrooms, are also banned.*

While a discussion of the current laws regarding these plants and chemicals is beyond the scope of the book, we believe in the maxim "The law of the land is the law." Therefore, the authors take no responsibility—legal, medical, psychological, spiritual, or otherwise—for any difficulty in which anyone may find him- or herself as a result of manufacturing, possessing, distributing, or using a psychedelic substance.

Nevertheless, the human drive to profoundly alter consciousness in the way that psychedelics do so reliably cannot be extinguished. Whereas there clearly are other legal ways in which we may alter our consciousness—meditation, prayer, fasting, extreme sports, and so on—few of us are able to attain a truly psychedelic state without using drugs or plants. Thus, some may consider the legal and other risks associated with taking psychedelic substances as less compelling than their perceived benefits.

Whenever possible, we advise using such materials in licit circumstances. There are countries and contexts in which the use of certain psychedelic substances is legal. Examples include Ayahuasca-using churches in the West, centers in Latin America that use Ayahuasca and other psychoactive plants, and peyote-using churches in North America, where jurisdictions allow its use for both Natives and non-Natives.

Those preparing for a psychedelic drug experience, even the most seasoned veterans, nearly always feel intense anticipation. The late Secret Chief, a San Francisco Bay–area psychologist who supervised thousands, if not tens of thousands, of psychedelic drug sessions, referred to this feeling of anticipation of a session as "[t]he trip has already begun."

The Secret Chief was uncannily, unerringly, and extraordinarily accurate—and it may require some deep thinking to fully understand what he meant. Obviously, the mere act of thinking about, discussing, and deciding to undergo a psychedelic drug session is not the same as actually taking a drug. Nevertheless, by making such a decision, we initiate a cascade of events within the matrix of set and setting, which form a continuum not only limited to the discrete time period during which we are under the influence of a psychedelic, but also spreading in all directions, like the proverbial pebble thrown into the pond. By embarking on the preliminary stages of taking such a trip, we set in motion certain feelings, thoughts, and actions that lead to a potentially life-changing event. Our lives have already come under the influence of the trip.

Set and setting, the two primary factors involved in determining the outcome of the inner journey to outer space, are themselves modifiable via the two primary tasks of that journey: getting ready and letting go.

GETTING READY

In order to derive the most benefit from making any journey, inner or outer, we must do what we can to minimize the risks of a negative outcome and optimize the chances for a positive one. Once we have established the most solid foundation possible, we can be more assured of the beneficial outcome that may result from truly letting go.

We possess the power to determine the nature and course of our trip much as we possess the power to determine the nature and course of our lives. On the one hand, our lives are undeniably constrained by the circumstances of our birth: our genetic makeup; who our parents are; and the chemical, social, and psychological environment into which we were born. In addition, we are subject to the "accidents" continuously coming our way: those chance encounters that play such an important role in who we are and what we do. On the other hand, we also have the choice of how to regard and react to these circumstances. This may be what is meant by the maxim "Everything is in the hand of heaven except the awe of heaven."

At the same time, we must not forget that the ultimate purpose and context of our lives is vast and ultimately unknowable. In this case, we can refer to the complementary maxim "The work is never done, but we must never cease from doing it." We must do everything we can to develop our intention and attitude toward what awaits us in the psychedelic state. Then, when we meet what awaits us, we can allow it to show us what it will and take us where it will.

There are several practical considerations in getting ready for a session. We can parse these into a general temporal scheme: long-term work, intermediate work, and short-term work.

LONG-TERM WORK

If we know ourselves—our state and traits—as best as possible, we will be able to contend with any likely resistance to the letting go that is requisite for the optimal journey. This self-knowledge cannot be acquired quickly but rather requires years and decades. Nevertheless, at some point, anyone who will make this journey must begin walking the path to inner knowledge.

The two most common ways of increasing self-knowledge and learning how we relate to ourselves and others—those enduring and deep-seated elements of our set—are *psychotherapy* and *spiritual practice*. Although some consider the two at cross-purposes, they may be combined in very useful ways, because they exhibit common elements in theory, technique, and goals. Both use focused self-awareness to observe, understand, accept, and modify our feelings, thoughts, and behaviors in order that we may live more fulfilling, satisfying lives. Whereas meditation may emphasize awareness of mental, cognitive, and perceptual processes, Western psychotherapy usually relates to working with emotional concerns.

Spiritual or religious practice may be shorn of much of its theological content and rituals by emphasizing primarily its benefits in the development of self-awareness and the cultivation of desired mental states. For example, sustained concentration on our bodies and minds in a regular meditation practice can help make apparent several core issues: How do we experience anxiety—in our bodies or mentally? If we perceive anxiety in both the body and mind, which perception comes first? What of vulnerability, happiness, and fear? What are our fears? Is it our nature to share with others or keep to ourselves?

Prayer, perhaps in a way we usually don't consider, also may provide access to helpful discoveries. Praying to an outside source of help or wisdom may result in many of the same answers regarding who we are and how we function in the world—answers similar to those that might arise in a meditation practice. Where we acquire such information may not matter fundamentally within the context of simply obtaining increased self-knowledge and efficacy. In addition, regular meditation or prayer practice does much to develop our muscles of attention, and we can then apply our strengthened ability to focus toward examining ourselves in ways we may not have been capable of engaging previously.

A reliable, dependable, empathetic, and admirable teacher can be of great help in this process. He or she can provide instruction and encouragement and serve as a role model who encourages us to persist in our practice. In addition to these more formal teaching functions, an effective meditation or prayer teacher allows for the development of a close relationship between him- or herself and students. An open-eyed examination of the nature of this relationship—its ups and downs, misinterpretations, and projections—can be invaluable to our process of discovering who we really are.

Effective psychotherapy shares features with an effective meditation of prayer practice. These include paying attention to areas of difficulty in our lives. By looking carefully at what situations stir up particular emotions, thoughts, and behaviors, we may discover previously unacknowledged emotional and cognitive habits that served us at one time but no longer do so. Within the traditional psychotherapeutic setting, we find the relationship that develops between student and therapist more commonly subject to careful examination. This *analysis of the transference* is especially the case within the psychoanalytic framework.

If our meditation or prayer practice is focused on more than self-examination and self-improvement, it will begin forcing us to ask larger questions that almost certainly will arise in any deep psychedelic work. These questions concern the existence, nature, and providence of God; the reason for our birth; the nature of this reality; enlightenment; and how to contend with nonphysical realities and encounters with alien or spiritual or noncorporeal beings. The deeper mystical teachings of the religions from which these meditation or prayer practices emerge are well equipped to provide answers to these questions. We may thus find ourselves pursuing a deeper involvement in a particular religion.

Conversely, the typical psychotherapeutic endeavor is not as concerned with spiritual issues—though any good psychotherapist knows the limits of his or her skill and will make a timely and appropriate referral to a spiritual teacher when necessary. In the same manner, a competent spiritual teacher will recognize the need for a psychotherapy referral when mood, thought, or personality issues appear to be interfering with progress in a meditation or prayer practice.

INTERMEDIATE WORK

Once we have decided to take a psychedelic journey, we can start preparing in specific ways. To the extent possible, we can educate ourselves regarding what to expect on our trip. Having some sense of the expected terrain, as described by those who have gone before, can be quite helpful. In this way, if others have alerted us to what to expect, we may not be surprised when we encounter phenomena far beyond the range of what is familiar to us.

The literature regarding near-death and out-of-body experiences, meditation, abduction, shamanism, and of course, the taking of psychedelic drugs contains a wealth of information about others' experiences. It can provide us with helpful background information as well as practical means of dealing with those states. Also recommended is speaking with others who have gone before, listening to talks, and getting involved in online groups of the various communities that discuss highly altered states of consciousness—and not only those concerned with the effects of psychedelic drugs.

Some might object on the grounds that these educational activities may bias us toward particular expectations that can lead to certain specific types of experiences at the expense of others—yet these arguments are not especially persuasive. The truly psychedelic experience is totally unexpected. Nevertheless, knowing how unexpected it can be may help us to keep our bearings when confronted with it. We will be ready for the unexpected.

Discuss the impending trip with your therapist or spiritual teacher if you have one. However, it should not come as a surprise if the stigma attached to drug use causes spiritual teachers to discourage the taking of them. This may be the case even if he or she has personally beneficial experiences with psychedelics. Faced with disapproval from someone in whom we have placed great faith and who has previously been very helpful to us, we may need to shelve the topic of psychedelic use and continue our work with him or her without any continued interference caused by such a discussion. Or perhaps we may decide to seek instruction elsewhere, in a context in which we can discuss how psychedelic drug experiences may work together with therapy or meditation or prayer.

Those who are taking medication should make certain that there are no possible adverse interactions with these medications and the psychedelic drugs considered. For those who are taking medications for conditions that can also be managed by lifestyle changes such as exercise; weight loss; diet adjustments; and the cessation of the use of alcohol, tobacco, caffeine, and other drugs, try to follow through with these changes first to see if some of the medications may no longer be necessary. The point is to simplify body chemistry as much as possible. Though the reasons behind the desire to stop medications may remain private, the actual process of trying to discontinue them must be taken up with your health care provider.

Intent

Once we have decided we want to experience a psychedelic drug session, we must home in on our intent. As the Secret Chief asked, "To what purpose?" Why are we doing this, and what do we hope to accomplish or gain from such an experience? Is it primarily curiosity that drives us—are we intellectually and emotionally drawn to novelty, to something new, exotic, and exciting? Do we wish to experience pleasure of an extraordinary degree? Do we have an emotional, artistic, creative, professional, spiritual, or interpersonal problem we want to solve? Are we seeking a spiritual experience or answers to our deepest yearnings? Do we wish to know God—to see him or her face-to-face? Do we hope for an encounter with the angels of the powers through which God manifests? Are we interested in outer-space travel, science-fiction revelations, journeys through time, and encounters with alien civilizations and their inhabitants? Do we wish to obtain information and power for good or for ill? Do we want to make the world a better place—or do we intend to hurt those who have hurt us? Do we wish to suffer? Do we want to create a situation in which we replay abusive past or present relationships?

There are so many possible motivations to take a trip—and any of these may compete and blend with one another. We must be as honest as possible with ourselves when deciding what our intentions are, realizing that having a particular intention doesn't necessarily guarantee the content of the session. We don't always have the trip we want; instead, we seem to have the trip we need. If we tell ourselves that our motivation is, perhaps, to learn more about our relationships, but more honestly, we want to have a good time, we may be unpleasantly surprised when we're actually confronted by deeper, more painful psychological issues. Conversely, we may approach the experience with deep solemnity and expectations for a divine encounter and then be similarly unprepared for the fun, lighthearted aspects of our session. Thus, it is important to understand the full range and complementary nature of our motivations. Ideally, this is accomplished through the use of the introspective skills we have obtained during our own inner work, either spiritual or psychotherapeutic.

It is worth noting that developing an intention to undergo a spiritual, otherworldly, near-death transcendent type of experience is, in some ways, the same as making the decision to subvert the dominant Western postindustrial worldview. That is, the total loss of self-control and our usual self-identity and the wish to interact with and be guided by spiritual entities whose mercy we count upon fly in the face of a materialistic, individualistic, and fear-based relationship to existence. It also runs contrary to a solely clergy-mediated relationship to the divine. If and when we do have this type of experience, we must realize that the mainstream, using the tools of ridicule and psychopathologizing, among others, will oppose our discussing and valuing it.

SHORT-TERM WORK

How do we prepare ourselves in the day or two before the psychedelic journey? First, it is paramount that we understand our intentions. Then, by attending to certain concrete matters, we validate our intention to mark this experience as unique. The essence of making something holy or sacred is to separate or distinguish between the sacred and the profane. Though at the absolute level of reality, there are no such differences between what is sacred and what is profane, at the relative level, in which most of us exist most of the time, the two do differ. Thus, it is important to manifest our inner intent through our physical reality. We want to perceive as clearly as possible our psychedelic experience without the muddying effects of influences such as fatigue and an unsafe environment.

It's important to approach the trip in good health and with a positive state of mind and to be well rested and have a clean body and clean clothes. Participants should be careful with what they eat, drink, and smoke several days before the trip. Further, are there loose ends requiring attention? Are these minor tasks, such as taking out the garbage, making a necessary phone call, and paying an overdue bill, or are some more significant, such as updating a will? Though updating a will may appear morbid, consider the prospect that while undergoing a near-death experience, you may recall that you have no will! Would your emotional reactions to your sense of dying be different if you knew you had taken care of those you were leaving behind?

Before taking any psychedelics, it is recommended that you check in with those who are most important in your life. Are we on good terms with our partner, spouse, family, friends, and business associates? An extra prayer, meditation session, or psychotherapy appointment or two in the days before a trip can make clear some internal or external issues that might require special attention.

SETTING

Clearly perceiving our intent naturally leads us to decide upon the setting, the circumstances in which we will be taking the trip. Earlier, we discovered different categories of experiences resulting from psychedelic-drug ingestion. We can use these categories as a model for conceptualizing the types of trips available to us:

- A pleasurable trip that fulfills curiosity
- A problem-solving session that addresses psychotherapeutic issues we want to work on or creative, professional, or other concerns
- A spiritual, near-death experience or otherworldly journey

Also to be considered are the particulars of the trip. These include:

- Environment—outdoors or indoors
- The dose of the drug
- Whether we will journey alone or in a group
- Whether we will have a sitter
- Accoutrements for our trip such as music or art supplies
- Supplemental techniques for reaching altered states of consciousness

Finally, we must consider if the session will take place in a research setting. All types of trips can take place in a research environment; it is important, however, to note the constraints and opportunities unique to this type of setting—the most important of which concerns the issue of altruism, the notion of giving up something in our own trip for the benefit of others.

IS THE SETTING OUTDOORS OR INDOORS?

An outdoor setting of natural beauty can lead to profound levels of identification or merging with the natural world, yet being outdoors is also less predictable than being indoors. These unpredictable factors include insects, animals, inclement weather, unwelcome intrusions by other people, dirt of all kinds, and lack of facilities if participants fall ill or feel particularly helpless.

An outdoor setting in a city or suburb can provide a unique perspective on humanity, but it lends itself more to an externally oriented and at times potentially chaotic experience. Such a setting requires us to be prepared for exposure to a wide array of interpersonal and technical challenges. An indoor setting in an area of natural beauty can combine the best of both worlds: the safety and predictability of an indoor space and the option of going outside to experience nature.

DOSAGE, ROUTE OF ADMINISTRATION, AND COMBINING DRUGS

We can divide doses into low, intermediate, and high. Usually, the higher the dose of drug, the more intense and longer-lasting the effects. Yet there are many cases in which the same person experiences a marked effect from a small dose and seems less affected by a large dose at some other time. Instead of serving as examples of tolerance, in which repeated dosing decreases subsequent responses, or sensitization, in which low initial doses increase the effects of subsequent low doses, there seems to be some poorly understood interplay among dose, set, and setting that results in dose not being invariably related to intensity and duration of effect.

There is merit in beginning with a low dose of any substance that is new to us, whether that "substance" is a relationship, an exercise routine, or a psychedelic drug. As is true most of the time, however, the true nature of any particular relationship is rarely known without receiving a full dose. Thus at some point, for the truly adventurous explorer of these realms, sooner or later a high dose plays a role in his or her work with the substance and the realms into which it leads.

Another consideration is route of administration. There are various ways to administer a drug. Intravenous injection, smoking, and snorting are the fastest ways to experience effects. Slower onset occurs with routes such as intramuscular and subcutaneous (under the skin) injection. Slower yet are gastrointestinal methods, such as swallowing or rectal administration. Topical application to the skin or mucous membranes varies in speed, depending upon the integrity of the tissue—that is, effects occur more quickly from applying a drug to a wound or open sore than from applying it to intact, calloused skin. In addition, the "carrier" for the topically applied drug, the solvent into which it is dissolved, can make a big difference in the speed of absorption. For example, DMSO (dimethylsufoxide) is a solvent that allows for very rapid skin absorption of a drug, whereas cocoa butter is absorbed by the skin more slowly.

It's also best to choose one dose of one drug for a particular session and then stick to that decision. Participants may feel the need to take more of a substance if the effects are not as hoped for—what some refer to as taking a "booster" dose. While there are instances of this booster being an integral part of the experience—for example, in indigenous Ayahuasca sessions—it is advisable to exercise caution in this area. Particularly when alone, impaired judgment may lead to making ill-advised decisions and can lead to taking a dose that is too high. Remember, there is always the next time to take more.

Neither is it advisable to mix substances. Doing so blurs the effect of one or the other and may produce toxic interactions.

SOLO OR GROUP: THE ROLE OF STRUCTURE

In this instance, the term *structure* refers to behavioral parameters that we impose upon ourselves during a session. Such parameters are for our own safety and comfort as well as the optimization of the trip. Further, when we are in a group setting, establishing a structure is intended to respect others' feelings and needs. There are several options regarding how many people we decide to journey with: we may travel solo, with a small group of friends or strangers, or with a larger group of friends or strangers.

SOLO

Safety concerns suggest having a trusted individual or individuals in our space when we take psychedelics, but sometimes none is available. In addition, we may want to journey free from interpersonal interference; we may not want company. Nevertheless, it is relatively imprudent to embark solo on a first trip. Even after we've gained some familiarity with a particular drug, it's wise to let a confidant know of our plans and whereabouts when we take the drug again.

If we do take the journey alone, it is important to think through certain issues beforehand and to decide upon responses to which we can adhere. It's important to gain familiarity with these structural issues from those who are more experienced with taking a drug, and that we spend some time establishing reasonable and appropriate guidelines for our session. Though we might hope to commit these guidelines to memory, once the time comes, it is helpful to have them available in written form in case we are unable to recall them. In most cases, when we are under the influence, it is ill advised to change the structure we have set up before taking the drug. It is important to remember that we can always change the guidelines for our next session, when we have had some time to think about these issues after we've had the experience of one journey.

There are many structural issues to consider, especially if we are taking the drug alone. Will we be listening to music? If so, will we set up our playlist beforehand or decide what we will listen to when we are in an altered state of consciousness? Do we intend to keep our eyes open or closed? Would we like eyeshades? Will we remain clothed? How much of the session will we spend lying down versus sitting up and walking around? When and what do we eat? How will we make sure we drink enough fluids? Under what circumstances might we take more of a drug or smoke a cigarette or drink alcohol or coffee? After our trip, when can we drive or leave the immediate premises? What about answering the telephone or making calls? How do we get help if we need it? What do we do if things become unbearable—do we want to have tranquilizer on hand to chemically abort the trip?

GROUP

Whenever more than one person in the room is under the influence, we must take into consideration other people's set and setting issues; however, this may quickly ferment into a frothy brew of personalities and interactions. Therefore, in group settings—particularly in a new group—it is important to have additional elements of the structure decided and agreed upon in advance. One way to minimize stresses associated with a group session is for each person to have his or her solo trip. The use of eyeshades and well-spaced, single-sized mattresses or pads will help effect well-demarcated, individual experiences in a group setting. As drug effects wear off, interactions might then begin outside the main room in order not to distract those who want to continue with a more inner-directed experience.

Ye the purpose of a group setting, particularly with lower and intermediate doses, may be to engage in some group activity such as playing or listening to music, sharing an aesthetic experience, or problem solving. In cases such as these, we might spend most of our time exploring how the group process is affected by the influence of the psychedelic. Most important, however, is that these expectations and ground rules be discussed and agreed upon before a session begins.

There are other concerns in a group: How do we signal that we are in need (that is, do we raise our hand or speak)? How would we like to be supported? Is support verbal or physical? How are decisions made regarding our welfare or behavior? If some find the music, incense, or room temperature or lighting unpleasant, how will this be managed? In addition, will others in the group be sober or intoxicated? If intoxicated, will everyone in the group be taking the same drug? How will we know?

Whereas certain variables lend themselves to more or less flexible responses, some structural issues are best adhered to rather strictly. For example, intercourse or sexual interactions of any kind between participants during the session should be prohibited, as should physical, verbal, or emotional acting out of aggression. It is unwise to ask for or accept material favors such as money or property during the group session. Certainly, we may ask for and accept favors whose consequences do not extend beyond the session, such as a blanket if we are cold, a book for viewing, and the like. Asking for favors that require follow-through outside of the session, however, should wait until everyone is back to a normal state of consciousness. In addition, everyone must remain in the group until previously agreed-upon criteria have been met—for example, the group leader has determined that drug effects are adequately resolved and, if there is no leader, everyone must get a good night's sleep before leaving. Privacy and confidentiality are crucial in the success of any such group, and therefore, everyone must agree never to mention with whom they took a group trip without the express permission of the others involved.

One of the advantages of the group setting is the option of having a period of organized sharing after the session, usually the day after the experience. This can be quite helpful in terms of the crucial reentry and reintegration necessary for optimal use of the session.

THE SITTER

Along with the question of who else is in the room tripping with us, an important question concerns whether anyone is "sitting" for those under the influence. The sitter supervises a psychedelic session much like a babysitter supervises children—those who take psychedelics may need the same kind of steering, restraining, and nurturing. In addition, it derives from the similarity between sitting in meditation and supervising a psychedelic session. The sitter must combine the skill of allowing people under his or her care to go through whatever takes place in a psychedelic trip and the skill of remaining alert and focused on the needs of those who are journeying. This combination of alert passivity and passive activity is a hallmark of many meditation practices.

Whether we are tripping on our own or in a group without a designated sitter, ostensibly there is a greater sense of freedom to have the type of trip we want—yet, particularly with high-dose sessions, it may be easier to let go more completely if we feel someone is taking care of us. In addition, the relative anarchy that may reign in a group setting, especially if people are on high doses, can be difficult to orchestrate. One or more sitters can provide a much needed supervisory function in such a setting.

Some sitters may lead sessions more actively rather than simply responding to the needs of participants. Those trained in a shamanic model may play musical instruments, sing, whistle, dance, shout, manipulate bodies physically and energetically, and pour, run, or spit various liquids, smokes, and powders onto participants.

SET OF THE SITTER

Though there are many reasons to trip with a sitter, it is important to be extraordinarily careful regarding under whose supervision we place ourselves when we are taking psychedelics. Such consideration both makes the most of sessions and works to avoid problems. It's useful to note that participants will be deeply involved with this person at all stages of a trip—before, during, and after. The sitter is in a position of authority, leadership, and support, and those who will participate in a session are well advised to learn what they can about that person.

Some questions include: Is he or she religiously or spiritually oriented? Is he or she a member of any particular religion or profession? What is his or her training? What about sexual orientation? Is he or she married, or does he or she have children? Does a potential sitter drink alcohol or use drugs, and if so, does he or she use them excessively or in moderation? Is he or she vegetarian? What are his or her motivations for supervising sessions—money, a desire to heal, sadism, curiosity, altruism, voyeurism, career advancement? How does he or she relate to the power and reputation that a sitter may accrue? What is his or her experience with these compounds in terms of administration to others as well as regarding personal use? Is this someone of whom we can ask questions and with whom we can work out plans for various situations that might arise during our trip? Do we feel we can trust this person to give us guidance and support when we are unable to provide these for ourselves?

We strongly encourage asking prospective sitters any or all questions whose answers will affect participants' feelings of safety and encouragement during a session. Included in these questions is a discussion of issues regarding structure. In addition, because it is so difficult to obtain psychedelic drugs, the person who supervises a session may be the one from whom participants obtain the drug. This is usually the case in small-group and shamanic sessions, and is always true in the research environment.

IS THE SITTER EXPERIENCED?

Within the shamanic tradition, it is axiomatic that the leader is intimately and thoroughly familiar with all manner of drugs and plants that he or she will administer to others. This is also usually the case in the West with those who sit for underground users of psychedelics. Empathy—knowing what another is feeling—is quite important in any healing or spiritual work and is found most often when the healer has previously undergone a similar experience. Even if the setting is not intended to address healing or spiritual issues directly, these may nevertheless arise at any time, and the sitter should be capable of responding appropriately.

Within the academic setting in the United States, a sitter's personal use of the psychedelic in question is discouraged. This is one of the unfortunate results of the Harvard research group's widely publicized personal use of psychedelics in the 1960s. Yet Western European researchers are required to "go first" in any of their own psychedelic studies. There are several reasons for this: in order to make sure drugs and doses are safe, these scientists believe it is more ethical to first self-administer an experimental treatment, especially if there is no significant therapeutic benefit expected. By going first, they bear the brunt of any adverse effects. In addition, European regulatory authorities believe that the informed consent process is better served if the researchers are personally familiar with the effects of the drug. As a result of their own experience, they then are more able to inform a prospective volunteer fully regarding what to expect, and they can be more empathetic during the actual drug studies.

IS THE SITTER TRIPPING AT THE SAME TIME?

It's important to know if, at the time of a session, a sitter is under the influence of a psychedelic. It's also important to determine how participants will know whether or not the sitter takes a drug. Often, in shamanic or indigenous settings, the leader also partakes of a psychedelic substance, though perhaps at a lower dose than the participants in order to retain the ability to move around and interact. This empathetic resonance among those who are experiencing a particular drug effect helps the sitter provide an especially deep level of support and guidance. In Western models, however, this is an evolving area; some leaders ingest psychedelics, others do not.

In an academic setting, it is unlikely that the researcher will also use the same psychedelic substance during the study period. The extraordinarily rare possibility exists that a sitter under the influence of the same drug would also be the object of study. For example, a research project might ask whether a therapist is more or less helpful while affected by the same psychedelic used by participants. Whatever the case, answers to the question of the leader's use of the drug should be addressed ahead of time. There have been a number of situations in which group leaders have acted inappropriately while intoxicated, crossing important boundaries and later using as an excuse the effects of the drug.

ACCOUTREMENTS

Music can evoke profound effects in a highly psychedelicized individual. It usually is easier to arrange music beforehand, either by the solo tripper or, in the case of a group session, in consultation with the sitter if there is one. In a group setting, it is advisable to consider a "veto" rule regarding music: If anyone finds the music intolerable, it must be discontinued. Music with understandable lyrics can sometimes be distracting or can constrain the experiences. Instrumental music or world music with lyrics that are unintelligible may allow for more fluidity in reaction to it. Playing musical instruments in a solo setting may help a participant express nonverbal, nonvisual elements of a trip. In a group setting, however, participants must take into account the reactions of other group members.

Art supplies, particularly during the "coming down," resolution period of a trip, can aid in giving form, shape, and color to otherwise nonverbal aspects of the experience. Writing materials also may be helpful, and in solo settings, a voice-recording device can capture fleeting ideas. Some people find looking into a mirror while tripping to be particularly evocative, especially in a session with a primarily spiritual or psychotherapeutic focus. Similarly, reviewing family photos from the past and present can stimulate the release of many emotions and insights.

SUPPLEMENTAL TECHNIQUES

There are many nondrug-based methods available for altering consciousness. These may be helpful in refocusing attention for those who might feel adrift in the psychedelic space or who might be physically uncomfortable. Examples of these techniques include yoga, massage, and a quiet form of meditation. Other techniques may help participants break through a particular psychic impasse in a trip. These include controlled hyperventilation, singing, dancing, and exercise. It's a good idea to be familiar and comfortable with these ancillary techniques before trying them in a psychedelicized condition. It's also important that participants not expose themselves to stressful or traumatic interventions unless that is one of the purposes of the trip. For example, participants may wish to work through their resistance to a particular yoga posture that they normally find too difficult to attain.

TYPES OF TRIPS

Keep in mind that despite the type of trip we wish to have, and despite deciding upon the dose, where we are, who we are with, and the activities available to us, we may not have the kind of experience we wanted. For example, we may expect a relatively minor, pleasurable experience, but we may instead reach a near-death state. We must be ready for anything to occur during a trip, no matter how much effort we expend in preparation. Also, it is rare that any one trip consists of only one particular type. Psychedelic experiences are notoriously varied. We enter and exit many levels during any one session. Nevertheless, there are general types of sessions and advisable related parameters.

AESTHETIC, PLEASURE-ORIENTED TRIPS

These journeys may occur outside, in an environment of natural beauty, or they may occur in a setting of manmade beauty that features music, art, or archaeological relics. Ideally, participants will have access to both environments. If we are alone, we may take a walk in the woods, visit a museum, play or listen to music, or get a massage. For this type of trip occurring solely in an urban setting, it is best to take a low dose of psychedelic.

These types of trips lend themselves to group experiences. Examples of large group settings include contemporary "raves"—large-venue dance events—and events such as Burning Man, in the Nevada desert, where tens of thousands of people congregate. Also fitting this type of intention are smaller groups, such as several friends who "hang out" together and enjoy each other's company in a psychedelic state.

Usually, there are sessions without a sitter or leader. The spontaneity and freedom that we seek in such a setting, with doses generally being relatively low, do not require much supervision. It's a good idea, however, to make certain that noninebriated people are available who know of participants' condition and whereabouts.

PROBLEM-SOLVING SESSIONS

We may decide to use a psychedelic drug to help work on personal, professional, or creative concerns. Lower and intermediate doses provide more ease in maintaining focus on these issues and recalling our solutions when we return from our journey.

Enhancing creativity with psychedelics may occur outdoors or indoors, depending upon the particular task. An unobtrusive sitter can help record our new approaches to problems and can provide encouragement and focus. We may want help within the context of a psychotherapeutic process, using the effects of psychedelics to modify the processes by which psychological healing occurs—that is, projection, transference, abreaction, and catharsis. In psychotherapeutic sessions, it's usually helpful to have someone acting as a sitter. This may be our own therapist or someone whom we only work with in psychedelic sessions. In a psychotherapeutic group setting, some people may be in therapy with the sitter, while others may not.

Lower doses in the psychotherapeutic setting allow for a better focus than higher ones and provide the basis of *psycholytic psychotherapy*. High-dose sessions, referred to as *psychedelic psychotherapy*, add the qualitatively unique spiritual, mystical, or near-death states to the quantitative augmentation of normal psychotherapeutic processes. Religious and spiritual issues often become conscious and important in psychedelic psychotherapy.

If we are working on interpersonal issues, we and those with whom we want to work through these problems might be journeying together. We may choose to begin the session solo and later come together with other group members. Because of the sometimes intense dynamics that may arise even with low or medium doses, it is helpful to have a sitter in this type of session.

One model of psychedelic psychotherapy combines high doses of drug with overpowering, multimodal sensory stimulation in an indoor group setting. This particular technique is intended to cause a breakdown of psychological defenses not deemed possible by any one modality alone. Yet such experiences are difficult to negotiate and later to integrate.

It is usually easier to work on psychological issues in an indoor setting, although access to the natural world can provide a necessary balance for the intense inner work that engages participants.

SPIRITUAL, NEAR-DEATH, AND OTHERWORLDLY EXPERIENCES

These breakthrough experiences usually lend themselves to large-dose, introspective, solo settings. They also require the most in terms of our ability to let go and open ourselves to highly unusual effects. If we choose involvement in a group setting, the emphasis usually remains on an individual's experience, at least in the initial and middle stages of the trip.

It is easier for us to maintain an inward focus in an indoor setting. Nevertheless, nature can provide powerful catalysts for such experiences. If we decide to take this type of trip outdoors, we must do our best to ensure that participants are safe and free from unexpected disturbances.

If there is a sitter, he or she is unlikely to be a minister of any organized religion. Rather, those trained in the shamanic tradition are usually capable of containing and guiding these types of sessions. In the postindustrial West, sitters are often psychologically or spiritually trained individuals with their own psychedelic experience. Supplemental techniques such as controlled hyperventilation can be useful in providing the final impetus for the desired breakthrough.

As alluded to earlier, these types of experiences usually require us to be placed into uncomfortable inner spaces. The giving up of cherished self-concepts and identifications necessary to emerge anew into our reality is nearly always quite distressing at some pint—and once we have had this type of experience, there is little social support for discussing its merits within the larger social mainstream. Social and spiritual support to help integrate such deep experiences is necessary and must be part of the preparation for any planned breakthrough session.

VOLUNTEERING TO BE IN A RESEARCH STUDY

Any of these types of trips can be experienced within the research setting. Volunteering to be a research subject, however, even for a study that may provide benefit—such as psychotherapy, mysticism, or creativity research—involves the element of altruism, of giving up something in our own trip for the greater good. This altruism generates a unique dynamic between us and our setting, particularly to those in the room with us. When we volunteer for a research study, the trip is not all ours. We are being asked—and are expected—to provide data and information rather than just have an experience for our own sake. While this is neither intrinsically good nor bad, the informed-consent process must be open and transparent, and this altruism must be acknowledged at the outset. From the beginning, there exist competing interests between our trip and the data we are generating—and we will not be allowed to forget this give-and-take that's superimposed upon our trip. It's important that research subjects not be surprised by, rebel against, or resent the exigencies of providing data. For example, as we may be traversing the deepest reaches of inner space, our vein may clot, and the nurse will flush the intravenous line with jarringly cold water or he or she might need to remove the line and replace it with another.

Those who are neophytes to psychedelic states must consider these issues carefully. "Sharing" a trip in this way can be likened to having our first sexual experience observed, with data and specimens collected. We might be more generous with our time, body, mind, and soul after we've gained some experience and familiarity with such new and intense experiences. Nevertheless, it is possible to participate in a research setting during our first psychedelic experience and have it turn out better than one we undergo alone or with friends. Perhaps the setting takes into account our inexperience and is designed to determine those factors that contribute to the best outcome. Such research projects are rare, though, and regardless of their intent, they must still collect data.

Research settings are characterized by a relatively constrained physical environment. They are almost always indoors, range of movement is restricted, and there are few surprises. Generally speaking, accoutrements or supplemental consciousness-altering methods are few or unavailable. These constraints are intended to keep constant as many variables as possible while modifying only those of interest. For example, the researcher may vary the dose of drug in the exact same setting to determine the effects of dose on the measured variables such as heart rate and blood pressure. It is interesting to note that though the usual hospital research unit is not especially peaceful, there we may have a sense of medical security—for instance, knowing that a cardiac resuscitation team is nearby—that is otherwise absent. In these studies, we are usually the only one in the environment taking a psychedelic drug.

Once we have decided to participate in research, there are two general types from which to choose: biological and psychological. The emphasis in the former is on data regarding our bodies, and the emphasis in the latter is on data regarding our minds. Biological studies may include subjective effects in their purview. They are called *psychopharmacological*—that is, seeking the pharmacological underpinnings of subjective experiences. *Psychobiological* studies, or *psychophysiological* studies, attempt to explicate the physiology of the mind. For example, these may assess the effects of psychedelics on involuntary aspects of perception, such as how we respond to images presented to one or both eyes using various sequences and time intervals.

The tools used in biological research may include brain-imaging equipment, some of which may be noisy and tight fitting and may involve being injected with a radioactive drug. Participants may have blood drawn to quantify levels of any number of factors: hormones, immune function, and metabolism of the drug in question or other drugs. Body temperature may be monitored, as may cardiovascular responses such as blood pressure and heart rate using an automatic blood pressure cuff.

Psychological studies can be divided into roughly two different categories: *problem solving* and *phenomenological*. We have previously discussed some of the parameters involved in problem solving with psychedelics as well as the difference in psychotherapeutic work between lower-dose psycholytic and higher-dose psychedelic therapy. In the research setting, the goals are similar, but the structure is more rigorously adhered to.

Phenomenologically based psychological studies focus on the mental rather than biological effects of psychedelics—that is, perception of time, color, distance, and depth. Rather than assessing perceptual, information-processing mental functions, psychoanalytic studies may investigate more complex phenomena such as projection, transference, mood reactivity, and free association.

Finally, studies may investigate the efficacy of psychedelics in eliciting mystical, near-death, and otherworldly experiences. These are somewhat more difficult to categorize within a research setting because they deal with concepts that, for many, fall outside of the purview of traditional scientific inquiry. Nevertheless, they partake of the general research model, limiting variables as much as possible and providing data to the research team.

LETTING GO

Once we have completed as much preparatory work as possible before a session and clarified our intent—thus choosing our setting—we are ready to turn our attention to the actual trip.

On the day of the session, we should be well rested and clear-eyed, feeling ready for whatever may come our way. Though it's a good idea to have water or ice chips available during the session to address thirst and dehydration, a person should not plan on eating any food or drinking alcohol.

The fundamental task required for an optimal psychedelic experience is somewhat paradoxical: it consists of actively establishing the direction in which we decide to let go. We consciously choose the cliff from which we will jump and with what attitude we make that leap. This is especially the case in high-dose sessions during which we hope to encounter the most radical and unusual experiences.

Resistance to high-dose, powerful trips can be extraordinarily painful and confusing. An open-eyed, level-headed surrendering of resistance is the most effective way to prevent being thrown into this maelstrom and is the best method for pulling ourselves out of it if we do find ourselves overboard. Prayers, mantras, mudras, visualization, music, bodywork, and other aids may be helpful at various points in our trip to redirect the flow of experience. At the deepest, most exposed, raw, and vulnerable moments of the psychedelic encounter, however, it is only through letting go that we find ourselves making the most progress. From the five minutes of the DMT flash to the twelve hours of an ibogaine ordeal, this surrender is the crux of a successful journey.

The foundation laid by any previous inner work will hold us in good stead at such times by virtue of the attention skills we have developed. These skills make it easier to remain focused when confronted with the unexpected. In addition, effective psychotherapy or spiritual practice will have made us familiar with the skeletons in our closets and will have better equipped us to contend with them if and when they emerge. Thus, not only do we clearly perceive what is garnering our attention, but also we subsequently open up and drop our resistances to it. We will know when we are resisting and when we are moving forward at any given moment of the psychedelic experience.

Yet it is not only in negative aspects of a trip that we may become blocked. We also might be unable to move out of pleasant or neutral states. For example, we might find ourselves deeply blissful but also sense that we can go even deeper into what lies beneath and supports that bliss. Seemingly innocuous images or feelings, such as the curtain of psychedelic lights that is often a hallmark of the drug experience, may stand in our way. We want to see even more, but we cannot take the next step.

All these states can be managed to facilitate our moving forward; we can slow down, right ourselves, and then go on. We regain our balance through the proper application of attention and awareness. This is the slowing down, which we can facilitate physically through relaxed, deep breathing and helps release any tension in our bodies. Once we've slowed ourselves down and replanted our psychic feet, it is easier to move our consciousness through the resistance or block. Sometimes, however, we may not feel we have a body to relax or lungs through which to breathe. At these times, it may be useful simply to bring our minds back to what is happening and to approach it in a positive, bright, and curious manner. For example, in my DMT work, I prepared volunteers by warning them that they might find themselves convinced that they had died. They could react in one of two ways: "Oh, my God, I'm dying—get me out of here!" or "I seem to have died. Very interesting. What's next?"

This approach creates the smallest space between being aware of an object (such as an emotion, thought, or perception) and having a relationship with it—in other words, just before we establish a relationship with it. The leverage exists in that microsecond gap; we become aware of the stuck or static nature of the relationship. Then, taking a psychic deep breath, we can pull back from it ever so slightly, enough to work ourselves through or out of the block. For example, with respect to the curtain of psychedelic lights, we can look for space or cracks within it and then pass through it.

ENCOUNTERING BEINGS

One of the most profound aspects of a psychedelic session is contact with alien or noncorporeal, spiritual, or invisible beings or entities. Upon experiencing such an encounter, the first task we must pursue is to regain our composure from the shock of meeting what appear to be sentient creatures in our newly discovered worlds—creatures that, in many instances, seem to have been waiting for us. Next, we are faced with how to relate to them.

Some beings appear to be kind, gentle, and concerned for our welfare. Others seem to be aggressive, angry, and hurtful. Some present in an ambiguous or mischievous manner. They may communicate more or less effectively, or they may ignore us altogether. While their sheer novelty and unexpectedness make us feel a sense of awe, it may be best, whenever possible, to appraise them with the same objectivity with which we would judge any chance encounter with strangers. At the time of such encounters, we don't know these beings' language or culture, nor do we know their intent. As with all elements of the psychedelic experience, it's important not to become obsessed with them or our reaction to them. Once we establish a modicum of stability in our interactions with them and have decided they are "safe," we can engage them in any number of ways—we can seek their help, advice, love, and healing. Keep in mind, however, the flux of the psychedelic experience, and do not be surprised if these beings morph readily into the opposite of everything that we had considered them the moment before.

Entities with fangs, poisonous-looking appendages, and other clearly menacing features usually are not benign, and it is best to be very wary of them. We can listen to what they have to say, but we ought not to be in any hurry to follow their advice. On the other hand, strange or frightening entities that seem to understand our fears may be more beneficent, particularly if they modify their behavior or appearance in response to our anxiety. Even if their appearance and behavior repel us, more benign entities usually do not force us to do or accept things or become angry with us if we do not agree to their requests. In addition, we should never make any contract with the beings for doing evil or harm to another person or thing.

THE BAD TRIP

Though we can try to ensure that we have a smooth session, it is the norm to have difficult, painful periods in at least part of any major psychedelic experience. These can range from transient anxiety to prolonged psychosis. More than 99 percent of the time in someone medically and psychologically healthy, properly screened, prepared, and supervised, such distressing moments are short-lived and leave little if any aftermath. Nevertheless, being prepared for difficult stretches in a session can help us manage them more easily.

Anxiety and fear are relatively common as we begin to enter into the psychedelic state—when we are "coming on" to the drug effect. Simply relaxing physically and mentally—for example, slowing and calming our breathing—is often sufficient to dispel these jitters. If we are with a sitter or in a supportive group, we may ask to have someone lay a hand upon us in a nonerotic manner or to hold our hand. Sometimes placing a blanket over the body or removing uncomfortably heavy clothes or coverings can also help by allowing us to reconnect with our bodies. Once we are in the midst of the experience, we can deal with unpleasant periods in a variety of ways. The simple breathing or physical contact suggestions outlined here can be helpful in refocusing us on the flowing, dynamic nature of the experience and can get us out of a rut. More intense or prolonged confusion, anxiety, fear, anger, or grief may require more active intervention, either on our behalf or on the behalf of those with us—that is, the sitter or group members.

Quieting the environment—turning off the music, turning down the lights, lying down—can be helpful. Such maneuvers allow us to pay attention to what is important: our inner state. Soothing interventions may be necessary, however. A warm or cool compress on the forehead; mild, nonintrusive, and nonsexual massage; and quiet, melodious humming or singing can help replace the more tumultuous inner workings of our minds with quieter thoughts and visions.

For more intense disturbances, there is a range of options: Someone may perhaps have to hug us or even lie on top of us to help us to ground ourselves. A cold shower, ice cubes down the back of our shirt, and other firmly yet gently administered strategies can help break any vicious cycles in which we find ourselves. Controlled hyperventilation can also help push us through any particularly tenacious disturbing states.

Finally, there is the option of using medication to interrupt an especially out-of-control situation—but such instances are extraordinarily rare. For many of us, however, it can be quite reassuring to know that a medication is available to pull us out of almost any negative spiral if we are unable to do so ourselves. Usually, a benzodiazepine such as alprazolam or lorazepam is sufficient, but the sedating side effects of these interventions—which can last for hours—must be taken into account. Antipsychotic medications are a last resort and come with their own host of unpleasant side effects.

COMING DOWN AND REINTEGRATING

After a trip, we must be kind to ourselves. It's best to allow for one or two days between a session and resumption of normal, everyday activities. It's also important to rest, eat healthy food, drink plenty of liquids, and get several nights of good sleep. Rest. Most of all, we must consider what we just experienced. After a session, we should write, draw, or record in some way the images, feelings, ideas, body sensations, and perceptions we contacted. We should share and process our experience with others whom we trust: we may share with someone who either did or did not join us for our trip; with our sitter; or with a shaman, minister, or therapist. We must review the aspects of the trip that continue to draw our attention.

GETTING HELP

While most people can integrate even major psychedelic drug experiences relatively well, some sessions—especially our first ones—may be traumatic. Generally, by the time the session is winding down, a well-integrated experience resolves itself into a sense of happy satisfaction with our session. Intense, unshakable, powerful emotions such as sadness, anxiety, fear, or anger may foretell unpleasant postsession feelings.

Intense or prolonged negative aftereffects may occur, and these can range from anxiety and depression to psychosis. Added to these potential negative outcomes are the stigma associated with psychedelic drugs and their illegality. These factors make seeking help more problematic. Nevertheless, when we feel we need help, we must search for it. If we have taken our trip with others of if we were supervised by a sitter, it is best to start with them when asking for appropriate referrals for follow-up. Such after-session follow-up may range from an hour or two decompressing with a knowledgeable friend to psychiatric hospitalization. In between these two extremes is the common feeling that we have confronted issues we are not psychologically or spiritually mature enough to integrate. We may recognize that a course of inner work must now ensue in order to use the session optimally and in a healthy way.

INTEGRATION

Even after relatively trauma-free sessions, we are faced with a daunting task: What do we do with all this information? It may be a case of "Now for the hard part . . ." We may ask ourselves if we will trip again, and we may wonder why or how we will if we choose to try another session. Perhaps most important, we may ask ourselves if we plan to change anything about our lives: our career, relationships, diet, drug use, or religious views or practices. Finally, we may ask whether we have begun a new phase of inner or outer work.

It may take awhile for a big trip to fully exert its effects—we need space and time for the ripples to reach the shore. We may have to live many years to fully digest and manifest the results of a big journey. It's important to be patient with ourselves and not to become frustrated that more has not changed in our lives as a result of what appeared, at the outset, to be a life-changing experience. More drug trips may not be the answer; perhaps what's necessary is a sober, concerted application in our everyday life of what we experienced.

Though we should not push ourselves, we also do ourselves a disservice by allowing a trip to be forgotten, filed away in some dusty recesses of our minds as just one more interesting experience. We must remember that in a psychedelic trip, we've been given a tremendous gift, one that very few people ever have the opportunity to receive and experience.

THE DIVINE SPARK

EXPERIENCING PSYCHEDELICS

AYAHUASCA AND THE CONCEPT OF REALITY: ETHNOGRAPHIC, THEORETICAL, AND EXPERIENTIAL CONSIDERATIONS[1]

BY LUIS EDUARDO LUNA, PH.D., F.L.S

Wasiwaska, Research Center for the Study of Psychointegrator Plants, Visionary Art and Consciousness. Florianópolis, Brazil. www.wasiwaska.org.

INTRODUCTION

Ayahuasca, a psychotropic preparation created by Upper Amazonian people since time immemorial, has been the subject of an increasing number of scientific and popular publications. Today, thousands of people from many countries and walks of life have had experience with it. Ayahuasca is the Quechua name, widely used in Peru, Ecuador, and Bolivia, and to a lesser extent in Brazil, where it has been adopted by religious organizations that refer to the beverage either as *Santo Daime* or *vegetal*. It is prepared by brewing the stem of *Banisteriopsis caapi*, a vine of the Malpighiaceae family, and the leaves of *Psychotria viridis*, in the Rubiaceae, locally known as *chacruna* or *chacrona*. In Colombia as well as areas of the Ecuadorean Amazon, *Diplopterys cabrerana*, a vine belonging also to the Malpighiaceae locally known as *chagropanga*, is added to *B. caapi* to prepare a beverage (as a cold infusion or as a brew) called *yajé* (also spelled *yagé*). Some indigenous groups make a drink of only *B. caapi*. This plant contains two main alkaloids, harmine and tetrahydroharmine (some contain traces of harmaline), while both *P. viridis* and *D. cabrerana* contain the powerful visionary alkaloid dimethyltryptamine (DMT), which is not orally active when ingested alone due to oxidation by the enzyme MAO (monoamine oxidase) in the liver and gut wall. In the presence of harmine, an MAO inhibitor, DMT crosses the brain-blood barrier and attaches to 2A and 1A serotonin receptors in the central nervous system, causing dramatic perceptual, cognitive, and mood changes.

Ayahuasca (as well as yajé) is thus the creation of Upper Amazonian indigenous groups, also famous for their discovery of the properties of other plants, such as those involved in the preparation of curare, a powerful muscle relaxant, and various species of rubber essential to the automobile revolution until the introduction of synthetic rubber in the 1930s. In addition, Amazonian indigenous groups brought about the domestication of

165

numerous plants, such as tobacco and many species of palms. The Amazon area is gradually being recognized as having been a center of high culture previous to the European invasion that brought unimaginable destruction to the whole continent. Within 150 years of the invasion, around 95 percent of the continent's population had disappeared, mostly due to contagious diseases for which the people had no natural defenses (see for example Mann 2005).

Ayahuasca (and yajé) is used within a shamanistic complex by numerous indigenous groups of the Upper Amazon with various purposes, such as divination, diagnosing illnesses, transformation into animals, or more generally to get in touch with normally unseen realms subjacent to ordinary reality, including visits to the primordial time where humans and animals acquired their present shapes. The concept of reality among indigenous groups suggests a many-worlds interpretation of the real. Ayahuasca and other sacred plants facilitate access to these other realities. Its importance is reflected in the myths of origin. Gerardo Reichel-Dolmatoff, who worked among Tukanoan indigenous groups of Colombia (also living on the Brazilian side of the border) collected a myth that I present here in a highly condensed form (Reichel-Dolmatoff 1975:134-136):

The Sun Father is the Master of Yajé. He impregnated a woman who looked at Him through the eye. She gave birth to the Yajé vine in the form of a radiant child. When she entered the *maloca*, or communal house, she asked, "Who is the father of this child?" One after the other, several men, the ancestors of the Tukano, said "I am his father," the first cutting his umbilical cord, others grabbing him by his fingers, his arms and legs, tearing him into pieces, each getting his own kinds of yajé. With it, they also got the rules by which to live and other things with which to reciprocate: conversations, songs, food, and also evil things. They found their place, their way of life.

Among the Cashinahua and other Pano indigenous groups of Peru and Brazil (who call Ayahuasca *nixi pae*), the origin of the vine is in the sub-aquatic realm. According to Lagrou (2000:33) the ancestor named Yube enters the water world of his spiritual kin, the snakes, to marry the beautifully painted snake woman whose vision had seduced him. He is initiated into taking Ayahuasca, but he fails to resist the fear induced by the visions. He cries out, offending his snake kin, owners of the brew, and escapes, only to be found and wounded by his angry kin a year later. Before he dies, he transmits to his people his knowledge of the brew's preparation and its song.

In other groups, the plants from which the beverage is prepared came from the bones, flesh, or blood of mythical beings. Numerous Amazonian indigenous groups consider *B. caapi*, together with tobacco and coca, as highly sacred, one of the greatest gifts to humanity.

Since at least the beginning of the 20th century, Ayahuasca has been adopted by segments of the mestizo population of Peru, Colombia, and Ecuador. In Peru Ayahuasca, along with other plants that are often psychotropic, is considered a *doctor*, a *plant-teacher* (Luna 1984, 1986). A new phenomenon took place in the states of Acre and Rondonia, in the Brazilian Amazon. Religious leaders originally from the mostly Afro-Brazilian Northeast created religious organizations, a mixture of popular Catholicism, in some cases Afro-Brazilian ideas, European esotericism, native Amazonian beliefs, and the use of Ayahuasca as a sacrament. There has been a rapid expansion of these religious organizations in urban centers of the whole country, and later with offshoots in other Latin American countries, Europe (mostly Holland and Spain), the United States, and Japan.

Consequently, in the last fifteen to twenty years, thousands of people have had access to the Ayahuasca experience, either by traveling to Amazonian countries, mostly Peru, or by joining the rituals of Brazilian religious organizations, or through practitioners from various backgrounds that offer Ayahuasca sessions in many countries. Significant religious syncretism has occurred since its use depends on cultural setting. A variety of therapeutic methods have also been incorporated within or around the ritual setting. Experiences are often extremely powerful, featuring contact with entities, animal or plant spirits, and journeys to other realms. In Westerners the Ayahuasca ingestion often elicits discussions of a philosophical nature, as people try to somehow make sense of their experiences. Many claim that Ayahuasca has been a veritable teacher to them, and it is not uncommon that Ayahuasca is considered as an intelligent being, a mother, grandmother, or grandfather. Such ideas are similar to those found among Amazonian indigenous groups.

It is my intention to present here some reflections on the Ayahuasca experience based on fieldwork I carried out among some indigenous groups in Colombia and Peru, Peruvian mestizo practitioners, members of Brazilian religious organizations as well as among contemporary Westerners from a number of countries. I will also draw materials from my contact with other researchers and my own investigations throughout the years with Ayahuasca.

THE ROLE OF AYAHUASCA AMONG INDIGENOUS GROUPS

The Amazon area is not only biologically but also culturally diverse. There are cultural differences between the various indigenous groups of the Upper Amazon in terms of social structure and habitats. There is, for example, a contrast between humans living in nutrient-rich vàrzea forests versus those living in relatively unproductive terra firma forests. There are also commonalities, such as the institution of shamanism and what has been called animism, the belief that nature, including rock and winds, rivers and thunder, is animated and intelligent, and that it is possible to establish a rapport with it. Another common belief is that human beings possess various souls, some of which transcend the dissolution of the body and may interact with the living. Certain plants, if taken under certain conditions, facilitate access to normally occult knowledge through altered states of consciousness. These are sacred plants such as tobacco (especially strong varieties of *Nicotiana rustica*), coca (there are 403 described species of *Erythroxylum*), *Anadenanthera peregrina* (locally known as *yopo, paricá, cohoba,* and many other vernacular names), *Virola* species, of which potent psychotropic snuffs are made, and of course the plants involved in the preparation of yajé and Ayahuasca.

Ayahuasca plays an important role in many Upper Amazon societies. Jean Langdon (2000:21), who worked among the Siona of Colombia, points out the centrality of yajé and its rituals for their notion of well-being and health as well as for their acquisition of knowledge about the occult reality. In Siona society, most narratives can be characterized as shamanic in the sense that they deal with shamans and/or with experiences in the occult world when dreaming or taking yajé. The Siona universe is characterized by two superimposed realities: "this side," everyday reality; and "the other side." It is composed of five disks arranged hierarchically beginning with the level under the earth and extending up to the end of the heavens, all populated by entities. Each domain has specific sounds, rhythms, music, smells, and colors that can be visited, although these are full of dangers, and the inexperienced can be trapped in the evil spirit domain.

Els Lagrou (2000:32) reports that among the Cashinahua of Northwest Brazil and Eastern Peru, "Ayahuasca is a means of transport and transformation, a means of reconnecting with invisible layers of the cosmos, as well as a way of making present the world and stories told in myth through imaginary experience." Osmani, one of her informants, told her, "You have to remember a myth before you drink the brew. If you concentrate well on the story, the story and its beings will appear to you in vision and you will understand the meaning this story has for your own life and experiences. You will feel the story. You will live it." (*Ibid.* p. 33).

This last report is similar to observations made earlier by Gerardo Reichel-Dolmatoff among the Tukano:

Taking yajé is called *gahpí irí-inyári* (from *iri*/to drink, *inyári*/to see), and is interpreted as a return to the cosmic uterus, to the 'mine,' to the source of all things. It has the objective of reaffirming religious faith, through the personal experience of seeing with one's own eyes the origin of the Universe and of mankind, together with all supernatural beings. On awakening from the trance, the individual remains convinced of the truth of the religious teachings." (Reichel-Dolmatoff 1971:174).

This idea is related to that of transformation into an animal, a common shamanistic motive in the Amazon area (as well as in traditional societies all over the world). The shaman is thought to transform into a predator of one of the three realms (earth, water, and sky)—jaguar, anaconda, harpy eagle—or into other animals, in order to perform certain tasks or to experience the world through them, a transformation of identity the Cashinahua referred to as a "change of skin," a symbolic death (Lagrou 2000:31). This is a radical epistemological possibility difficult to imagine without direct experience. If true, it would mean alternative consciousness and transpersonal perception of whatever is out there, of the "real."

Contemporary members of Brazilian religious organizations that use Ayahuasca as a sacrament exhibit similar ideas. Among members of the UDV (União do Vegetal), one of these organizations, the central doctrine is embedded in certain *histórias,* stories or myths, which are recited (not written down) during rituals, the memorization of which would determine the advancement in the organizational hierarchy. I participated in some rituals, hearing several times the main central myth, the *História da Oaska,* which in fact is a variation of a myth of origin found among indigenous groups and among mestizo practitioners by which the origin of the two plants involved in the preparation comes from the bones and blood (or simply from the grave) of human beings. I was struck at how vividly the story unfolds in the mind while under the effect of the brew, how easily it would be to believe the myth to be true. Ayahuasca may in fact reinforce any religious beliefs, hence its potential for being adopted by other religious organizations and as a facilitator of syncretism.

Mestizo shamanism in Peru is the result of the syncretism of popular Catholicism, Amazonian, and Andean ideas (as well as some European esoteric elements). Furuya (1994) has pointed out the gradual *umbandization* (from *umbanda,* an Afro-Brazilian religion) of CEFLURIS, the largest of the Brazilian religious organizations that use Ayahuasca under the name Santo Daime. Afro-Brazilian ideas are even more evident among members of Barquinha, an organization I studied carefully (Luna 1995). They have the concept of "incorporation," different from "possession" in that the person remains conscious of his normal self. Members are believed to be able to incorporate four types of spirits: *pretos velhos* (old and wise black slaves), *caboclos* (the spirits of Indians), *erés* (the spirits of children), and *encantados* (princes or princesses "enchanted" or transformed into certain animals). This is close to the Amazonian idea of transformation. Once while harvesting the vine in the forest with a group from Barquinha, one of the men told me the story about one of the members that once was gripped by extreme anxiety while harvesting the vine up to about twenty meters above the ground. He solved the problem by "incorporating" the spirit of a preto velho, a black slave, and descended easily to the ground. This suggests that accessing such states of consciousness may have had an evolutionary advantage.

SUPERNATURAL ENTITIES

Shamanism, which implies altered states of consciousness and the activation of what seems as common archetypes beyond ethnic and cultural differences, may have had a role, as Winkelman suggests, (2010) in the emergence of modern humans. This may have its roots back in ancient primate ritual heritage from our evolutionary past. Winkelman attempts "to understand the original manifestation of shamanism and the diversity of manifestations of shamanistic phenomena produced by social influences on our innate potential for ritual, alterations of consciousness, and endogenous healing responses."

Contact with supernatural entities of some sort is documented since Upper Paleolithic time, the so-called therianthropes, part human and part animals, found in rock art of all continents (Hancock 2003:69–93). Lewis-Williams (2005:10) explores the possibility that people from that period "harnessed what we call altered states of consciousness to fashion their society and that they used imagery as a means of establishing and defining social relationships." The same author summarizes thus one of the chapters in his extraordinary research on Upper Paleolithic Art:

> Most researchers have consistently ignored the full complexity of human consciousness and have concentrated on only one slice of it and made that slice the defining characteristic of what it is to be an anatomically and cognitively fully modern human being. Here I examine interaction of mental activity and social context: how, I ask, do notions about human experience that are shared by a community impinge on the mental activity of individuals and how does socially controlled

access to certain mental states become a foundation for social discrimination?

When I was doing fieldwork among the mestizo riverine population of the Peruvian Amazon, I marveled at what seems to me complete sincerity when, for example, a fisherman described the mermaids he saw once in the river, or when another man vividly told me of the apparition at night of a frightening huge water snake, the *Yakumama*. Mermaids, dolphins turning into human beings in order to seduce, bird spirits announcing a death in the family—all are to be expected given the shared notions about human experience of that society. Actual apparitions are usually extraordinary events, often connected with altered states of consciousness, the same way that UFO apparitions often are (see Vallee 1969, Hancock 2005). Culture has been, no doubt, a powerful influence in the way we perceive the world and ourselves. It is well-known that anthropologists sometimes are afflicted by the so-called ethno-specific illnesses of the human groups they study.

At the same time this would also explain why Westerners (except children) seldom see fairies. They are said to live in the forests. Most Westerners live in cities, far from nature, and their notions of reality would usually preclude this kind of belief beyond a certain age. I read fairy tales to my mother when she was in her deathbed, and I know of psychologists who read those stories to very old people. The results are often simply extraordinary, as if in this way we connect with something deep inside us with which we were in touch as children.

NEW INFORMATION

There is no doubt that experiences with Ayahuasca and other psychointegrator (a term coined by Michael Winkelman) plants and substances bring forth not only ecstatic but also sometimes terrifying emotions. Information may also come from long-forgotten or repressed memories. New information may come from such channels as de-familiarization, when everything is seen as new, most eloquently expressed by Huxley (1954) in his experiments with mescaline: "I was seeing what Adam had seen on the morning of his creation—the miracle, moment by moment, of naked existence." This is something I have often experienced, "discovering" new qualities in what was familiar, objects, plants, or human beings. When anthropologists have gone to the field, their first notes are invaluable, as they record what they have seen as new in the societies and the environment is portrayed as seen with greater clarity. As time goes by, what was strange becomes familiar, and therefore becomes practically invisible. To have the chance of seeing all, in the cosmic sense, once more like "in the beginning" (in mythical times) is a precious gift.

When asked about the origin of their body painting, their art, or other products of their culture, indigenous Amazonian groups often refer to sacred plants. "We see this in the visions." "These are songs we learn from the plant spirits." "Ayahuasca taught us the right way of living." Michael E. Brown reports that among the Aguaruna of the Alto Río Mayo in Peru:

"Men continue to recognize the important role that the visions obtained in their youth had in promoting their moral education and physical well-being, and in helping them make the transition to the responsibilities of adult life" (Brown 1985:59).

According to Lagrou (2000:31) "The cosmic snake Yube has mastered all possible appearances of form, color and design that can be perceived by human eyes. All the phenomena of this world are said to be inscribed in the designs of its skin and can be visualized through the (metaphoric) ingestion of his blood (*nawa himi*) or his urine (*dunuc isun*), which are the names of Ayahuasca in ritual songs."

Among members of the Brazilian religious organizations, the songs sang during the rituals are called hymns by those organizations that refer to the sacrament as Santo Daime, or *chamadas* by members of the UDV (União do Vegetal). These songs are said to have been "received" from the astral plane, not composed by the founders or their disciples.

ALTERED STATES OF CONSCIOUSNESS

Consciousness in general was until recently almost a taboo in academic circles. Roger Penrose (1994:8) states, "A scientific world-view which does not profoundly come to terms with the problem of conscious minds can have no serious pretensions of completeness. Consciousness is part of our universe, so any physical theory which makes no proper place for it falls fundamentally short of providing a genuine description of the world." Western rational thinking, as pointed out by Frecska (2005), continues to marginalize—and even pathologize—ASCs (altered states of consciousness), considered deviant states. It is unable to differentiate between disintegrative and integrative forms, and cultivates only the basic state of consciousness. It is unfortunate that the theme of ASCs is still anathema in most learning centers, even more so in therapeutic practice.

In a much-quoted paragraph, William James (1929:378-9) affirms:

Our normal waking consciousness, rational consciousness as we call it, is but one special type of consciousness, whilst all about it, parted from it by the filmiest of screens, there lie potential form of consciousness entirely different. We may go through life without suspecting their existence; but apply the requisite stimulus and at a touch they are there in all their completeness, definite types of mentality that probably somewhere have their field of application and adaptation. *No account of the universe in its totality can be final which leaves these other forms of consciousness quite disregarded.* [italics mine].

The belief in spirits is nearly universal across ages. Shall we just dismiss, in the name of advanced rational thinking, the existence of other intelligent realms right here under our noses, only were we able to attune ourselves to these other realities? Roberts (2006) proposes the idea that our minds function in many mindbody states. Consequently, he rejects what he calls the "single state fallacy": the erroneous assumption that all worthwhile thinking, behaving, and emotions occur only in our ordinary, awake mindbody state. Could it be, then, that there are mental state-bound realities, only manifested under appropriate circumstances? Traditional societies usually consider the cosmos as multilayered, normally depicted by anthropologists as worlds above and below a middle plane representing this reality. Could it also be conceived as multidimensional from within, depending on the state of consciousness? Is not this perhaps the reason why ideas, events, and imagery during our dreams (as well as often in the hypnagogic state previous to falling asleep) lose all their meaning immediately after waking, even though apparently our other self, the one in the dream, found no contradiction? Dreams and visions are equated in many cultures. Perhaps visions are a form of conscious dreams. According to Winkelman (2010), the physiological properties of ASC indicate that the visionary experiences are produced by the information capacities of the lower brain systems, and tap in to the dream capacity, an ancient mammalian adaptation for integrating information in the pre-language symbolic capacity represented in the visual system.

Neurons alone aren't sufficiently complex to explain all brain phenomena and provide a computational model for thought. Roger Penrose and Stuart Hameroff (Penrose 1996) propose that consciousness emerges from biophysical processes acting at the subcellular level involving cytoskeletal structures. Consciousness is attributed to quantum computation in cytoskeletal proteins organized into a network of microtubules within the brain's neurons. Ede Frecska (2005) proposes the existence of a dual foundation of knowledge. The first one would be the ordinary, perceptual-cognitive-symbolic,whichisneuroaxonallybased,iselectrochemical(basedonlocaleffects), and relies on sensory perception, cognitive processing, and symbolic (visual, verbal, logical) language. It performs modeling, with an implicit split subject-object: it peaks in Western scientific thinking. The second one is the direct-intuitive-nonlocal, its medium being a subneural network, such as the micro-tubular network, which connects the whole body, from head to toe, and based on nonlocal correlations, so small (measured in nanometers) that they are close to quantum physical measures. The cytoskeletal matrix, with 10 million more units than neurons may be immense enough to contain holographic information about the whole universe via nonlocal interaction. It may mediate direct, ineffable experiences without subject-object split. It is perhaps the realm from where shamans and mystics, the masters of nonlocality, after rigorous training and symbolic death, get their information and powers when in altered states of consciousness. This direct-intuitive-nonlocal knowledge is perhaps "The Forgotten Knowledge" in Western civilization, deemed non-existent by academic Western science.

MIND AND MATTER

Among some indigenous groups of the Amazon, there is the idea that people take Ayahuasca not "to see the future" but "to create the future." Brown (1985:60), who worked among the Aguaruna of Peru, writes: "The future exists as a set of possibilities that are given shape by the effort to bring them into consciousness within the visionary experience." Rafael Karsten, who worked among the Shuar of Ecuador, writes that in the victory feast, celebrating the acquisition by a warrior of a new *arutam* spirit by slaying an enemy, both men and women, even half-grown children, take part: all "who want to dream" being allowed to drink *natéma* (Ayahuasca). The drinking has a ceremonial character throughout. During the victory feast celebration, half a litre of natéma was drunk by each person three times followed by vomiting. The participants did not eat or drink before the ceremony nor after they had slept and dreamed. After the ceremony the dreamers left the house and remained in shelters in the forest, where they slept until the afternoon. After they woke up, they took a bath in the river and returned to the house where they told the older Indians what kind of dreams and visions they'd had. The object of the drinking of natéma at the victory feast was to dream of the house of the slayer and his closest relatives:

> Surrounded by large and flourishing plantations of manioc and
> bananas, they see his domestic animals, his swine and his hens, numer-

ous and fat, etc. At the same time the persons who have drunk the sacred drink will be purified from impure and disease-bringing matter, and gain strength and ability in their respective work and occupations. (Karsten 1935:345).

Fericgla (2000), who worked much later among the Shuar, reports that when they take Ayahuasca and have visions referring to their lives, this is because what they see is either happening to them, or is about to happen. If they see something negative to happen in the future, they take the brew again and try to correct it. If they are not able to do so, and they again see the same thing, they look for a shaman stronger than them in order to be able to change what would happen. In other words, they have the belief that the visions influence reality.

I have witnessed extraordinary synchronicities in this respect happening to contemporary Westerners. It is as if having a vision had enough power for the universe to conspire toward its completion. Perhaps mind and matter are two apparently contradictory manifestations—like the wave and particle properties of light—of an underlying ultimate reality. Perhaps consciousness is an essential part of reality. It is urgent to have a deep understanding of this paradigm in a world of increasing environmental degradation, alienation from the natural world, and consequently our proneness to violence and/or depression. Whatever may reconnect us with our past, with nature, and with our inner self is of vital importance for our own survival.

Shamanism is ultimately about healing in the highest sense, a reintegration of all levels of existence. Ede Frecska (2008:146-8) suggests an extension of the biopsychosocial paradigm in contemporary medicine proposed by George Engel (1997), including also the spiritual dimension: therapy *sui generis* is reintegration *in toto* on biological, mental, social, and spiritual levels; the identification with higher realms of reality, with the psyche, with the community, and at the end with an entity above community (i.e., environment, nature, Universe, Mother Earth, etc., depending on culturally determined worldviews). A process contrary to what has happened to modern humanity who lost first the connection with any kind of supernatural world, then got alienated from nature and from his/her community, including the extended family, being then reduced to an often depressed individual devoid of their dreams and creativity. A concept of reality restricted to the measurable material world is certainly impoverishing.

BY WAY OF CONCLUSION

It is not at all strange that plants with the properties of altering the mind have been considered sacred by traditional cultures. It is now forty years since my first encounter with such a powerful medicine. I have witnessed and participated in hundreds of sessions in different settings, and I have been in touch in one way or another with most of the people who have been doing research on the subject. The most important questions have not been answered. What is the nature of the worlds and the entities one may encounter in such experiences? What is their level of reality? Are they simply "creatures of imagination," as proposed by Reichel-Dolmatoff (1975:5)? Do they have any kind of reality outside our own experience? Are certain plants really intelligent and able to communicate with us through real "communion" (and even more convincing than is claimed for the Catholic Eucharist)? Are the supernatural powers residing in these plants "organic chemical constituents that allow mortal man to communicate through visual, auditory and other hallucinations with the spirit world that controls every aspect of man's earthly existence"? (Schultes 1975). Is the brain more a receptor than the originator of all experience? Are we really able to communicate with normally unseen intelligences, perhaps in other dimensions? Are spirits real? Is there a multidimensional ecology of beings? What is the relationship between mind and healing? What about those very common motifs—the serpents, for example? Are they part of our mind, and therefore universal?

Under the effects of Ayahuasca and other psychointegrators the mind seems to open to higher, more comprehensive dimensions. One is confronted in a very real and profound way with the mystery of existence, of life and death and the great enigma of the relationship between mind and reality. Few people are left indifferent to such experiences, if done in a respectful, controlled setting and under the guidance of an experienced facilitator.

I would like to present here, as way of illustration, two accounts of recent experiences I had with Ayahuasca:

> I see a strange, floating, irregular, nearly transparent bubble with alien organs. I cannot make sense of it. It comes toward me slowly from the left. I let it happen. It stops in front of me. I enter it with my intention, look at it from inside with total clarity. I go through it and enter a world of threatening beings in the shape of brownish intricate surfaces with protruding tentacles that go for my forehead. I hum and lift my arms, protecting it. Then from the right, almost out of my visual field, comes another attack. I search for my rattle with eyes closed. To open them would mean defeat. I rattle, blow, hum—they seem unaffected by

what I do and persist in their attack. In front of me I have the perfect perception of three-dimensional space. Tall shapeless beings, perhaps five of them, occupy the space that expands in front of my closed eyes. I think of the water from the Sangoma Valley in South Africa, that was brought to the house by a friend. My wife had used it on me on a previous occasion in which I was attacked, with almost instant results. I call Rodolfo, a friend, to bring the bottle that is with my wife.

Almost immediately after my request, there is a change in the visions. There is light to my left; the creatures all seem to look toward the light, pointing at something to come. There is the feeling of reverence in the strange creatures of this world. Is it due to the bottle that is coming? The bottle comes to my hands. I continue with my eyes closed. Open the cork, moisten my fingers, there is now color, flowers spring out, movement toward the sacred water, almost formless beings rushing toward the moisture that crossed from this reality to the other world. Then gifts come, like other times, small objects, perhaps some sort of jewelry, nothing I can fully recognize as anything concrete corresponding to my world.

The "beings" rush toward me, appearing in several irregular layers. I am in a more familiar territory. I have seen this many times before. I am less interested and begin to pay attention to the exterior world. I open my eyes, still seeing forms in the darkness. I am in both worlds, but more here than there. Everything is all right. I close again my eyes. I am again in a world that seems to be made of a light-brown continuous material, almost like a kind of plastic. I have the feeling of intelligent presence. There seems to be some sort of technology. I think: *How could I keep this channel open? How could I always get in touch with "them"? As they seem to be ahead of my own time, they know what is coming (the principle of divination).* The thought of an implant comes to mind but no; I do not wish anything inside me. I would not allow this to happen. I think of finding out about lottery numbers, and faintly I see some numbers appearing but then reject the thought. This is cheap; this is not the way divination should be used, for personal gain. I am taken again by the thought of communication with this other reality. But then I come back, I have to take care of other people, choose the appropriate music for the moment. This reality is calling me now.

On another occasion I had the following experience:

Even with my eyes open, I can see with dismay, once more, the black ants that were almost constant in my visions of some years ago. I close my eyes. There they are against a familiar background that seems to be underground. This has been my specialty, the visitation to subterranean worlds. I follow a row of ants going somewhere.

I notice that without any effort, my mind is following, and I begin to zoom in. I see the ants bigger than any other time before. I continue zooming, or better, zooming is taking place almost without my volition. I get closer and closer to some sort of nodules that separate small areas from others within that, somehow lightly illuminated organic environment. I get excited. The zooming continues, and I am now seeing tiny organelles that become bigger as I continue getting closer and closer. I begin a narrow deep descent, and then suddenly I am in a new place.

It is lighter here. I can see everything with total clarity, sharper than everyday vision, mediated by the eye anatomy. Round, relatively bright, softly colored organisms covered by some sort of moving filaments approach me. The feeling is good. No danger here. I let them come very close, just a few centimeters from my inner eyes. More come behind. I let them also come to just what seems as millimeters from my eyes. I have no apprehension. They are curious. Again, they bring presents. That is at least what I believe they are, as they come with all these objects that I cannot recognize as anything belonging to my world.

Then something is happening to my left. The attention of all those beings turns toward something coming from a seashore that I see upside-down as I am lying down. I understand I have to get up. I get to my knees, facing a sort of wall with sort of pre-Columbian anthropomorphic figures. I have the feeling that there is a ceremony, and it has to do with me. I am humbled by the situation. I tell them that I do not want anything for myself, but I would like to be able to help other people. More than asking to be a healer, I simply ask that healing may take place through me. Two figures, which I cannot distinguish well, are above me, carrying some sort of flags, or floating veils. I am struck by how when I move my head, the whole perspective changes, as if I was really in a three-dimensional space. If the visions were projected on my vision, the same image should follow my head. This is not the case. I can turn around. There is space all around me.

In another experience, I saw what riverine people of the Peruvian Amazon call the *Sachamama,* the great serpent of the jungle realm, powerful yet completely indifferent to my presence. In yet another, I was riding the Yakumama, the great serpent of the water realm, down to the bottom of a lake. There is often a certain consistency, familiar places that I visit again and again. I know more or less their geography. In some cases, I get to places and see people who seem to go on with their own business without paying any attention to me. *Just one more tourist,* they seem to think. In others, I am welcomed, there is a rapport, they seem eager to meet me. How can I explain such experiences to myself in a satisfactory way?

First of all, it is obvious that stories like this are universal. Experiences like these are deeply ingrained in human physiology. They are part of us. I was simply experiencing aspects of reality in remarkably similar ways to those of human beings across time and space (Winkelman, personal communication). There are plenty of similar contemporary accounts of journeys to other realms with various (potentially) psychointegrator agents, including of course Ayahuasca. The Internet is of course an extraordinary source in this respect. These extraordinary inner worlds, beyond normal imagination, seem to be too organized to be disparate constructions of the mind under the effect of alien alkaloids, just hallucinations without any value. The feeling is rather that these plants and substances are extraordinary tools for the study of consciousness. They may give access to infinite treasures of beauty and mystery, perhaps to the source from which all human construction finally emanates.

NOTE

1. Published earlier in Ascott, Gangvik & Jahrman (eds) *Making Reality Really Real. Consciousness Reframed.* Trondheim: TEKS Publishing, 2010. Permission was granted for this publication.

BIBLIOGRAPHY

Brown, Michael F. 1985. *Tsewa's Gift. Magic and Meaning in an Amazonian Society.* Washington and London: Smithsonian Institution Press.

Engel, George. 1977. The need for a new medical model: a challenge for biomedicine. *Science,* 196:129–136.

Fericgla, José María. 2000. *Los Chamanismos a Revisión. De la Vía del Éxtasis a Internet.* Barcelona: Kairós Ed.

Frecska, Ede. 2008. "The shaman's journey: supernatural or natural? A neuro-ontological interpretation of spiritual experiences." In Rick Strassman, Wojtowitz, Slawek, Luis Eduardo Luna, and Ede Frecska *Inner Paths to Outer Space: Journeys Through Psychedelics and Other Spiritual Technologies.* Vermon: Park Street Press.

Furuya, Yoshiaki. 1994. "Umbandização dos Cultos Populares na Amazônia: A Integração ao Brasil?" in Hirochika Nakamaki and Américo Pellegrini Filho (Eds.) *Possessão e Procissão. Religiosidade Popular no Brasil.* Osaka: National Museum of Ethnology.

Hancok, Graham. 2005. *Supernatural. Meetings with the Ancient Teachers of Mankind.* London: Century.

Huxley, Aldous. 1959 (first published in 1954). *The Doors of Perception* and *Heaven and Hell.* London: Penguin Books.

Lagrou, Els. 2000. Two Ayahuasca Myths from the Cashinahua of Northwestern Brazil. In Luna, L.E. and White, S.F. Ayahuasca Reader. *Encounters with the Amazon's Sacred Vine.* Synergetic Press, Santa Fe.

James, William. 1929. *Varieties of Religious Experience.* New York: Modern Library.

Lewis-Williams, David. 2002. *The Mind in the Cave. Consciousness and the Origins of Art.* London: Thames and Hudson.

Luna, Luis Eduardo. 1984. The Concept of Plants as Teachers Among Four Mestizo Shamans of Iquitos, Northeast Peru. *Journal of Ethnopharmacology* 11:135–56.

———. 1986. *Vegetalismo: Shamanism Among the Mestizo Population of the Peruvian Amazon.* Stockholm: Almqvist & Wiksell International.

———. 1995. "A Barquinha. Una Nueva Religión en Río Branco, Amazonía Brasileña." *Acta Americana* 3:2:137–151. Stockholm.

Luna, Luis Eduardo & Amaringo, Pablo Amaringo. 1991. *Ayahuasca Visions: The Religious Iconography of a Peruvian Shaman.* Berkeley: North Atlantic Books.

Mann, Charles C. 2005. *1491. New Revelations of the Americas Before Columbus.* New York: Alfred A. Knopf.

Penrose, Roger. 1994. *Shadows of the Mind: A Search for the Missing Science of Consciousness.* Oxford: Oxford University Press.

Reichel-Dolmatoff, Gerardo. 1971. *Amazonian Cosmos. The Sexual and Religious Symbolism of the Tukano Indians.* Chicago: The University of Chicago Press.

———. 1975. *The Shaman and the Jaguar. A Study of Narcotic Drugs Among the Indians of Colombia.* Philadelfia: Temple University Press.

Roberts, Thomas B. 2006. *Psychedelic Horizons.* Exeter, UK: Imprint Academic.

Schultes, Richard-Evans. Foreword to Gerardo Reichel-Dolmatoff *The Shaman and the Jaguar. A Study of Narcotic Drugs Among the Indians of Colombia.* Philadelphia: Temple University Press.

Vallee, Jacques. 1969, 1993. *Passport to Magonia: On UFOs, Folklore and Parallel Worlds.* Chicago: Contemporary Books.

Winkelman, Michael. 2010. *Shamanism A Biopsychosocial Paradigm of Consciousness and Healing.* Santa Barbara: ABC-CLIO Publishers.

COMMUNION WITH THE GODDESS: THREE WEEKS OF AYAHUASCA IN BRAZIL

BY MARK SEELIG

I just got back from a shamanic seminar in South America involving a number of fascinating lectures by world authorities on South American culture and shamanic wisdom. The seminar included seven nightly ceremonies of drinking the jungle brew Ayahuasca, a potion containing DMT and harmaline known to bring strong visions and communion with the divine.

This is an attempt at reporting things that cannot really be put into words. Since many have asked me to send a recollection of my impressions, I am doing so in a form that is somewhat like a travel report. This account also contains content of the visionary journeys that addresses philosophical and contemporary issues.

But before I begin, a warning and disclaimer is in order:

1. What follows is in no way intended as an incentive to ingest substances that are illegal in most countries.

   In other words: Be sure to protect yourself against the idiocy of current legislation!

2. What follows is entirely my subjective experience and does not claim authority over anyone else's experience.

   In other words: Be sure to protect yourself from "gurus, methods, and teachers" (Van Morrison), and seek out your own personal experience in a safe setting!

3. What follows is an entirely personal and subjective mixture of highly ecstatic and poetic descriptions mixed with spicy and aggressive criticism of what I believe to be a global misunderstanding of why humanity is here.

   In other words: Do not read what follows unless you enjoy a good rant and a good portion of spiritually poetic bliss!

Ayahuasca makes us see what's real. This can be something collective and global, and it can also be very much about oneself. One of the many things I was shown again and again was this:

Given my personal history as a former theologian turned clinical psychotherapist and student of shamanic traditions, I have very deeply looked into the endless destruction and genocide that religious ideologies and dogma have inflicted upon human beings. After having worked with hundreds, if not thousands, of people for about thirty years now, I have seen how damaged human souls are, how deeply depressive, meaningless, and prone to exploitation are the lives that many live. Religious dogma is at the root of this epidemic meaninglessness. Behind that is a thirst and cry for love.

My past and present prompt me to make no bones about what lies at the core of the human soul: the deep longing to experience communion with the divine, to be received and loved. I take issue with anything that stands in the way of this calling of the human species. I consider it my obligation to do so, simply because I have repeatedly and deeply experienced this communion and because I have witnessed more than enough of what the lack of this communion does to human beings.

With these warnings and disclaimers in mind, I enjoy the thought of you reading the sharing of my ecstasy, of my aggressive rants against the destructive and violent constructs of religious dogma, against the schizophrenia and superstition called "science," against contemporary legislation, which in its utter arrogance criminalizes plants that grow from the earth while at the same time endorsing, promoting, and profiting from lethally dangerous and addictive substances such as alcohol, nicotine, etc.

These things have to be said. And they cannot be said loudly enough. And I deeply admire all those who speak their respective truths about these matters.

The Brazil report: I want to begin by describing how the fabulous lectures, usually given from about five to seven in the afternoon, kind of set the stage for the Ayahuasca journeys that began at nine in the evening. It is one thing to move into the mystery of a shamanic journey, particularly if we're talking about the order of what can be expected with good Ayahuasca. It is yet another when, prior to the actual vision quest, a world authority on shamanism, someone who has studied the history *and* has submitted themselves to the shamanic experience—to my mind, the only credible qualification and trustworthy authority to speak about such matters—has shared her or his wisdom and thus prepared the "neurological stage" for the journey and its meaning.

I consider myself incredibly fortunate having had the opportunity to share the sacred space of such a gathering with a wonderful group of seekers, among whom were three people who full-heartedly embrace the abovementioned credibility and authority. Precisely because they do not hide behind theories but base them on their own repeated personal experience, I consider these people world teachers who should be heard and read by as many as possible. One of these folks arguably is the world's most knowledgeable person on Ayahuasca and South American shamanic traditions, the next arguably is the world's most exciting authority on ethnopharmacology, and the third arguably is the world's most fascinating expert on the hidden mysteries and wisdom of ancient cultures. For reasons of privacy, I do not want to name them here.

It is very difficult to put into words the excitement that builds as a precursor to Ayahuasca experiences in such company. It is even more daunting to describe what transpires during an Ayahuasca ceremony, as it is very different for each individual. The experiences I had are therefore entirely subjective and have to do with my personal history, with the way my life is at the moment, and with the way I relate to Spirit and to people.

This said, there also are some general qualities to Ayahuasca journeys that are similarly experienced by most everyone drinking the brew, for example:

- A sometimes extremely challenging and at times very frightening encounter with what shamanism refers to as the "Underworld." In "modern" and more psychological terms, the Underworld would include dimensions of existential and object-related fears; shadow sides of the human personality; repressed, forgotten, and denied contents of the psyche; as well as collective symbols for the difficult aspects of being human (see the 'DSM-4' and the 'ICD-10' for psychology's attempt to group and categorize—and severely pathologize—these experiences). All these "energies" can appear in the form of menacing visions of demons and dark forces that at times seem to threaten one's very life.
- At other times, the journeyer will experience highly ecstatic phases during the visionary quest, blissful encounters with divine beings waiting to teach the shamanic traveler about her/his life, about how to collaborate with the divine in saving planet Earth, how to change one's life toward supporting and helping all sentient beings, and how to be a happy, spiritual, and compassionate human being.

In spite of the fact that magazines such as the *Men's Journal* should be taken *cum grano salis*, with the proverbial "grain of salt," there is a very reasonable and interesting, if somewhat brief article in the March 2013 issue (Link: http://www.mensjournal.com/magazine/ayahuasca-at-home-an-american-experience-20130215).

Ayahuasca ceremonies are usually held in a group setting. It is almost uncanny to witness how in a very short time people who have never met before, and who speak different languages and have grown up in different cultures, bond in a deeply heartfelt way when they journey together. This type of gathering is a role model for community building because it also immediately becomes evident that this kind of healthy family has a strong capacity to expose, make visible, and help grow out of, immaturities that we all carry as baggage from our respective pasts.

Inconceivable depth of healing is possible. Human beings have an almost unlimited potential for ecstasy, love, compassion, support, and reciprocating nourishment. These strange creatures called humans have been given bodies that have a capacity to feel the deepest ecstasy, joy, and comfort when touched and caressed. They have been given souls that can commune with the divine and thereby experience the highest spiritual bliss. They have been given hearts that can feel the deepest love. They have been given eyes to behold the breathtaking beauty of life, of other beings, of nature, of art. They have been given ears to listen, to share words, and to revel in one of the most beautiful and soul-inspiring mysteries conceivable: music.

How is it, then, that so few of these strange creatures, these earthlings, make use of this unbelievable abundance of talent? How is it that so many of them prefer to hunger and lust for power, status, money? Well, because they have forgotten to regularly thank the universe for the gifts they have been given. Because they have forgotten to hold sacred ceremonies. In simple words: most of them have forgotten how to love. This is all of us, guests on planet Earth!

My own seven journeys have mainly consisted of deeply blissful and ecstatic communion with what I very clearly experience as a feminine energy that I like to call "Mother Ayahuasca" or "The Goddess." Hardly ever do I only have ecstatic communion without first, or somewhere along the journey, being challenged by being shown demons, frightening visions, etc., but the more I learn to trust that SHE is always working for our best, the more I am able to let myself go through these fearful moments and be moved on to ecstatic communion with HER spirit of cosmic wisdom, healing, and revolutionary inner freedom that SHE infuses me with.

There is no question: this is by far the deepest, most profound teaching, and the greatest adventure that I or any human being, I believe, can submit themselves to, and the most rewarding one at the same time, right next to a deep love relationship. I do not have the notes to sing and play the beauty of HER. I do not have the words to praise the utter devotion I feel toward HER. I live for HER, and SHE has told me many times that I am HER child (as we all are), HER student, HER collaborator when it comes to making a contribution to the growth of consciousness and conscientiousness on this planet. There can be no greater honor for me. I was saved from sure death several times; I was invited into the highest heavens several times; I was shown the deepest meaning of what human existence is meant to be; I was told how to help preserve our sacred abode Earth. The questions I ask HER are always answered, either through the words I hear HER speak during the journey, or through the visions SHE gives me. SHE awakens the poetic nature of the soul. SHE awakens the warrior of the heart.

Music is playing throughout the whole journey. For me and many others, music becomes "visible" during the ceremonies in a way that is hard to put into words—rainbow colors shape-shifting into garlands, ornamented with billions of glittering crystals and jewels, twist and turn around their own axis and explode into kaleidoscopic supernovae that dance with every note of the track. It becomes visible what Mozart "saw" when he wrote his symphonies. I feel the incredible passion and love of the rock singer putting her soul into a song, having devoted years of hard work practicing her instrument and voice . . . "show your true colors . . . they are beautiful . . . like a rainbow." On top of a simple but heavenly composition of guitar music, I hear Terence McKenna speak about what a shaman is, and I explode into deep longing for divine communion, forever grateful that the Goddess has invited me into HER realms. No greater ecstasy for me to behold.

One of the most powerful and moving visions that came to me happened in the middle of the third journey. It sounds almost pathetic when I put it into writing: how could a moment that most probably changed the entire course of human history (see the vibrant writing of Graham Hancock, particularly his new book, *War God*) appear in a vision of a German person? That doesn't make sense. At least not from a purely rational perspective. However, Ayahuasca does not adhere at all to what we consider rational faculties. It actually couldn't care less. It will just give us what it decides we must see. The challenge, then, is not so much the reality of the visions; they are way more real than some of the stuff we see through our eyes on any given day shopping for groceries. The challenge is to accept that there is more to reality than meets the eye.

The vision: I saw the initial encounter between the South American native peoples and the first vessel of the Spanish conquistadors reaching the shores of South America. I was alternating back and forth between being two persons: A native man looking on in awe as the giant wooden ship slowly closed in on the banks, recollecting the prophecies of my scriptures. And I was a Spanish soldier on the ship looking on in awe as I beheld the abundant beauty of the land and its people. I remember very clearly the feeling of that moment, which lasted for quite some time. It was actually a moment of deep reverence, utter beauty, and endless potential, of mutual admiration and silent communion. And then the lightning of dogma struck: the Spanish soldier remembered what he had come here for, what he was supposed to carry out as his duty, and the rest is history, as they say. One of the most brutally violent and destructive genocides in human history ensued. In the name of "god" entire populations were annihilated within a matter of a few years, and in the wake of this disaster, thousands of years of spiritual wisdom and healing arts were obliterated and lost forever (see *American Holocaust* by David E. Stannard). The magnitude, horrifying brutality, and pseudo-religious delusion of this frenzied extermination committed in the name of the "Christian" "god" is beyond anything the human mind can imagine.

Since then, the planet has never recovered. In many parts of the world, humanity has long since fallen prey to the delusional and inflated dogma of monotheistic religions and their angry and jealous gods that seek revenge against each other and try to kill whatever is in their way. Their followers to this day do not believe what their own scriptures have been trying to teach them for millennia: that there is only one god. Instead, they continue to live in paranoid fear of "other gods" that might threaten theirs, and they wage war on everyone that triggers this fear.

This devastating monotheistic rampage then spread throughout South America. The reality of a giving, caring, feminine universe that loves its children and provides for them was lost. The experience that nature is benign, that it must be cherished and preserved, that it holds all the healing secrets that humans need was forgotten. The communion with the Goddess, with the creative principle of a mothering abode—Earth—with a cosmic intelligence is only now being rediscovered as some of us, scattered across this globe, are privileged enough to be reintroduced to the ancient wisdom that shamanic traditions have cherished for millennia. Some call this emergence the "rise of the divine feminine."

I had the great fortune of being joined in the last two ceremonies by my beautiful lover and partner. Some say, a "good tripping buddy" can be as important as a love relationship. How about if one's own lover and partner is that good journey companion? Can there be a greater blessing? In one of the journeys, my lover sang along with the music, and I had to get my ears close to her so that I could drink her voice; it was incredible, this beautiful feminine energy.

The masculine world is so starved for feminine beauty and tenderness, and it has lost the ways to be nourished by it, instead trying, but never succeeding, to find it in glossy magazines and many other venues that sell women's bodies. What a teaching to listen to that song being sung into my ears and to see how the feminine, Shakti, always holds the universe together so that the masculine can do Shiva's dance without getting lost in space, i.e., in the spacy-ness that frustrated men lose themselves in: the airheaded and retarded pseudo-masculine spacy-ness of academia, the power-driven madness of politics, the fear-based and frenzied propagation of ideologies, the spiritually destructive and deluded evil force of religious dogma. Make no mistake here: these energies have almost completely destroyed ancient spiritual wisdom and human sanity.

Most of academia is nothing but a pursuit of scientific superstition, the unfounded belief that measuring and reproducing is the only valid means of acquiring knowledge. That's a fear-based ideology; it has nothing to do with science.

Most established religions are dogmatic constructs serving the purpose of power and influence of a few leaders who like to oppress and exploit fellow human beings; these leaders promote fear-based ideologies, not authentic spiritual communion with the divine. Legislation follows and condemns and criminalizes everything that might truly liberate people. As the notorious Tim Leary has so mischievously and beautifully stated: psychedelics cause schizophrenia and paranoia in those that have not used them. Or as the beloved Terence McKenna had it: psychedelics dissolve boundaries.

Behind these stupid endeavors that too many men waste their beautiful potential for—and as collateral damage, so to speak, tear the planet to pieces—behind these activities rings the muffled scream to be held, protected, mothered, and loved by the divine feminine. Like small children, these lost men throw temper tantrums all over the globe, abusing their talents and gifts to gain power, influence, status, and a kind of recognition that leaves them empty at heart and prone to fight for more. To make a blunt statement: Ayahuasca can fix this schizophrenia. As one of our experts so aptly stated: all political leaders should be obliged to go through ten Ayahuasca sessions before being admitted to office.

Really, the deepest thirst of the masculine is to be of service to the feminine, to protect and shield the loved ones, to go out into the world with a powerful vision and be lovingly welcomed back home, to adore and be blown away by the beauty of the feminine, to be fully and completely received and be nourished that way. Really, the deepest longing of the feminine is to be protected and held, to be cherished and adored, to support the masculine in its visionary power, to drink the heart-centered strength of the masculine and be nourished that way.

Another deeply instructive vision was one that was at times unbearable because of its threatening character. An energy of utter darkness and destruction crept into the overall quality of that particular journey. This was felt by a number of people as an immediate threat that went against everything that was good, true, and beautiful—an utterly destructive attempt of unknown origin, seemingly bent on annihilation. It was extremely mysterious in that we all felt it had nothing to do with the life-affirming power of Ayahuasca. Some very deep teaching was afoot.

It took quite some time to come to grips with what had happened. Our discussions afterwards were filled with a sense of deep recognition for the polarity of existence. It is difficult to grasp when just told as a story, at times mind boggling or even seemingly crazy, but there was a very acute sense that we had been exposed to the eternal struggle of darkness and light that is being told about in all mythologies, all sacred scriptures, and all spiritual teachings. It was scary enough, all right, but the subsequent blessing was of such incredible beauty and spiritual depth that once again, there was not the slightest trace of doubt: to go through this together was well worth it.

We emerged feeling that this sister- and brotherhood can weather the storm of the assault of evil and emerge with an even stronger resolve to hold on to the light, to everything we humans know as good, true, and beautiful. Needless to mention, the sense of belonging to each other was acutely felt by everyone. But what's more important was nothing short of miraculous: many felt that by going through this ordeal, we had helped the eternal cause of the very essence of Mother Ayahuasca's teaching, the teaching of all good forces, the teaching of the creative principle of the universe: to prioritize our working together at bringing Love, Healing, and Wisdom to this planet.

Filled with remaining awe and wonder from that session—and with a clear sense that we must always be conscious of the reality of these challenging forces—I went into the next quest two days later. At some point, I directly asked what I always experience as the spirit of "The Goddess" or Mother Ayahuasca. I flat-out posed the question to HER: "What the hell was *that?*" The reply came as straightforward and as clear as a bell. SHE said: "Now you know what I'm having to struggle with *all* the time, and I need you beautiful and courageous people to help me!" I was speechless. I felt so deeply validated as a human being. In spite of all my frailties, my feelings of powerlessness to make a difference in this world, in spite of feeling so incredibly small in the face of the magnitude of destruction that our species visits on this planet, I felt acknowledged and appreciated by the divine in my effort to gain insight and to receive HER teaching by moving into these journeys with HER. It was clear beyond any doubt: this was a calling. The call of the mystic to pursue the path toward the divine, to follow that which brings peace, healing, and love to all sentient beings.

I returned from Brazil, acutely aware that I cannot even begin to think that my experiences can be expressed in words. Believe me . . . what I tried to hint at above is less than a far cry from what really happened inside. The human soul finds rest only if it finds a way to fully surrender and open to the divine communion. Wise women and men in tribal cultures have preserved the sacred art of holding ceremony and have passed on the wisdom and tools to us so that we can now study this art and learn what it means to live in harmony with all sentient beings and with the universe.

The tea served was one that made only very few people throw up, yet it's very strong and spiritually powerful. Volume was freely and individually chosen, so plenty of cautiousness was possible in working toward a level that doesn't scare the living daylights out of one. Obviously, and as demonstrated by the above, I constantly went way beyond that level and did get those daylights scared out of me, but I knew things to be safe. The learning was incredible. All in all, an experience I would most emphatically recommend to anyone inclined to inner exploration of depths, provided they seek out a safe setting.

Ayahuasca even teaches Buddhism . . . HER comments on the essential wisdom of the Buddhist teachings are priceless. But this is yet another story of many that will follow. I hope and pray that this experience becomes available to you and that you'll go and seek it out in a safe surrounding.

Namaste

IS ALCOHOL A SPIRIT? OR, MY GOODNESS, MY GUINNESS!

BY ROBERT TINDALL

The word *spirit*, the "animating or vital principle in man and animals," comes to us via the Latin *spiritus*, "soul, courage, vigor, breath," and is related to *spirare*, "to breathe." Its plural form, *spirits*, or a "volatile substance," is an alchemical idea, and it was only in the 1670s that its usage narrowed to its present meaning: "strong alcoholic liquor."

Yet lurking within our modern, dry categorization of strong alcohol as "spirits," this original sense of animating power remains firmly entrenched.

As Shakespeare's Falstaff put it, a good sherris sack "ascends me into the brain, dries me there all the foolish and dull and crudy vapors which environ it, makes it apprehensive, quick, forgetive, full of nimble, fiery, and delectable shapes, which, delivered o'er to the voice, the tongue, which is the birth, becomes excellent wit." Not only that, it breathes courage into the soul, it "illumineth the face, which as a beacon gives warning to all the rest of this little kingdom, man, to arm, and then the vital commoners and inland petty spirits muster me all to their captain, the heart, who, great and puffed up with this retinue, doth any deed of courage, and this valor comes of sherris."

This is the language of spiritual inspiration, not mere infatuation with a physical effect!

Perhaps we should take ourselves at our word. What if alcohol really is a spirit?

In a recent interview with Erik Davis on his program *Expanding Mind*, our discussion turned to the nature of addiction and the healing potential of traditional, and psychoactive, plant medicines such as Ayahuasca and peyote.

To illustrate these plants' mysterious capacity to cleanse us of addictive patterns, I disclosed an experience I'd had not so long ago, one which ended a decades-long fierce attachment to red wine.

Indeed, I loved red wine. Holding a wine glass was like cupping a rosy heart in my hand, transparent, almost pulsing, catching the light like blood.

Ancient, celebrated by song, wine even had its own deity! A good wine tasted of the roots of the earth, of her fruit, even the sunshine, and its relaxation was, to quote the Cyclops in Homer's *Odyssey*, "Ambrosia!"

Although I knew full well my life had been fraught with addictive struggle, I hadn't ended that particular love affair. When I did, it was with a finality that will endure until my dying breath.

It happened deep in the ocean of an Ayahuasca ceremony. Accompanied by the otherworldly, Asiatic tones of the Shipibo icaros of the Amazon rainforest, I had found myself in deep trance, holding my water bottle and praying for the health of the waters of our planet: thanking the ocean for giving birth to us and sustaining us, apologizing for our contamination of her precious being.

Suddenly, I caught a glimpse of something dark flickering over my right shoulder. My hand, like a cat's paw, shot back and, seizing whatever it was, thrust it into the water bottle.

"Okay," I said to myself, sitting there bemused in the dark, "I've just gone and trapped a spirit in my water bottle. Now what do I do?"

I directly knew I needed to go outside and toss out the water, dispersing the spirit back to the elements. Getting up, I carefully walked through the crowded room, slipped out beneath the stars, and scattered the water.

Returning to my seat, charmed, I asked, "Okay, what was that all about?"

I then saw it. The dark, flickering thing had been the spirit of red wine, and the entity had been feeding off of my energy like a succubus. I thought of all the evenings I had hastened home from a long day of work to relax into the amber red cave of her intoxication, reading my books, disappearing from my family, escorted into a sodden sleep by her liquid embrace. She had been a dark lover.

And I was done with her.

Returning home, I emptied my house of my stockpiled bottles of organic red wine, and wondered to myself, "How am I going to do this?" I was already aware of a hollow yearning within me, one I would never feed again, left gasping for air in the dust. I felt a smidgen of dread in my soul. So many years seeking solace in the opiate embrace of red wine—could that yearning ever fade away?

Well, it did. So clean was the excision of the spirit that some nights ago, watching an Italian priest pour himself a well-deserved glass of red wine across the table from me, I felt not a trace of yearning arise in my being.

After relating this story, I received this message from a listener to that episode of *Expanding Mind*:

I have had a complicated relationship with alcohol for years. Just last night I was alone and decided to have some beers while watching hockey. I ended up drinking too much. It hurt my work production today and I decided to go and do some errands. That's when I heard you talk.

Hearing you tell your red wine entity story was the second thing that was hugely helpful. The first was that over the weekend I had a powerful dream. I was in a big, old library with the comedian Greg Fitzsimmons, who is sober and in his mid-forties like me. Greg was guiding me through the shelves and we were looking for a spirit.

At one point, he disappeared and it was just me. I knew the spirit was just around the corner and suddenly I was terrified. I let out this huge scream that scared the crap out of my wife. She said it sounded as though I was going to attack something.

This dream really rattled me. Then yesterday I didn't plan on drinking but I just did. Then I heard your red wine story and I immediately knew that there is a spirit of alcohol that feeds off my energy.

Is this so strange? Do we not call distilled alcohol "spirits"? Don't we celebrate so, from Shakespeare's Falstaff to the Captain Morgan rum ads, where a piratical, intensely colorful, mischievous spirit manifests like a jinni in the company of young drinkers at a party?

From an indigenous perspective, it isn't odd at all. As anthropologist Frédérique Apffel-Marglin points out, among traditional cultures:

> Concerted actions between humans and certain nonhumans that have been crucial for human welfare and carried out over long periods of time have given rise to entities, or rather beings, who embody those concerted actions. For example, the soil becomes Mama Allpa, a being to whom prayers and offerings are made, who is endowed with understanding, agency and sentience and responds to the actions of humans. In modernity the soil has become a "natural resource" bereft of agency, sentience and understanding.[1]

If this has been characteristic and true (the ethnographic records clearly indicate it is) for human culture for thousands of years, why should we be an exception? Why should alcohol, to whom we do indeed offer up a steady stream of addicts' prayers and offerings, not be an entity in its own right?

My own innate resistance to this concept, which I presume is shared with most of my readers, is actually a product of my own historical conditioning. As Apffel-Marglin points out regarding ancestral practices of making offerings to the Earth:

> The Reformers in 16th century Europe called such rituals "magic" due to their insistence on the total separation between humans, nonhumans, and the religious, namely a God removed from the material world. For the Reformers, agency, voice, and meaning became exclusively human attributes. Ever since the Reformers' separation between matter and spirit, such rituals of regeneration could only be understood as humans representing symbolically or metaphorically the nonhumans who became passive and silent.[2]

Does not her argument, which applies to all concerted action between human and nonhuman agencies carried out over long periods of time, apply equally well to alcohol? Are we really justified in claiming that all the spiritual manifestations of alcohol are mere representations of something actually inert and without sentience?

For "passive and silent" alcohol is not, not by a long shot.

This essay is not, by the way, an argument for a ban on alcohol or any other consciousness-altering substance. It's a call to get our relationships straight with them, which indigenous peoples can teach us a lot about. Whatever our take may be on the metaphysics of indigenous worldviews, their efficacy is undeniable.

Wine with admixtures was once used medicinally in medieval Europe; tobacco and coca in indigenous cultures are sacred plants that allow us to commune with divinity and heal; and if I'm ever seriously injured, please give me a preparation from the opium plant! Opium, according to the indigenous ancient Greeks, is sacred, a gift to humanity from Prometheus. I have entire faith in its curative properties.

By treating our plant allies with respect and veneration, we protect ourselves. A quick glimpse at any tobacco addict, who believes tobacco a mere "natural resource" and consumer product, is sufficient to support that argument!

Even if not taken in an explicitly sacred context, it's still good to know what being you are communing with. For myself, although my relationship with red wine is sealed, because of the cultural richness and personal significance of enjoying a glass of stout, I still leave that possibility open for myself.

Yet I haven't taken that opportunity in many moons, and I don't know if I ever will again. First, I'll be sussing out how my relationship stands with that other old friend of mine, that pint of Guinness, once enjoyed in many a convivial gathering in the local pubs in Connemara, Ireland.

NOTES

1. Apffel-Marglin. "The pre-Columbian Amazonian Black Earth Re-emerging," 6.
2. Ibid., 10.

BIBLIOGRAPHY

Apffel-Marglin Frédérique. "The pre-Columbian Amazonian Black Earth Re-emerging Today. A source for Global Regeneration." Selva Vida: De la Destrucción de la Amazonía al Paradigma de la Regeneración. eds. Stefano Varese, Roger Rumrill and Frédérique Apffel-Marglin. UNAM, Mexico: IWGIA, Denmark; and Casas de las Americas, Cuba. Forthcoming.

DMT: THE THINKING MAN'S MOONSHINE?
BY GABRIEL ROBERTS

Did you know that you are presently "holding" a schedule 1 psychedelic drug in your brain right now? Unfortunately as soon as that shit is anywhere other than in your brain, it's as illegal as heroin or crack.

You may be wondering what it is. Well, psychnautical guru and all-around interesting guy Terence McKenna said DMT was the most shocking thing a human can consume this side of the yawning grave. Coming from a guy who was to psychedelics what Lil Wayne is to "Sizzurp," this is quite an astonishing claim.

Due to its difficulty to get ahold of, some have gone through the work of figuring out how to get this mystical substance from their expanding little minds. A friend of mine was one of those people. He, like many others, had been hearing wonderful and sometimes terrifying stories of DMT's transformational power. He had read books like *The Cosmic Serpent*, *Supernatural*, and *DMT: The Spirit Molecule* and watched all kinds of YouTube stuff.

By this time, something in him just had to make his first encounter with DMT happen. It's not like you can just score some on a street corner, and it's not exactly an easy thing to casually bring up, so with no other option seemingly available, he did what any resourceful young man would do; he made it himself.

Before he knew it, he had the bark he needed from an online source and a recipe from the Internet. Lo and behold, he had (with some trial and error) the real deal. After he had made a batch of his own and tried it, he was now on a mission to let other people know about his wild journey through hyperspace.

I had come to many of the same conclusions as him about the nature of consciousness and spent many nights talking about the mysteries of the world, so when he revealed to me that he had figured out how to make DMT, I jumped at the chance to try it.

Though he was very excited to share with me (free of charge), he was also very stern that this was not some lighthearted deed. He offered that I take a moment to be at peace with myself and make sure I wasn't going in half-cocked. I took his advice and gave it a whirl.

Upon first inhalation, I was staring at my bookcase, which now looked like a giant smile with six rows of book-teeth. It smiled at me because "it held so much wisdom in its mouth." During this first time, the plants in the room all reached out to me and telepathically told me that they were always there for me.

Something was not quite right, though; when I closed my eyes, it looked like I was staring at a giant mandala that was ever changing. It also felt like I was on some cosmic swing and needed a push in order to swing higher. There was this frustrating feeling of not being all the way there, even though I didn't know where "there" was.

I committed to a larger dose of his home-brewed paradigm changer, and off I went! This time, everything was left behind, including my sense of self. In fact, self was a laughable concept. While the set of eyes that made up the perceptive character I knew as myself floated in a Technicolor clusterfuck, every digital media I had ever seen in my life spun like a trillion rainbow dervishes and transformed into "people."

I use the term *people* very lightly—these were like a million-year-advanced species of light serpents making love and tangling like earphones in Jerry Garcia's pants pocket. Through all of this, they spoke to me in jokes and riddles, telling me the mysteries of the universe in a Fourth of July finale.

The illusion of disconnection had been so powerful in my life just moments before, and now it was laughable. Everything and everyone was a mechanical part in a giant machined object; one of love and hate, of all manner of feeling. It was amoral; it was loving, it was alien in a way that beggared any Hollywood depiction of alien.

I came back with tears in my eyes having witnessed a wild spectacle that only the closed eye can reveal. The potential of the human mind walked into the room like an unexpected visit to your home from your favorite movie star.

My friend and I suddenly spoke a language of symbol and metaphor, because everything seemed to be exactly that. I understood finally what the mystics of the ages saw. No wonder they seemed so otherworldly! They very well may have seen these things from a natural outburst of DMT in their own system. Religion was someone else's trip report sadly misunderstood!

Two years and many trips later, my life was changed by an experience that my own brain holds the key to. Holy shit.

THE DIVINE SPARK

This leads us to the question of whether or not it is responsible to even try such a thing. I cannot tell other people that this is the be-all and end-all, because it isn't. I can't say that it's advisable to try, but I can say that I should be able to make those decisions for myself as an adult. If I'm going to live and die, I'd like to think it's on my own terms.

So is DMT the thinking man's moonshine? It might be. My friend burned a hole in his floor and stained his toilet purple as Grimace's ass. He set his first batch on fire because he forgot to do some sort of chemical wash before he tried it. Trial and error made mayhem and peril possible as well.

Like moonshine, people can make DMT at home, but with no small amount of legal risk and pharmacological uncertainty. Hopefully, like moonshine, the psychedelic helper known as DMT will become like booze: legal.

DMT—THE FINAL FRONTIER: WHAT DO HALLUCINATIONS, ANGELS, ALIENS, DREAMS, AND NEAR-DEATH EXPERIENCES ALL HAVE IN COMMON?

BY MIKE ALIVERNIA

Your brain on DMT! I believe that it would be hard to *disprove* the connection between all those words above, in bold print, and the chemical DMT produced within each of our brains as the mysterious link at the center of so many misunderstood moments in human history! Simply stated, our brains *function differently* in reaction to *any* chemical. There is no doubt that your reaction to any external form of DMT (either smoked or injected for a shorter but extremely effective result, or drank as a simple but serendipitous concoction in the form of an ancient Amazonian brew known as Ayahuasca) allows for your brain to explode into other realms of consciousness while your heart beats and your body stays piled in its seat. There is also no doubt that our bodies produce the chemical dimethyltryptamine: DMT *http://en.wikipedia. org/wiki/Dimethyltryptamine*. Dr. Rick Strassman's almost exclusive, yet extensive work has shown the effects of a DMT "trip" to be most likened to reports of near-death experiences, alien abductions, encounters with spiritual beings, or feeling wide awake in the most incredible of dreams. Indeed, our bodies take a required, daily physical and mental break from our reality that we accept as sleep. During which, I believe there is a mechanism that releases the appropriate amount of DMT required for your mind to peacefully enjoy whatever hallucination it can conjure—dreaming in REM. (Does the pineal gland produce or simply regulate the chemical? This seems to be the final wrangling point for science. *http://disinfo.com/2013/05/breakthrough-dmt-found-in-the-pineal-gland-of-live-rats/*)

With the acceptance that there is no other reasonable definition for what a dream is—save a hallucination while your body lies incapacitated—it should be noted that this is the exact state induced by a DMT or Ayahuasca "trip." One is left to realize that while we not only don't understand the reasons humans are born equipped to access a naturally available, nightly neuro, carpet ride, we seem to be ignoring the answer as to *how* we sail uninhibited in dreamscapes un-mappable, all from the comfort of our down pillow. Recently, I've been afforded the opportunity to listen in on firsthand, graphic retellings of more than a handful of hallucinations, a few rare cases of "bipolar 1 with psychotic features" patients have had to endure. More importantly, they were retellings of these brave souls trying to survive within the midst of the never-ending wake of confusion and fear these prolonged parallels of perception leave behind. It was during one of these sessions that I truly had that aha moment, in which I was flooded with the obvious connections in all of their stories and the work Graham Hancock clearly laid out in "Elves Aliens, Angels, and Ayahuasca" *http://www.youtube.com/watch?v=0qgMFO0KU-I.*

There was one fact that every story shared, but every patient would naturally gloss over, that struck me as most important. These were altered realities that would uncannily occur at night, during a period of high anxiety or manic-induced insomnia, or during an unusually difficult night of sleep and were nonetheless eerily similar to the narratives in the relatively recent flux of "alien abductions" and the equally unexplainable "breaks from reality" that medicine currently classifies as "schizophrenia." The resulting altered realities share strikingly similar reports of geometric shapes, animals, or creatures that have humanoid features that usually share animal features or have "otherworldly" characteristics, knowledge, and settings that are far more powerful and/or frightening than that moment of confusion right before you wake—when you can't quite put your finger on the fact that you're still dreaming. Let's not forget the peculiar pasttime as old as man itself, for those rare individuals with a "more close relationship with God." Why have they been able to have face-to-face, seemingly flesh encounters with Angels, have conversations with God Himself, or put into words divinely inspired wisdom? The vast majority of these people have, indeed, induced altered states of consciousness through meditation; fasting by deprivation of sleep, food, or water; severe stress or trauma; eating or drinking "spiritual sustenance"; or otherwise been deemed to be "special" or "touched."

WHAT DOES IT ALL MEAN?

What makes these human beings enter into states that they perceive to be "not our shared reality"? I purpose it to be quite simple. It is the altering or *malfunctioning* of the natural mechanisms we all use to dream while asleep— and for our soul to escape the body upon its demise. I won't go into my thoughts as to why we are intended and readily equipped to enter into a dream state every single night—or why DMT is released at the moment the brain believes the body is dying—here. What I want to get across is that indeed, *things that cannot currently be explained have a remarkable way of being connected!* Whatever the trigger—be it REM sleep, lack of sleep, extreme anxiety, a malfunctioning of our brain's internal regulator, lack of food and water, purposeful deprivation and meditation, or the introduction of external DMT or psilocybin—the result is the same. Our brains use all their naturally equipped physical pathways necessary for DMT to produce alternate states of perceived realities. How can we begin to understand our true purpose here on this planet, with a dualism as perverse as a fleeting mortal body, carrying within it a super computer of soft membrane encased in fluid, firing on electricity and chemicals in ways we'd rather ignore than embrace?

WOULD IT BE THE END OF THE WORLD AS WE KNOW IT?

If every culture openly partook in spiritual rituals (freely and religiously practiced in the Americas from antiquity until the bloody Spanish conquests of the 16th century, and *surely* the lost key used by the ancient Middle Eastern, Indian, and Far Eastern religious originators) of using either plants or chemicals, or fasting and meditation methods for encountering spiritual realms currently either feared or deemed to be worthy of only prophets or sick minds, would *anything on this earth* be the same? I don't know, but I presume such a worldwide movement to be the awakening, rebirth, revival, or revelation so many have feared or foreseen.

As the ever-churning motor of science's boat keeps us moving forward, in an unfathomable ocean of physics and chemistry, mysticism and magnetism, and the light of life and the dark of matter, the only things changing are the make and model of the engine and the perception of the brain instantly analyzing the images taken in by the eye peering into the scope placed firmly on "our reality" *http://www.youtube.com/watch?v=5UwvaSLbIgc.* That is to say, wake up! The future is arriving at an exponentially escalating rate. The shift in understanding necessary to realize that we have the keys to answer spiritual, religious, esoteric, theosophic, and all other philosophical questions and ideas with scientific proofs will be as mute in its infancy as Christ's death on a cross. Just as it took some three hundred years for one man's death in the desert to show its value in the manifestation of His messianic, cult-based following becoming His executioner's mandated orthodox, it will take time to relearn what has been oppressed and forgotten to the point of near spiritual extinction. While they don't draw fish in the sand, perhaps there are enough brave souls making rifts in the newly (re)constructed and ever-evolving web of consciousness that can bring whoever you are now and whoever I was when I wrote this together to enjoy a fulfilling reality in which we embrace each other for what we are. Star-crossed souls, blessed with the chance to experience everything our brain and soul, have the ability to access here—knowing love, pain, gain, loss, sharing, and caring in the miraculous manipulation of matter that is our only chance at *this* physical life. One with a transparent ceiling. Don't fear the images on the other side—simply looking through it won't crack the glass!

Resources

Watch DMT: The Spirit Molecule, here: *http://www.youtube.com/watch?v=c4FaDMak-TQ*; and here: *http://www.youtube.com/watch?v=eMOC44vby9g*

Terence McKenna rapping about DMT, here: *http://www.youtube.com/watch?v=EZAMKn2xr9E*

Watch Rupert Sheldrake, get banned from TED here: *http://www.youtube.com/watch?v=1TerTgDEgUE*

Watch Graham Hancock, get banned from TED here: *http://www.youtube.com/watch?v=YIjYA_X4ivg&feature=c4-overview-vl&list=PLAFA58CE2C884BBCC*

Graham Hancock Interview on Consciousness, Ayahuasca and more: *http://www.youtube.com/watch?v=B1Ne6rTo_5U&feature=c4-overview-vl&list=PL4E62628231F3DD64*

WHY I DON'T DO PSYCHEDELICS VERY OFTEN ANYMORE

BY THAD MCKRAKEN

I feel like I should start this off by saying that I'm never going to stop doing psychedelic drugs and to say that I don't do them very often anymore would sort of ignore the fact that I get high almost every day. In my mind, weed's a bit more of a hallucinogen than most people like to acknowledge—it just takes a bit more focus to be used in that capacity and people are lazy. Things like acid and mushrooms come right into your headspace and impose their essence into the very fiber of your world. They're the only reason I'm writing this weird shit for you today. I took mushrooms when I was eighteen and saw a universe of transcendent, shape-shifting, mutant space art that no one will ever be able to explain to me with conventional thought.

One of the more mind-blowing aspects of randomly experimenting with psilocybin as a teenager had to do with reading people like Carlos Castaneda shortly thereafter. Whatever you think about the guy's work, I can absolutely say that I was completely unfamiliar with the concept of sorcery or shaman-ism until that exposure. Most of us tune it out. I wasn't crazy. People had been basing their spiritual beliefs on the ritualistic use of entheogens ever since we can remember there being people, and yet, we've outright rejected this philosophy in Western culture. I just can't figure out why everything's fucked. I just can't figure it out.

The sensory fireworks of psychedelic high strangeness eventually led me into the even freakier spectacles of astral projection and chaos magick. I can say with all certainty that these things have led to more coherent cosmic informational downloads than psychedelics ever have. Hands down. The psychedelic experience is almost too powerful. You get a constant invasion stream of more than you can take, which is why it's so awesome, but it's also easier to process the information more effectively in alternate formats like sex ganj-i-tation and dream analysis. It typically takes me months to process a single trip, but there was a time when I didn't take them so sparingly.

The problem is the drug war. Set and setting largely dictate the resulting imprint of any entheogen voyage, and in this day and age, your average teenager dives into them like they would any other illegal substance. You could argue that the majority of our spiritual beliefs are backhandedly diluted shamanism when you get down to it. This is some powerful shit. And most of us just throw ourselves into it as if it's no different than choogling cheap beers and trying to get laid. I had absolutely no idea what I was getting myself into when I first tripped out. It was a Friday night—I was looking to party. What happened changed me forever. Not many people are going to tell you that's a possibility. The psychedelic experience has never really grown up past its frat boy party phase in Western culture. I'm still not of the mind that going to a crowded concert or festival is the best way to get something profound out of them, as hyper rad as that can be. Optimally, I think sex should be involved, but that's another story.

What I'm really getting at is that I sort of find psychedelic culture embarrassing to a certain extent. I remember reading about research done back in the sixties that indicated that without the implementation of an alternate spiritual practice, the long-term effects of a given acid trip on an individual's behavior were often negligible. I've known a crap ton of people who have taken a bunch of psychedelics, and very few of them have adopted any sort of alternative spiritual discipline whatsoever. It usually seems to be about, again, taking drugs as a means to escape life's bullshit and little more. A lot of times, it almost turns into a pissing contest, a sort of I-can-handle-more-than-you-can competition. Granted, I know a lot of other people who use it to inspire art, and that's a spiritual discipline unto itself, but very few people I've known take on even basic things like regular meditation or intentional dream manipulation. For most casual trippers, it doesn't change them much at all in the long term. If I were to put a finger on why this is, I'd wager it has something to do with the set and setting in which we take them, which is typically "at a party or party environment" under the impression that "they're just drugs fucking with your head." That's a pretty good setup for a failure to learn anything. Basically, just edit out all the freaky shit to the best of your abilities because there's no reason to pay much attention to it anyway. That's the attitude a lot of us are launching ourselves heavenward with.

God, the dumb shit I did in my youth. I have multiple stories of being drunk at like three a.m. at some random party and one of my friends finding acid. Yeah, let's take that, right now, after seventeen beers. It's not like it wasn't fun. I had the free time, and I used to be able to handle these shenanigans. On the other hand, it's also kind of stupid. I knew one girl who took mushrooms and had to be forcefully evacuated from a concert because she wigged the fuck out. I knew another guy who on several different occasions ate 'shrooms and wound up in a mental institution not really having any idea how he got there. He lost a couple jobs because of that. Right after high school, I sold a dude some and he went home and took them by himself. Ended up freaking and his mom took him to the hospital in the middle of the night to get his stomach pumped. That has to be one of the worst trips on record, and I still sort of feel bad for selling him those. Why doesn't anyone say obvious shit about psychedelic drugs? Why is it always just "Goooooo Teeeaaaam Druuugs!!!!!"?

No seriously, I'm about the biggest advocate for the stuff imaginable, but if someone who's never tried them asked, I'd tell them to try weed first. If you can't handle what that does to your brain (and a lot of people struggle with it), you really have no business going any further. Try smoking pot and meditating, and if you like that, by all means proceed. If you have a predilection to things like manic depression, schizophrenia, or spontaneous schizophrenic experience, taking acid or mushrooms might just push you way over the edge, which we've seen time and time again. When you do try them, take a small dose and wait for a couple hours. If you want more, take more, but increase the dosage in small increments to test what you can deal with. I so did not take this advice or think this way when I was younger. Even years back when I took mushroom chocolates with my wife, who had never done them, I accidentally gave her way too much because I'd never tried that batch and had no idea how strong they were. As a result, she had a rough first few hours (although she learned a few things) and I had to put in a bit of effort to pull her out of it, which worked. You'd think I would have figured the protocol out by this point, but it's not like you learn it in schools or on TV. They tell you to party.

The other important point is: don't do them all the freaking time. I'm of the mind that Timothy Leary's idea that you can take these things weekly without frying your brain is 100 percent off. When I read about the sixties, it never ceases to amaze me how large they went on that front. There is absolutely no way that wouldn't have made me go all Syd Barrett bat shit—which is quite depressing, I might point out. And it's not like I've never gone over the edge tripping balls too much like those guys did. When I moved out to Seattle twelve years ago, I arrived with a half sheet of acid in tow. On top of that, mushrooms just kept finding me. This of course led to some of the most transcendent sexual experiences of my life, but eventually an eerie communication started reverberating through the ether of psychic waves. I kept seeing the exact patterns repeating themselves over and over again.

Nothing new was piercing the veil of novel experience. It wasn't just that, but as with everything telepathy, I was starting to understand that the repeating feedback loop was meant to tell me something, and I'll try and translate it into English for you:

> Hey, Thad, it's us, the mutating hive-mind super gods. Yeah, we dig you too. I get that you like making us do this little trick we do, but guess what. We've shown you everything we can, little guy. Go out and, like, accomplish something with your life before you summon us again. Impress us and we'll impress you. Thanks for leaving us alone until you do.

Of course I didn't really listen to all that because back in the day, I was actually quite a bit denser than I am now, which is hard to believe. I did slow it down a bit, though, but of course I suppose a true lesson had to be imparted for them to get through to me. That happening took some of my most irresponsible drug behavior ever. I got promoted into this new management gig where I had to be on call and carry a pager regularly. The very first night that I had this responsibility, I showed up at home, and my girlfriend at the time was cutting up lines of coke. We bumped those, and then at like two in the morning, decided we're going to do the ecstasy we had lying around. That got weird and really sort of fun and emotional. We talked about a lot of repressed things we'd never touched on before. I actually answered a call from my work no problem despite being completely out of my head. Then when the E wore off at, like, six in the morning, we had the brilliant idea of taking the last bits of acid we had in the fridge. This is the problem with thinking about psychedelics as party drugs in a nutshell.

Now, it should be noted that before this happened, we'd done this stuff a few times and it was super weak, which is what influenced the decision. We thought it'd just put a perma-grin on our faces, which is what it did before. An hour later, though, while we were walking around the park, it somehow came on fiercer and more sinister than anything I've ever had creep up on me. The next ten or so hours were the most demonic horror-show invasion-type vibes that have ever slipped into my micro-verse. The spirits were fucking pissed. Now the message was:

> Hey, dipshit. We told you! *We told you!* What the fuck are you doing with your life? Jesus Christ, get a fucking hold of yourself. Go out and do something to impress us or never summon us like this ever again.

It was absolutely brutal, and one of, like, only two bad trips I've ever had. I remember at one point actually having sex with my quite gorgeous girlfriend and just stopping. I wasn't even into sex. That's how nuts it was. Eventually, she had the quite brilliant idea of giving me a bunch of Benadryl, which finally ended the ordeal and knocked me out. Thank god no one else paged me. It should be noted that it wasn't nearly as negative a vibe for her and I had way more experience with acid at that point.

After that, I didn't do hallucinogens at all for like two and half years, and I, you know, actually sort of accomplished some things with my life. I got into magick. Then next time I took them was again at, like, one in the morning when I was sort of drunk with the same girl, who called me out of nowhere. It ended up being one of the better trips I've had, and I've actually written about it fairly extensively. The spirits were pleased with me again. There sure is some potent psilocybin in the Pacific Northwest. The trip started with this kitten on a calendar someone gave me shooting psionic neon-red laser beams out of its eyes and into my eternal structure. Hadn't seen that trick before.

In the seven or so years since, I usually embark on one or two cosmic voyages a year, max. I typically do it to reward myself for some sort of accomplishment, which for me typically involves the completion of an album that I ritualistically listen to. I've been increasingly trying to plan these things out and hone the ritualistic element more precisely. This is all new, honestly. I did a 2012 audio acid ritual that quite quickly pointed out to me what the next step in my magickal evolution is: communion with my Holy Guardian Alien. Abduction basically, but from my body, not of my body. I've got a long way to go as far as mastering that goes, but until then, further figuring out how to maximize the set and setting of the psychedelic experience is sort of what I'm up to.

On that note, part of the reason I'm talking about all this is because I took a chocolate and went to the first Hypnotikon psychedelic music festival in 2013. Aces. Just top-shelf psychic residue spewing forth from that camp. I was peaking in the front row while an unholy Night Beats freak-out was going down. Amazing. Like going on a hyper-color great-space roller coaster. Did I gain any real new spiritual insights? Not really, but it certainly was mind blowing in epic proportions. So mind blowing that my head wasn't entirely back to normal for four whole days afterward. Christ, I'm getting old. It used to take me, like, a day to bounce back from that kind of madness overload. On the other hand, just kind of verifies my point. You probably don't want to be doing this sort of thing too often, but rather, ritualistically and with respect. The term *acid casualty* exists for a reason. Let us not forget that.

THE DIVINE SPARK

GIVING UP THE GREEN BITCH: REFLECTIONS ON CANNABIS, AYAHUASCA, AND THE MYSTERY OF PLANT TEACHERS

BY GRAHAM HANCOCK

I have some personal stuff to share here, and I intend to do so with complete openness in the hope that my experiences will prove helpful to some, thought provoking to others, and might stir up discussion around issues of consciousness and cognitive liberty that are often neglected in our society.

I'll soon be on my way to Brazil for what has become pretty much an annual pilgrimage to drink the visionary brew known as Ayahuasca, the "vine of souls," sacred among shamanistic cultures of the Amazon for thousands of years.

I'm not doing this for fun, or for recreation. Drinking Ayahuasca is an ordeal. It is, for a start, among the most horrible tastes and smells on the planet—a mixture of foot rot, raw sewage, battery acid, sulfur, and just a hint of chocolate. Within about forty-five minutes of drinking it, you frequently begin to suffer bouts of severe nausea, vomiting, and diarrhea. It is not for nothing that it is also known as "the purge" in the Amazon! And then, alongside the light and joy and valuable life lessons that are often part of Ayahuasca journeys, there are the sometimes terrifying psychic challenges including visionary encounters with seemingly malevolent entities in convincingly freestanding parallel realms that can be distressing to say the least.

So . . . I'm bracing myself. But I don't feel too much fear because of the deep understanding, which has gradually settled on me during the ten years I've worked with Ayahuasca, that a being of pure and boundless love—who may even be that being recognized by some ancient cultures as the Mother Goddess of our planet—has harnessed the brew in the context of time-honored ceremony to gain access to human consciousness and to teach us to do the best we can with the precious gift of our life on this earth.

I know how strange this may sound to those who have never drunk the Amazonian brew and never encountered "Mother Ayahuasca" in one of her many forms. Moreover—let me be clear—I am not making any empirical claims about the reality status of the sorts of experiences I'm talking about here. Perhaps they *are* all "within the brain," as skeptics say. Perhaps they *are* all imaginary (although if so, we must explain the transpersonal character of these imaginings). Perhaps they *are* "just hallucinations." Or perhaps what is going on here is that our brains are transceivers rather than generators of consciousness, in which case, could it be that Ayahuasca temporarily "retunes the receiver wavelength of the brain," giving us fleeting access to other levels or dimensions of reality not normally accessible to our senses? This is a serious question, and one that is taken seriously by increasing numbers of scientists working at the cutting edge of consciousness studies.

But setting aside the unsolved problem of whether Mother Ayahuasca is real or not, what is interesting is that at the level of phenomenology, many, many people have undergone encounters with her during Ayahuasca sessions and have had their behavior and their outlook profoundly changed as a result. Those changes are real even if materialist science would like to reduce the entity who inspires them to a mere epiphenomenon of disturbed brain activity.

Very often this entity (who, I repeat, may or may not be real but is experienced as real) gives us profound moral lessons in the depths of the Ayahuasca journey. We may be shown episodes from our lives in which we have behaved unkindly or unjustly to others, or been mean-spirited and unloving, or failed to live up to our own potential, and we will be shown these things with absolute clarity and transparency, with all illusions and excuses stripped away, so we are confronted with nothing more or less than the cold, hard truth about ourselves. Such revelations can be very painful. Frequently, people cry during Ayahuasca sessions because of them. But they bring insight and give us the chance to change our behavior in the future, to be more nurturing and less toxic, to be more considerate of others and to be more aware than we were before of the incredible privilege the universe has given us by allowing us to be born in a human body—an opportunity for growth and improvement of the soul that we absolutely must not waste.

Perhaps this is one of the reasons why Ayahuasca has been so very successful in getting people off addictions to harmful hard drugs. For example, Dr. Jacques Mabit has for many years been offering heroin and cocaine addicts incredibly effective treatments with Ayahuasca at his Takiwasi clinic in Tarapoto, Peru, where they might typically undergo twelve sessions with Ayahuasca in the space of a month. See here: *http://www.takiwasi.com/docs/ arti_ing/ayahuasca_in_treatment_addictions.pdf.*

A very high proportion of participants have such powerful revelations about the roots of their own problems and behavior during the sessions that they leave Takiwasi completely free of addiction, often without withdrawal symptoms, and never resume their habit. The success rate is far better than any of the conventional Western treatments for drug addiction.

Likewise in Canada, Dr. Gabor Mate was offering phenomenally successful Ayahuasca healing sessions to his drug-addicted patients before the Canadian government stepped in and stopped his work on the grounds that Ayahuasca itself is an illegal drug—see here: *http://www.theglobeandmail. com/life/health-and-fitness/bc-doctor-agrees-to-stop-using-amazonian-plant- to-treat-addictions/article4250579/.*

Yes, indeed, Ayahuasca *is* an illegal drug in the narrow Western definition of the term, which allows big pharmaceutical companies to make billions out of marketing consciousness-altering substances like Prozac or Ritalin but will send us to prison for exploring our own consciousness with time-honored sacred plants such as those that go into the Ayahuasca brew.

The plants concerned, which are simply cooked together with water, are the Ayahuasca vine, *Banisteriopsis caapi*, and a shrub from the coffee family, *Psychotria viridis*, called *chacruna* in the Amazon. (Very few other plants are also known to produce an effective brew, but *B. caapi* and *P. viridis* are probably the most widely used.)

The illegal element, contained in the leaves of *P. viridis*, is dimethyltryptamine (DMT), is arguably the most powerful hallucinogen known to man. Normally in the West, when we encounter DMT, it must be smoked—producing a rapid, overwhelming, but short-lived (twelve to fifteen minutes) alteration of consciousness, with which there is no negotiation. The smoking route has to be taken because there is an enzyme in our gut called monoamine oxidase that switches off DMT on contact. The ancient shamanistic societies of the Amazon, however, have found a workaround for this problem in the form of *B. caapi*, the vine itself, the other ingredient of the Ayahuasca brew, which it turns out, contains a monoamine oxidase inhibitor that switches off that enzyme in our gut and allows the DMT in the *chacruna* leaves to be absorbed orally. The result is a long, reflective (up to four-hour) visionary journey with which a great deal of negotiation is possible and that is very different qualitatively from the intense but brief experience of smoked DMT.

How, thousands of years ago, did shamans manage to select these two plants out of the estimated 150,000 different species found in the Amazon and learn to marry them together with water to produce the extraordinary potion that we know as Ayahuasca? It is a bit of a mystery, but shamans today claim it was not done by trial and error. Their ancestors, they say, were taught the secret by spirit beings as a gift to mankind.

Certainly those who have experienced the profound healing of harmful addictions that Ayahuasca can bring would agree that the brew is a very special gift. And on this matter, I speak not only from my knowledge of the research but also from personal experience.

In my case, the addiction was not to heroin or cocaine but took the form of a twenty-four-year cannabis habit that I began in 1987 at the age of thirty-seven and that I stopped abruptly at the age of sixty-one after five traumatic—but ultimately positive and life changing—Ayahuasca sessions in Brazil in October 2011.

In what I have to say next, I want to make a number of things extremely clear.

1. I am not putting down or disparaging cannabis or those who choose to use it. The "Green Bitch" in the title of this article is not cannabis itself but the abusive, self-indulgent relationship, entirely my own responsibility, that I had developed with the herb.

2. I recognize that cannabis can be an immensely helpful plant ally and that it has uniquely beneficial medicinal applications.

3. Quite apart from these medicinal properties, I recognize that the sensual qualities of cannabis can also be of great value—enhanced appreciation of food, music, the joys of lovemaking, the wonders of nature, and so on and so forth

4. I believe absolutely and unconditionally that it is the right of adults— an inalienable and fundamental human right—to make sovereign decisions over their own consciousness, including the right to enjoy the effects of cannabis and to benefit from its medicinal properties, should they choose to do so.

5. I remain as strongly opposed as I have ever been to that wicked and evil enterprise called the "war on drugs," which only serves to empower criminal gangs on the one hand and the worst and most controlling elements of government on the other. My views on this matter have not changed a jot since I wrote the article, "The War on Consciousness," in 2009 (*http://www.grahamhancock.com/features/the-war-on-consciousness.php.*).

6. Last but not least, I fully recognize that I myself benefited greatly from some aspects of my long relationship with cannabis. It lightened me up a lot in all sorts of ways and encouraged me to explore unusual connections between things that I would not normally have connected. I was a current affairs journalist when I was thirty-seven (that was in 1987—I was born in 1950) and I had written some nonfiction books on travel and current affairs issues, but I don't believe I would ever have moved on to writing about ancient mysteries (still nonfiction, although

many of my critics would disagree!) if it hadn't been for the new way of thinking that cannabis drew me into.

My first investigation of an ancient mystery was *The Sign and the Seal: A Quest for the Lost Ark of the Covenant*, which I began to research seriously in 1987, shortly after getting into cannabis (*http://www.grahamhancock.com/library/sats.php*). *The Sign and the Seal* was published in 1992. During the writing of that book, it was my habit to smoke cannabis only in the evenings for an hour or two before going to bed, but things changed from 1992 onward when I began to work on my next nonfiction historical mystery *Fingerprints of the Gods*. This was when I began to smoke cannabis all day long and to experiment with writing while I was stoned. I liked the result, and it soon became my practice to light up my first joint (or pipe if it was hash) the moment I sat down at my desk in the morning and then just to carry on smoking all day long until I went to bed—often in the small hours of the morning. This remained my habit thereafter—smoking continuously from morning to night, whether writing or not, and gradually seeking out stronger and stronger strains of the herb.

In 2006 or 2007, I switched from combustion products to a Volcano Vaporizer and at the same time began to buy from a grower who has amazing green fingers and produces incredibly powerful varieties of bud, most usually a variety called "Cheese"—I guess because of the smell—but way stronger than anybody else's product of that name that I have sampled.

Cannabis had always exaggerated paranoid tendencies that I probably have already, but these began to come more and more to the fore from 2007 onward with very negative effects on my behavior. The worst was that with absolutely no real-world justification at all, I began to become increasingly jealous and suspicious of my beloved partner, Santha, who is the most honest and true person I could ever hope to know. We would have increasingly frequent shouting matches, always initiated by me, as I accused her of all sorts of things that she had not done and would never do. And while part of me knew I was behaving in a more and more crazy way I couldn't stop the behavior or the feelings that were causing it. We still had happy times, but the jealousy and suspicion kept tightening their grip on me, and I can honestly say that I made Santha's life a misery between 2007 and 2011. It is a miracle and a tribute to her goodness of heart, care, and love for me that she didn't simply walk out and leave me but instead patiently and tolerantly persisted with me and tried to get me to see sense.

So what did those five sessions of Ayahuasca show me in October 2011 that led me abruptly, overnight, to end my cannabis habit? After all, I had already been smoking cannabis for sixteen years when I first began to drink Ayahuasca in 2003, initially as part of the research for my last nonfiction book *Supernatural* but later as a form of regular spiritual work. I drank Ayahuasca at least three times a year every year after that—so what changed? What was so different about those sessions in 2011?

When I look back on the whole process now, I can see that right from the very first session, Ayahuasca was giving me messages about the need to moderate my cannabis habit and showing me how my obsessional relationship with the herb was feeding and empowering negative aspects of my character. What's more, I received those messages loud and clear! But by then, I was already so involved with cannabis, so convinced that I could not live my life without its help, and so sure that all my creativity would dry up and wither if I did not continue to smoke it, that I simply ignored and blanked out what Ayahuasca was trying to tell me. Perhaps if I hadn't done that and had listened carefully instead, I could have got my relationship with cannabis into some sort of constructive balance and stayed within the boundaries of responsible use rather than self-indulgent abuse, and perhaps then I would never have needed to reject the herb completely, as Ayahuasca finally compelled me to do in 2011.

The process began on September 30, 2011, just before Santha and I flew down to Brazil. We were in the United States, at a location I won't disclose, where I smoked a pipe of pure DMT.

I had smoked DMT before. My first two experiences, in England in 2004, were terrifying (for those who are interested, I describe them in my book *Supernatural*). Then in 2009, I had three pipes in one night in the same US location I found myself in in 2011 and had amazing, healing experiences. Rotating lights moving all over my body, a sense that I was being scanned and that something was being fixed, some (slightly scary) computer-like circuitry that seemed to be sentient, an encounter with a sorcerer/magician figure who opened a rip in the earth for me and showed me an ancient buried city, etc. It was all great fun and rather exciting. Same thing happened in 2010—two pipes that time, separated by about an hour—and more beautiful, healing experiences.

So when I found myself back at the same location in the United States in 2011, I felt relaxed, and I welcomed what I expected would be another pleasant healing excursion to the DMT realms. I certainly had no expectation that anything particularly disturbing or terrifying would happen to me.

Turned out I was wrong.

As soon as I took my first long draw, I had the unsettling feeling that something intelligent and not necessarily friendly had leaped into my head from the spherical glass pipe. I held in the smoke as long as I could and then took another long draw. By now, there was a crackling, buzzing sound in my ears, and I felt utterly overwhelmed and had to lie back at once (I always lie back; no way can I stay sitting up!). Immediately, things were very different (though with some similarities) from all my previous smoked DMT experiences. The first thing I saw was something like a mandala with an ivory background and intricate brick-red geometric lines—like tracks—inside it. Between the lines, or tracks, imposed on the ivory background, were a large number of clock faces with weird hands. I'd seen something like this before, not under smoked DMT, but under a very strong dose of Ayahuasca. It terrified me then, don't know why, and it proceeded to terrify me again. Then I realized that the mandala (only an approximation; there was something very like computer circuitry about it as well, or even like one of those toy race-car tracks where little electric cars whiz round and round) was sentient and focused on me. I got a hint of eyes or feelers. There was something very menacing about the whole scene, and I began to feel uncomfortable and restless in my body. I had enough of my everyday consciousness left at that point to wish profoundly that I hadn't smoked the pipe, and I felt myself struggling— uselessly of course—against the effect. Then I heard an ominous voice, filled with a sort of malicious glee, that said very clearly, "*You're ours now.*" And I thought, *Shit, yes, I am yours now, not much I can do about it, but it's only for about ten more minutes and then I'm out of here.*

Since it was pointless to struggle, I resigned myself to the situation and thought, *Okay then, get on with it,* and immediately the mandala/intelligence and lots of its little helpers (who I felt but cannot describe) were all over me. I had the sense that my body was a huge, fat, bloated cocoon and that these beings were tearing it apart, tearing off lumps of matter and throwing them aside, getting access to the real, hidden me. I was aware that this was a place of absolute truth, like the Hall of Maat in the ancient Egyptian tradition, and that everything about me was known here—every thought, every action, good and bad, throughout my whole life—and the sense that the real hidden me within the cocoon was utterly transparent to these beings and that they were finding me wanting. About as far from being "justified in the judgment"—as the Egyptian texts put it—as it is possible to be, I realised that therefore I might face annihilation here. And I heard something like a trumpet blast and a loud voice that announced, as though this were a proclamation at court: "*Now the great unfolding will begin.*" Or possibly: "*Now the great transformation will begin.*"

That was the point where I lost consciousness of the material realm completely, and indeed of everything else. Feeling utterly helpless, utterly in the power of whatever process I was going through and of the intelligence that was running it, I fell into a darkness that seemed to last forever. I have no conscious recollection of what happened to me in there, only the conviction that it was something massive. When I began to come out of it, there were some moments—though this felt much longer than moments—when I was deeply confused and disoriented and had absolutely no idea where I was or why I was there. I could see the room around me but didn't recognise it, didn't even know it was a room at first, or even what a room is, and it kept melting back into that other terrifying reality out of which I was emerging. This has never happened to me with DMT before—I've always known, even in the depths of the experience, that I was having that experience because I had smoked a pipe of DMT and my body was in a specific place, which I did not forget, at a specific time. This was completely different and very, very scary.

Gradually my eyes began to focus, I remembered I had smoked DMT, and I looked around and saw Santha sitting on the edge of the bed, very calm, and incredibly strong. I was immersed in a wild melting storm of colours, and the only clear, sure thing in the whole place for me was Santha with her amazing strength and beauty and lines of light emerging from her body and rising up out of her and surrounding her. I remember falling to my knees on the floor in front of her and telling her, "I found you again," or something such (the sense was that I had known her in a past life and had found her again in this one) and also telling her that she is a goddess. I felt shaken but basically happy to be back on planet normal and was able to witness the sessions of several other participants without actually falling apart or melting down.

Over the next two days as we left the United States and made the journey to Brazil, I thought quite a lot about what had happened to me and began to feel very apprehensive. If I had been "theirs" for ten minutes and it had been so overwhelming, what was it going to be like for me being "theirs" for four hours at a time in the upcoming Ayahuasca sessions (since DMT is, of course, the primary active ingredient of Ayahuasca)?

Accordingly, on the night of the first session in Brazil (Monday, October 3) I chickened out and had a (for me) small cup of just 80 mililitres. Nothing much happened that night. Just restlessness and annoyance at myself for not taking a bigger dose.

So on the night of the second session—Wednesday, October 5—I increased the dose to 140 mililitres. The first two hours passed uneventfully and I was thinking, with some relief, that nothing was going to happen. That's when I became aware of a great serpent looking at me. Just the eye filled with wisdom and compassion. I got the message—"I can work with you but you have to surrender to me." So I did surrender and in fact said out loud, "I surrender." Immediately, she was inside me—a huge, very warm, almost hot presence inside my chest. I was immobilised, literally pressed down onto the mattress, and felt a tremendous vibrating sensation inside my chest and along my arms, and I thought—*Wow! This is weird.* But I could no longer resist or do anything about it, and the presence (whom I construe as Mother Ayahuasca) worked her way down into my abdomen and then down to my groin, and then back up again all the way up my trunk, up inside my chest, into my neck, and finally into my head, where she spent a very long time. I felt I was in the hands of a great power that was doing stuff with me whether I liked it or not. I have always trusted Mother Aya, so I didn't feel fear and stayed calm while this was being done to me.

Then suddenly the presence left, and I could move again, and I thought, *What an amazing blessing Mother Aya has just given me, to work with me for so long, and I felt sure that I had been healed.* But just when I was feeling that, I was suddenly back into the same DMT space that I had gotten lost in in the United States, and the feeling of calm and healing gave way to terror. I was aware once again of an entity (one this time, not many) all over my body, dancing around me, filled with malice, and I spent the next half hour or so in utter terror and also feeling in some way betrayed by Mother Aya—that she had left me in the hands of this, that she had let me be "theirs" again.

The third session, I took a low dose and pretty much escaped under the radar.

The fourth session, I increased the dose, and Santha also took a larger dose, and we went through an extraordinary series of traumas together. Santha had the sense of some terrible dark being pulling out her heart and saying to her, "I'm going to take you to teach Graham a lesson." She communicated this to me—and I at this point had the DMT trickster all over me again— and I totally freaked out. I had a massive realization of all the pain I had caused Santha in recent years and how this was a black mark on my soul and how I absolutely had to do something about it and stop living selfishly and start being a nurturing, loving, giving, and above all *trusting* presence in her life—otherwise I would be doomed, and I would doom her too. I was filled with grief and terror that she would die right there on the mattress beside me. Both of us were sobbing and crying. Santha grabbed hold of me and said, "Don't let them take me," and our shaman came over to help and began singing just an amazingly poignant and beautiful song, which in due course helped to ground both of us.

The next morning in the sharing (a common feature of Ayahuasca sessions worldwide), I expressed my intent to change my behavior and be a better partner to Santha in the future, and I said I was determined to change my relationship with cannabis. I didn't think it was realistic, after twenty-four years, to give it up completely, but I resolved to go back to my pre-1992 pattern of only smoking at night and never again all day.

On the fifth session, after the traumas of the fourth, I took a very small cup of Ayahuasca—less than 50 militres; still, I didn't quite get under the radar. I was approached by entities offering me food and drink, but I remembered the rule expressed in many ancient cultures that one should never eat food in the Underworld (witness, for example, the story of Demeter and Persephone), so I refused and opened my eyes to stop the vision.

At the final sharing, I once more expressed my intent to rid my life of all jealousy and suspicion toward my wonderful Santha and to get my relationship with cannabis under tight control, smoking only at night, not all day.

We flew home on October 14, arriving October 15. It was a very tiring and uncomfortable journey with no legroom and the fasten-seat-belts sign on almost all night. I naturally wanted to comfort myself with a little cannabis when we got back, so I fired up my Vaporiser and filled a nice fat bag. But as soon as I started to smoke it, I began to feel really awful—as though I had a poisonous fog inside my head. Immediate massive paranoia set in, and I felt I was on the edge of going completely insane. I persevered and took a few more puffs, but the feeling of madness just got worse and worse. Panic and total self-revulsion seized me—things I have never felt before with the herb. The upshot was that I squeezed out the rest of the vapor in the bag to get rid of it without smoking it and put the Vaporiser away. As I walked upstairs from my office, shuddering with paranoia, convinced I was going crazy, and disgusted at myself, I suddenly realised that my stated intention in Brazil "to change my relationship with cannabis and use less of it" just wasn't enough. It wasn't good enough just to use it less. It hit me with the force of a revelation. I could never smoke cannabis again, or I would be doomed. I had become a complete slave to my abusive, seductive relationship with the herb; it had exacerbated the worst aspects of my personality, and my only hope was to give it up completely. Sure, I reasoned, it might be difficult for me to write without it (since for so long it had been inextricably interlinked with my writing life), but I was just going to have to deal with that.

So I have not smoked any more, well over a year has passed, and I remain resolutely determined never to smoke again. I feel free now. Liberated. As though a whole new chapter of my life has opened up in front of me. I find myself enjoying little things I didn't enjoy before, appreciating every moment that I am not stoned and that my head is clear. It feels *great* to have a clear head! My concerns about the effect on my writing have also turned out to be completely groundless. I had feared I would lose my inspiration without the herb as my muse, but quite the opposite has turned out to be the case. I am buzzing with new ideas and creativity. Also, I'm *much* more efficient—writing between three and five times as many words a day as I did before.

Last but not least, my crazy jealousy and suspicion of Santha have evaporated like a bad dream. I simply don't have those feelings anymore, or the toxic behavior that used to go with them. We're having lots of fun together and have rediscovered the positive and beautiful basis for our love.

As to my soul, I think I've been given another chance—a chance not to be found wanting in the judgment when death finally comes. I am grabbing that chance with both hands.

SUPERNATURAL

TOWARD AN EXPLORATION OF THE MIND OF A CONQUERED CONTINENT: SACRED PLANTS AND AMERINDIAN EPISTEMOLOGY[1]

BY LUIS EDUARDO LUNA

INTRODUCTION

The conquest of the Americas by the empires of Europe resulted in the nearly total loss of the cultural, technical, and intellectual achievements of one-third of the population of the world of that time. The Amerindian crops adopted by the European conquerors spread around the world: corn, potatoes, manioc, tomatoes, pepper, calabash, certain beans, as well as stimulants such as cacao, coca, and tobacco. Yet the advanced technical capabilities of many Amerindian societies in the fields of astronomy, engineering, medicinal plants, ceramics, weaving, basketry, and—as is becoming increasingly evident—the sophisticated and efficient use of the land, did not have any significant impact on the home countries of the conquerors.

Apart from the academic work of relatively small circles of historians, ethnologists, and anthropologists and the obscure accounts of travelers, there was no European acknowledgment of a single philosophical idea from the people of the Americas prior to the recently awakened interest in Amerindian shamanism.[2] There was no technical or philosophical/theological exchange between the peoples of the two continents. Europeans viewed the Amerindian population as objects of conversion, assimilation, subjugation, or annihilation.

The sacred books of the Maya were burned in 1562. The quipus of the Andes—a work of the Devil according to 16th-century friars—were destroyed by a decree in 1583.[3] The sacred groves, temples, and places of worship of the Amerindians were desecrated. Revered works of art were melted down for the price of their gold. The repository of Amerindian traditions, the bearers of wisdom who "remembered" and knew "how to speak," were hunted and killed. Their knowledge was treated as the work of Satan, still today a powerful archetypical figure in both the Christian and Islamic worlds.

It was the obliteration of the wonderings about the nature of reality of a whole continent with the transplantation into the Americas of an Indo-European syndrome that, according to Gimbutas (1989), had already destroyed the spiritual manifestations of European Neolithic cultures, the "Old Europe," largely associated with the natural environment. At the time of the arrival of the European conquerors, the "Old World" for a long time had been engulfed in ideological religious wars in which deviation from pronounced dogmas could be punished with death.[4]

All of this went hand in hand with deforestation, a development that in the West goes back to Greco-Roman times, if not even further back in time to the fear of forests: it can be traced to the Mesopotamian myth of Gilgamesh, the first hero in world literature, who embarked on a quest to kill Humbaba, the demon of the forest, who lived in the mountainside cedar groves harvested to the last by the ancient Sumerians (Harrison 1992).[5]

The deforestation of Europe was carried out in the interests of agriculture; the conversion to grasslands for the grazing horses, cattle, sheep, goats, and pigs to satisfy an insatiable appetite for meat and milk; the construction of houses, palaces, fortresses, boats, and weapons, and for strategic or religious reasons.

The Americas are still being subjected to the kind of devastating deforestation that already by the time of the conquest of America had decimated the forests of much of Europe, North Africa, and the Middle East.[6] Domesticated plants and animals from Eurasia accompanied the conquest of the Americas, destroying much of the original biota, a phenomenon referred to by Crosby (1986) as "ecological imperialism." At the same time, the indigenous population was condemned to humiliation, subjugation, and poverty, barely surviving history's greatest ethnocide. Almost by a miracle after five hundred years of persecution, one aspect of Amerindian cosmology did survive, although in an attenuated form: shamanism.

SHAMANISM IN THE AMERICAS

The term *shamanism* is used here to refer to an innate human capacity, culturally manifested in various ways, which include several universal elements: altered states of consciousness (ASC), community rituals, spirit world interaction, and healing (Winkelman 1992, 2010). The ASC produce a cognitive and personal transformation by means of various techniques used to enter into an "integrative mode of consciousness" (Winkelman 1996, 2010), which include sensory overload or sensory deprivation, drumming, chanting, fasting, isolation, meditation, and hyperventilation. Both in the past as well as in the present, numerous examples can be found of the use of psychotropic plants, often in combination with one or more of the other techniques.

The cognitive changes thus achieved may involve journeying to complex, stratified, and interconnected worlds perceived as ontologically real, and contacting entities often related to the natural environment, such as animal spirits, or the spirits of the dead. These changes may involve a symbolic death or experiencing a transformation into an animal such as a bird or a powerful predator to visit specific realms or to better perform a certain task.

Understood in this sense, shamanism entails a socially recognized status that includes the possibility of certain individuals being able to heal, cause harms, prophesize, mediate in situations of social conflict, or obtain leadership capacities by means of the knowledge and power acquired by such techniques and supernatural contacts.

Shamanism was of central importance in the Americas prior to the arrival of the Europeans and still plays a central role among contemporary indigenous groups as well as among certain segments of the mestizo population. Its ethnography has been extensively and widely documented.

When examined from the perspectives of the shamanic paradigm, much of the art left behind by pre-Columbian societies as well as specific paraphernalia, point in this direction. The archaeological record suggests that shamanism may have often been intimately associated with the use of certain plants, usually considered as sacred, and as proposed by Winkelman, now known as psychointegrator plants.

Winkelman (1996, 2010) uses the concept of psychointegrator plants and the related concept of integrative modes of consciousness to postulate that they reflect not only what happens at the level of the self but also at the biological level, manifested in theta wave synchronization, i.e., at three to six cycles per second. The Winkelman model posits an accessing of information from the lower levels of the brain, the brain stem or reptilian brain that regulates vegetative processes such as breathing, heartbeat, and the fight-or-flight mechanism as well as accessing the paleomammalian brain or limbic system that supports functions such as emotion, behavior, long-term memory, and olfaction. Winkelman suggests that in this way, the information that is normally habituated or relegated to the subconscious is made available through a reverse inhibitory process.

In addition, Winkelman posits that at the physiological level, psychointegrator plants and substances enhance the way the serotonin system functions, modulating and integrating information within the brain. They also inhibit very specific mechanisms, releasing certain dopamine-related capacities of the brain normally repressed by serotonin, and consequently enhancing the functioning of the dopaminergic system, which is fundamental to motivational and learning processes of the brain.

Winkelman uses the concept of psychointegrator plants to refer to experiential, phenomenological, or psychological aspects of their physiological effects. He suggests that the resulting mentation (how you think) and emotion (how you feel) may produce a holistic state of psychological integration and emotional growth.

Some of the alkaloids found in psychointegrator plants are surprisingly similar to human brain neurotransmitters, reflecting adaptations made by human ancestors in the course of evolutionary processes. Psychointegrator plants are traditionally used across cultures in a religious, spiritual, and often therapeutic context and may enhance some of the innate capacities of consciousness, integrating various forms of information. They seem to enhance the innate capacities of human beings for spiritual experiences as well as the presentiment of spirits embodied in nature.

The standard Eurocentric worldview has no place for the powerful cognitive transformation facilitated by psychointegrators. For this reason, the typical inhabitant of a Eurocentric worldview is unable to make any sense of examples of Amerindian art such as the extraordinary Tolita ceramic from Ecuador shown in Figure 1 (Klein & Cruz 2007). In Europe, prior to the advent of modern art, there were few representations of the cognitive changes such as of body perception, of the disintegration of the self, or of the perception of nonnatural entities that may be produced by psychointegrators. But once shamanism and integrative states of consciousness are taken into account, a great deal of Amerindian art begins to make sense.

A case in point is the pioneering work of the "Father of Colombian Anthropology" Gerardo Reichel-Dolmatoff and his study of the pre-Columbian gold work in the Gold Museum in Bogotá (1988). He argues that by recognizing the relationship between ritual objects and the subjacent shamanic ideology, a deeper significance is revealed. In fact, the greater part of the figurative representations constitutes a consistent and articulated complex of shamanic art, with transformation as the unifying theme (Reichel-Dolmatoff 1988). He contends that much of the artwork preserved can be explained in terms of the shamanic paradigm. Certain iconographic elements may serve to identify particular figures as shamans, such as special headdresses, specific postures, rattles, and more significant representations of animal transformation or journeys by means of animal auxiliaries.

Figure 1: Tolita ceramic, Ecuador

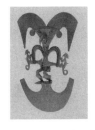

Figures 2: Pre-Columbian
gold work

The ritual objects include several golden snuff trays from the territory of the Muisca people in the central highlands of present-day Colombia. The snuff trays, decorated with felines and birds commonly associated with shamanism, were once used for the storage of small amounts of the highly psychoactive powder obtained from the crushed roasted seeds of *Anadenanthera peregrina*. The ritual objects also include golden poporos once used for the storage of small amounts of lime as well as poporo sticks once used in the consumption of coca—the poporo sticks are topped with tiny and complex heads with apparent shamanic motifs.

Representations of birds or winged objects are also predominant in the goldwork. Reichel-Dolmatoff suggests that the winged motif is connected with the shamanic sphere and is a conscious or unconscious allusion to shamanic flight. In many instances he recognizes, in different styles and variations, the figures as that of a shaman transformed into a bird, a "bird-man" (two examples from Reichel-Dolmatoff 1988). There are also highly abstract examples of goldwork, which are variations of the birdman motif, once the basic elements are recognized.

Effigies of various animals—sometimes of a fantastic, nonnaturalistic nature—sometimes accompany the central figure, which the author interprets as animal auxiliaries perhaps representing qualities such as sharpness of sight or hearing, aggressiveness, the ability to undergo metamorphosis, etc. The incorporation of animal qualities—in its more radical form being complete transformation into an animal—or the transference of those qualities to their patients being one of the characteristics of shamans in many cultures (Luna 1992).

Reichel-Dolmatoff also presents examples of golden figurines with a toad spread on the head of the central figure, perhaps a reference to *Bufo marinus,* whose parotid glands produce bufotenine, a psychoactive alkaloid, as well as figurines in which semispherical bodies appear on the head, possibly a reference to psychoactive mushrooms according to Schultes and Bright (1979). In some of these figures, both elements appear.

The goldwork preserved at the Museo del Oro is thus for Reichel-Dolmatoff "a treasure of shamanic art, a treasure of forms and ideas which for thousands of years have constituted one of the cornerstones of the Indian cultures of this country," and the bird-man, the ecstatic shaman, one of its key symbols.

Rebecca R. Stone in *The Jaguar Within: Shamanic Trance in Ancient Central and South American Art* examines what she calls "shamanic embodiment," which may be artistically expressed along a continuum that may go from predominantly human to creative mixtures embedding animal selves to images almost wholly given over to the ineffable. She argues that in order to represent a shaman, a liminal being who is both Here and Not-Here, there is a deliberate engagement with ambiguity, perhaps the essential feature of shamanism, which "productively fires the artistic imagination, catalyzing inventive ways to express the ineffable cosmic flux," and using such strategies as "juxtaposition, conflation, substitution of parts, *pars pro toto* (the part stands for the whole), inversion, double reading (through contour rivalry, figure-ground reversal, and three-dimensional versus two-dimensional aspects), mirror-imaging, abstraction, and interiority" (Stone 2011:67).

Among the myriad possible artistic approaches to the paradoxes intrinsic to embodying of the shamanic Self, she proposes four general traits: creative ambiguity, authority, cephalocentrism, and the trance gaze. By way of evidence, she cites examples of ancient Costa Rican and Central Andean art, at the same time pointing to the possibility of subjecting thousands of works of art from all over Central and South America to a similar analysis making use of the concepts she has presented.

Stone's compelling and encompassing well-crafted argumentation is impossible to encapsulate in a few paragraphs. Here are some ideas I found particularly attractive. How can the artist through colors, shapes, and lines in a static image capture the flux of liminality, of existing somewhere suspended between states of being, of true multiplicity in the Self? Amerindian art gives a plethora of solutions. The artists, without the constraints of an artistic mandate to reproduce terrestrial appearances, have as their goal the recorporealization of the shaman, something that entails a decorporealization, just as does the visionary experience, and then the rebuilding of a different idea of a spirit-body as a holder for the being in trance. The visionary experience, on the other hand, requires a participation in a convincingly nonhuman-centered gestalt of all nature infused with life and obviates the need to make hard-edged visual distinctions between a person and a bat or a peanut and a divine being. The artist is able to throw aside discrete categories and mimetic attachments to this world and its static constituents by exploring possibilities beyond how things look under normal conditions, creating combinations that defy description. The Western worldview limits our understanding of such art objects because seemingly neutral terms such as *image, depiction,* and *representation* inevitably communicate the opposite of the shamanic approach to the object. Amerindian artists, on the other hand, "embrace creative ambiguity." Stone proposes that the object we call an effigy of a shaman served as both a visual rendition of the shaman's many selves and as one of the shaman's subjective selves.

We may infer that seen as a whole, totally unrecognized by most people, pre-Columbian art is full of allusions to unseen realms, shamanic transformation, subjective states, and alternative modes of cognition. One of the most common themes is the jaguar transformation. The human/feline motif is found in South America from the earliest cultures, such as in Caral (ca. 4,600 B.P.) in coastal Peru. The idea that shamans are able to transform into jaguars is widespread even today in the Amazon, as shown by Reichel-Dolmatoff (1975) in his monograph on this subject. Transformation into other animals, such as serpent, harpy eagle, or whatever animal it would be necessary to acquire certain qualities or cognitive abilities is also believed to be possible. Therianthropes, a composite of human and animal, sometimes of several of them, as well as many other motifs expressing various inner states are thus common in Amerindian iconography. Therianthropes may be either a representation of entities acquiring anthropomorphic features in order to communicate with human counterparts, or an expression of a subjective perceptional mode in which the human acquires animal qualities. These images would instantly evoke in Amerindian people particular cognitive states related to multidimensional, multilayered cosmologies, spaces in the mind (perhaps the perception of alternate realities) nowadays mostly forgotten but once visited by the ancestors of all of us, as may be deduced from numerous examples of Paleolithic rock art (Clottes & Lewis-Williams 1998; Lewis-Williams 2002; Hancock 2005).

PSYCHOINTEGRATOR PLANTS

Throughout the Americas in the past and in some places still today, shamanism has gone hand in hand with the use of psychointegrator plants. The best known are peyote (*Lophophora williamsi*) and psilocybin mushrooms in Mesoamerica; several species of *Brugmansia, Anadenanthera colubrina,* and *Anadenanthera peregrina* in South America (also introduced in pre-Columbian times in the Caribbean); the various San Pedro cacti (*Trichocereus pachanoi* and other *Trichocereus* species) in Andean and coastal areas of Peru; Ayahuasca (*Banisteriopsis caapi* with *Psychotria viridis*) and *yajé* (*B. caapi* with *Diplopterys cabrerana*) in the Upper Amazon; and of course tobacco, sacred in the whole of the Americas. In more restrictive areas, many other psychotropic plants were or are still used.

According to Alicia Fernández Distel (1980), *A. colubrina* was already being used in Inca Cueva, Puna de Jujuy, Argentina, around 2100 BCE. It played a central role in the extraordinary Tiwanaku culture, from roughly 300 to 1000 AD, as evidenced in representations of snuff paraphernalia in monoliths and the ubiquity of snuff kits, including tablets, inhalators, spoons, and pouches with powder from seeds of this plant, conserved in San Pedro de Atacama, Chile, an area heavily influenced by the Tiwanaku culture (Torres & Rebke 2006; see figures 3–4, courtesy of C. M. Torres).

According to Gordon Francis McEwan (2001:197) prehistoric agricultural groups associated with the Saladoid tradition (ca. 5300–2000 BCE) transplanted *A. colubrina* into the West Indies from the Orinoco valley, reaching Puerto Rico by 2300–2000 BCE. Several pre-Columbian mortars from the Amazon area probably associated with the use of *cohoba* or *yopo* have been preserved (McEwan 2001). The use of *A. peregrina* was witnessed during his second trip (1497–98) to the Americas by Columbus, who had the Catalonian friar Ramón Pané document its use in the very first book written in the Americas in a European language.[7]

The oldest evidence of the use of *Trichocereus pachanoi* dates from around 2000–1500 BCE in Las Aldas on the north-central coast of Peru (Fung 1972; Polia Meconi 1996: 289). The San Pedro cactus played a central role in Chavin culture in the northern Andean highlands of Peru, as evidenced in figures from the religious and political center of Chavin de Huántar (900–200 BCE, see Figure 5) as well as from Nazca (100 BCE to 700 AD).

The oldest known dates for tobacco are from the north coast of Peru, with dates ranging between 2500 and 1800 BCE (Pearsall, 1992: 178). Coca chewing in northern Peru began in at least 6000 BCE (Dillehay et al. 2010).

PRE-COLUMBIAN AMAZON

Compared to the extraordinary cultures found in coastal Peru, the Andes, and Mesoamerica, until recently the pre-Columbian Amazon area was considered to be devoid of high culture. It is now clear that human beings

THE DIVINE SPARK

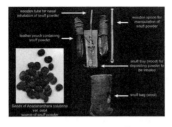

Figure 3: Paraphernalia from San Pedro de Atacama (Courtesy C. M. Torres)

Figure 4: The Ponce monolith in the Kalasasaya yard of Tiwanaku

Figure 5: Therianthrope with feline characteristics holding a stalk of San Pedro cactus, Circular Plaza of the Old Temple, Chavin de Huántar (Photo C. M. Torres)

were living in the Amazon area at least twelve thousand years ago or even longer (Roosevelt 1994). The oldest ceramics in South America, from 5080 BCE, were found in Taperinha, near Santarem, in the Brazilian Amazon area (Roosevelt et al. 1991). Several agricultural centers have been localized in the Amazon area, perhaps independent of those where agriculture was autonomously originated in the Americas (Mesoamerica, the Andes, and eastern North America). Archaeologists such as Clark L. Erikson, William L. Balée, Michael Heckenberger, Eduardo Neves, Augusto Oyuela-Caycedo, and others are changing our ideas of the pre-Columbian Amazon with the discovery of the vast manmade channels, raised fields, mounds, and forest islands connected by earthen causeways in various parts of the Amazon, and the existence over large areas of the so-called *terra preta do indio* (Amazonian Dark Earths), or manmade soils of the highest quality, and at times two meters deep in areas where natural soils are no more than a few centimeters, as well as large orchards of semidomesticated fruit trees (see, for example, Woods et al. 2009). In Acre, Brazil, a large number of geoglyphs, geometric earthworks, have been localized (Schaan et al.) and a large circle of granite stones found in Calçoene, near Macapá, in Amapá state, also in Brazil, dating back to between 700 AD and 1000 AD suggest a knowledge of astronomy.

The indications of large sedentary populations, perhaps in the millions, and levels of civilization much higher and complex than previously thought, lend credence to the picture painted in 1542 by Friar Gaspar de Carvajal in his chronicle of the odyssey of Francisco de Orellana and his men, the first Europeans to travel down the Amazon River from the Napo River to the Atlantic Ocean. Carvajal wrote of great "capitanías," large human settlements on both sides of the river, and of extraordinary ceramic work, "the best in the world" even "better than then of Málaga."

It is difficult to imagine the kind of cultures that occupied this vast area, given the cataclysmic decimation of up to 95 percent of the population throughout the Americas following European contact (Stannard 1992). In 1634, Acuña still talked about myriads of people living along the rivers and cultivating soils of great fertility. Nearly one hundred years later, Charles-Marie de La Condamine reported on his journey into the Amazon, which started in 1743, that the area was to a great extent empty. The most probable cause was the diseases brought by the European conquerors.

The material culture of the inhabitants of the Amazon of today and probably even more so of the Amazon of the distant past is based on a sophisticated use of plant material. The inhabitants have proved to possess a great knowledge of edible, venomous, medicinal, and psychoactive plants. Amazonian Indians discovered the properties of latex from the *Hebea* genus, the source of rubber: the rubber boom in 1850 to 1914, which was to become a pillar of the automobile and weapon industries, resulted in the enslavement of local populations; a similar havoc was also suffered by the local populations in the Congo Free State, the personal fiefdom of the ill-famed King Leopold II of Belgium. Quinine from the bark of Ecuadorian cinchona trees was used until the 1940s in the treatment of malaria. Plants containing curare have not only been used for various types of arrow poisons but have also been vital for the development of the techniques of open heart, radical brain, and craniofacial surgery as well as organ transplants.

The people of the Amazon live in one of the areas of largest biodiversity on the planet. It is becoming increasingly evident that the biodiversity of the Amazon is to a great extent the result of the natural resource management of the pre-Columbian people of the Amazon. Some of this knowledge is still preserved today by the Cayapó of the Brazilian Amazon, who demonstrate a great understanding of ecosystems, plant and animal species association, insect-plant interaction, as well as sophisticated soil taxonomy (Posey 1984,

1991, Posey et al. 1989). The Cayapó have been credited with the creation of forest islands on mostly savanna covered territories, with the recognition of marginal or open spots within the forest that have micro-environmental conditions similar to those in the savannah, as well as with the exchange and spread of useful species between ecological zones through the transplantation of seeds, cuttings, tubers, and saplings (Posey 1984, 1991, Posey et al. 1989).

To a certain extent, the Amazon is an anthropogenic forest, a gigantic garden partially created by human beings through millennia of interaction with the natural environment.

THE AYAHUASCA/YAJÉ COMPLEX IN THE UPPER AMAZON

The knowledge of the people of the Amazon of what may be called the pharmacology of consciousness needs perforce to be placed within the context of such a sophisticated high culture.

Snuffs made from the seeds of *A. peregrina* or from the sap of *Virola theiodora*, are still used today to induce altered states of consciousness. Various indigenous groups of Colombia and some areas of the Ecuadorian Amazon as well as indigenous groups belonging to several linguistic families in the Upper Amazon still today use the pounded stem of the vine *B. caapi*, often in combination with *Diplopterys cabrerana*, a vine in the same family (Malpighiaceae), either as a cold infusion or as a decoction called yajé (also spelled *yagé*). In other areas of Ecuador, as well as the Peruvian, Bolivian, and Brazilian Amazon, indigenous groups use the stem of *B. caapi* in combination with the leaves of *P. viridis* (Rubiaceae), usually as a decoction, under the Quechua name *Ayahuasca* (also spelled *ayawaska*). There are other vernacular names for both yajé and Ayahuasca.

There is no clear evidence of the earlier use of either of these plant preparations beyond the statements by 18th-century missionaries, who considered the preparations to be agents of the Devil. However, given the antiquity of the use of other psychotropic plants, it seems unlikely that yajé or Ayahuasca is a relatively recent innovation. It is little more than speculation to claim that knowing how to prepare yajé or Ayahuasca derives from some kind of higher psychopharmacological knowledge of indigenous Amazonians. But what is beyond speculation is that the preparation of yajé or Ayahuasca requires the mastery of a sophisticated technique.

D. cabrerana and *P. viridis* contain the alkaloid DMT (dimethyltryptamine), which is orally inactive due to its degradation by the monoamine oxidase (MAO) present in the human gut and liver. The MAO-inhibitor harmine in *B. caapi* protects the DMT in *D. cabrerana* and *P. viridis* from oxidative metabolism, thus allowing the transport of the DMT through the intestinal wall and liver and making it available for the central nervous system. The serotonin reuptake inhibitor tetrahydroharmine in *B. caapi* most probably adds to the overall effect of Ayahuasca on consciousness. In addition to the two main alkaloids harmine and tetrahydroharmine, some varieties of *B. caapi* contain active amounts of harmaline.

Yajé and Ayahuasca are still used by numerous indigenous groups of the Upper Amazon for contacting normally hidden spiritual realms, for hunting, for learning about the plans of other people, for finding the etiology of illness, or for divination. Yajé or Ayahuasca is frequently a source for their art, expressed in body painting or the decoration of their material culture. It may also be used for memorizing myths or tales important to their communities; for reinforcing the social moral values, especially among the youth; and for getting in touch with the spirits of other plants to learn about their properties (all uses are not necessarily present in each and every indigenous group).

The importance of the plants involved in these preparations is reflected in myths and narratives. They may have been revealed by beings living in underwater realms—considered especially powerful—or the offspring of the Sun after impregnation of a woman through her eyes (Reichel-Dolmatoff 1975, Lagrou 2000, Luna 2011). The plants are considered sacred, with their collecting and handling often ritualized and their consumption occurring in special ceremonies, either collective or intimate.

In some areas, these and other plants are considered teachers, a commonly held idea the author first encountered while doing fieldwork in the Peruvian Amazon among *mestizo vegetalistas,* or practitioners, specialized in certain especially powerful plants, or *vegetales* (Luna 1984, 1986), many of whom primarily used Ayahuasca for the diagnosis and treatment of illness as well as for divination. Another commonly held idea is that by taking Ayahuasca and other sacred plants, it is possible to have a clearer mind and focus, enhanced sensory perception and imagery (and therefore the possibility of learning more easily), in addition to access to information not readily available in everyday life. It is commonly held that the plants strengthen and protect people from illnesses, including those caused by living agents such as other human beings or spirits.

Practitioners often talk about *la ciencia de la Ayahuasca,* a concept that describes the ability to find the plants in the forest, the knowledge of the kind of soil where they grow, their color and shape, the part of the plants used, as well as the way to prepare them such as the amount of plant material and water added, the intensity of the fire, the point of boiling, the moment at which the pot is taken off the fire, even the thoughts, songs, or prayers of the person who is preparing the brew.

Plant teachers include not only the plants involved in the preparation of Ayahuasca but also other plants that are used either as occasional admixture plants, such as several species of *Brugmansia* and *Brunfelsia grandiflora,* or are used by themselves, such as *Couroupita guianensis* that is said to teach in the dreams, which are not necessarily psychotropic (Luna 1986, Beyer 2009). The subjacent idea is that by ingesting these plants, one gets in touch with their spirits and learns from them, either directly in the visions that they may produce, or in dreams. Practitioners claim that it is possible to fine-tune one's psyche in a controlled way in order to acquire certain cognitive abilities to perceive aspects of reality not available in normal consciousness. The Aguaruna of the Peruvian Amazon, for example, believe it is not enough simply to know the facts: one must learn how to bring the body, the intellect, and the emotions together into the epiphany of the visionary experience (Brown 1985). The acquired knowledge inspires cultural creations such as song, dance, body painting, or narratives, or otherwise benefits the individual or group. In contemporary terms, we could say that for the practitioners, the plants are cognitive tools to enhance their cultural production.

A NOTE ON AYAHUASCA SHAMANISM AND ART AMONG THE SHIPIBO OF THE UCAYALI RIVER, PERU

In 1987, I spent a month in Santa Rosa de Pirococha, a small Shipibo settlement of around seventy inhabitants on the left bank of the Ucayali River approximately between the cities of Pucallpa and Orellana. The Shipibo are famous for their elaborated designs—*kené* in their language—with which in earlier times they decorated the objects of their material culture and their bodies. Nowadays, Shipibo women still embroider their skirts with elaborate geometrical patterns. Originality is emphasized so that within their overall particular style, all the skirts are different (Figure 6). Nowadays, Shipibo women also produce high-quality ceramics, which they also decorate with elaborate geometrical patterns (Figure 7). The Shipibo seem to see themselves as not only covered but also surrounded by a normally invisible field of colorful tridimensional patterns.

The Shipibo are locally known for their shamanic traditions associated with the use of *shori,* their vernacular name for Ayahuasca. The reason for my visiting Santa Rosa de Pirococha was to study the process of "learning from the plants," which involves a certain diet and the repetitive ingestion of Ayahuasca. During the one-month stay, I was guided by Don Basilio Gordon,

Figure 6: Young Shipibo Women,
Santa Rosa de Pirococha, 1987

Figure 7: Shipibo woman decorating
a ceramic, Santa Rosa de Pirococha,
1987

at the time a reputed shaman and now deceased. For one month, I followed the prescribed traditional diet consisting of only manioc, plantains, and at times a little fish, and did not consume any salt, sugar, or alcohol. I drank Ayahuasca thirteen times. As I do not know the language, my training basically consisted of following the melody of the songs while under the effect of the brew and accompanying Don Basilio in his trips to the forest to see various plants.

Don Basilio told me that when you know the songs of a given plant, it is not necessary to use the physical plant, as all their physical properties are embedded in the song. In this tradition, healing is basically done through the songs. There were always a few mestizo patients attending the ceremonies during my stay, but no members of the Shipibo community, except Irineo, a man in his thirties, who often sang along with Don Basilio.

At the end of my stay, Don Basilio told me that he was going to sing a song to protect me when going back to Pucallpa. When I asked him what he meant, he took one of the cloths richly embroidered with geometrical patterns. "I am putting this on you," he said. This was, for me, a confirmation of the work by German anthropologist Angelika Gebhart-Sayer, who to my knowledge was the first person to find a relationship between the songs sung under the effect of Ayahuasca, Shipibo art, and healing, which involves the restoration of the beauty and harmony of the invisible patterns surrounding the body of the patients. She writes:

Under ayahuasca influence, the shaman perceives, from the spirit world, incomprehensible, often chaotic, information in the form of luminous designs. He then "domesticates" this information by converting it into various aesthetic notions: geometric patterns, melodies/rhythm and fragrance which play a key psychological and spiritual role for both the patient and society. Only through this mediating step the awesome and

234   THE DIVINE SPARK

incomprehensible become an applicable corpus of shamanic cognition suitable for the mundane village (Gebhart-Sayer 1986).

Shipibo art is one of the many examples of Amerindian art that point to another reality, to perhaps the threshold of geometric patterns that often appear at the onset of the visionary experience with Ayahuasca. The current interest of Westerners in Ayahuasca has provoked an interest in Shipibo textiles and ceramics that has created a renaissance in Shipibo art, body painting, and cultural identity.

AYAHUASCA TRANSFORMATION NARRATIVES

Yajé and especially Ayahuasca already by the beginning of the 20th century were adopted by a segment of the mestizo population of the Western Amazon. In the 1930s, 1940s, and 1960s, they gradually gained a foothold among the urban population of non-Amazonian towns in Brazil, becoming a part of organized religions. Beginning in the 1980s with the experimentation of Westerners with Ayahuasca and its various associated traditions, interest in Ayahuasca has become an international phenomenon (cf. Labate & Jungaberle 2011). The numerous narratives about Ayahuasca encounters and other plant preparations with a similar phytochemistry, i.e., the so-called Ayahuasca analogues (Ott 1994), have made possible comparative studies.

Among the narratives available, I decided to concentrate on the theme of transformation, which are so common in indigenous accounts and pre-Columbian iconography, particularly on that of jaguar transformation. Here are two examples of transformation from an anthology on Ayahuasca encounters (Luna & White 2000). The first, a jaguar transformation experienced during an Ayahuasca session by French anthropologist Dr. Françoise Barbira-Freedman. The second example is transformation into a water molecule and witnessing of the photosynthesis process experienced by American ethnopharmacologist Dr. Dennis McKenna during a ritual of one of the Brazilian religious organizations that use Ayahuasca as a sacrament.

Barbira-Freedman studied shamanism among the Lamista during the early 1980s. She partook in ceremonies and participated in an apprenticeship process, gradually penetrating into a worldview that challenged her own ideas about power and morality. She was being "put right" by her shaman informants in the sense that she was becoming spiritually and physically stronger to be better able to cope with the cosmological realities of that culture. She relates how in one of her experiences with the brew, she came face-to-face with a large female jaguar following her. She goes on to relate how other jaguars she saw became angry when she picked some flowers and how she became transformed into a jaguar and began to fight:

A wave of intense aggressiveness unfurls in my solar plexus. This causes me to vomit, later than usual after taking Ayahuasca, and the process of "becoming jaguar" takes me over irresistibly. I feel it all at once, paws and claws, spine and tail, nose, whiskers and tail; I see with a jaguar's eyes, suddenly encompassing a wider field of vision, prick a jaguar's ears, open my jaws in practice. "My" jaguar has gone; It dawns on me that I have become her, am her, yet at the same time I retain the awareness of her merged with my consciousness. I find it easy to signal to the other jaguars to go away with mere body language, arching my back intensely. As I do this, I have a flashback of my cat standing up to the stray cats of a new neighborhood when we moved house in Cambridge.

Nothing I ever read about shamanic animal metamorphoses could have prepared me for the total involvement of my senses, body, mind in this process. I am fully experiencing it, I am it, yet at the same time I retain the awareness of who I am, albeit in jaguar form, partaking with other people clearly dealing with intense experiences of their own in an Ayahuasca ceremony. The female jaguar whose form I have entices me to go into the forest where she will teach me the ways of jaguars. Suddenly I am in a swampy area near an ox bow lake which is my home and instantly I am made to understand/feel stalking prey, jumping and killing, ripping, spreading fear and also feeling fear myself, being lonely and shy and even cowardly among the other animals there; surprisingly lounging and relaxing in the water. ...

It does not surprise me that the other shaman present, as an eagle, comes to find me and blows gently on my crown. It is even reassuring, as surprised as I am to know that this large harpy eagle is him, that as a jaguar I can physically relate to the being of the eagle, particularly eyes, beak and talons. I respond to the ritual blowing and feel very calm and at ease in my jaguar self, keenly sensing my surroundings. (Barbira-Freedman 2000:115)

Particularly noteworthy are the author's comments:

This vision engaged my whole self experientially in a phenomenological approach, which was blatantly at odds with the empiricist standpoint I intellectually favoured. There was no longer any other possible standpoint for me as an anthropologist than that of the shamanic rainbow, forever bridging between incommensurable perceptions and perspectives within highlands and lowlands, earth and sky, earth and water, from a constantly changing in-between." (p. 117)

The full text merits a close reading.

Dennis McKenna was one of the invited guests at the first scientific conference organized by the União do Vegetal (UDV) in Brazil. The UDV, created in Porto Velho in 1968 by José Gabriel da Costa, is the youngest of the Brazilian religious organizations that use Ayahuasca as a sacrament, to which they give the name of *vegetal*. The UDV conceives the brew as having two basic components: *força* (force) and *luz* (light).

At the end of the conference, a ritual was held involving the consumption of the sacrament. After a second cup, McKenna found himself changed into a disembodied point of view, suspended in space, thousands of miles over the Amazon basin" seeing a World Tree in the form of an enormous *Banisteriopsis* vine, "the embodiment of the plant intelligence that embraced and covered the earth, that together [with] the community of the plant species that existed on the earth provided the nurturing energy that made life on earth possible."

McKenna "understood" that photosynthesis was the "force" the UDV were talking about, "indeed the force on which all life depends." He relates:

> I found myself "instantly transported from my bodiless perch in space to the lightless depths beneath the surface of the earth. I had somehow become a sentient water molecule, percolating randomly through the soil, lost amid the tangle of the enormous root fibers of the *Banisteriopsis* World Tree." (McKenna 2000:154–7)

McKenna continues with an extraordinary, detailed narrative about his journey through the roots and vascular system of the vine, his arrival at the surface of a leaf, and how as a water molecule, he not only witnessed but also participated in the process of photosynthesis.

Accounts by educated Westerners such as Barbira-Freedman and McKenna echo ideas found in pre-Columbian art and in indigenous narratives. They point to a new alter-ego, to an alternative epistemology: the gaining of knowledge through a radical self-transformation, by taking an alternative—nonhuman—point of view, by cognitively merging with the focus of one's attention.

The techniques for achieving such cognitive states are culture specific. Like the mastery of any other technique, they require a special form of training. However, the various techniques have a biological dimension that is common to all human beings. The first steps in the scientific study of this biological dimension have already been taken in what amounts to an immense field of future research. Hopefully the development of some of the new theories of human consciousness will take into account tools that traditional societies have used for thousands of years.

An example of one such new theory of human consciousness is Ede Frecska's theory of the dual complementary methods of knowledge acquisition (Frecska 2008). The author proposes that the duality and complementarity in the physical universe where there are particles and waves, mass and energy, local effects and nonlocal connections is also found in a duality and a complementarity in knowledge acquisition. Frecska posits the existence of two sources of knowledge: perceptual-cognitive and direct-intuitive, with the former having fewer problems than the latter with replicability. Perceptual-cognitive knowledge is electrochemical (based on local effects), operates via neuroaxonal networks, is linguistic albeit not necessarily verbal, and relies on a modeling with a subject-object division. It peaks in Western scientific thinking. Direct-intuitive knowledge is quantum-physical (based on nonlocal connections), operates via subneural networks, it is ineffable, and relies on direct experience with no subject-object division. It is the source of contemplative traditions.

Winkelman, on the other hand, suggests evolutionary mechanisms by which early primates would be able to metabolize substances toxic for other organisms found in the natural environment, and which may have contributed to human evolution.

CONCLUDING REMARKS

Clearly, psychointegrator agents do not simply disrupt normal perception. It seems that through them, by mysterious ways of mind exploration not yet understood, it is indeed possible to access valid information not readily available by ordinary means. Psychointegrator agents offer complex, often beautiful, coherent, and useful experiences not normally accessible, to which some traditional societies assign great value. To dismiss such experiences as aberrations of the mind under the effect of drugs, which is the ordinary accepted discourse, is quite biased. Unbiased attention needs to be given to such phenomena. As William James pointed out, no account of the universe in its totality can be final, which leaves these other forms of consciousness quite disregarded (James 1929:379).

The religious use of peyote by Native Americans in the United States and Ayahuasca among the general population in Brazil and a few other countries has been accepted. This is of course a great step forward. However, this is still too short. Ferguson (2011) points out that one of the reasons for the scientific superiority of Western Europe over the Ottoman Empire in the 16th century was the unlimited sovereignty religion in the Muslim world: in 1515 a decree of Sultan Selim I had threatened with death anyone found using the printing press. To allow the religious use of Ayahuasca but to prohibit it as a tool for scientific and personal exploration would be a similar mistake. Science explores today the vast riches of outer space as well as the minute yet immense realms of subatomic particles. We explore the depth of the oceans and the forests, the high mountains and the deserts. Yet the exploration of consciousness is still a forbidden realm, vastly explored by shamanic societies yet neglected in contemporary science due to a great extent to religious preconceptions carried throughout centuries.

Amerindian art, largely inspired by altered states of consciousness, has perhaps a message for us. It expresses forms of cognition neglected by most but still accessible to all of us as humans. The ontological reality of the worlds perceived through psychointegrator agents in the final analysis depends on the perceiver's worldview. Many traditional societies would not doubt the existence of parallel and multidimensional worlds. With the exception of contemporary theories in physics and cosmology, modern thinking does not admit the existence of parallel and multidimensional universes. Short of direct experimental verification, orthodox scientific thinking treats talk of parallel and multidimensional universes as fiction if not as the projections of a deranged mind. This is not usually corroborated by those who have immersed themselves deeply in the study or experimentation of integrative states of consciousness.

As a researcher, I often ponder about the reality of the worlds I perceive through Ayahuasca. A recent study on visual perception using functional MRI concludes that practically neural activity observed in the primary visual cortex when having visions under the effects of Ayahuasca was indistinguishable than during normal perception. According to the authors, this means that visions have a real, neurological basis; they are not made up or imagined (Araújo et al. 2011). Certainly this somehow explains why these alien perceptions often seem to subjectively have the qualities of reality, at times even more so than normal reality. Interaction with normally invisible beings, visitation of apparently coherent—at least subjectively—other worlds are commonly reported by educated individuals. The fact is that, whether we want it or not, these other dimensions—whatever their ontological reality—constantly emerge in our daily life, either through the stories we tell our children—we all lived once in those forested and magical worlds—in the arts everywhere, in some of the religions we create, and certainly in our dreams. These other worlds and beings greatly enrich our existence. Without them, as without our remaining forests and their animals, the world would be a duller place.

NOTES

1. A shorter version of this chapter was published in Adams C, Waldstein A, Sessa B, Luke D, King D, eds. *Breaking Convention: Essays on Psychedelic Consciousness.* London: Strange Attractor Press. 2013.
2. A remarkable exception would be the influence of Iroquois Confederacy ideas on the Constitution and Bill of Rights of the United States (see *http://www.senate. gov/reference/resources/pdf/hconres331.pdf*).
3. Consider the following paragraph from the 1583 Decree of the Church Council of Lima, Declaring the Quipus to be the Work of the Devil: "Consider prohibited in full books that deal directly with, or recount, or teach lascivious or unchaste things, for one must keep in mind that which undermines the faith but also that which undermines good behavior—which reading such books usually does. And so those who have such books shall be rigorously punished by the bishops. However, ancient books in Latin, written by non-Christians, shall be permitted, because of the elegance and propriety of the Latin language, provided that these lascivious books, even if they are in Latin, not be read to young boys. And because in lieu of books the Indians have used, and some continue to use, registers made of different threads, that they call quipus, and with these they preserve the memory of their old superstitions, rites, ceremonies, and perverse customs, the bishops should diligently try to take away from the Indians completely all the records or quipus that facilitate their superstition." (*Organización de la Iglesia y órdenes religiosas en el virreinato del Perú en el siglo xvi: Documentos del Archivo de Indians.* Ed. Roberto Levillier, vol. 2 (Madrid: Sucesores de Rivadeneyra, 1919), pp. 213–214. This selection was translated by Cheryl E. Martin.
4. In Mann's view (2011) it was the 1492 collision of two Old Worlds that resulted in a New World.
5. Plato, in his unfinished dialogue *Critias*, wrote a moving account of the damage done in his time: "What now remains compared with what then existed is like the skeleton of a sick man, all the fat and soft earth having wasted away. . . . Mountains which now have nothing but food for bees . . . had trees not very long ago. [The land] was enriched by yearly rains, which were not lost to it, as now, by flowing from the bare land into the sea; but the soil was deep, and therein received the water, and kept it in the loamy earth . . . feeding springs and streams running everywhere. Now only abandoned shrines remain to show where the springs once flowed" (Quoted by Wright [2004:87–8]).
6. It is estimated that the amount of pristine forest in Western Europe is just 2–3 percent. In the European part of Russia 5–10 percent of the forests can be classified as pristine or near-pristine natural forests (*http://www.saveamericasforests.org/ europages/history&geography.htm*).
    Deforestation in the Amazon area is well-known. Less so is the near-total loss of Brazilian Atlantic Coastal Forest, one of the areas of richest biodiversity and

high endemism in the world—even more so than most of the Amazon area—of which only around 7 percent remain of a million square kilometers of forest due to urbanization, agriculture, and cattle ranching (Thomas 2008).

7. Fray Ramón Pané; Translated by Susan C. Giswold (1999). José Juan Arrom. ed. *An Account of the Antiquities of the Indians.* Durham, NC ; London: Duke Univ. Press. A New Edition, with an Introductory Study, Notes, & Appendixes by José Juan Arrom.

BIBLIOGRAPHY

Albuquerque, Maria Bethania. 2012. *Epistemologia e Saberes da Ayahuasca.* Belém, Brazil: Eduepa.

Barbira Freedman, Françoise. 2000. The Jaguar who would not say his Prayers: Changing polarities in Upper Amazonian Shamanism. In Luna, L.E. & White, S.F. *Ayahuasca Reader: Encounters with the Amazon's Sacred Vine.* Santa Fe: Synergetic Press.

Beyer, Stephan V. 2009. *Singing to the Plants. A Guide to Mestizo Shamanism in the Upper Amazon.* Albuquerque: University of Mexico Press.

Brown, M.F. 1985. *Tsewa's Gift: Magic and Meaning in an Amazonian Society.* Washington: Smithsonian Institution Press.

Clottes, Jean & Lewis-Williams. 1998. *The Shamans of Prehistory. Trance and Magic in the Painted Caves.* New York: Harry N. Abrams, Inc. Publishers.

Crosby, Alfred. 1986. *Ecological Imperialism: The Biological Expansion of Europe, 900–1900.* Cambridge University Press.

De Araujo, D., Ribeiro, S., Cecchi G.A., Carvalho, F.M., Sanchez T. A. , Pinto J.P., de Martinis B.S., Crippa, J.A., Hallak, J.E.C., 3, Santos, A.C. 2011. "Seeing with the eyes shut: Neural basis of enhanced imagery following ayahuasca ingestion." *Human Brain Mapping* first published online on 16 SEP 2011.

Ferguson, Niall. 2011. *Civilization. The West and the Rest.* London: Penguin Books.

Fernández Distel, Alicia A. 1980. "Hallazgo de pipas en complejos precerámicos del borde de la Puna Jujeña (Republica Argentina) y el empleo de alucinógenos por parte de las mismas culturas." *Estudios Arqueológicos* 5: 55–75, Universidad de Chile, Antofagasta.

Frecska, Ede. 2008. The Shaman's Journey. Supernatural or Natural? A Neuro-Ontological Interpretatin of Spiritual Experiences. In Strassman, Rick; Wjojtowicz, Slawek; Luna, Luis Eduardo & Frecska, Ede. *Inner Paths to Outer Space. Journeys to Alien Worlds through Psychedelics and Other Spiritual Techniques.* Rochester, Vermont: Park Street Press.

Frecska E, Magyar V, Móré Cs, Vargha A, Luna LE. 2011. "Enhancement of creative expression and entoptic phenomena as after-effects of repeated ayahuasca administration." *Journal of Psychopharmacology.* In press.

Fung, Rosa. 1972. "Las Aldas. Su ubicación dentro del proceso histórico del Perú antiguo." *Dédalo* 9–10, Museu de Arte e Arqueologia, Universidade de Saô Paulo, Brazil.

Gimbutas, Marija. 1989. *The Language of the Goddess.* HarperSan Francisco, a division of HarperCollins Publishers.

Hancock, Graham. 2005. *Supernatural. Meetings with the Ancient Teachers of Mankind.* London: Century.

Harrison, Robert Pogue. 1992. *Forest. The Shadow of Civilization*. Chicago and London: The University of Chicago Press.

James, William. 1929. *Varieties of Religious Experience*. New York: Modern Library.

Klein, Daniel & Cruz Ceballos, Iván. 2007. *El Arte Secreto del Ecuador Precolombino*. Milán: 5 Continentes Ediciones.

Labate, Beatriz Caiuby & Jungaberle, Henrik (Eds.). 2011. *The Internationalization of Ayahuasca*. Zurich and Berlin: LIT Verlag.

Lagrou, Els. 2000. Two Ayahuasca Myths from the Cashinahua of Northwestern Brazil. In Luna, L.E. and White, S.F. *Ayahuasca Reader. Encounters with the Amazon's Sacred Vine*. Synergetic Press, Santa Fe.

Langdon, Jean. 1992. A cultura Siona e a experiencia alucinogénica. In Lux Vidal (Ed.) *Grafismo Indígena. Estudos de Antropologia Estética*. Sao Paulo: Studio Nobel.

Luna, Luis Eduardo. 1984. "The Healing Practices of a Peruvian Shaman." *Journal of Ethnopharmacology* 11:123–133, 1984.

———. 1984. "The concept of Plants as Teacher Among Four Mestizo Shamans of Iquitos, Northeast Peru." *Journal of Ethnopharmacology* 11:135–156, 1984.

———. 1992. Therapeutic Imagery in Amazonian Shamanism. Some Observations. *Scripta Ethnologica* Vol. XIV:19–25. Centro Argentino de Etnología Americana.

———. 2011. Indigenous and mestizo use of Ayahuasca. An overview. In: Santos, R.G. *The Ethnopharmacology of Ayahuasca*. Research Signpost, Trivandrum.

Lewis-Williams, David. 2002. The Mind in the Cave. Consciousness and the Origins of art. Thames and Hudson, London.

Luna, Luis Eduardo & White, Steven F. 2000. *Ayahuasca Reader. Encounters with the Amazon's Sacred Vine*. Santa Fe: Synergetic Press.

Mann, Charles C. 2011. *1493. Uncovering the New World Columbus Created*. New York: Alfred A. Knopf.

McEwan, Colin. 2001. "Axiality and Access to Invisible Worlds." In McEwan, Colin, Barreto, Cristiana and Neves, Eduardo *Unknown Amazon. Culture in Nature in Ancient Brazil*. The British Museum Press.

McKenna, Dennis. 2000. An Unusual Experience with "Hoasca": A Lesson from the Teacher. In Luna, L.E. & White, S.F. *Ayahuasca Reader: Encounters with the Amazon's Sacred Vine*. Santa Fe: Synergetic Press.

Ott, Jonathan. 1994. *Ayahuasca Analogues. Pangæan Entheogens*. Kennewick, WA: Natural Products CO.

Polia Meconi, Mario. 1996. "*Despierta, remedio, cuenta . . .": Adivinos y Médicos del Ande*, 2 vols. Lima: Fondo Editorial, Pontificia Universidad Católica del Perú.

Posey, Darrell A. et al. 1984. 'Ethnoecology as applied anthropology in Amazonian development'. *Human Organization* 43: 95–107.

Posey, Darrell. 1991. Kayapo Indians: experts in synergy. *Leisa Magazine*, Vol 7 no 4, 3–5.

Posey, Darrell A. & W. Balée (eds.). 1989. 'Resource Management in Amazonia: Indigenous and Folk Strategies. *Advances in Economic Botany* 7. New York Botanical Garden.

Reichel-Dolmatoff, G., 1975. *The Shaman and The Jaguar. A Study of Narcotic Drugs Among the Indians of Colombia*. Philadelphia: Temple University Press.

——— 1988. Goldwork and Shamanism. An Iconographic Study of the Gold Museum. Medellín: Editorial Colina.

Roosevelt, Anne Curtenius. 1994. *Amazonian Indians from Prehistory to the Present*. University of Arizona Press,

Schaan, Denise; Ranzi, Alceu; Párssinen, Martti. 2008. *Arqueologia da Amazonia Ocidental: Os Geoglifos do Acre*. Belém: Editora Universitaria UFPA.

Schultes, Richard Evans & Bright, Alec. 1979. Ancient Gold Pectorals from Colombia: mushroom Effigies? *Botanical Museum Leaflets*, Vol. 27, Nos. 5–6: 113–141. Harvard University, Cambridge, Massachusetts.

Stannard, David E. 1992. *American Holocaust: The Conquest of the New World*. Oxford University Press.

Stone, Rebecca E. 2011. *The Jaguar Within: Shamanic Trance in Ancient Central and South American Art*. University of Texas Press.

Thomas, William Wayt (Ed.). 2008. *The Atlantic Coastal Forest of Northeastern Brazil*. Bronx, New York: New York Botanical Garden Press.

Torres, C. Manuel & Rebke, David B. 2006. *Anadenanthera: visionary plant of ancient South America*. New York, Oxford, London: The Haworth Press.

Winkelman, Michael. 1996. Psychointegrator plants. Their role in human culture and health. In *Yearbook of cross-cultural medicine and psychotherapy 1995, Sacred plants, consciousness and healing*. Vol. 6, ed. M. Winkelman and W. Andritzky. Berlin: Verlag und Vertrieb.

——— 2010. *Shamanism. A Biopsychosocial Paradigm of Consciousness and Healing*. Santa Barbara, California, Denver, Oxford: Praeger.

Woods, W.I., Teixeira, W.G., Lehman, J., Steiner, C., WinklerPrins, Rebellato, L. (Eds.). 2009. *Amazonian Dark Earths: Wim Sombroek's Vision*. Berlin: Springer Science. Berlin.

Wright, Ronald. 2006. *A Short History of Progress*. Edinburgh, New York, London: Canongate.

THE SOUL CLUSTER: RECONSIDERATION OF A MILLENNIA-OLD CONCEPT

BY EDE FRECSKA[1], LEVENTE MÓRÓ, HANK WESSELMAN

While I am not so foolish as to make rash assertions about these things [i.e., the substantial nature and possible immortality of the soul], still I do claim to have proofs that the forms of the soul are more than one, that they are located in three different places . . .

—GALEN OF PERGAMON

ETERNAL RETURN . . .

Every era is unique, but our age is unprecedented in that for the first time in recorded human history, the myths and spiritual teachings of almost every living tradition have become accessible to all as a common cultural treasure. One hundred years ago, the *Rigveda*, an ancient Indian sacred collection of Vedic Sanskrit hymns and one of the oldest religious texts (ca. 1700–1100 BCE) in continual use in any Indo-European language was accessible to the curious mind, but information about the Hawaiian mystical Kahuna tradition, or about the worldview of the Inuit circumpolar peoples was entirely lacking. As always, many pieces of the overall human cultural spectrum are still missing, but the teachings derived from a wide variety of cultures about the Great Mystery of human existence can now be studied from different perspectives, and the cross-cultural similarities are stunning.

Ethnographic data collected over the last one hundred years has generated a fertile field for those interested in studying cross-cultural commonalities. Frecska and Luna (2006) have discussed why the ideas of soul, spirit, or rebirth echo across the ages and why these concepts repeatedly appear in entirely different cultures. The belief in the existence of soul(s), spirit guides, spiritual forces, and other worldly realms appears to be universal in the human species. Edward Osborne Wilson (1998) has noted that sociology has identified the belief in a soul to be one of the universal human cultural elements, and he has suggested that science needs to investigate what predisposes people to believe in a soul. With our coauthors, we have made efforts to overcome the typical rational interpretations that deem such ideas to be superstition, originating in delusion or the fear of death. We accept that these recurrent, prevailing themes ("elementary ideas"—as they were called by Adolf Bastian, one of the founders of ethnography) (see Koepping, 1983) are not just products of wishful thinking, and represent more than irrational coping mechanisms against the anxiety of ego-dissolution at death.

The focal point of the current paper is the observation that the concept of soul is noticeably complex in aboriginal cultures, and its plural—especially tripartite—nature is the rule rather than the exception. Curiously, this perception is getting clearer and more pronounced when one considers our shamanic origins. Herewith, we refer to Wilhelm Wundt (1920) who gave much attention to the point that the animistic perception of the soul is pluralistic. Among aboriginal groups, the term *soul* cannot be used as it is in the Western tradition because indigenous peoples widely hold the belief in multiple souls (or aspects) of a human being. There are advanced cultures where the number of principles defining the human essence is reduced to a number smaller than three (e.g., the duality of *ling-hun* in Chinese traditional medicine), but a thorough look reveals that such dualism (or monism) is a deflation of an earlier trinity (Harrell, 1979). Taoism, which has shamanic origins (Stutley, 2003), teaches that there are three souls, one of which remains with the corpse after death (like the *Ka* of the ancient Egyptians), while another resides always in the spirit world, and the third that transmigrates between the physical back to the spiritual realms. Shinto lore suggests the soul has multiple sections that can act and move around independently, so it may be that different parts have different afterlives—one being reincarnated, one becoming a guardian, etc. As far as advanced Mesopotamian civilizations are concerned, there seems not to have been any clear concept of a soul in neither Sumerian, nor Babylonian, and Assyrian religions. One may just speculate if these advanced civilizations have moved far from their source.

Swedish Sanskritist Ernst Arbman (1926/1927) analyzed the Vedic beliefs in India and found that the concept of the soul (*atman*) was preceded by a duality. In his analysis, Arbman separated the soul inhabiting the body and endowing it with life and action from the free-soul, an unencumbered soul-aspect embodying the individual's nonphysical mode of existence not only after death but also in dreams, trances, and other altered states of consciousness (ASCs). According to his classification, the free-soul doesn't have any physical or psychological attributes; it simply represents the immortal spiritual essence of the individual.

In this regard, Arbman addressed the issue of duality but implicitly wrote about tripartition since he combined two soul parts for which different cultures have separate names (see Table 1). In addition to the free-soul, the physical soul or body-soul is often divided into several components. Usually it falls into two categories, one of which is the "life-soul," the vital force, frequently identified with the breath, while the other is the "ego-soul," the source of thoughtful action and decision making. In the Vedic tripartite soul concept, the free-soul incorporated the psychological attributes of the body-soul, a development that occurred among a number of other cultures.

One of Arbman's most gifted pupils Åke Hultkrantz (1953) followed his master's lead while studying Native American Indians and took the same stance, speaking about dualism while describing a trinity. Bremmer (1983) has addressed how multiplicity can be obscured by the focus of interest and the concepts of the soul held by the field investigators themselves. In this regard, Arbman and Hultkrantz were clearly more interested in the free-soul and in its evolution over time and accordingly paid less attention to the "life-soul" and "ego-soul" as independent entities. Their predecessors and contemporaries were also more interested in the myths of Afterlife than in tribal psychology. The main goals of this publication are: 1) to give a detailed analysis of ancient and indigenous soul concepts within the framework of tripartition, 2) to outline a dynamical relationship between the soul components, and 3) to provide a tentative "neuro-ontological" interpretation based on a biophysical approach.

SOUL CONCEPTS IN EARLY CIVILIZATIONS

Ancient Egypt

The conception of the soul in Ancient Egypt was complex. The Egyptians conceived of a person's individuality as being made up of several independent beings, each of which was a distinct personality seen as a whole having a separate existence both during life and after death. Their belief system that appears to have been based in direct shamanic experience included a number of souls or soul aspects and auxiliary entities that together constituted the individual. According to Egyptian funerary texts, man was composed of a mortal body, the *Kha*, and at least three soul principles: the *Ka, Ba,* and *Akh* (Hall, 1965).

- *Ka* represented the spiritual essence, which made the difference between a living and a dead person. It was received at the instant of birth by breath, and death occurred when Ka left the body. The ancient Egyptians contributed life-giving energy to the Ka. This characteristic makes Ka similar to the concept of "life-soul" or "spirit" in other religions and the "energy body" in contemporary Western thought.

- Ba referred to all those qualities that make up a person, including everything nonphysical that makes an individual unique, similar to the Western view of personality. In this regard, Ba is the closest to the contemporary notion of "ego-soul" or "mental-soul." Ka and Ba were held to be very much attached to the physical body: they had physical needs, like food and water, confirming their resemblance to Arbman's two body-souls.

- The most important player who has the leading role in the Afterlife was the immortal soul called the Akh. Following the death of Kha, the Ba and Ka had to be reunited to reanimate the Akh. The Egyptian funerary customs were intended to aid the deceased in becoming an Akh, to prevent rebirth and "dying a second time in the Afterlife." In the Egyptian religion, this second death was possible and permanent. Akh was associated with thought, but not as an action of the mind; rather, it was a form of pure consciousness, analogous to the higher self or immortal spiritual Oversoul in Western thought. It was believed to be able to wander away (Ka and Ba could also do that), to haunt the deceased body if the tomb was not in order, and it could either do harm (sickness, nightmares, and bad feelings) or extend good (protection) toward persons still alive. Within the frame of the ancient Egyptian belief system, Akh corresponds the best to the "free-soul" or higher self of a human being.

In addition to the Ka, Ba, and Akh, there were further principles, which make the comparison more difficult: the *Ib* (metaphysical heart center of compassion), *Sheut* (shadow aspect of the person), *Ren* (name soul aspect of the person), *Sahu* (spiritual body for the Akh), and *Sekhem* (spiritual-energetic entity dwelling in the Afterlife in association with Akh). An interesting parallel can be noticed here with the Taoist conception of the "immortal spirit body."

Accordingly, it can be observed that the ancient Egyptian soul concept is an example of the inflation of the number of soul aspects: In comparison to other traditions (Table 1), a segregation and transformation of soul elements is presumable. The idea of an independent and pure immaterial existence was so foreign to Egyptian thought that it assigned spiritual body (Sahu) and spiritual force (Sekhem) to the potentially eternal soul form (Akh), and delegated the other soul forms (Ka and Ba) for its help. It also seems that by Sekhem, ancient Egyptians introduced a complementary, ethereal version of the "life-soul" (vital force) by granting it to the deceased person's Akh as an energetic force. After all, in Egyptian cosmology, nothing existed in isolation, and duality was a norm.

PRE-CLASSICAL GREECE

The Christian worldview is monistic, allowing for only one soul per human body. The Trinity applies only to God, but not to man. However, centuries before, there were many discussions of the pluralistic concept of the human soul. In the early Greco-Roman period, the mindbody problem was complex: On the one hand, there was the *psyche* (Greek), or *anima* or *genus* (both Latin), an unencumbered soul that survives death. The Greek concept of the psyche is confusing to Western investigators. While on the one hand, it can closely correspond with Arbman's free-soul, some regard the psyche as passive while the body is alive. Its presence is the precondition for the continuation of life, yes, but—following the Greek tradition—Western scholars hold that it has no connections with the physical or psychological characteristics of the individual. In other words, it doesn't carry over one's personal identity or memories after death but instead enters the Underworld as a shadow of the living person (Bremmer, 1983).

On the other hand, there was the Greek concept of the *thymos,* or in Latin *animus* or *fumus,* which is the seat of personal identity and personal memories, but which dies with the physical body. It is this soul part that is the seat of emotions. Unlike psyche, thymos was believed to be active only when the body is awake. Thirdly, *noos* was a soul form representing the intellect and generating the willful actions of the person. There also was a soul component called *menos,* which can be described as a momentary impulse of combined mental and physical agencies directed toward a specific act. It was said to be able to manifest itself in a berserk-like fury. After the Archaic Age (800–500 BCE), there was a gradual incorporation of thymos and the noos into the psyche, which made the latter the center of the self—the organ of both thought and emotion. Accordingly, Plato goes as far as to include all intellectual functions (originally belonging to the noos) into the psyche.

The resemblance of the Archaic Greek soul belief to that of most indigenous peoples (to be discussed) strongly suggests that it belongs to a type of tribal society consciousness in which the individual is not yet in the center of focus (Bremmer, 1983). It may also reflect the effect of a tradition based less on philosophical speculation but rather more on the direct experience of which shamans and tribal healers were masters. Hultkrantz (1953) cites Edward Tylor, the 19th-century scholar of comparative religion who observed that the belief in a personal supernatural aspect or soul formed the original foundation for religious awareness: "The material shows that the greatest importance should be ascribed to such experiences and observations for the development of the ideas of the soul." Apparently, a "direct-intuitive approach," "the second foundation of knowledge" (Strassman et al., 2007) is the source that was suppressed with the unfolding of Western civilization, dominated by Judeo-Christian overlay.

CLASSICAL GREECE

Lack of direct experience can partly explain—at least—that in our own time, the concept of the soul is one of the most ambiguous, confusing, and poorly defined of our human ideas. As the antipode of the material essence, it exists as an entity substantially different from the body. Within this concept, the soul is the principle of life, action, and thought, and in this framework, body and mind can depart from it and go on in separate paths (like in Hindu mythology) . . . or they cannot be separated but can be opposed to each other (as in the three Abrahamic religions). In other approaches, the soul designates the totality of the self, refers to every level of the individual, and represents both the essence and the wholeness of human nature.

In this essay, we are going to refer to it in the latter meaning.

Discovering the "true" nature of the self has always been part of the Great Mystery, for unless one understands who and what we are, one cannot experience the mantle of authentic initiation. In Western philosophy, the 5th century BCE Ionian philosopher, mathematician, and mystic Pythagoras was the first to express his ideas about this during the classical period, proposing that every human being has three *principia*: a physical aspect (body, or *soma*), an intellectual-emotional aspect (mind, or psyche), and an immortal spirit. Pythagoras's three principia have influenced numerous thinkers and philosophers across time—among them Plato, Aristotle, Galen of Pergamon, and the Renaissance physician Paracelsus. One must also keep in mind the Freudian "Id—Ego—Superego," or the Jungian "conscious—subconscious—collective unconscious" personality models, both of which converge on this ancient perception.

Yet the tripartite division of human nature was probably recognized far earlier than Pythagoras since we can find its categorical depictions in the many millennia old shamanic traditions of the indigenous peoples. In fact, it is conceivable that the Greek philosopher himself was drawing on the shamanic traditions of tribal cultures. Christopher Janaway (1995) wrote: "The body of legend which grew around Pythagoras attributes to him superhuman abilities and feats. Some think these legends developed because it is more likely that Pythagoras was a Greek shaman." Indeed, Aristotle described Pythagoras as a wonder-worker and somewhat of a supernatural figure. According to Aristotle and others' accounts, some ancients believed that he had the ability to travel through space and time, and to communicate with animals and plants, all features that link him with the shamanic tradition (Huffman, 2009). Herodotus and modern scholars (Dodds, 1951) admit that Greek civilization was greatly influenced by the shamanistic culture of the Black Sea Scythians in the 7th century BCE. Kingsley (1999, 2003) presents evidence through the fragmentary writings attributed to the 6th-century mystic and shaman Parmenides of Velia, a small town in southern Italy, that the shamanistic tradition (*iatromantis*) actually formed the foundation for Western thought and philosophy, one that Plato did not fully understand. Seen in this perspective, Pythagoras and his fellow "Pythagoreans" were most definitely practitioners and teachers in the shamanic foundation.

SOUL CONCEPTS IN INDIGENOUS CULTURES

Africa

According to the view of the Kwawu people in Ghana, three soul categories animate each human being. "At the time of conception, blood and flesh come from the mother. The person's body comes from his mother, belongs to his mother's matrilineage, and ultimately returns to the Great Mother: Earth." It is occupied by the bodily soul form *saman*. A person receives semen from the father at conception. By this medium, a child gets fertility and cleanliness. Cleanliness means morality in a spiritual sense, while fertility is closely linked to personality by them. The soul component associated to it is called *sunsum*. "In contrast to blood and semen that a child obtains at conception, the breath of life is received from the God[2] at time of birth." The soul part entering the body this way is called *ɔkra*. Death means that *ɔkra* is taken back by the God (Bartle, 1983).

ASIA

Surprisingly similar to this African soul concept is that of the Mongolian shamanic tradition that also considers that people have three souls. According to the *Darkhad* shamans, one soul comes from the maternal side (the soul that governs flesh and blood), a second is a bone soul from the paternal side, and the third soul comes from the Spirit World. The third one, the immortal soul, transmigrates from the Spirit World to a fetus in the womb. After death, it stays for a short while in the body, and then later, seeing the light, it moves back to the Spirit World and, eventually, transmigrates back into another baby (Purev, 2004).

In other parts of Mongolia, the soul form *ami* is held to be the soul that enlivens the body. It is related to the ability to breathe—in other words to the breath. After death it returns to the Upper World in the form of a bird (like the Ba of the Egyptians). During an illness the ami soul may temporarily be displaced, but it does not leave permanently until death. Ami may reincarnate among the relatives of the dead person. The *suld* is the most individualized of the human souls. It lives in a physical body only once; after death it remains around the body for a while, and then it takes residence in the Middle World. The *suns* soul, like the suld, also contributes to the formation of personality, but it carries the collected experiences of past lives. The suns reincarnates and stays in the Other World between incarnations but may return as a ghost to visit friends or relatives. Among the two reincarnating souls, the suns usually bears the strongest past-life memories. The suns soul may also temporarily leave the living body and sometimes wander as far as the Lower World, which may require a shaman to negotiate for its return. This Mongolian tripartite soul concept clearly reflects the three-tier shamanic cosmology (Sarangerel, 2000).

Throughout Siberia, it is widely held that all humans possess at least three souls; some groups such as the Samoyedes believe there are more: four in women and five in men. Not every author agrees on the concept of multiple souls. Shirokogoroff is skeptical of this notion: "I believe that in some instances of very multiple souls . . . we have the ethnographer's complex, his creation and not that which exist in [the indigenous population's] mind" (Shirokogoroff 1935/1982, p. 54). Some sort of deculturalization process adds to the confusion: Western influences and missionary assimilations have greatly adumbrated the soul concept of numberless tribes. Even so, the examples above suggest that humanity's archaic culture—the hunter-gatherer culture—perceived the reality of the soul trinity over thousands of years, and the commonality, even perhaps universality of the tripartite soul concept is plausible. Like in the case of the shamanic cosmology: the three-tier view is the most common worldwide, despite numerous deviations (for example, the twelve-level worldview of the South American Yagua tribe) (Fejos, 1943).

The Puyuma people—indigenous in Taiwan—believe that each person has three souls, one of which resides in the head, and the other two reside on each shoulder. Chinese aborigines belonging to the Hmong tribes follow their ancient shamanic tradition and believe that each living body has many souls (not in full agreement on the numbers, though). For a newborn infant, one soul enters his or her body when he or she is conceived in the mother's womb. Another soul enters when the baby has just emerged from the mother's body and taken its first breath. A third one will have to be called on the third morning after birth. The first soul is the one that normally stays with the body. The second soul is free, it wanders; this free-soul causes a person to dream while asleep. The third soul is the protective soul that tries to protect its owner from harm (Symonds, 2005).

AMERICA

The Native American Lakota Sioux distinguish the *woniya* (physical self), *nagi* (cognitive self), and *nagila* (spiritual self). Similarly, the Inuit Eskimos separate three souls: an *anerneq* soul, which we receive with the first breath at the moment of birth, an *ateq* soul, which we get with our names after birth, and a *tarneq*, our immortal soul. The Caribbean Voodoo religion also differentiates three forms of soul: *gros bon ange, ti bon ange,* and *z'étoile* (Wesselman, 2008.)

The Shuar (Jívaro) headhunter tribe living in the Upper Amazon regions of Ecuador also believes in the trinity of the soul (Winkelman and Baker, 2008). In their culture, everyone bears a "true soul," the *nekás wakanl,* which arises at the moment of birth. This soul resides in the blood of an individual, and therefore blood loss equates to partial soul loss to a Shuar. The "true soul" leaves the body when one dies, and it starts an immortal existence reliving the entire life of the individual that it belonged to. After reliving this life, it may become a forest demon, or after several transformations, it evolves into mist and in this form unifies with the cloud of every deceased person's "true soul." The war-cultivating Shuars are pragmatically minded and preoccupied with their everyday warfare. Therefore, the "true soul" interests them the least among the three, since—they suppose—it has minimal effect on their actual affairs.

The second soul is the *arutam wakanl,* which brings vision (*arutam*), and provides protection to the person. This "protecting soul" is so important that no one can reach adulthood without it, and it has to be gained before puberty. To acquire this soul, a young Shuar boy must go out into the forest for a vision quest of about five days. It is the vision (arutam) that brings power and intelligence; it shields against malevolence and witchcraft. Over the course of a lifetime, a warrior acquires several "protecting souls," or helping spirits that give him extra protection.

The third one is the "avenging soul," the *muisak wakanl,* which takes the stage when an arutam bearer is murdered. The function of muisak wakanl is revenge. When an individual with arutam wakanl is killed, his "avenging soul" leaves through the mouth and proceeds to try to kill the murderer. Because the Shuars are frequently engaged in killing raids, it is important for them to come up with a mechanism to stop the "avenging souls" from coming after them. This is the reason why the shrunken heads (*tsantsa*) are made. Shrinking the head prevents the muisak from leaving the body, and covering it with charcoal blinds this "avenging soul." Moreover, the preparation moves the power of muisak to the killer's family (for example awarding them with more food). However, the muisak means potential danger for the tribe even when it is incarcerated into the tsantsa, so after a while, they excommunicate it to its village of origin, or sell the head to someone passing by (e.g., a tourist). In the belief system of the Shuars, the three-soul concept serves a double function: the conservation of tribal warfare and the protection of the individual's well-being (Winkelman and Baker, 2008).

According to the view of Hawaiian aboriginals (Kahuna mysticism), everybody has a lower soul—the *'unihipili,* connected to the body and feelings, a medial soul; *'uhane,* related to mentality and thinking; and a superior, immortal *'aumakua* (Wesselman and Kuykendall, 2004, Wesselman, 2008, 2011). Ancient Greek thinkers would definitely ponder upon the tripartite definition of the Kahuna tradition, as in classical Greek thought, the psyche subsumed the emotional and the cognitive functions into one, while the Polynesians perceive these to be functions of two quite different souls.

THE TRIPARTITE "SOUL CLUSTER"

The composite picture derived from the concepts of the soul in numerous cultures outlines meaningful commonalities and offsets insignificant differences. The results suggest that the singularity defined as "self" by Westerners is actually a cluster, a personal "soul cluster" (Table 1). All aspects of the soul cluster are combined to create a functional self, and all of them are part of the same totality, originating from the same source, yet they exist in very different states of quality. In considering the Hawaiian Kahuna teachings, we find a psychodynamically intriguing interplay between the three soul components, a sort of *soul dynamic* that has been utilized in treatment concepts and enjoys an extensive multicultural acceptance spanning across space and time. It has been my experience (Frecska) that my psychiatric patients can relate to this tripartite soul division more easily than to the terminology and psychodynamic approach of classical psychoanalysis.

The indigenous peoples understand that the harmony between the components of the self (i.e., the soul forms) is essential for physical and mental health. If the relationship between them is well-balanced and the unity of the three soul components is maintained, then health persists. In other instances where there is disharmony within and between them, healing intervention is necessary.

In the following, we plan to cast light upon the benefits of this perception that are not quite present in Western teachings and practice. Conversely, the traditions of the indigenous cultures can provide this to us if we are open to them. Concretely, as it is expressed in the Kahuna protocol, every soul

Table 1: The Various Presentations of the Tripartite "Soul Cluster"

	SOUL ASPECTS		
	Physical	Mental	Spiritual
Ancient Egypt	Ka-Ib	Ba-Ren-Sheut	Akh-Sahu-Sekhem
Archaic Greece	thymos	noos, menos	psyche
Mongolian shamanism	ami	suld	suns
Lakota Sioux	woniya	nagi	nagila
Inuit Eskimo	anerneq	ateq	tarneq
Shuar (Jívaro)	arutam	muisak	nekás
Kwawu tradition	saman	sunsum	okra
Kahuna teaching	'unihipili	'uhane	'aumakua
Caribbean Voodoo	gros bon ange	ti bon ange	z'étoile
Christianity	Son	Father	Holy Spirit
Kabbalah	nephesh	ruach	neshamah
Ernst Arbman	life-soul	ego-soul	free-soul
Hank Wesselman	body-soul	mental-soul	Oversoul

In the complex soul-concept of ancient Egypt, the precise meaning of the individual components Ka, Ba, Akh, Sekhem, etc., is not clear. "Well-meaning scholars try again and again and again to force the Egyptian idea of the soul into our traditional categories without enabling us to understand even a little of it any better" (Poortman, 1978, p. 108). Bewaring of this while still maintaining good intention, we would dare to say that several Egyptian soul parts can be merged under the auspices of tripartition. We are unprepared for a theological discussion, so we abstain from disrupting and classifying the Holy Trinity (we mean, whether the Father corresponds to body-soul or mental-soul). In the table, we just mention it to emphasize the consistent appearance of tripartition.

form can act both independently—in different roles according to their special attributes as well as in special intra- and transpersonal dynamics. Long-term or even complete and final healing may be based on the practical use of this recognition.

HAWAIIAN KAHUNA THOUGHTS ON THE SOUL ASPECTS

'Aumakua: The Immortal Free-Soul

As mentioned above, the Hawaiian expression *'aumakua* refers to the supreme, immortal aspect of the self and can be translated as "utterly trustworthy ancestral spirit," or as "the spirit that hovers over me." In Western teachings, this component of the self appears as the "overself," the "higher self," the "divine me," the "angelic self," the "transpersonal witness," the "god self," and the like. Symbolic illustrations of it in the West depict it typically as a benevolent winged creature, a guardian angel. In Polynesia, it is associated with the creator deity Kane or Tane, and is depicted by an upright stone monolith. Following Wesselman and Kuykendall (2004) and Wesselman (2011), we call it Oversoul, which can be conceptualized as our personal share of the all-encompassing Holy Spirit, or as some call it "the Human Spirit." Originally, it was Ralph Waldo Emerson who coined the word *Oversoul* while a divinity student at Harvard University.

The visitation of something magnificent, benevolent, and divine is a frequent subjective experience during mystical altered ASCs, either occurring spontaneously or induced by transpersonal techniques. Those who are less familiar with direct transcendent experiences may interpret this presence as a divine visitation of an angelic greeting or even as a manifestation of the Almighty father-God, and we must always observe that such visitations cannot be ruled out. However such a transpersonal connection is interpreted, one can observe a tendency for the mystical presence to be perceived as being outside the subject's self, although it most likely may be the manifestation of one's own Oversoul. Such a claim must be validated by the words *most likely*, as—paradoxically—similar interpretations tend to be more accurate when they are less categorizing (i.e., not the "either–or" kind).

In the Polynesian Kahuna tradition (Wesselman and Kuykendall, 2004; Wesselman, 2008, 2011), our Oversoul is observed to be in permanent connection with us in every moment of our lives, both waking and sleeping, whether we are aware of it or not. This connection appears to be surprisingly easy to manifest or activate, and those who practice meditation have a greater ongoing access than those who do not. As part of our soul matrix, the Oversoul monitors all our deeds and thoughts, actions and reactions, emotions and relationships, revealing that privacy is truly an illusion. This self-aspect is passive but not dispassionate toward us, silently feeling concern for our wrong decisions and silently rejoicing upon our successful choices. The Oversoul is a silent observer, as the responsibility for decision making belongs to another self-aspect, the mental-soul or egoic self. This reveals that for most of our lives, our Oversoul does not interfere with our mundane affairs, and neither does it dictate what to do—it respects the right of free choice. However, its protection and guidance can be asked for and invoked. Without such a request, it is only in the rarest cases—perhaps to avoid an "untimely end"—when such an "angelic intervention" or miraculous avoidance experience may happen.

As our wise spirit teacher, our Oversoul is also the source of our inspiration and intuition. It may send us dreams and visions in which it may appear in the image of a spiritual teacher or other wise being, depending on the person's culture, belief systems, and mythical world. Cross-cultural examples reveal that people who have been raised in European traditions may have transpersonal experiences of discarnate entities known in Polynesian or Mesoamerican civilizations. In a relaxed meditative state of perfect calmness and inner peace, such connections can be achieved . . . and then, upon recalling a certain problem, an answer to the dilemma may suddenly appear within the meditator's conscious awareness revealing that the Oversoul is passive only for the passive person. Through personal divination, it may serve as a source of information, and this service can be cultivated with practice.

The Kahuna tradition reveals that the 'aumakua, the Oversoul, is also our personal creator: the primordial source of our self. At birth it divides itself, sending in a seed of its light that takes up residence within a new body for a new life with the first breath, revealing the breath to be the vehicle of transfer. As our "divine source," it projects a hologram of its immortal soul-character into the newborn, including all its cosmic information content. Similar to many other cosmogenic myths, the Kahuna tradition emphasizes that our personal creator is not a monotheistic off-planet father god, but rather our own divine and immortal part of our self.

All individual Oversouls create a holographic field—the spirit of humankind, termed *ka po'e 'Aumakua* (Wesselman and Kuykendall, 2004). As the Oversoul resides outside space and time (i.e., it is nonlocal), the result of this summation is the cumulative (past + present + future) experience and wisdom of our species *Homo sapiens*. This database corresponds to the "collective unconscious" in Carl Jung's terminology. In Kahuna thought, it is an inexhaustible resource of information, which has been and is being tapped by mystical philosophers and shamanic healers, and which is theoretically accessible to all of us, all the time. Connection with it is often realized during rituals and ceremonies, and in integrative forms of ASCs, with the body-soul being the mediatory agent between our mental-soul and our Oversoul.

'UNIHIPILI: LIFE-GIVING FORCE, THE BODY-SOUL

Upon its arrival in the biological medium, the nonlocal Oversoul seed must achieve a successful relationship with another soul already in residence: the body-soul sourced into us from our mother and father. The usage of the terms *local* and *nonlocal* is essential for us, as they serve as the basis for a rationalizing approach that will be explicated. The body-soul approximates what psychoanalysis calls the "personal unconscious." In the Kahuna tradition, this self or soul aspect is the source of all our emotions and feelings and is in charge of the entire operation of the physical body, including its repair and restoration. Next to the energetic matrix of the body-soul and that of our own Oversoul, the third soul form, the mental or egoic soul, takes form in response to life as we live it and is shaped by our life events.

According to the Kahuna thought, the body-soul, being energetic in nature, serves as the location of our personal memory storage, and so it is this soul that may recall all personal events upon request by the mental-soul. It is the database of all instinctual and learned behavior and thus serves as our personal operating system and inner hard drive.

The body-soul communicates to the other soul components, the mental as well as the spiritual, by reacting to our life events with emotional responses, expressing what it likes or dislikes. The body-soul does not lie; it expresses itself without inhibitions in the language of emotions, revealing exactly how it feels about a family member, a friend, a job, or a life opportunity. As the interface between our inner and outer worlds, it vividly monitors both the realities in which we act as well as those in which we think, feel, and dream. We could describe it as the mind of the body, which uses our sensory organs to gather information, then forwards the data to our receiving self (mental-soul). This *interface* function should be emphasized, because the body-soul is both the sender and receiver of all psychic experiences as well as shamanic visions. It is thus the part of our self that makes the spiritual world accessible, according to Kahuna teaching and practice. The inner portal, through which we may make contact with our spiritual guardians and teachers, is located just there, within it. Even the Oversoul part of our self communicates through it to the third soul aspect, the mental-soul or intellect.

The body-soul is the soul of great possibilities. It is at one and the same time material and immaterial, bound by matter and yet free. When Wilhelm Wundt (1920) combined the breath-soul with the idea of the free-soul, he did that on good grounds as both are unsubstantial and unstable. From a psychological viewpoint, the conception of the free-soul, Oversoul, is identical with the memory image of the dead person projected back into the supernatural reality—the airy, ethereal shape of the deceased like a condensation of human breath. The Oversoul and the body-soul thus have qualifications favoring a meeting and merging.

The body-soul—although not by logical abstraction—is able to reason. It provides us with conclusions based on immediate experience. It remembers everything that succeeds or that which causes pain and damage. It is programmed in such a way that induces such behavioral output that helps survival. The body-soul is a fundamental driving force toward our growth, upon acquiring new skills that help us to grow, increase, and become more than we were.

As mentioned above, the body-soul is also our inner healer, programmed to repair our bodies. It restores us based on our genetic as well as our energetic inheritance, and as such, it works with the interactive field of our body components. According to Kahuna thought, these two sources—genetic and energetic—are essential in the healing function because the body-soul is not creative; it is not able to invent and does not draw a plan, but it follows the genetic and energetic blueprint around and with which the body was formed. It is not a leader, but it executes commands as a good subordinate, and it functions at its best when getting unambiguous directives from the mental-soul—from the soul form (self aspect) that is named ego in the West.

'UHANE: OUR EGO, AS THE MENTAL-SOUL

Next to the Oversoul and body-soul, the third aspect of our self is the mental-soul, which takes form in the process of our reactions to life events. Well known to the West, this is the intellectual part of the "I" that thinks, analyzes information, integrates, adjudges, assigns meaning to, and functions as our chief executive. It is the source of our rational mind and intentions, and the realizer of our creative inspirations. The mental-soul conceptualizes new ideas, thought forms, and goals, and then aspires to reach them. However, as we have mentioned earlier, the source of this inspiration is the Oversoul, which is accessible to the mental-soul via the *interface* of the body-soul. In other words, the mental-soul is our intellectual, rational, creative, coping apparatus—our inner director. It is the side of our self that is continuously changing on the basis of our experiences and collected knowledge. The mental-soul is also the bearer of our belief systems that it holds to be true, those same convictions that underlie how well it directs. If the mental-soul faces a challenge that it deems uncontrollable, then it may become inefficient. For example, if one accepts that his or her illness is incurable (and this often happens by external influence, like a medical opinion), then the mental-soul may surrender to the illness.

In Kahuna teaching, a connection exists between feelings and emotions generated by the body-soul and the belief systems held by the egoic self, and long before Aaron Beck, the Kahunas assumed that the former depend on the latter. They understood that feelings inform the mental-soul about which belief is currently the operative one, and that the body-soul expresses its opinion about the dominating schema in the form of feelings. The mental-soul then has a choice, whether to accept the subconscious message and to act accordingly, or to discard it by declaring as invalid. Mental and physical health presumes a good working relationship between the mental-soul and the body-soul. Indeed, this is not a democratic relationship; the mental-soul is the master, and the body-soul is the servant. As the superior agent of our coping mechanism, the mental-soul directs the activity of the body-soul, which serves as its executer. However, this dominance is maintained only in the ordinary state of consciousness, when orientation to the outer world is adaptive and the main daily task is coping. Meditative, contemplative, and ritual techniques may break the mental edges and the dominance of the ego, and may evoke a state in which the mental-soul introspectively receives signals coming from the Oversoul, crossing the bridge (or interface) of the body-soul.

The mental-soul has a rather heterogeneous and sometimes obscure nature. In its "pure" form, it constitutes a hypostasis of the stream of consciousness, the center for thinking and willing—the intentional mind in a broad sense. But at the same time, the mental-soul manifests certain peculiar features, which makes it clear that it is not just an expression of the individual's own personality but also functions as a being within the individual which endows him with thought, will, and so on. This "soul of consciousness" is motivated by order (this influence is coming from the Superego in Freudian theory); the body-soul by comparison is motivated by desire or pleasure (a characteristic of the Freudian Id). The conscious content of the ego may thus manifest certain independence—especially when neurotic persons are found to be in conflict with compulsive notions, acts, phobias, etc., sourced by the body-soul. This peculiarity of the mental-soul explains why we find it now split into several potencies, now taking up an exaggeratedly independent, at times superior, attitude toward its owner. On the other hand, most addictive or impulsive behaviors are expressions of the body-soul that may assume dominance over a poorly developed mental-soul.

THE TRIPARTITE SOUL-CONCEPT IN EUROPEAN AND NEAR-EASTERN CULTURES

The Polynesian teachings draw upon the dynamism and essence of much the same trinity that accompanies the history of many other cultures, including the significant tradition in Western thinking. It is indeed thought provoking for us that at the dawn of European philosophy, expressed through Pythagoras and Plato, the transcultural similarity is demonstrable. Pythagoras believed in the immortality and transmigration of the soul. Plato understood that the soul differs from the body and that it can exist separately as pure thinking, but his thoughts do not reflect whether the soul can or cannot survive death (Janaway, 1995). Plato argues that the human soul has three parts: *Logos* (an intellective, rational part), *Thymos* (a spirited part, having to do with emotion and will), and *Eros* (an appetitive part, having to do with drives and basic impulses). Each of us has two mortal soul parts—appetite and spirit—plus one, the intellect, which is immortal (Sedley, 2009).

Aristotle avoids addressing the principle of immortality. He thinks of the soul as a substance, the form of a potentially living natural body, which accomplishes and consummates the possibility of supplying bodily functions. Aristotle attempts to explain life processes with the soul; he distinguishes three soul parts, according to three assumed life processes: nutrition–reproduction, sensation, and cognition. In his case, the unity of the self is already far away. Aristotle did not consider the soul in its entirety as a separate, ghostly occupant of the body (just as we cannot separate the activity of cutting from the knife). As the soul, in Aristotle's view, is an actuality of a living body, it cannot be immortal. Perhaps it was the influence of his physician father that caused the narrowing of his soul concept to biological and psychological relations. Following Aristotle's footsteps, Western scientific thinking was influenced accordingly, until it reached the point where the notion of the soul had eventually become completely disqualified. We take it that, avoiding the metaphysical, "direct-intuitive" experience (Strassman et al., 2007) provided by integrative forms of ASCs (like the shamanic state), the idea of immortal soul has gradually lost ground in Western philosophy.

Yet Aristotle also described a quality of being that is closely allied with the perception of the Oversoul. He called it the *entelechy*—that which is already realized as opposed to the *energia* (the energy body) that carries the life force that motivates and orients an organism toward self-fulfillment. The entelechy was understood in classical philosophy as a fullness of actualization that requires ongoing process and effort in order to continue to grow and thus exist, perpetually becoming itself . . . a good description of the Oversoul.

Plotinus of Lycopolis (205–270 CE) presents arguments for the *tripartition-cum-trilocation* of the soul (Plotinus, 1991) advanced by Plato in *Timaeus* (2001). His version is marked by a clear spatial separation between the three parts of the soul: reason in the brain, will in the heart, and desire in the liver. Plotinus refers to the ideas presented by Galen of Pergamon in his work *On the Doctrines of Hippocrates and Plato* (Galen, 1978/1980). At the same time, he takes stance for the unity and incorporeality of the soul. From Galen's perspective, the parts of the soul are not located in the three bodily organs in an ordinary sense—only their activity takes place there.

In Islam, the human soul is also split into three parts: the *Qalb* (heart), the *Ruh* (blood), and the *Nafs* (passion of the soul). In the words of Ibrahim Haqqi of Erzurum: the heart is the home of God. Qalb enables the individual to perceive God as the All-Helping and All-Maintaining. Interestingly, the immortal Oversoul seed is also felt by the Kahunas to reside in the heart.

The *Zohar*, a classic work of Jewish mysticism, separates three soul parts as *neshamah, ruach,* and *nephesh*. They are characterized in this way (Von Rad, 1965): Neshamah is the higher soul, or Oversoul. It allows man to have awareness of the existence and to feel the presence of God. It is the bearer of intellect and provides us the gift of immortality. This part of the soul is implanted at birth. After death, neshamah returns to the source. Ruach is the middle soul. It carries the moral virtues and gives humans the ability to distinguish between good and evil. Ruach corresponds to the ego, to the mental-soul in our terminology. Nephesh is a living mortal essence: it feels pain, hunger, and emotions, and most importantly, it eventually dies. It is the source of one's physical and psychological nature. The last two elements of the soul are not given at birth but are continuously created over time; their maturation depends on the beliefs and deeds of the person.

THE TRIUNE MAN³

"Man is a bundle of relations, a knot of roots, whose flower and fruitage is the world."

—RALPH WALDO EMERSON (1841/1979, P. 20)

One could raise a justified doubt about the fundamental basis for using the notion of the soul at all. As an answer: the Kahuna can "psychodynamize" and elucidate by using the three soul forms, and can even build a healing praxis on this basis. Of course, this does not necessarily mean that the thing must be more than just a hollow metaphor (even the phlogiston theory was capable of explaining certain phenomena). The Kahunas knew that metaphors work powerfully because the body-soul takes everything literally and does not distinguish between reality and illusion. It perceives both as real.

Rational content can be given to a metaphor by deducing or transferring it into other metaphors that have been approved in other fields of science. If we discern a premise which is extremely reductionist and which constricts our aspects, then questioning the given starting point can take us forward on the cognitive path. What we are questioning here is that our self, our human essence, and all of our experiences would be reducible to the operation of one and only one network: the neuroaxonal network. If we accept that other networks—operating by other and different types of information processing strategies—may also contribute to our human essence, then we may reasonably address many concepts that so far have been excluded from the reference framework of rational thinking.

Table 2 summarizes the levels of organization supposedly involved in generation of the conscious experience. Since the topic of consciousness is mostly ignored by mainstream neuroscience, it is difficult to determine the opinion of prominent brain researchers. Despite some positive trends in other disciplines (for example, physics), orthodox neuroscientists avoid the issue, and unorthodox ones use the politically correct term *awareness* when preparing their grant proposals. Nevertheless, with the exception of the very top level and one at the very bottom, most neuroscientists would not disagree with the assumption that all these levels represented in Table 2 are involved in the process.

To avoid the trap of radical reductionism, one must assume that all levels are at work with bidirectional interrelated causative processes (*bottom-up* and *top-down* reciprocal interactions). Let us pay attention to the position of the dashed line in Table 2. Illustrating the contemporarily accepted view,

Table 2 : Organizational Levels That Play a Role in the Human Experience

a l t e r e d c o n s c i o u s n e s s	something else? culture individuum, the brain brain subsystems (e.g., triune brain by MacLean) corticothalamic loops brain modules neurons synapses, neural membranes – microtubules microfilaments cytosol proteins hydrophobic pockets van der Waals forces electron superpositions, photon polarizations spin networks, space–time geometry	o r d i n a r y c o n s c i o u s n e s s

it divides levels based upon their assumed causational role in generating the conscious experience.

According to the theories on the neural correlates of consciousness, the neuroaxonal system has a pivotal role both in the emergence of conscious experience and in the function of levels above it. In his book, *The Blank Slate: The Modern Denial of Human Nature*, Steven Pinker (2003, viii) writes, "Culture is crucial, but culture could not exist without mental faculties that allow humans to create and learn culture to begin with." The effect of culture in shaping brain structure and neuroaxonal function is also permitted. In cogent and convincing writing, Bruce Wexler (2006) argues that our brain does not merely dictate how we respond to changes in the environment but is also itself shaped through interaction with the social world. Briefly, social relations, even culture and ideology, affect neurobiology.

This means that above the dashed line *bottom-up* and *top-down* interactions are at work, and every level is supposed to have an active role. This is not the case below it: the assumption here is that subcellular levels are passive, subserving higher levels by permitting, but not shaping, their function. Here the causation operates only from *bottom-up*, but the role of *top-down* effects is not believed to operate at this level in mainstream neuroscientific thinking. Above the horizontal line, there is a well-balanced "cooperative hierarchy"; below it, "oligarchy" is the rule. Of course, this is an arbitrary delineation with broken symmetry. It lacks an explanation about why only the upper half has active and reciprocal interactions. Perhaps it would be more consequent and congruent to suppose that subcellular levels also have an active role in the creation of the human experience and that they add something to the self, which is a characteristic of their level. Considering their size, this characteristic could be their relation with quantum reality.

So what is this quantum characteristic that subcellular parts can enrich the human experience with? We assume that it is "nonlocality" (more specifically "signal nonlocality"), which is an important property of the quantum processes. In brief, *nonlocality* means that if two elementary particles were once part of the same quantum system, then they remain in immediate interaction, regardless of their position in space and time. If the quantum state of one particle changes, then the state of the other *quantum entangled* particle will also change simultaneously—no matter how far apart they are from each other in space and time. "Signal nonlocality"—a new fertile term in 21st-century physics—means that a change in the state of a system induces an immediate change in an interconnected (*entangled*) system. A subcellular network (perhaps the lipoprotein membrane complex) might enable the brain to receive "nonlocal" information and to transmit it toward the neuro-axonal network (Figure 1). A tentative function of subcellular components by forming a "quantum array antenna" of the brain is discussed in our book (Strassman et al., 2007). A biological model of information processing is proposed there, in which subcellular, cytoskeletal networks serve as the basis for quantum computation and represent a medium of quantum holography.

The connection to quantum reality can be mediated by a subcellular network that presumably covers the whole body and represents a space- and time-independent holographic image of the Universe inside the body by "nonlocal" connections, in other words, by quantum correlations (Figure 1). "Nonlocal" information about the physical Universe provides the missing link between objective science and subjective experience, including the mys-

Figure 1: The hierarchy and speculative interaction of networks related to human experiences.

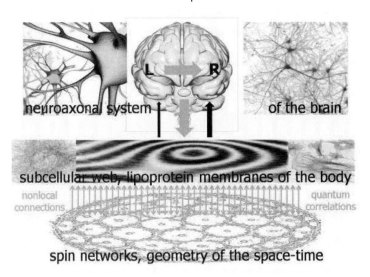

neuroaxonal system of the brain

subcellular web, lipoprotein membranes of the body

nonlocal connections

quantum correlations

spin networks, geometry of the space-time

Crossed gray arrows between the left and right hemispheres, as well as between the neuroaxonal and subcellular networks, denote inhibitory effects (left–right hemisphere and "up–down" network dominances) in the ordinary state of consciousness. "Nonlocal" interactions (marked with uncrossed grey double arrows) are persistent and independent from the state of consciousness. It is primarily during the integrative forms of altered states of consciousness (e.g., in meditation and contemplation as opposed to psychosis, delirium, or intoxication, which are disintegrative forms of ASCs) when a minimal and very uncertain information transfer may occur emerging from the subcellular matrix to the neuroaxonal network via visions (i.e., presumably by visual cortical input) or revelations (i.e., presumably by verbal cortical input), as shown by black arrows.

tical experience. Based on the principle of "nonlocality" and with the "quantum array antenna" of subcellular networks, the brain (and the full body) is in resonance with the whole Universe. A faint hologram of the Cosmos emerges inside the body, and regardless how pale it is, it is able to present wholeness and can elucidate teachings like: "The kingdom of God is within you" (Luke 17:21, in Greek, *entos hymon*), or "Look inside, you are Buddha" (Humphreys, 1987). The perennial wisdom of "As above, so below" (or: "As within, so without") obtains a fresh perspective and there is hope for the integration of similar teachings into Western rational thinking. Subcellular matrix can be the mediator of the Jungian "collective unconscious," and cytoskeletal quantum holography can explain a very common but obscure phenomenon known as "intuition."

We represent a radical idea that the world of well-integrated ASCs is related to quantum processes, while the reality of ordinary consciousness belongs—beyond doubt—to classical physics. Their boundary is probably not sharp at all; ordinary conscious experience can be affected by quantum processes as well (in some cases of intuition), and many features of the experiential world of altered states can also be deduced from classical physics. We see a seamless continuum with phase transitions from the classical-physics based neuronal brain functions all the way to the quantum-physics based subneuronal "direct intuitive" information processing.

While the "nonlocal" connections are permanent, in ordinary states of consciousness, there is only a very limited and mostly unconscious shift of the "nonlocal" information into the neuroaxonal system—since the coping apparatus, the "survival machine," is mostly focused on the more reliable "local" signals coming from the perceptual organs—so only a little or none can get into the focus of attention of the "I." In integrative forms of ASCs (e.g., meditation and contemplation), coping, planning, and task-solving functions are put into the background along with the agent (ego) bearing those functions. Thus, a chance appears for fragments of "nonlocal" information—present already in subcellular networks—to be projected and transferred into the neuroaxonal network and to be experienced also by the ego. This outlined hologram can be a stage for out-of-body experiences: consciousness does not leave the body, but its introspective attention sweeps the "matrix," i.e., the field of "nonlocal" correlations mediated by the subcellular network.

In biological systems, everything that involves a transfer of energy (i.e., of mass—by the Theory of Special Relativity), leads inevitably to a change in space–time geometry (by the Theory of General Relativity), and shows up by making imprints in complex nonbiological networks (spin network—Penrose, 1971.) Where there is a complex network, there must be a function, and an agent can be assigned to that function. Thus, the mental-soul (ego) can be assigned to the neuroaxonal system, the body-soul to the subcellular networks (lipoprotein membrane complex), and the Oversoul to a nonbiological, basically physical network (spin network, space–time geometry). The referred native peoples and antique philosophers (namely Pythagoras, Plato, and Galen) may have intuitively sensed the presence of these network functions representing "agents" in their soul concepts. Based on the association above, a careful watch on Figure 1 reveals that the presented model reflects quite accurately the dynamics of the Kahuna soul forms: the Oversoul ('aumakua)—the agent of the nonbiological network—is in a permanent connection with us in every moment of our lives; the body-soul ('unihipili')—the agent of the subcellular matrix—is the bridge between the Oversoul and the mental-soul ('uhane')—the agent of the neuroaxonal system—and serves as an inner portal to receive transpersonal information. Moreover, the model shows an analogy with the Shuar concept in that the arutam wakanl (which corresponds to the body-soul in Table 1) is the bearer of visions. As we have earlier mentioned, biological metabolism, conformation change of molecules can affect space–time geometry. By the Kahuna teachings, this can also hold in reverse: see above the detailed "download" of the Oversoul at the formation of the body-soul.

There is another benefit of the presented model—it may explain away the confusion in the classification of soul components: Soul dualism results from combining the biological network agents (life-soul and ego-soul) in contrast to the nonbiological one (free-soul). The tripartite soul concept emphasizes more their unique role and sets the foundation of "soul-dynamic psychotherapy."

Several arguments can be raised against the outlined model questioning the special role of each presented network. Within the matrix of the lipoprotein membranes, is it the microtrabecular lattice that makes humans (and other cellular organisms) capable of carrying an albeit faint hologram of the Universe, or is it something else? Is it—alternatively—the microtubular cytoskeleton, which is the proposed medium of quantum computation in the Penrose-Hameroff model (Penrose, 1996)? At the bottom rung, others would not put space–time geometry—an already outdated concept, some experts believe—but entangled quantum holograms in the universal ("Akashic") field (Laszlo, 2009). Ervin Laszlo argues (personal communication) that space-time is itself a manifestation of the field—there is neither space nor time prior to the quanta that arise in the topological field. Moreover, what functions as the source of information on that fundamental level is not "geometry"—he goes on—but the "nonlocal" network of quantum holograms: the informational structure of the field. Nevertheless, the strength of our concept is not tied to the successful proposal of one specific network, but to the argumentation that there must be "nets" other than the neuroaxonal for shaping human experiences, and there must be at least three, with one of them being nonbiological.

We consider as the miracle of nature not only that the three soul forms can have a material basis—although it can already be unacceptable for many. Their interaction, which catapults the human experience to the infinite, fascinates us more, and so does the fact that a rational explanation can be created even for this relation-dynamics—although by stretching academic frames. These and similar thoughts are explicated in detail in the book *Inner Paths to Outer Space* (Strassman et al., 2007) for readers who are open to interdisciplinary trespasses. As we are not sure about the same attitude at present, we have shortened our discussion—which may sound cumbersome and far-fetched for many—as much as we could. On the other hand, we cannot see any other way to authentically interpret these and similar teachings. To ignore or to belittle them is another possible way—but it does not lead to progress. Evidently, these are concepts and theories that need to be discussed and developed.

NOTES

1. Address correspondence to Ede Frecska, Department of Psychiatry, University of Debrecen, Nagyerdei krt. 98., 4012 Debrecen, Hungary. E-mail: *efrecska@hotmail.com*
2. Instead of God we would prefer the use of Great Spirit, which is more consistent with the tribal, shamanistic worldview.
3. Coined by following the triune brain model of Paul MacLean (1990).

REFERENCES

Arbman, E. 1926/1927. Untersuchungen zur primitiven Seelenvorstellungen mit besonderer Rucksicht auf Indien, Part 1 and 2. Le Monde Oriental 20:85–222 and 21:1–185.

Bartle, P. F. W. 1983. The Universe has three souls: notes on translating Akan culture. Journal of Religion in Africa 14(2):85–114.

Bremmer, J. 1983. The Early Greek Concept of the Soul. Princeton: Princeton University Press.

Dodds, E. R. 1951. The Greeks and the Irrational. Berkeley and Los Angeles: University of California Press.

Emerson, R.W. 1841/1979. The essays of Ralph Waldo Emerson. Cambridge: The Belknap Press of Harvard University Press.

Fejos, P. 1943. Ethnography of the Yagua. New York: Viking Fund, Inc.

Frecska, E. and Luna, L. E. 2006. Neuro-ontological interpretation of spiritual experiences. Neuropsychopharmacologia Hungarica 8(3):143–153.

Galen 1978/1980. De placitis Hippocratis et Platonis (On the doctrines of Hippocrates and Plato). In Corpus Medicorum Graecorum, Vol. 4.1.2, Part 1 and 2, Ed. De Lacy, P., 1:65–358 and 2:360–608. Berlin: Akademie-Verlag.

Hall, M. P. 1965. The Soul in Egyptian Metaphysics and the Book of the Dead. Los Angeles: Philosophical Research Society

Harrell, S. 1979. The concept of soul in Chinese folk religion. The Journal of Asian Studies 38(3):519–528.

Huffman, C. 2009. Pythagoras. In The Stanford encyclopedia of philosophy, Ed. Zalta, E. N. First published on February 23, 2005, Revisioned on November 13, 2009,

Retrieved on August 14, 2010 from *http://plato.stanford.edu/entries/pythagoras/*.

Hultkrantz, Å. 1953. Conceptions of the Soul Among North American Indians: A Study in Religious Ethnology. Stockholm: Caslon Press.

Humphreys, C. 1987. The Wisdom of Buddhism. London: Curzon Press.

Janaway, C. 1995. Ancient Greek philosophy I: The pre-Socratics and Plato. In Philosophy: A Guide Through the Subject, Ed. Grayling, A. C., 336–397. Oxford: Oxford University Press.

Kingsley, P. 1999. In the Dark Places of Wisdom. Inverness: The Golden Sufi Center Press.

Kingsley, P. 2003. Reality. Inverness: The Golden Sufi Center Press.

Koepping, K.P. (1983). Adolf Bastian and the Psychic Unity of Mankind: The Foundations of Anthropology in Nineteenth Century Germany. St. Lucia: University of Queensland Press.

Laszlo, E. 2009. The Akashic Experience: Science and the Cosmic Memory Field. Rochester: Inner Traditions.

MacLean, P. D. 1990. The Triune Brain in Evolution: Role in Paleocerebral Functions. New York: Springer-Verlag.

Penrose, R. 1971. Angular momentum: An approach to combinational space–time. In Quantum theory and beyond, Ed. Bastin, E. A., 151–180. Cambridge: Cambridge University Press.

Penrose, R. 1996. Shadows of the mind: A search for the missing science of consciousness. Oxford: Oxford University Press.

Pinker, S. 2003. The blank slate: The modern denial of human nature. New York, NY: Penguin Group.

Plato 2001. Timaeus. Newburyport: Focus Publishing.

Plotinus 1991. Enneads. London: Penguin.

Poortman, J. J. 1978. Vehicles of consciousness: The concept of hylic pluralism. Wheaton: Theosophical Publishing House.

Purev, O. 2004. Darkhad shamanism. In Shamanism: An encyclopedia of world beliefs, Practices, and Culture, Eds. Walter, M. W. and Fridman, E. J. N., 545–547. Santa Barbara: ABC-CLIO.

Sarangerel (Stewart, J. A.) 2000. Riding windhorses: A journey into the heart of Mongolian shamanism. Rochester: Destiny Books.

Sedley, D. 2009. Three kinds of Platonic immortality. In Body and soul in ancient philosophy, Eds. Frede, D. and Reis, B., 145–162. Berlin, New York: Walter de Gruyter.

Shirokogoroff, S. M. 1935/1982. Psychomental complex of the Tungus. Original edition, London: Kegan Paul, Trench, Trubner. Reprint, New York: AMS Press.

Symonds, P. V. 2005. Calling in the soul: Gender and the cycle of life in a Hmong Village. Seattle: University of Washington Press.

Strassman, R., Wojtowicz-Praga, S., Luna, E. L., and Frecska, E. 2007. Inner paths to outer space. Rochester: Inner Traditions.

Stutley, M. 2003. Shamanism: A concise introduction. London: Routledge.

Von Rad, G. 1965. Old Testament theology. San Francisco: Harper.

Wesselman, H. and Kuykendall, J. 2004. Spirit medicine: Healing in the sacred realms. Carlsbad: Hay House, Inc.

Wesselman, H. 2008. Hawaiian perspectives on the matrix of the soul. The Journal of Shamanic Practice 1:21–25.

Wesselman, H. (2011, in press). The bowl of light: Ancestral wisdom from a Hawaiian shaman. Boulder: Sounds True.

Wexler, B.E. 2006. Brain and culture: Neurobiology, ideology, and social change. Cambridge: The MIT Press.

Wilson, E.O. 1998. Consilience. New York: Alfred A. Knopf.

Winkelman, M. and Baker J. R. 2008. Supernatural as natural: A biocultural approach to religion. Upper Saddle River: Prentice Hall.

Wundt, W. 1920. Völkerpsychologie, IV. Band: Mythus und religion, I. Teil. Leipzig: Engelmann.

THOUGHTS ON PARAPSYCHOLOGY AND PARANORMAL PHENOMENA[1]

BY ROBERT SCHOCH

For more than two decades, I have advocated the idea that civilization dates back thousands of years earlier than previously believed (a generally cited date for the origin of civilization is circa 4000 to 3000 BCE). My position was initially based on my work on the Great Sphinx in Egypt. In the early 1990s, I demonstrated, using geological data, that the statue's origin is thousands of years older than the generally accepted date of circa 2500 BCE. Initially, I "conservatively" suggested that the core body of the Sphinx dates back to 5000 BCE or a bit earlier. I made my case comparing erosion and weathering profiles on the Sphinx to the ancient climatic history of Egypt.

In brief, the Sphinx sits on the edge of the Sahara Desert, a hyperarid region for the past five thousand years; yet the statue shows substantial rain-induced erosion. The original structure must date back thousands of years prior to 3000 BCE (the head was re-carved in Dynastic times). Seismic studies, carried out in conjunction with geophysicist Thomas Dobecki, confirmed that the oldest portion of the Sphinx dates well prior to Dynastic times. Over the years, as I continued my studies and collected more data, I slowly revised my estimate, considering progressively earlier possible dates for the statue. I am now comfortable with the notion that possibly the Sphinx's earliest origins go back ten thousand years or more, perhaps even to the period of circa 10,000 BCE to 9000 BCE; that is, the end of the last ice age.

For many years, one of the harshest criticisms of my redating of the Great Sphinx was that it apparently stood in stark isolation at such a remote period in time. The people who carved it must have been extremely sophisticated culturally and technologically. They were civilized. But where was corroborative evidence of such sophistication, of true civilization, at such an early date?

Over the last quarter century, I have traveled to numerous parts of the world searching for further evidence that civilization began earlier than standard archaeologists would have us believe. However, it was not until 2010 that I visited Turkey. In Anatolia, I found evidence that demonstrates beyond doubt, in my assessment, that true civilization arose before the end of the last ice age some twelve thousand years ago.

In southeastern Turkey, there is a site known as Göbekli Tepe. Here, immense finely carved T-shaped limestone pillars, many in the range of two to five and a half meters (two and a half to eighteen feet) tall and weighing up to an estimated ten to fifteen tons, form Stonehenge-like circles. Various pillars at Göbekli Tepe are decorated with bas-reliefs of animals, including foxes, boars, snakes, aurochs (wild cattle), birds, and arthropods (scorpions, ants, or spiders). The level of sophistication seen at Göbekli Tepe clearly, in my opinion, indicates that a true civilization existed here. What is really amazing, and corroborates my work on the redating of the Great Sphinx, is the age of Göbekli Tepe. Based on radiocarbon techniques and geological studies, the site dates back an astounding ten to twelve thousand years ago.

The evidence of Göbekli Tepe confirms that civilization dates back to the end of the last ice age (circa 9700 BCE), a concept that was unimaginable when I was a graduate student at Yale University back in 1979–1983. And I have come to realize that there may be many things that just might be true even if they once were, or for many people still are, unimaginable.

In addition to my work pushing back the age of civilization, I have always had a deep and abiding interest in matters of spirit and consciousness—subjects often viewed as outside of the domain of serious modern scientists (and I am a scientist, with a PhD in geology and geophysics)—and as a result I have extensively researched the field of parapsychology.

I am commonly asked how my studies in parapsychology relate, if at all, to my studies of ancient monuments. Even though I am a geologist and my initial concern was dating various ancient structures, I could not help but wonder why they were built, especially given the enormous efforts that must have gone into their construction. The why behind the monuments, more often than not, apparently included religious beliefs and practices, initiation rites, and rituals, which in many cases seemed to have an ostensible paranormal aspect, whether it was clairvoyance, divination, or manifestations of higher levels of consciousness. The temples and tombs of ancient Egypt, Mexico, and Peru seemed to cry out "paranormal." So was it all a mixture of ancient myth, superstition, and downright fraud on the part of many a seer, priest, and priestess, or could there be something to it? Were the ancient structures used, at least in part, to alter consciousness and possibly enhance paranormal phenomena?

In all honesty, I have always been highly skeptical of any alleged paranormal phenomena. However, my concept of skepticism is not the same as dismissal, and in my studies of ancient and traditional cultures, alleged paranormal phenomena kept making an appearance. When a former Boston University student, Logan Yonavjak, encouraged me to delve deeply into the serious parapsychological literature, I found the topic both fascinating and enlightening. The immediate tangible result of our research was the book *The Parapsychology Revolution: A Concise Anthology of Paranormal and Psychical Research*, in which we include selections from fourteen seminal papers, dating from 1886 through 2007, by major figures in the field plus a hundred pages of our own commentary. For me, however, the real result of my immersion into parapsychology was a new appreciation for human potentiality and the connections we share with all of life and ultimately, perhaps, with the cosmos. This is something I address to a certain extent in the final chapter of my latest book, *Forgotten Civilization: The Role of Solar Outbursts in Our Past and Future* (Inner Traditions, 2012) and I anticipate will be the subject of future articles and books.

People often ask me if I now "believe" in the paranormal. Let me just say that after looking at the hard evidence, and sifting out the fraud and bunk, I have come to conclude that there definitely is something to such phenomena as telepathy and psychokinesis. Here I should point out that in *The Parapsychology Revolution,* we discuss paranormal and psychical phenomena in a strict sense, including the concepts of ESP (extrasensory perception: telepathy, clairvoyance, and precognition) and psychokinesis (PK, or mind over matter, on both micro and macro scales). Certain topics that are sometimes included in more general definitions of the paranormal and parapsychology, such as UFOs, aliens, Big Foot, and so forth, were not our concern in this book. Likewise, our primary focus did not include evidence bearing on survival beyond the grave (though we do briefly discuss evidence for reincarnation). The survival issue is highly controversial, and the evidence typically used to support life after death is subject to many interpretations. We felt it was important to first establish what is possible in terms of paranormal phenomena while people are still alive. Perhaps the survival issue will be the subject of a future book on my part.

Most people who have seriously studied the subject conclude that telepathy (mind-to-mind interactions) is the best-supported class of paranormal phenomena. There is strong laboratory evidence for telepathy, such as classic card-calling experiments as well as many more sophisticated tests of telepathy, clairvoyance, and remote viewing. There is also a large and compelling body of evidence from spontaneous cases supporting the reality of telepathy. For instance, crisis apparitions, veridical hallucinations, or "ghosts" are well-known, as documented in the classic two-volume scientific monograph of rigorously authenticated events produced by the Society for Psychical Research titled *Phantasms of the Living* (first published in 1886; an excerpt from this work is included in *The Parapsychology Revolution*). The evidence for PK is also strong, including micro-PK studies using random event generators and similar devices, such as the evidence developed by the PEAR (Princeton Engineering Anomalies Research) labs over more than a quarter of a century, and the carefully studied incidents of macro-PK associated with genuine spontaneous poltergeist cases. Another line of compelling evidence for the reality of paranormal phenomena is the study of presentiments or "pre-sponses," essentially a form of short-term precognition as measured by physiological parameters (heart rate, electrodermal activity, and so forth). Numerous replicated experiments have demonstrated the physiological responses of individuals to, for instance, disturbing photographs a second or two before they are actually viewed by the person. According to conventional science, this should not be possible.

As a natural scientist, I expect genuine phenomena (be they psychical and paranormal phenomena, or more conventional phenomena) to exhibit patterns and share elements in common, and this is just what has been found in spontaneous cases of the paranormal. Even when viewed cross-culturally, such commonalities persist.

Perhaps even more compelling for me is the work of various modern researchers that has demonstrated a weak but persistent correlation between low levels of geomagnetic activity on planet Earth and cases of apparent spontaneous telepathy (based on records going back to the latter half of the 19th century). This, in my opinion, is a very strong argument supporting the contention that there is something genuine to the concept of telepathy. It suggests that spontaneous telepathic phenomena are real and natural and, as might be expected of natural phenomena, their manifestation is influenced by other natural parameters. Alternatively, are we to hypothesize that hundreds of hoaxers over nearly a century and a half have conspired to fake telepathic incidents in identical correlation with geomagnetic activity? This latter hypothesis strikes me as rather far-fetched, if not downright ludicrous. It has also been found that incidents of the paranormal correlate with Local Sidereal Time (which relates to the position of the horizon at any particular point on Earth relative to the center of our galaxy).

Note that a correlation between geomagnetic activity and spontaneous telepathy does not necessarily imply that the "telepathic signal" is magnetic or electrical in nature. The human brain is influenced by magnetic and electric fields, and whatever may be the carrier of the telepathic signal, the transmission, reception, and manifestation of the message by the brain could be hampered or enhanced by differences in the magnetic and electric fields that the brain is subjected to.

For many people a phenomenon is not "real" unless it can be duplicated in a laboratory setting under controlled conditions. Being a natural scientist and field geologist, I have never agreed with this contention. After all, can we create a genuine volcanic eruption in the laboratory or even on command in the field? Until about two centuries ago, the scientific community routinely rejected the concept of rocks falling from the sky (meteorites). Still, attempting to induce, capture, observe, and experiment with apparent telepathy under controlled conditions is a worthy endeavor. Unfortunately, however, to this day it is fraught with problems, and though numerous experiments have tested positive for apparent telepathy, others have had negative results and replication is a persistent problem. The bottom line is that we really do not know exactly what parameters or variables make for good telepathic transfer (or the elicitation of other types of paranormal phenomena), much less how to control for them.

> There are major issues that remain unresolved concerning paranormal and psychical phenomena. We don't fully understand what conditions are best to elicit paranormal phenomena, and thus these phenomena are not easily replicated on command (such as in a laboratory setting). There is often a very low signal-to-noise ratio when it comes to psychical phenomena, there is no single physical theory to account for paranormal phenomena, and there is the issue of fraud and charlatans. Fraud is a very real and persistent problem in the field of psychical research, and it's one reason to undertake large statistical studies of average persons (as opposed to so-called psychic superstars) and search for the regularities and patterns one would expect among any genuine natural phenomena. Also, paranormal studies have extended to animals (and in some cases, even plants). One of the strengths of nonhuman

studies is that it is less likely that animals will cheat and lie. It can also be noted that many "powerful mediums" who appear to have genuine paranormal abilities also apparently have low moral values and will cheat and commit fraud, perhaps unconsciously, at times, especially when their genuine paranormal powers fail. This is a pattern that has been noted over and over among parapsychologists working with human subjects. All of these topics are discussed in *The Parapsychology Revolution*.

A popular approach to possible paranormal phenomena is simply to dismiss such as impossible—impossible either in an absolute sense or as being of such a "low probability" as to be unworthy of consideration. For example, Sean Carroll (senior research associate in physics at the California Institute of Technology) has posted on his blog, *Cosmic Variance*, a diatribe against parapsychologists and the very idea of studying possible paranormal phenomena (*http://cosmicvariance.com/2008/02/18/telekinesis-and-quantum-field-theory*). The core of his argument is as follows:

> The main point here is that, while there are certainly many things that modern science does not understand, there are also many things that it does understand, and those things simply do not allow for telekinesis, telepathy, etc. Which is not to say that we can *prove* those things aren't real. We can't, but that is a completely worthless statement, as science never proves anything; that's simply not how science works. Rather, it accumulates empirical evidence for or against various hypotheses. [Italics in the original.]

I am classically trained in the sciences, and I understand where Carroll is coming from philosophically when he states that "science never proves anything" (and I agree that, epistemologically at a deep level, proof is not the domain of science). However, Carroll contradicts himself when he states:

> The crucial concept here is that, in the modern framework of fundamental physics, not only do we know certain things, but we have a very precise understanding of the *limits of our reliable knowledge*. We understand, in other words, that while surprises will undoubtedly arise (as scientists, that's what we all hope for), there are certain classes of experiments that are guaranteed not to give exciting results—essentially because the same or equivalent experiments have already been performed. [Italics in the original.]

Here Carroll is clearly, and for all practical purposes, arguing that certain things have been "proven" when he asserts that "we know certain things." This strikes me as a modern version of the famous (famously wrong) 1894 pronouncement by Albert A. Michelson, 1907 Nobel Laureate in Physics:

> The more important fundamental laws and facts of physical science have all been discovered, and these are now so firmly established that the possibility of their ever being supplanted in consequence of new discoveries is exceedingly remote. . . . Future discoveries must be looked for in the sixth place of decimals. (Quoted in Neil deGrasse Tyson, "The Beginning of Science." Natural History, March 2001.)

Michelson made this statement before the elucidation of X-rays and the structure of the atom, and before the discovery of radioactivity and the development of quantum physics and relativity theory. Despite his scientific brilliance, Michelson did not prove himself a very good diviner of the future.

> Returning to Sean Carroll, he states, "The main point here is that, while there are certainly many things that modern science does not understand, there are also many things that it *does* understand, and those things simply do not allow for telekinesis, telepathy, etc."

If in place of "telekinesis, telepathy, etc." we substitute "continental drift," I could easily imagine this statement being made in the early 20th century. The very concept of moving continents was lambasted from some quarters, despite the strong evidence in support of the theory, because it was deemed "impossible" and utterly "inconceivable," based on the science of the time, that continents could move. There was no known mechanism, until, that is, the development of plate tectonic theory. (Yes, as a geologist, I am aware of the various criticisms and possible shortcomings of tectonic theory, but that is not the point or issue here.)

Analyzing further the selected quotations from Sean Carroll, they actually expose the weaknesses of like-minded individuals who insist that science in its modern Western guise should have the last word or, to put it another way, be the final arbiter of truth (even if only a provisional truth). Again, the Carroll quotation is:

> The main point here is that, while there are certainly many things that modern science does not understand, there are also many things that it does understand, and those things simply do not allow for telekinesis, telepathy, etc. Which is not to say that we can prove those things aren't

real. We can't, but that is a completely worthless statement, as science never proves anything; that's simply not how science works. Rather, it accumulates empirical evidence for or against various hypotheses.

To say that something is "worthless" is a value judgment, and in an ultimate sense, one can argue, value judgments are outside of the realm of science and dependent on an emotional investment and context, among other factors. I would argue that the fact that "science never proves anything" is quite valuable, as it precludes the "sleight-of-hand" dismissal of the very possibility of any supposed paranormal phenomena ever being genuine.

As far as empirical evidence is concerned, for many people, this is the heart of the issue when it comes to alleged paranormal phenomena. Exactly what is evidence? Are anecdotal case studies evidence? Are card-guessing experiments in one lab (with good controls and taking all precautions against possible fraud) which give positive results for telepathy not "evidence," whereas similar experiments in a comparable lab (whatever "comparable" is in this case, given how poorly we understand the aspects that influence paranormal phenomena) which give negative results "solid evidence" against the telepathic hypothesis, as some critics and debunkers would contend? In fact, what is and is not "empirical evidence" is not a black-and-white matter, either in parapsychology or in many other scientific disciplines. Rather, evidence—any evidence—is a matter of degree and also carries a subjective and value-based component. The criteria that make for convincing evidence on the part of one person are not necessarily the same as the criteria for another person. Precluding obvious fraud and the like, there is no single magical scientific way to determine "objectively" the ultimate value of any particular alleged evidence. Science, any science, is not quite as "objective" as some would assert.

NOTE

1. Many of you reading this piece may know me from my work on the Great Sphinx, the Great Pyramid, and other ancient monuments, as discussed in various articles and my books *Voices of the Rocks* (1999), *Voyages of the Pyramid Builders* (2003), *Pyramid Quest (2005), and Forgotten Civilization* (2012; see also my website, www.robertschoch.com.

ACKNOWLEDGMENTS

For references and further discussion on various topics mentioned in this essay, see especially *Forgotten Civilization* and *The Parapsychology Revolution*.

I thank John Anthony West for reading and critiquing an earlier draft of this piece. In part, this article developed from correspondence with Greg Taylor of *The Daily Grail* (*www.dailygrail.com*). I thank Greg for his perceptive questions. This essay is a slightly modified version of an essay that was first posted in April 2008 on Graham Hancock's website for his "Author of the Month."

ROBERT M. SCHOCH:

Dr. Robert M. Schoch, a full-time faculty member at the College of General Studies at Boston University since 1984, earned his Ph.D. (1983) in Geology and Geophysics at Yale University. In the early 1990s, Dr. Schoch stunned the world with his revolutionary research that recast the date of the Great Sphinx of Egypt to a period thousands of years earlier than its standard attribution. In demonstrating that the leonine monument has been heavily eroded by water despite the fact that its location on the edge of the Sahara has endured hyper-arid climatic conditions for the past 5,000 years, Schoch revealed to the world that mankind's history is greater and older than previously believed. More recently Dr. Schoch has determined the astronomical cause of the demise of antediluvian civilizations, which he describes in his book *Forgotten Civilization: The Role of Solar Outbursts in Our Past and Future*, along with the scientific and archaeological evidence that supports his conclusions.

LETTERS FROM THE FAR SIDE OF REALITY[1]
BY GRAHAM HANCOCK

LETTER 1, FRIDAY, JANUARY 25, 2013

Santha and I are in Brazil after a long flight cramped up in the back of a British Airways 747. The seats seem to have been designed like the medieval torture called "Little Ease" where it is impossible to find comfort in any position. I'm due to have my right hip replaced in April and spent the twelve-hour journey in something approaching excruciating pain. What a relief to arrive into the Brazilian summer and be able to stretch my legs!

Now we're at the retreat where I had the extraordinary experiences in October 2011 that I describe in my article "Giving Up the Green Bitch: Reflections on Cannabis, Ayahuasca, and the Mystery of Plant Teachers." (p. 207) In the coming weeks, together with a group of a dozen other people and our facilitator (who resists being called a shaman despite his enormous depth of experience), we will participate in a series of Ayahuasca sessions. As well as drinking the sacred Amazonian brew and learning the lessons it has to teach me this time around, I will be presenting several talks to the group on various aspects of my work. The other presenter here is the renowned ethnopharmacologist Dennis McKenna, brother of the late, great Terence McKenna. I first got to know Dennis well during a lecture tour that we did together in Australia last year and am looking forward to renewing the acquaintance and to the further deep connection that shared journeys with Ayahuasca always bring. If you haven't read it yet, I urge you to get ahold of a copy of Dennis's new book, *The Brotherhood of the Screaming Abyss*, about his life with his remarkable brother Terence, see here: *http://www.grahamhancock.com/grapevine/McKennaD1/McKennaD1.php*.

So yesterday, Friday, January 24, we rested, relaxed, and recovered from the long flights we'd all made to get here (the other participants come from as far afield as the Middle East, Australia, and the United States). Today, Saturday, January 25, the work begins with the first all-night Ayahuasca session.

I have some trepidation—as Dennis puts it, anyone who approaches deep work with Ayahuasca without at least some trepidation doesn't really know the brew. But I have made a sincere effort since October 2011 to implement the changes in my life and outlook that Mother Ayahuasca required of me. I'm hoping to be handled gently this time and to experience beautiful visions, healing, inspiration, and love.

Above all, love.

That, I know from long experience, is the essence of the intelligence behind the vine.

I'll report back tomorrow.

LETTER 2, SATURDAY, JANUARY 26, 2013

So Santha and I are in Brazil for a series of sessions with Ayahuasca, the sacred visionary brew of the Amazon. *Ayahuasca* means "the vine of the dead" or "the vine of souls." It is given this name for a number of very good reasons. One is that it can allow the experience of contact with those who have passed on. I make no claims here as to the reality status of that experience, although I do have an opinion. Another is that aspects of it are so similar to some of the well-known features of the near-death experience, notably a life review, that some feel it may provide us with a dress rehearsal for death itself and for whatever we may encounter when we pass beyond the veil. Again, while I have my own opinion, I make no specific claims here as to the "reality" of such experiences. I give some further thoughts on this in my article "Giving Up the Green Bitch."

Last night's session was very mild, and for many in the group, it was not visionary at all. This is sometimes the case with Ayahuasca; one should not go into a session with expectations of seamlessly convincing and overwhelming visions. Often the brew will give you these, but not always, and not reliably. Last night, however, there was an additional factor of uncertainty, and this was that the maestros had provided a new batch of the brew that they believed to be very strong and which was indeed thicker and more syrupy than the brew we normally drink here in Brazil. It reminded me in its consistency of the very concentrated brew, sometimes with bits of plant matter floating in it, usually offered by Peruvian shamans (where, accordingly, rather small cups—about 25 milliliters—are the norm). At our Brazilian retreat, on the other hand, it is the practice to offer a less concentrated brew but in larger doses, and in past visits here, I have frequently drunk cups of 100 or 150 and sometimes even 200 milliliters.

Because last night's brew was new and was said to be strong, our facilitator proposed cups of just 25 milliliters or less for each of us and we would then discover its strength, or otherwise, for ourselves. If it was not as strong as expected, we could always drink a "booster" cup after an hour and a half or so.

The effect was not strong, and after ninety minutes, almost the entire group queued up for a booster, again of 25 milliliters. Still, in my case, this had no—or almost no—effect, and I began to contemplate a third cup. This is not an exact science, and it is never good to be too eager with Ayahuasca. In other words, you can go for a booster after experiencing no effect with the first cup only to discover that it was merely slow kicking in and that suddenly, with the booster, you have had more than you want. So I waited awhile, but when it was clear I was still not entering the Ayahuasca realm, I did go for a third cup. So three cups, each of 25 milliliters, making 75 milliliters in total.

There was no purging—i.e., (apologies for being graphic) neither I nor anyone else in the group vomited last night. This is most unusual although I have found as the years go by that I do purge far less than I used to when I started out. But within half an hour of drinking my third small cup, I did gradually begin to enter visionary space. These visions were mild and a little "flat" or two-dimensional by comparison with other fully immersive visions I have experienced in the past. The visions were of intricate geometrical and cursive patterns presented as though on separate individual cards, but when I studied each card, the patterns proved to be in movement and resolved into the forms of entities, rather scary in appearance, and I felt somewhat menaced. Go to Google Images, search "Codex Borgia" and/or "Codex Nuttal" and you may get some inkling of the atmosphere, if not the exact details, of these images. I felt myself to be in the presence of intelligence, and I tried to focus on that intelligence rather than be repelled by the menacing images, and in due course, I moved on to the next stage of the journey in which I was filled by powerful feelings of empathy and compassion for my fellow human beings.

These feelings began with reflections on the other members of our group who I had begun to get to know, and whose stories I had heard, over the past two days. Often in my daily life, I become absorbed selfishly in my own immediate worries and concerns, certain problems and issues that are confronting me which seem to loom large, and matters that are causing me emotional or spiritual pain. I am incredibly privileged and live a blessed life, yet still I find reasons to feel victimized or hard done by and sorry for myself! In an instant last night, I was shown how ridiculous and self-indulgent and

THE DIVINE SPARK

uncalled for such feelings are as I reflected on what I knew of the difficulties and challenges and real worries and pain that members of our group, in their own ways, are confronting bravely and without complaint in their own lives. I thought of some cases in particular, the strength, the dignity, the goodwill, the cheerfulness in adversity, of certain individuals, and I felt myself brimming over with compassion and love and admiration for them. And it came home to me in a real and immediate way that each one of us here on earth, not only the members of the immediate group surrounding me in the Ayahuasca session, but every one of the billions of my fellow humans going through this incarnation in this time are bright and luminous individual flames of light—each with his or her own special gifts and creativity and imagination, each with his or her own strengths and weaknesses—and every one of us faces challenges and difficulties and ordeals and pain and is confronted daily by defining choices, some small, some momentous, that write the pages of the stories of our lives.

And the only right response is gratitude, gratitude, gratitude to the universe for working the high magic that has made it possible for us to travel the path of human experience, and to learn and grow and develop in the process, and to practice love.

LETTER 3, WEDNESDAY, JANUARY 30, 2013

This is the third of my series of letters about the Ayahuasca sessions I'm presently participating in here in Brazil. Ayahuasca is a visionary brew that marries leaves containing dimethyltryptamine (DMT) with a monoamine oxidase inhibitor contained in the Ayahuasca vine itself; these two primary ingredients are cooked together in water to produce a foul-tasting but highly psychoactive beverage that has been drunk for at least three millennia by the indigenous peoples of the Amazon rainforest who value it as a portal to the spirit world. In the past decade, it has begun to acquire a global reputation and has been described as "twenty years of psychotherapy in one night."

So our second session took place on the night of Monday, January 28 into the small hours of Tuesday, January 29. This time I drank 80 milliliters of the brew in a single cup—as against three doses of 25 milliliters each in the previous session. With too small a dose of Ayahuasca, it is perfectly possible to have no experience at all; with too large a dose, it is possible to have an experience that is completely overwhelming—perhaps far more so than you would like. It is not an exact science, and it is complicated further by differences in one's own body chemistry from day to day that can result in widely varying effects.

I'm here together with a group of more than a dozen people and, as in previous retreats for serious work with Ayahuasca that I've participated in over the last ten years, it is noticeable how close and trusting of one another we have become. The Ayahuasca experience has a very special way of doing this—of opening the heart and breaking down barriers so that you feel intense empathy and a deep connection with others at a level that is near to impossible in the often angry, often competitive, frequently loveless hustle and bustle and grind of daily life. It is a great privilege to be able to know this empathy and connection, and it reminds me that all of life could be like this should we consciously set out and be willing to do the work to make it so. It is not oil, or water, or mineral deposits, or food, or land, or any other economic resource that is truly scarce or precious or "running out" in this bountiful earth of ours. What we are short of as a global species, what we seem reluctant to manifest, what we are failing to express and act out, is simply love, and in a way this should be the easiest problem in the world for us to solve—for it is within the capacity and the power of each and every one of us to give love if we choose to do so.

It is *such* a good feeling just to lay down the barriers of suspicion and fear and self-interest, and to trust others completely and know that the trust is shared and that the love you put out is the love you get back.

So, we all gathered round and raised our cups, mine containing 80 milliliters of Ayahuasca, and thanked the spirits and the ancestors for giving us this blessing, and drank. I then went to the bathroom and washed the acrid taste of the brew from my mouth before sitting down on my mattress with my back propped against the wall of our large ceremonial room surrounded by the rest of our group. Our facilitator turned off the lights and put on a CD of the sounds of nature—the ocean, rainfall, birdcalls—and through the open windows came a soft, cooling breeze. Stillness descended like a blessing, and for the next half hour or so, we all simply sat there staring into the darkness, thinking our thoughts. It is best to sit up at first—some prefer to sit up the whole night—as it allows swifter and more efficient digestion of the brew than can be achieved lying down. Nausea and vomiting commonly accompany the consumption of Ayahuasca, but it is a really good idea not to purge for at least an hour to allow full absorption of the medicine from the gut into the bloodstream. Vomit before the hour is up and you will likely need to drink some more brew.

Mercifully, as I have become more experienced with Ayahuasca during the past ten years, I find that I vomit less and less, and usually not at all—although I do still suffer episodes of nausea.

After forty-five minutes, I felt I was ready to lie down and stretched out on my mattress. Music is a constant accompaniment of our sessions here—the facilitator sensing intuitively the needs and mood and individual journeys of the members of the group and adjusting the playlist and his own instrumentals and vocals accordingly. He practices within the Peruvian, Shipibo tradition (though these ceremonies are taking place in Brazil), and at the point where I lay down he had begun to sing a series of *Icaros* (*http://en.wikipedia.org/wiki/Icaro*), traditional songs that provide an excellent waveguide into the profound meditative state that Ayahuasca can bring, or equally Ariadne's threads that can help to lead us out of labyrinths we might prefer not to find ourselves in.

These days, I rarely go into an Ayahuasca session without some fear, and this has much to do with a terrifying session on pure (smoked) DMT that I had in the United States in 2011 (described on my website). The Ayahuasca experience is not the same as the DMT experience, even though DMT is the primary active ingredient of Ayahuasca, but sometimes a strong Ayahuasca journey will plunge me squarely back into what I think of as DMT space. I feel vulnerable there, sometimes unprotected by the kindly, healing spirit of the vine, and my fear derives from this sense of raw exposure to elemental intelligences.

I suppose an hour had passed when I first became definitely aware of the effects of the brew in the form of intense visuals, seen best (even in the darkness) with my eyes closed. They took shape at first, as they often do, as swirling patterns of deep, richly saturated colours, but almost from the first moment, they had the slightly menacing undertones of my 2011 DMT trip. How can I describe them? Patches of colour all joined to one another, here purple, here ochre, here a strange deep brownish red, here a luminescent green, here blue—each patch about the size of a human hand and shaped into oblique, rhomboidal geometric forms, and all joined together in a mean-ingful swirling dance. This was not simply the entertaining pattern flow of a kaleidoscope. The patterns radiated intelligence, sentience, intent, and I felt my fear rise up another notch, and at the same time I exercised my will and said to myself, "I will not be afraid; I will journey into this without hesitation and see where it leads me." As soon as I had made that decision, I felt my fear subside and I journeyed deeper and then, emerging from the patterns, and shaped out of them, appeared the beautiful, glittering, sinuous form of a serpent seeming to radiate compassion and concern for me, and I sensed the presence of the great spirit, Mother Goddess of our planet, who I think of as Mother Ayahuasca, and I felt her healing energy. She worked on me for some time, swirling around my body, fixing parts of me that were broken, right down to the deepest level of my DNA and of my psyche.

At this point, it was all extremely gentle. I saw faces I did not recognize. A great bird, a raptor of some kind, took wing amidst a nimbus of supernal light. The serpent became a jaguar. And still I was not afraid, and I began to think, *Well, this is going to be fine.* My 80 mililitre cup was just right, just enough to enter healing visionary space but not so much that the visions would overwhelm me and swallow me up. And as is often the case with Ayahuasca, the visions came and went in waves—sometimes quite intense, sometimes falling away almost to nothingness.

I drifted into thoughts about my relationship with my wife, Santha, how I am so blessed to have her in my life, how she is in fact a goddess who manifests in human form, and how incredibly privileged I am that she permits me to go through this incarnation with her and learn from her how to be a better human being. And I realized how so much of our life together has been very selfishly about *me*, about my work, my creativity, my concerns, and it was brought home to me with the force of a revelation that the next stage of our partnership has to be about *her* and that my role now is to be of service to her and help her in every way possible to express and manifest her own wonderful creative gifts and to fulfill herself.

I spent some time in the presence of our children—Santha and I have six children between us, all young adults now, and they are a tremendous blessing to us and the light and joy of our lives. And I thought about how wonderful and full of love they all are, and what good people they are, and I reflected on the struggles and challenges they face, and the elegant, generous spirit in which they are all maturing and developing and travelling their own journeys.

Next came thoughts about the state of the world. I found myself dwelling on the terrible, inhuman way the state of Israel behaves toward the Palestinians, and on that hideous wall that Israel has built, and about its constant aggressive seizure—in the name of God, no less!—of more and more land on which Palestinian families and communities have traditionally lived. The more power we have—and Israel has immense power—the more it is our responsibility to love, and I realized that the great task facing Israel now, even though its people themselves feel threatened and fearful and unloved, is to desist forthwith all acts motivated by hatred and fear and to act instead with love and generosity toward all neighbouring peoples, to dismantle that abominable wall, to stop aggressively expanding settlements, and to carry the entire region forward into a new era based on trust and the mutual benefit of all. It will be difficult, incredibly difficult, and every attack on Israel by those

THE DIVINE SPARK

communities that Israel has monstrously abused for so long will be used as an excuse and a justification for more acts of hate and cruelty by Israel itself, but the vicious cycle must be broken, and as the most powerful player on the regional stage, it falls to Israel to change the destructive, hateful, violent pattern that has been in place for so long. At first, acts of love will be rejected, thrown back in Israel's face, even punished, but love is giving, love is persistence, love is kind, and if Israel adopts a policy based on love and shows as much kindness and compassion toward non-Israelis—and concern for their needs and interests—as it presently shows toward its own people, then little by little, the injuries of the past will heal and a way will be found to bring peace and security to all humans, regardless of their creed, colour, ethnic origin, or nationality, whose fate it is to live in that tortured region today.

It would be a good thing, I couldn't help thinking, if every military leader, every religious fanatic, every president, every prime minister, every dictator presently exercising power in the world were to be required to undergo ten sessions of Ayahuasca before being allowed to make a single other decision.

By this point in my journey, my head seemed completely clear. I thought the visions had stopped. I gave thanks that nothing too terrifying had happened to me, and I got up and walked around for a while. As I was walking, however, a new wave of visions descended on me like a storm, and I retreated once again to my mattress where the next phase of my night's journey began.

I was immediately in the presence of the entity I saw when I last smoked DMT in 2011 and who I think of as "the Trickster" or "the Magician" or "the Sorcerer" and whose aura, quite unlike that of Mother Ayahuasca, is entirely male. I do not know who this entity is or where he comes from. It is perfectly possible that he is simply one of the many transformations of Mother Ayahuasca herself—and indeed the healing female spirit that many of us experience through the brew is construed as male by a number of traditional cultures in the Amazon rainforest.

So there was the Trickster, and he was dancing, dancing, his face long and thin, severe and yet sensual, with steep, angled planes as though drawn by Aubrey Beardsley. And he wore a cloak of many colours made up of a patchwork of those same richly saturated rhomboidal forms I had seen earlier in the session. He made elaborate, skillful, elegant arm movements, as though he held silver threads in each hand and was stretching these threads out and showing them to me, and it came to me that his dance was the dance of creation and that with each gesture and movement, he was bringing reality into being—fabricating, generating, and manifesting reality—and that in his dance some kind of immense cosmogenic power was at work.

My feelings of fear were very strong now, quite overwhelming, and I wanted to flee, to run away from this scene, to open my eyes wide and stop the visions, but again I exercised my will, placed myself under control, and stayed put to let this magnificent, terrifying, cosmogenic dance unfold before me. I could not banish the fear entirely, but I began to realize that perhaps there is nothing to be afraid of here, and then just as this became clear to me, I was overtaken by a giant wave of nausea and had to shuffle round on my mattress and bring up my bucket to my face (we all have buckets) in case I would vomit.

In the end, I didn't vomit and after a few moments the nausea began to subside, and then Santha, who was beside me, suggested that we go out into the middle of the floor and dance. Sensing the change in mood, our facilitator began to play rhythmic, vital, energizing music, and other couples and individuals joined us in the clear area of wooden floor at the centre of the room, and I felt no pain whatsoever in my severely osteoarthritic hip, on which I am due to undergo surgery in April, and we danced and danced and were overtaken by joy and the celebration of the magnificent and generous and precious, precious gift of life.

LETTER 4, MONDAY, FEBRUARY 4, 2013

I make no claim as to the reality status of the entities and realms encountered in Ayahuasca visions and described in the account that follows. It is possible that they are real but only accessible to our senses in altered states of consciousness; but it is equally possible that they are projections with no fundamental reality whatsoever. There are many other possibilities, ranging from archetypes to the imaginal, that are also worthy of consideration. All I can say for sure is that they are experienced as real, and I claim nothing more than that.

I'm still in Brazil, still working with Ayahuasca. See earlier letters in this series for my accounts of sessions one and two.

Our third session took place on the night of Wednesday, January 30, 2013, into the small hours of Thursday, January 31. I drank the same dose, 80 mililitres, that had taken me on a complex and thought-provoking journey during the second session, but this time the effects were very different. Perhaps it was the music, which often sounded to me like panes of glass being broken with a hammer, or sometimes like a pneumatic drill breaking up a road, but I was for a long while completely unable to drift into a visionary state. I felt distressed and unhappy, with a slight admixture of relief that at least I would not have to confront the entity I call the Trickster that night.

This absence of visions, which I experienced as a gulf, a void, seemed to go on for a very long while, but gradually an odd state of mind began to overtake me. I had glimpses of a whole other life that I was living somewhere else, where I was me and yet had a different biography from the one that defines me in this life. I knew different people, did different things, and was living out that parallel life completely oblivious to this one. So it was an odd thing, lying in the darkness in our ceremonial space here in Brazil, under the influence of Ayahuasca but not very much—if at all—carried away by visions, to experience these strange episodes of crossover, of intersection, in which I became aware of both lives simultaneously, with each life seeming like a dream—ephemeral, fleeting, and yet haunting—that I was experiencing in the other.

I stood, visited the bathroom, and came back to my mattress. I could not shake the feeling of being haunted. Then dizziness swept over me and suddenly, precipitously, as though falling off a cliff, I tumbled into the realm of vision.

It was as though I were within a gigantic serpent. Its body, which had engulfed me, was transparent, allowing me to see through the patterns of its skin into the room beyond. At the same time, the feelings of unhappiness and distress that had set in very early in the session remained with me, and I found that I was unable to surrender to the experience as I knew I should and unable to master my fear. I was haunted by that dream world that was my other life, suspecting that in some way something, some entity, some intelligence was seeking to possess me and not liking or welcoming that feeling at all.

I continued to wrestle with it. I would not surrender to it, and at the same time, it would not leave me alone.

Eventually, I went down to the kitchen and dining area, where in the winter months, there is often a fire for participants to gather round in the late stages of a session. Tonight, in the Brazilian summer, there was no fire, but other members of our group were already there, and I fell into a conversation with them that helped to distract me from my haunted state and draw me out, little by little, into a sense of normality with myself.

Our fourth session took place on the night of Saturday, February 2 into the small hours of Sunday, February 3. I drank 90 millilitres of a different batch of the brew. The effects were immediately powerful but quite pleasant. Not at all threatening. I felt strongly the presence of Mother Ayahuasca, Mother Goddess of our planet, guardian of the great forests and of the wise and ancient trees, spirit of the oceans in her manifestation as Yemanja, the Blue Angel, whose special day in Brazil is February 2.

Time passed. The brew worked its way through me, and I tottered out to the bathroom, sat myself on the throne (sorry to be graphic, but it is not for nothing that Ayahuasca is also called "the purge" in the Amazon), and lost track of time there. It was absurd in a way. There I was sitting on the toilet, doing this very mundane and earthy thing, and at the same time, I could feel the presence of Mother Ayahuasca, of this deeply compassionate, unutterably beautiful goddess who became present to me in her serpent form and seemed to wrap me up in her coils and just loved me, loved me, for the longest while. I was very strongly given the message that I am too hard on myself, that I do not appreciate myself enough, that, yes, I have made errors in my life, yes, I have caused pain to others—as we all do—but that I am, nonetheless, fundamentally a good person and that perhaps the time has come for me to stop beating myself up about my mistakes and even to celebrate myself.

So I was surrounded by this lovely warm energetic glow, and I took it with me when I returned to the ceremonial space. My intention was simply to lie quietly back on my mattress and resume my discourse with Mother Ayahuasca, and if possible to experience even more of that healing love that she had bestowed on me. Instead, however, I gradually became aware of the malevolent attention of someone . . . or something.

After my encounter with the Mother, I still felt full of confidence, protected by a great and powerful Goddess, able to handle whatever was thrown at me, but at this precise moment, I came under an intense and focused psychic attack, and matters grew very strange. I was still in the ceremonial room in Brazil, but at the same time, I was not—as though everything had been shifted half a step to the side into some parallel dimension that had always been there, overlapping with ours, but had hitherto remained unseen. So at one and the same moment, I was in my body, on my mattress in the ceremonial space, and at the same time, out of my body in this other simulacrum of the room half a step to the side on another plane of reality.

The entity that was attacking me stood very close to me. It had human form—in fact, it looked like one of the other members of our group, but it was immediately obvious that it was not a physical being.

Was it the Trickster again?

Sparks of light flashed from its eyes, and there was sorcery in its hands and its gestures, and the confidence I had felt just moments before that I would be able to handle this malevolent force, that I might somehow meet it on equal terms and defend against it, was blown away like mist. I realized I was completely powerless and incompetent in its presence, utterly overmastered by it, out of my league. If this were a spiritual dojo, I would be the novice wearing the white belt and this thing, whatever it was, would be the ninth dan black belt here to wipe the floor with me.

I tried projecting love at it. It wouldn't work. The sense of threat and danger continued to mount. I tried to invoke Mother Ayahuasca in her manifestation as the Blue Angel. This did no good at all. I tried to raise a barrier of light. Failure again. Finally, my out-of-body self just curled up into a ball while I was pummeled and beaten and humbled on that etheric plane.

I endured the continuing psychic attack for a while, but then when I could bear it no longer, I decided the only course open to me was to leave the room, so I staggered out—the Ayahuasca was very strong, and I was a little unsteady on my feet—went downstairs, across the dining area, and out through the porch into the lush tropical gardens that surround this property.

Immediately, the atmosphere changed again, the psychic attack ceased, and I was in the domain of Mother Ayahuasca. I walked amongst the trees and bushes, touching each one, and entered into some kind of intense communion. Scintillating light and patterns, alive with energy, filled with sentience, sparkling with magic, emanated from every leaf, every branch, and I was, for the longest time, completely surrounded by and immersed in enchantment and beauty.

Later as I began to process the experience and talked with others in the group, it became clear that everyone had experienced a powerful, unusual, truly extraordinary night.

And I thought, Well, working with Ayahuasca is sometimes very strange, and it can be terrifying, and one faces challenges not often met in everyday life, but what an incredible blessing it is and what an incredible opportunity it is to learn and grow and develop and fortify oneself against the dangers of this and other realms. And I thought about the entity I had encountered, the Trickster in one of his many disguises and my lost bout in that spiritual dojo, and I suddenly realized that I had not lost at all—I had gained an important lesson, and I no longer felt afraid.

LETTER 5, TUESDAY, FEBRUARY 12, 2013

Warning before you begin reading: In what follows, I am reporting experiences and also interactions with others. I give my interpretations of those experiences and interactions, but I make absolutely no claim that my interpretations are correct.

Very strange and disturbing events around our fifth Ayahuasca session here in Brazil, which took place on the night of Monday, February 4 into the small hours of Tuesday, February 5.

I mentioned in my previous letter on this subject that during the fourth session, something happened to me that I experienced as an intense and focused psychic attack. To provide context, I cite extracts from that account here:

> I was still in the ceremonial room in Brazil, but at the same time, I was not—as though everything had been shifted half a step to the side into some parallel dimension that had always been there, overlapping with ours, but had hitherto remained unseen. So at one and the same moment, I was in my body, on my mattress in the ceremonial space, and at the same time, out of my body in this other simulacrum of the room half a step to the side on another plane of reality.
>
> The entity that was attacking me stood very close to me. It had human form—in fact, it looked like one of the other members of our group, but it was immediately obvious that it was not a physical being. . . . Sparks of light flashed from its eyes, and there was sorcery in its hands and its gestures, and the confidence I had felt just moments before that I would be able to handle this malevolent force, that I might somehow meet it on equal terms and defend against it, was blown away like mist. I realized I was completely powerless and incompetent in its presence, utterly overmastered by it, out of my league. If this were a spiritual dojo, I would be the novice wearing the white belt and this thing, whatever it was, would be the ninth dan black belt here to wipe the floor with me.
>
> I tried projecting love at it. It wouldn't work. The sense of threat and danger continued to mount. I tried to invoke Mother Ayahuasca in her manifestation as the Blue Angel. This did no good at all. I tried to raise a barrier of light. Failure again. Finally, my out-of-body self just curled up into a ball while I was pummeled and beaten and humbled on that etheric plane.
>
> I endured the continuing psychic attack for a while, but then when I could bear it no longer, I decided the only course open to me was to leave the room, so I staggered out—the Ayahuasca was very strong, and I was a little unsteady on my feet—went downstairs, across the dining area, and out through the porch into the lush tropical gardens that surround this property. . . .

So that was the fourth session. Now just before the start of the fifth session, something even stranger and utterly unexpected happened. Having already stated our individual intentions for the evening, we began to queue up to receive our cups of the brew from our facilitator.

Often during this moment, members of the group embrace and wish one another a good and safe journey; that is quite normal. But this evening, I heard a sudden cry of shock and one of the women in our group—I must respect privacy and will not name her—protested that another member of the group, a man (again, no names) had approached her making a series of bizarre and threatening hand gestures and at the same time projected his breath forcefully into her face. For those of us familiar with Amazonian shamanic traditions, it was immediately obvious that this was a very serious act, for it is by blowing with the mouth that the *brujos*—sorcerers—of the Amazon project the magic pathogenic darts known as *virotes* at their enemies in order to do them harm. Virotes may also be projected through a sorcerer's arms and out of openings in his hands.

"Did you do that to anyone else?" asked the woman who had been the victim of this sinister assault.

The man admitted that he had not.

"Then why did you do it to me?" she asked.

"I was blessing you," he said.

"I don't even let my husband blow in my face like that," she objected, "and I certainly didn't ask for your blessing! What were you trying to do to me?"

"Pah!" he replied, turning his back "You wouldn't understand."

It seemed that what had been, just a few days before, a peaceful, trusting, cooperative group had suddenly been exposed to some malignant energy or intent. And for me, the strangest thing of all—the very strangest thing—was that the man who had blown into the woman's face, who had so aggressively stepped into her space and infringed her sovereignty, was the very same man I had been attacked by the night before in my visions.

Except then I had convinced myself that it could not be him ("It had human form, in fact it looked like one of the other members of our group, but it was immediately obvious that it was not a physical being.").

Now, I was not so sure.

After such a disruption of the flow, it would probably have been wise if no one had drunk the brew that night but, having come so far, we all did, including the woman who had been assaulted—although she asked our facilitator to clear the negative energy that she felt had been projected at her first.

I took my largest dose yet in this series of sessions, 100 milliliters, composed myself for whatever lay ahead, and instantly regretted drinking so much. In the end, however, I was hyperalert, jangled, and so afraid that whenever an intense visionary state threatened to creep up on me, I resisted it, actively and consciously fought against it, and willed it away. The plain truth was that I did not wish to become vulnerable again to that malevolent force that had overmastered me and psychically bullied and terrified me during the previous session, and since it could not get at me in the physical realm, but only in the visionary or astral realm, my instinct was not to allow myself to go there.

And I found myself wondering, What are we dealing with here? Is it in fact what it appears to be? Is this individual who tonight so blatantly transgressed the sovereignty of another member of the group in physical space, somehow manifesting a spirit body and using it to transgress also on the astral plane? Or is it, as I originally suspected, some powerful etheric entity that is not him at all but simply disguising itself as him? Or could it be a bit of both? Could he be a weak, perhaps psychopathic, individual who has made some sort of Faustian bargain with a dark and hungry supernatural force and is serving as a more or less willing lightning rod to channel it to others around him? Or might it be none of the above?

Here, before going further, I feel compelled to repeat that I make no claim as to the reality of the entities and realms encountered in Ayahuasca visions. It is possible that they are real but only accessible to our senses in altered states of consciousness; but it is equally possible that they have no fundamental reality whatsoever. There are many other possibilities, ranging from archetypes to projections to the imaginal, that are also worthy of consideration. All I can say for sure is that they are experienced as real, and I claim nothing more than that.

About two hours into the session, we all heard a crashing sound somewhere below. Along with our facilitator and a couple of others, I hurried down the stairs, and we found another member of our group, a strong young man in his early thirties, collapsed on the floor. He said he did not understand what had happened to him. Something dark had attacked him, swarmed over him, overpowered him, and he had felt certain he was going to die unless he got out of the ceremonial space. On the way down the stairs, he had become faint and fallen. "I looked death in the face," he kept on saying. "I looked death in the face."

Our facilitator went to work on him. There are certain techniques—the use of a rattle, a thumb placed firmly on the center of the brow, the chanting of the special songs called icaros—which are helpful in clearing away negative psychic energies and, after about half an hour, the young man was able to stand and walk around. "I looked death in the face," he repeated—but this time with a smile—"and I survived."

Later in conversation, our facilitator told us that when he had begun to work on the young man, he himself had been seized by a feeling of absolute terror—a powerful and overwhelming dread that he was only able to master with great difficulty and by drawing on everything he had learned in more than forty years of working with the brew.

Later still, another member of our group, a trained psychotherapist who is also enormously experienced with the sacred use of psychedelics, came down from the ceremonial space to join us in the kitchen, took a seat, and said calmly and reflectively: "What the hell was *that?*" He then reported that he too had been terrorized in the visionary realm by some dark entity that he too associated with the individual who had blown in the woman's face at the beginning of the ceremony. "I tried very hard to rationalize what was happening," he said. "I tried to convince myself that what I was experiencing was just my own shadow side taking illusory form, that this was something I was projecting, but in the end, I became certain it was a real force, something utterly alien and deeply, deeply evil and completely external to myself. I tried every technique I know to keep it at bay, but nothing worked."

The following day, I talked to the individual who had blown in the woman's face. "I'm a basement shaman," he said. He sounded quite proud of himself. "I make DMT and smoke it a lot at home, exploring visionary worlds, and I go around Ayahuasca groups doing this work. Sometimes people don't like it, but I just withdraw within myself so they can't get to me." He told me he hoped I appreciated how much courage it took for him to talk to me openly like this about the disruption his behavior had caused. I told him that my advice was that he should cultivate humility and not imagine that he has any "work" to do with anyone else, only with himself. After speaking to me, he spoke to the woman whose sovereignty he had transgressed the night before and apologized to her, again repeating that he hoped she appreciated what tremendous courage it took for him to come out in the open like this. She found herself unable to accept his apology. "You're trying to make it all about you," she told him, "with all this crap about your courage. That's not a genuine apology at all."

Two days later, mercifully, the man left. Indeed, most of the group has now gone. Just seven of us remain for the final two sessions, the first of which took place on the night of February 10 into the small hours of February 11. It was a blissful, openhearted night with a great feeling of love, security, solidarity, and trust. I am not going to describe it further here except to say that the same member of our group who had asked, "What the hell was *that?*" after the fifth session had a new insight during the night. He experienced a direct, personal encounter with the loving entity whom we call Mother Ayahuasca (who is perhaps a goddess, though she does not wish to be worshipped), and he asked her the same question: "What the hell was *that* thing that attacked us during the fifth ceremony? Why did we have to go through that?"

"You needed to see it," she replied. "Now you know what I have to deal with all the time. It's the evil that is loose in the world, twisting and destroying the human spirit, and I need your help to fight it, the help of good people everywhere, the help of the power of love."

I realize how strange all this must sound to those (undoubtedly the vast majority who read this) who have not drunk Ayahuasca and perhaps do not wish to. All I can say, as my good friend Dennis McKenna puts it, is that Ayahuasca is the ultimate skeptic's challenge. It is not an intellectual argument. It is not a matter of empirical, scientifically verifiable proofs. It is quite simply an experience. Once you've had a deep and powerful encounter with the brew, you can make of it what you will, but until you have had such an encounter, it is better to withhold judgment.

I hope with these personal accounts that I have added some quantum of useful data to the body of available information about the Ayahuasca enigma. I have not held back and have shared with you both the dark and the light sides of the realm of experience into which this mysterious, ancient, and sacred Amazonian brew can plunge us. It is as though a doorway is opened into a parallel universe in which—as in the universe we inhabit in our daily lives—there is both good and evil, but in which—both there and here—we as conscious human creatures are gifted with the power of choice. Sometimes we must face evil, sometimes it may do us harm, but we do not have to join forces with it, we do not have to make compromises with it, we do not have to bow down to it, and we do not have to serve its purposes. Evil cannot always be defeated, but it can always—always!—be resisted.

So the Ayahuasca experience is by no means all sweetness and light, and if you go into a session with that naïve expectation, you may well, at some time or other, find yourself unpleasantly surprised. Ayahuasca is extremely serious business, and this is one among many reasons why I would not advise anyone to partake of it without skilled and well-intentioned shamanic guidance—though such guidance, these days, is available from a small but growing number of goodwilled and completely un-egotistical Western shamans as well as from Amazonian shamans. Indeed, the fact that a self-styled "shaman" hails from the Amazon is no guarantee whatsoever of the quality of care and service he will provide; in this, as in all adventurous journeys where hazards can be expected, you should do your research carefully, consult others, and rely on word of mouth before committing yourself to a particular path.

With these necessary cautions expressed, however, I conclude by affirming that the Ayahuasca experience is, above all else, about love and that there is openness of heart in it and a tremendous sweeping away of the blockages and mechanisms of denial that prevent us from getting to grips with and resolving fundamental issues in our lives. Truly, it is not for nothing that a very strong Ayahuasca session has been described as twenty years of psychotherapy in one night! In this regard, I have already set before readers here the radical change in my own life initiated by a series of Ayahuasca experiences I had during October 2011—see my article "Giving Up the Green Bitch: Reflections on Ayahuasca, Cannabis and the Mystery of Plant Teachers." (p. 207)

And above and beyond all that, as I've tried to show, the great virtue and promise of Ayahuasca is that it raises profound questions about the nature of reality itself. There are, as yet, no definite answers to those questions—perhaps there never will be—but to confront the experiences that give rise to them, while sometimes terrifying and often chastening, is, I believe, ultimately of the greatest value.

NOTE

1. These five letters, originally written as status updates for my Facebook community, describe a series of sessions with Ayahuasca, the "vine of souls" that I participated in in Brazil in January and February 2013. They are written in real time and reflect the changing dynamics of these unusual experiences over a period of two weeks. Something very strange happened in sessions four and five, something sinister that I could not have anticipated from my previous work with Ayahuasca, and looking back through the whole sequence of letters now, I am struck by how it took me, and others, by surprise and how we at first sought to intellectualize it and even explain it away.

COULD PSYCHEDELICS SAVE THE WORLD?
BY GREGORY SAMS

The psychedelic experience appears to have been, at one time or another, part and parcel of human cultures throughout the world; with or without assistance from the plant world, and usually with. Today, as our civilization careens mindlessly out of control and we face rejection by the planet that is our only home, it is appropriate to ask whether the virtual absence of the psychedelic experience in modern culture might be connected with the predicament in which we find ourselves.

The fields of ecology and green consciousness are products of the sixties hippy movement, now branched and developed far beyond the first "back to the land" aspirations of the time. Before then, a few select and far-sighted individuals primed the pump, from Rachel Carson to Bertrand Russell, Aldous Huxley to George Ohsawa. But it was the wholesale ingestion of psychedelics that enabled large numbers of a new generation to break out of a mental straightjacket that has constrained our dominant Western thought processes for far too long.

Psychedelics can transport us into an unfamiliar space. The familiar world in which we live, with houses, plumbers, parliaments, cell phones, cars, advertising, restaurants, and so forth is but one channel on the set of all possible channels. Because this is the reality we have created within the world around us, we are tuned to it to such a degree that we easily become oblivious to the deeper nature of this intricately interwoven world, of which we are but a part, living upon our little speck of dust within the Universe.

The psychedelic experience is not embraced as an escape from our world but as a ticket to escape from the single channel; to see the bigger picture and the smaller picture; to see our world from a different perspective, even from a different dimension. It is hard to emerge from this voyage without developing a realization, amongst many others, that those "in power" are possessed of a narrow vision fuelled primarily by the desire to stay in power. Their viewpoint is of one channel only—the one that represents the status quo they understand, in whatever country they control—and their efforts to control and fine-tune this channel to a micro-degree can often appear ludicrous.

The "alternative" culture that developed in the sixties was the first mass-movement to recognize that the channel we are tuned to is incompatible with the fostering of health, happiness, or peace and goodwill among humankind. Perhaps we did not recognize the coming of climate change and the scale of the threat. But we certainly recognized, through a new and spiritual perspective, that our communal ship was in danger of sinking. The state's natural response was to do everything in its power to prevent us from building lifeboats, to stop us from tuning in to new and experimental channels. And what may have most frightened the maintainers of the status quo was the prospect of a generation who were inserting flowers into gun barrels; embracing threatening concepts like love, peace, oneness, and nonviolence; looking inside themselves; and rejecting a nine-to-five future as tax-paying consumers in an untenable endless-growth economy. Who would need Big Government anymore? The psychedelic experience reconnected us with our inner self and a world of spirit; with concepts such as harmony and good vibrations; practices such as meditation and yoga; values such as conservation and recycling; organic farming and natural eating; alternative healing techniques from acupuncture to herbal and the laying on of hands. It is difficult, today, to imagine just how grey and disconnected from our true reality was the pre-sixties culture of the Western world. Opening the doors of perception in those days was a much greater surprise than it is today. Yet it is depressing to see just how little has changed in the core mind-set of those who profess to run our world; those who rely upon the power of coercion and propaganda to achieve their ends; those who ban cannabis and psychedelic drugs; those who seek to restrict and even ban the expression of dissent and protest; those who would drill holes in the lifeboats.

But how did we get disconnected in the first place—how did we get to the point where things that come naturally would be part of an "alternative" culture—be a "movement" instead of the mainstream? In the same way that we would not need a nutritional supplements industry were our food not refined and denatured in the first place, there would be little need for ecological awareness and a green movement had our culture not come to be isolated and disconnected from the world around it.

Though our profligate consumption of the world's oil reserves can easily be seen as a root cause of our ecological crisis, it is important to recognize that our disconnection from the planet was in place long before the Age of Oil. It is complex, bordering on the impossible, to conceive just how the discovery of cheap and transportable power would have impacted upon a culture that had not banned shamans and the shamanic experience. Those who developed the oil industry were of the same stock as those who slaughtered herds of buffalo in order to sell their tongues, the same who would destroy beautiful landscapes to extract a few pounds of yellow metal, the same who ardently believed in a universal god whose prime purpose lay in producing, providing for, and monitoring the human race.

Perhaps we can track the original suppression of the shamanic, psychedelic experience right back to Adam and Eve in the Garden of Eden, described in the Bible's opening pages, and the most commonly known Bible story of all. In this fundamental story, the fruit-pushing snake is portrayed as an agent of the dark side for telling Eve that "when you eat of it your eyes will be opened, and you will be like God, knowing good and evil" (Genesis 3). The snake, of course, has been symbolic of knowledge and divinity across many religious and shamanic traditions throughout the world. An angry God, as punishment for being disobeyed, visits toil and suffering upon the human race thereafter, especially targeting women by promising to "greatly multiply your pain in childbearing" and decreeing that men shall "rule over you." It's a peculiar story, to be sure, and one that has impacted upon us ever since.

An alternative interpretation of this Adam and Eve story was held by the widespread Gnostic sects known as the Ophites, who revered and recognized the serpent as man's benefactor and saw Jehovah as the bad guy who sought to keep us in ignorance by denying us knowledge of our potential divinity. The Ophites were declared heretics and brutally extinguished by the spread of an organized and intolerant Christianity in the 4th century. One could be forgiven for suggesting that had our species embraced the serpent's gift, we might still be living in harmony with each other and our planet—enjoying life in the paradise that we inhabit. Instead, a lack of differentiation between good and evil seems to be the hallmark of those in power today.

The powerful post-Constantine Church claimed a monopoly on spirituality, banning or destroying anything they thought to be in conflict with their religious hegemony. Witchcraft, astrology, spiritualism, soothsaying, and worshipping the Sun or Moon could all get one into serious trouble. A patent was effectively put upon the ecstatic state, with punishment meted out to those caught seeking a "religious" experience by any means other than those approved by the Church.

The psychedelic experience and shamans were out—thought control was in. A select group of people now decided what we could think and how we should behave, assuming a mandate from God to do so. The natural world was not supposed to be able to teach us things, and our intuition was not to be trusted in matters which had been divinely decreed, or decreed by those who claimed divine responsibility to do so. We could use our intellect to learn about the natural world, usually for the purpose of exploiting it, but that world itself was stupid and could not inform us, and to believe it could was to indulge in superstitious pagan behaviour. That was a dangerous place to be.

The natural world had been provided by our divine creator as little more than a store cupboard for humanity. A common mind-set believed that we were specifically given "dominion over the fish of the sea, and over the fowl of the air, and over the cattle, and over all the earth, and over every creeping thing that creepeth upon the earth" as well as "every herb bearing seed, which is upon the face of all the earth, and every tree, etc." It says it all, right there in the Bible (Genesis 1).

A consequence of this assumption of human dominion over all was to invest Western civilization with a God-given license to take from this planet with unabashed greed, wiping out species and blithely destroying landscapes and cultures in the process of "developing" them. Humanity was relieved of the need to show any consideration or thought to the land or its other residents, except for their utility to the intelligent human race. Everything else in the Universe was seen as stupid or inanimate, other than creatures kind of like us, and the denizens of Heaven. It is becoming more and more apparent that this viewpoint is ungrateful, thoughtless, plain stupid, and as damaging to us as it is to the planet that hosts us. Yet it has infused the culture of the so-called "developed" world for seventeen centuries.

Doors opened by the psychedelic experience allow us to blow this crippling mental straightjacket right out of our mind space, revealing a world more interconnected, alive, and wonder-filled than we had ever realized; a world in which we may feel like gods, but not a world that we can rule over like deterministic kings; a world that is our host and teacher as well as our conscious provider. We learn to respect the world, and wonder at how we could have ever done otherwise.

For the shaman in all of us, spirit is out there and is as real a part of our world as the physical stuff we can see and touch. When we recognize the spirit in the trees, the spirit in the mountain, the spirit in the earth and the Sun and its fellow stars, we live in harmony and respect with our environment—it comes naturally.

PERMISSIONS/CREDITS

Alivernia, Mike. "DMT—The Final Frontier." Reprinted with permission from Mike Alivernia. First published online on *http://www.grahamhancock.com*.

Brand, Russell. "Why Richard Dawkins Is the Best Argument for the Existence of God." Reprinted with permission from *New Statesman*. First published online on *http://www.newstatesman.com*, April 7th, 2011.

Brown, David Jay. "Transcending the Medical Frontiers." Reprinted with permission from David Jay Brown. This essay also appears online on *http://acceler8or.com* and in *The New Science of Psychedelics*, published by Inner Traditions, 2013.

Devereux, Paul. "Whispering Leaves: Interspecies Communication" Reprinted with permission from Paul Devereux as an adapted excerpt from *The Long Trip* (1997; 2008 Daily Grail Edition).

Doblin, Rick. "Pahnke's Good Friday Experiment." Reprinted with permission from the original source: Doblin, R (1991). Pahnke's "Good Friday" experiment: A long-term follow-up and methodological critique. *Journal of Transpersonal Psychology*, *23*(1), 1-28

Frecska, Ede, Moro, Levente, and Wesselman, Hank. "The Soul Cluster: Reconsideration of a Millennia Old Concept." Reprinted with permission from Ede Frecska. Also published online on *http://www.grahamhancock.com*.

Grey, Alex, with thanks to Grey, Allyson. "The Creative Process and Entheogens." Reprinted with permission from Alex Grey. Previously published by MAPS, 2000.

Haramein, Nassim. "To Infinity and Beyond: The Holographic Nature of Mass." Reprinted with permission from Nassim Haramein. First published online on *http://www.grahamhancock.com*.

Hoffmann, Martina. "How Expanding Consciousness and Our Connection to the Spirit Might Help the Survival of Life on Planet Earth." Not previously published.

Lattin, Don. "The Second Coming of Psychedelics." Reprinted with permission from Don Lattin. First published in *Spirituality and Health* magazine.

Luna, Luis Eduardo. "Ayahuasca and the Concept of Reality: Ethnographic, Theoretical, and Experiential Considerations." Reprinted with permission from

Luis Eduardo Luna. First published in *Making Reality Really Real*. Consciousness Reframed. Trondheim: TEKS Publishing, 2010. Also published online on *http://www.grahamhancock.com.*

Luna, Luis Eduardo. "Toward an Exploration of the Mind and a Conquered Continent: Sacred Plants and Amerindian Epistemology." Reprinted with permission from Luis Eduardo Luna. Also published online on *http://www.grahamhancock.com.*

McKenna, Dennis. "Reflections in a Rear View Mirror: Speculations on Novelty Theory and the End Times." Not previously published.

McKraken, Thad. "Why I Don't Do Psychedelics Very Often Anymore." Reprinted with permission from Thad McKraken. Previously published online on *http://www.disinfo.com.*

Razam, Rak. "From Cosmic Consciousness to Convergence." Not previously published.

Roberts, Gabriel. "DMT: The Thinking Man's Moonshine?" Reprinted with permission from Gabriel Roberts. Previously published online on *http://www.disinfo.com.*

Roberts, Thomas B. "Three Humungous Ideas and a Dozen Merely Big Ones." Reprinted with permission from Thomas B. Roberts. First published as excerpts from *The Psychedelic Future of the Mind* online on *http://www.grahamhancock.com.*

Sams, Gregory. "Stellar Consciousness." Reprinted with permission from Gregory Sams.

Sams, Gregory. "Could Psychedelics Save the World?" Reprinted with permission from Gregory Sams. Previously published by MAPS.

Schoch, Robert. "Thoughts on Parapsychology and Paranormal Phenomena." Reprinted with permission from Robert Schoch. First published online on *http://www.grahamhancock.com.*

Seelig, Mark. "Communion with the Goddess." Reprinted with permission from Mark Seelig. First published online on *http://www.grahamhancock.com.*

Strassman, Rick. "Preparation for the Journey." Reprinted with permission from Inner Traditions. An excerpt from *Inner Paths to Outer Space* first published by Inner Traditions, 2008.

Tindall, Robert. "Is Alcohol a Spirit? Or My Goodness! My Guinness!" Reprinted with permission from Robert Tindall. First published online on *http://www.grahamhancock.com.*

CONTRIBUTORS

David Jay Brown is the author of *A New Science of Psychedelics*, and 10 other books about the evolution of consciousness and the future. Visit him online at: *www.mavericksofthemind.com*.

Don Lattin is the author of *The Harvard Psychedelic Club: How Timothy Leary, Ram Dass, Huston Smith and Andrew Weil Killed the Fifties and Ushered in a New Age for America*, published by HarperCollins. His most recent work is a memoir titled *Distilled Spirits: Getting High, then Sober, with a Famous Writer, a Forgotten Philosopher and a Hopeless Drunk*, published by University of California Press. To learn more, go to *donlattin.com*.

Thad McKraken is the author of the book *The Galactic Dialogue: Occult Initiations*. In addition to contributing regularly to Disinfo.com and writing about music at Redefinemag.com, he's also a musician, visual artist, and Occult film maker who can be followed on Twitter @Thad_McKraken.

Rak Razam is the world's "leading experiential journalist" and the author of *Aya Awakenings*, a unique spiritual adventure into the jungles of South America and the psychic landscapes of Amazonian shamanism. It has recently been adapted into a critically acclaimed, feature-length shamanic documentary of the same name: *http://www.aya-awakenings.com*

Dr. Robert M. Schoch, a full-time faculty member at the College of General Studies at Boston University since 1984, earned his Ph.D. (1983) in Geology and Geophysics at Yale University. In the early 1990s, Dr. Schoch stunned the world with his revolutionary research that recast the date of the Great Sphinx of Egypt to a period thousands of years earlier than its standard attribution. In demonstrating that the leonine monument has been heavily eroded by water despite the fact that its location on the edge of the

Sahara has endured hyper-arid climactic conditions for the past 5,000 years, Schoch revealed to the world that mankind's history is greater and older than previously believed. More recently Dr. Schoch has determined the astronomical cause of the demise of antediluvian civilizations, which he describes in his book *Forgotten Civilization: The Role of Solar Outbursts in Our Past and Future*, along with the scientific and archaeological evidence that supports his conclusions. Robert Schoch's website: www.robertschoch.com.

Mark Seelig was born in the Western part of Berlin, Germany in 1957. He has been an academic theologian for 15 years, holds a Ph.D in Psychology of Religion (Frankfurt-Main University, Germany), and he has worked as a professor of psychology at Columbia Pacific University, Novato, CA. He is a founding member of Ken Wilber's Integral Institute in Boulder, CO, a founding member of the German College of Transpersonal Psychotherapy, and he has trained and worked with Stanislav Grof, Ralph Metzner, and several other teachers in the field of Transpersonal Psychology.

Mark has lived in Germany, the USA, and in India. He is a clinical psychotherapist, facilitator of shamanic ceremonies, and a musician. He plays Indian classical, and shamanic-ambient music, and he has released several CDs collaborating with Byron Metcalf and Steve Roach. *www.mark-seelig.com*

Born in Geneva, Switzerland, in 1962, **Nassim Haramein** from as early as nine years old was developing the basis for a unified hyperdimensional theory of matter and energy, which he eventually called the Holofractographic Universe theory. He has spent most of his life researching the fundamental geometry of hyperspace.

Combining this knowledge with a keen observation of nature, he discovered a specific geometric array that is fundamental to creation. His unification theory, known as the Haramein–Rauscher Metric (a new solution to Einstein's field equations that incorporates torque and Coriolis effects), and his recent paper "The Schwarzschild Proton" lay down the basis of what could be a fundamental change in our current understandings of physics and consciousness.

In the past 20 years, Mr Haramein has directed research teams of physicists, electrical engineers, mathematicians and otherscientists. He founded a non-profit organisation, The Resonance Project Foundation, where as Director of Research he continues exploring unification principles and their implications.

The foundation is actively developing a research park in Hawai'i which combines science, sustainability and green technology.

Nassim Haramein has been giving lectures and seminars on his theory for more than 10 years.

Russell Brand is an English comedian, actor, radio host, author, and activist.

Gregory Sams is a pioneer of food for the body and food for the mind. He co-founded, with his brother Craig, Seed restaurant, the first natural and organic eatery in the UK, followed by Ceres Grain Store in the Portobello Road because people wanted to cook this food at home, and then Whole Earth foods, the all-organic brand. In 1982, he launched the first VegeBurger, a product he developed and christened. Craig went on to found Green and Black's chocolate. Aged 18, Greg founded *Harmony Magazine* in 1968 to which John Lennon dedicated an 8-frame cartoon, and later co-published *Seed: The Journal of Organic Living*. He founded Strange Attractions, the world's first ever shop dedicated to chaos theory. His interest in chaos led to an interest in consciousness that led to writing *The State Is Out of Date*. He is also the author of the *son of gOd*. He lives in London.

Dennis McKenna is an ethnopharmacologist who has studied plant hallucinogens for over forty years. He is the author of many scientific papers, and co-author, with his brother Terence McKenna, of *The Invisible Landscape: Mind, Hallucinogens, and the I Ching*, and *Psilocybin: Magic Mushroom Grower's Guide*. He holds a doctorate from the University of British Columbia, where his research focused on ayahuasca and oo-koo-hé, two hallucinogens used by indigenous peoples in the Northwest Amazon. He received post-doctoral research fellowships in the Laboratory of Clinical Pharmacology, National Institute of Mental Health, and in the Department of Neurology, Stanford University School of Medicine. In 1990, he joined Shaman Pharmaceuticals as Director of Ethnopharmacology, and in 1993 became the Aveda Corporation's Senior Research Pharmacognosist. Dennis has been an adjunct assistant professor at the Center for Spirituality and Healing at the University of Minnesota since 2001, where he teaches courses in ethnopharmacology and botanical medicine. He has taught summer field courses in Peru and Ecuador, and has conducted fieldwork throughout the upper Amazon. He is a founding board member of the Heffter Research Institute, a non-profit organization focused on the investigation of the potential therapeutic uses of psychedelic medicines.

Gabriel D. Roberts was born in Tacoma, WA. The value of seeking the truth wherever it may be found was instilled in him at a very young age. At 7 years old he was street preaching in Salt Lake City, Utah and by 10 years old he had traveled to China, Japan, Hong Kong, South Korea, Macau and The Philippines as a missionary. Having grown up in a fundamentalist Christian environment, his perspective on the world was greatly influenced by the Bible and the fundamentalist view of its teachings. Having come to adulthood, Gabriel moved from his hometown of Tacoma to the more cosmopolitan Seattle to get his theology degree at Seattle Bible College. Through his studies and endeavors to live the truth and find a spiritually fulfilling life, Gabriel felt that there must be something more to the story than a contest of sin and salvation. After many years of study and with a lifetime of effort to connect with something greater, Gabriel stepped away from his Christian faith. The details and reasons are catalogued in his book, *Born Again To Rebirth*. Like many others who have had an earnest thirst for the answers to the big questions of life, Gabriel was not satisfied to settle for not knowing more. His continued research in the fields of Science, Spirituality and Psychedelics continue to yield more and more exciting discoveries. Not being afraid to challenge his own cosmologies in light of new information, Gabriel D. Roberts continues to put together the puzzle pieces of life in a continued effort to bring enlightenment to himself and to his readers. Foremost among his influences are great writers, researchers and scientists like Terence McKenna, Jonathan Talat Phillips, Graham Hancock, Dr. Jeremy Narby, Russell Targ, David Wilcock and Rupert Sheldrake. Gabriel is currently a contributor for *Disinfo.com* and *Realitysandwich.com*.

Rick Strassman, MD, is clinical associate professor of psychiatry at the University of New Mexico School of Medicine and the author of *DMT: The Spirit Molecule*.

Luis Eduardo Luna, PhD, is co-author (with Pablo Amaringo) of *Ayahuasca Visions*, and director of Wasiwaska, Research Centre for the Study of Psychointegrator Plants, Visionary Arts and Consciousness in Florianopolis, Brazil.

Ede Frecska, MD, is chief of psychiatry at the National Institute of Psychiatry and Neurology in Budapest, Hungary, and a contributing author to *Psychedelic Medicine*.

Robert Tindall is a professor of English, writer, and classical guitarist. With his wife, Susana Bustos, he leads groups into the Amazon rain forest to encounter the healing traditions there. He is the author of *The Jaguar that Roams the Mind* and *The Battle of the Soul in Sir Gawain and the Green Knight*.

Martina Hoffman works as a painter and sculptress. Her paintings offer the viewer a detailed glimpse into her inner landscapes—imagery that has been inspired by expanded states of consciousness: the realms of the imagination, meditation, shamanic journeys and the dream state.

"The visionary artist makes visible the more subtle and intuitive states ofour existence and creates maps and symbols reflecting consciousness. My work is an attempt to show spirit as the universal force which unifies us beyond the confines of cultural and religious differences. By accepting the interdependency of all life and our universal interconnectedness we have a chance to heal and transform the planet's general state of woundedness.In using art as a tool for transformation, we have the opportunity to create a reality as beautiful, healthy and strong as our imagination permits."

Martina Hoffmann, has exhibited her work and spoken on behalf of visionaryart and culture internationally. Together with her husband the AmericanFantastic Realist, Robert Venosa, she teaches visionary painting workshops.

Paul Devereux is co-founder and managing editor of the peer-reviewed *TIME & MIND—The Journal of Archaeology, Consciousness and Culture* (*www.tandfonline.com/rtam*), a research affiliate with the Royal College of Art, and a columnist with *Fortean Times*. He has written 28 books since 1979 and many articles and academic papers. He gives lectures, presentations and workshops in the UK, Continental Europe and the USA. His main research interests include ancient sacred sites and landscapes, sound at archaeological sites, and the anthropology of consciousness (ancient worldviews) along with modern consciousness studies. His books include, *Secrets of Ancient and Sacred Places*, *Re-Visioning the Earth*, *The Long Trip*, *Lucid Dreaming*, and *Sacred Geography*. Website: *www.pauldevereux.co.uk*.

Mike Alivernia writes *The Mind of Mike* blog featured on Graham Hancock's website.

Alex Grey is an American artist specializing in spiritual and psychedelic art.

Allyson Grey is an artist and the co-founder for the Chapel of Sacred Mirrors.

Thomas B. Roberts, PhD, is a founding member of the Multidisciplinary Association for Psychedelic Studies, co-founder of the Council on Spiritual Practices, creator of Rising Researcher sessions, and originated the celebration of Bicycle Day. He teaches Psychedelic Studies in the Honors Program of Northern Illinois University. Taught since 1981, it is the world's first university-catalogued psychedelics course. He was a Visiting Scientist in the psilocybin research team at the Johns Hopkins Behavioral Pharmacology Research Unit in 2006. More publications, PowerPoints, and info are at *http://niu.academia.edu/ThomasRoberts*. Dr. Roberts is the author of *The Psychedelic Future of the Mind*, *Spiritual Growth with Entheogens*, *Psychedelic Medicine*, *Psychedelic Horizons*, and *Religion and Psychoactive Sacraments*.

Rick Doblin PhD, is the founder and executive director of the Multidisciplinary Association for Psychedelic Studies (MAPS). He received his doctorate in Public Policy from Harvard's Kennedy School of Government, where he wrote his dissertation on the regulation of the medical uses of psychedelics and marijuana and his Master's thesis on a survey of oncologists about smoked marijuana vs. the oral THC pill in nausea control for cancer patients. His undergraduate thesis at New College of Florida was a 25-year follow-up to the classic Good Friday Experiment, which evaluated the potential of psychedelic drugs to catalyze religious experiences. He also conducted a thirty-four year follow-up study to Timothy Leary's Concord Prison Experiment. Rick studied with Dr. Stanislav Grof and was among the first to be certified as a Holotropic Breathwork practitioner. His professional goal is to help develop legal contexts for the beneficial uses of psychedelics and marijuana, primarily as prescription medicines but also for personal growth for otherwise healthy people, and eventually to become a legally licensed psychedelic therapist. He founded MAPS in 1986, and currently resides in Boston with his wife and three children.

ABOUT THE EDITOR

Graham Hancock is the author of the major international bestsellers *The Sign and the Seal*, *Fingerprints of the Gods*, and *Heaven's Mirror*. His books have sold more than five million copies worldwide and have been translated into 27 languages. He has written for many of Britain's leading newspapers, including *The Times*, *The Sunday Times*, *The Independent*, and *The Guardian*. He was co-editor of *New Internationalist* magazine and East Africa correspondent of *The Economist*. He lives in England.

E1P5 P$ K567
!!! P dsd 1 $21